THE GREAT BETRAYAL

THE GREAT BETRAYAL

India's Development Experience Since Independence with Reference to Central and Western India

Kalipada Deb

KALPAZ

ISBN: 978-93-5128-002-6

Price: ₹ 990/-

Third Edition 2014

Published by

Kalpaz Publications
C-30, Satyawati Nagar,
Delhi - 110052
E-mail: kalpaz@hotmail.com Ph.: 9212142040

Laser Typesetting: Gyan Print AB-I
Printed at: G. Print Process, Delhi

Cataloging in Publication Data—DK
Courtesy: D.K. Agencies (P) Ltd. <docinfo@dkagencies.com>

Deb, Kalipada.
The great betrayal : India's development experience since independence with reference to central and western India / Kalipada Deb. -- 3rd ed.
p. cm.
Includes bibliographical references (p.) and index.
ISBN 9789351280026

1. Economic development--India. 2. India--Economic policy--1947- I. Title.

DDC 338.954 23

Contents

PART IV: THE ECONOMY OF MAHARASHTRA

PART V: THE ECONOMY OF GUJARAT

PART VI: SUMMING UP

PREFACE

"Thank you
I'm here for a few days, Bapu said
No place now to step in this country.
I know my photo hangs in courtrooms,
Government offices and banks
But no place to step – in your hearts.
I know your wallet is full of bank notes
With my famous head, some of them forged.
Look, how dark the marks are under my eyes
I'm smeared all over with corruption.
Surely some ominous plague has seized this country
My head reels even to estimate how badly it is abused."
(Boudhayan Mukherjee, The Statesman 2009)

The development objective of a nation must primarily be total removal of absolute poverty among the people, while pursuing overall growth. Extreme of inequality in the levels of living can never be in the long-run interest of a nation, as the saying goes, 'Poverty anywhere is a danger to prosperity everywhere'. If a small segment of population is wallowing in riches, while the vast majority is steeped in poverty and ignorance, it is bound to breed violence and disorder. The strategy of growth must, therefore, incorporate strong measures for equitable distribution of income.

India's development was also envisaged to proceed on this line. The Constitution of India that came in 1950, promised to the people in the Preamble itself: "Justice, social, economic and political; Liberty of thought, expression, belief, faith and worship; Equality of status and of opportunity; and to promote among them all, Fraternity assuring the dignity of the individual and the unity of the Nation...." The Directive Principles of State Policy contain a variety of assurances in these directions. Section 43 states: "The state shall endeavour to secure, by suitable legislation of economic Organisation or in any other way, to all workers, agricultural, industrial or otherwise, work, a living wage, conditions of work ensuring a decent standard of life and full enjoyment of leisure and social and cultural opportunities...." Similarly, Section 46 states: "The state shall promote with special care the educational and economic interests of the weaker sections of the people, and, in particular, of the Scheduled Castes and

Scheduled Tribes, and shall protect them from social injustice and all forms of exploitation."

Such pronouncements were there in the Plan and other documents also. The First Five-Year Plan underscored the need for changing the socio-economic framework in order to "accommodate progressively fundamental urges which expressed themselves in the demands for the right to work, the right to adequate income, the right to education and to a measure of insurance against old age, sickness and other disabilities." (p. 8). The document of the Second Five-Year Plan expressly incorporated the objective of bringing a Socialist Pattern of Society.

What happened to these lofty objectives ultimately? How much could be achieved after six decades of development efforts? Did the government try its utmost to provide food and other basic necessities to the semi-starved billions? Were there adequate efforts to reduce the regional imbalance in development? How far the rural-urban disparity could be reduced over the decades? Did the government exert itself fully to mobilize all possible resources? This study makes an in-depth analysis of these questions with reference to the Central and West Indian states.

The Central and Western regions of the country presently comprise of six states, four in the former - viz., Uttar Pradesh (UP), Uttarakhand, Madhya Pradesh (MP) and Chhattisgarh - and two, Maharashtra and Gujarat, in the latter. These two regions together account for 39.2 per cent of the country's total population, the former having 24.9 per cent. Uttar Pradesh is the largest state in the country, with a population share of 16.2 per cent in 2001. MP's population is around half of UP's. In the Western region, until 1960, there was only one state, Bombay. Maharashtra is the third largest state in the country, with a population share of 9.4 per cent. Gujarat is much smaller. In terms of development, to begin with, the Central India was very backward, whereas the Western India relatively developed.

The study is divided into six parts, comprised of 23 chapters. The first part is introductory, and has two chapters. The first one deals with the nature of the Constitution, the quality of governance, and the pattern of planning and development over the entire period since Independence. The second chapter is a state-wise general review of the resources and the nature of development over the years. The focus is on the relative position among the states on various aspects of development. The following four parts have five chapters each, making a detailed analysis of the situation in each of the states. The chapters are on resource mobilisation, human resource development, transformation in agriculture and allied sectors, nature of industrial growth, and changes in absolute poverty and the measures taken.

Some of the salient findings of the study may be noted here. The way the state machinery worked, soon it became transparent that the Constitution is in reality a propaganda material. All the assurances made in the Directive Principles of State Policy were thrown to the wind. The deceptive nature of the democracy soon became apparent. The government formed at the Centre never represented the majority of voters. The conducting of elections turned out to be largely a game of money and muscle power. The Constitution was distorted to suit vested interests. The President of India became only a titular head. The Parliament's nature of working became a matter of shame. Lows of behaviour and highs of privileges for parliamentarian became an integral part of the Parliament. The legislators and bureaucrats enriched themselves by both fair and fowl means. Corruption became rampant everywhere in the country. India became a patent example of mockery in democracy.

In this situation, the planning and development that came could not be anything but anti-people. The resource mobilisation was low, and even this was misdirected to serve a small segment of population at the top. The beneficiaries from the development efforts were confined to less than a quarter of the population. The common man's basic needs were totally neglected. The diversification in economic activities was very low. Large proportion of the workers continued to be engaged in the low productive agriculture, and their wage levels remained extremely low. The inter-state and intra-state disparities in development accentuated, and this resulted in demand for creation of more and more new states. Gradually, it took a violent form. The absence of justice in the operation of the government led people to take law into their own hands. The so-called Maoist movements spread to many states over the years.

Among the states under study, the western two are much better placed than the central ones on every parameters of development. Maharashtra's per capita income was generally the second highest in the country. Gujarat's was also higher than in most of the states. The largest state, UP's per capita income, on the other hand, was generally the second lowest, and MP's just above it. In reducing absolute poverty, none of the states performed well. But most shameful was the situation of Maharashtra. The proportion of BPL population here in 2004-05 stood at 31 per cent - a gross underestimation - which was significantly higher than at the national level. Even in Gujarat, where the proportion had declined noticeably, the situation worsened in recent years. The implementation of poverty alleviation programmes nowhere received the attention it deserved; corruption was rampant almost everywhere.

In the social sector, UP's situation was distressingly poor. The literacy rate in 2001 was only 56.3 per cent, with females at 42. MP made a significant progress in the last decade, and its proportion was seven percentage points higher than UP's. Both the western states were in a much better position. However, Gujarat's latest, at 69 per cent, was eight points below Maharashtra's. The position of human development index was below expectation for both the western states; Maharashtra's was fourth in 2001 and for Gujarat sixth. UP's position was 13th and MP's just above it.

Industrially, the western states were very well placed. Maharashtra has always been at the top, and in 2004-05, in the all-India total factory sector output its share came to 21.5 per cent; Gujarat's was 15.6 per cent. A very disturbing aspect of the industrialisation is, however, that the industries were very heavily concentrated in a few districts in both the states. In Maharashtra, Konkan and Pune division together accounted for 70 per cent of total factory workers even in recent years. The Central region was very poor industrially. UP accounted for only seven per cent of all-India factory sector output in 2004-05; and MP a mere 4.5 per cent, despite having large natural resources.

The inter-regional disparities in development remained very high in each of the states, and it was not solely due to the difference in resource endowment. The government's efforts at decentralised development were insignificant. Particularly glaring was the situation in the developed states. In Maharashtra, the per capita income of Gadchiroli in 2002-03 was a mere 42 per cent of the state average. In the social sector, the literacy rate in 1991 was less than 50 per cent in five of the districts as against 65 at the state level. In Gujarat, the lowest literacy rate was less than half the state average this year. The proportion of urban population was less than 15 per cent in four of the districts.

This nature of neglect and exploitation of a vast majority cannot go on for ever. If the nation is not to be engulfed in total chaos and disorder, certain steps are urgently called for. These are:

(i) The poverty line be redefined appropriately, and the proportion of BPL population reduced to less than five per cent within the next five years. Cent per cent literacy should also be reached at the earliest.

(ii) The education system should be thoroughly overhauled to make it strictly need-based and value-oriented. Every student after passing out be made to render social services in rural areas at least for two years.

(iii) Eradication of corruption from government departments should get the highest priority; without it all development expenditures will continue to be largely infructuous. Strict accountability and punishment for failures have to be introduced at every level.

(iv) The destruction of environment has already gone too far and must stop without any further delay. Industrialisation should not be pursued at the cost of agriculture, and in setting up industries the environmental clearance must be very rigorous. In agriculture, the soil health must be kept under close watch.

(v) Due to resource limitations, the growth in population has to be drastically reduced, and a simple life-style encouraged everywhere. It must be impressed on the people that this earth is not meant for mankind only and the natural habitats of different creatures should not be destroyed beyond a point.

(vi) The decentralisation of power from the state to district level and below needs to be increased greatly without any further delay. The panchayats have to be strengthened adequately so that self-rule becomes a reality in near future. A massive transfer of resources to rural areas is urgently called for to meet all the basic needs of the people.

These changes will not be brought by the present self-seeking, corrupt leadership on their own. They have to be forced by the masses through all possible means to bring them. There appears to be need for a second Independence movement in the country to get rid of the criminal elements in the government and bring a truly democratic pattern of development. The Constutution has to be implemented both in letter and spirit.

In the completion of this work, my debt is indeed very extensive. A variety of materials has been collected from different government departments, research institutes and university libraries. In this process many people came to my help. Among the government departments, particularly helpful were the Directorate of Economics and Statistics and planning department of the relevant state governments. Among research institutes, particularly useful was the Gujarat Institute of Development Research (GIDR), Ahmedabad and Gokhale Institute of Politics and Economics, Pune. The universities that need a special mention are Mumbai, Lucknow, Gujarat Vidyapith and Barkatullah in Bhopal.

Due to lack of space, acknowledgment of debt individually to all the people that came to my help is not possible. The range is very wide, and I express my deep gratitude to every body. To name a few of the persons: At Lucknow: in the Lucknow University, Prof. S.B. Singh, Prof. A.K. Sengupta, Dr. Pradeep Misra and Dr. F.H. Hashmi; in the government Directorate of Economics and Statistics (DES), Om Kumar Sharma, R.N. Sharma, Ilias Khan and Surya Prakash; and in the Planning Department, Mrs. Amita Srivastava. At Bhopal: Prof. Hanuman Singh Yadav at the Barkatullah University; in the DES, Mrs. Mitra Tripathy, P.D. Joshi and Ahmaduddin; in the Rural Development Department, S.N. Srivastava; and in the Planning Department, Kiran Misra; in the MP State Industrial Development Corporation, S.D. Sharma. At Ahmedabad: Sudarshan Iyengar, Minal Seth and Chandra Krishnamurthy at the GIDR; Kiran Shah at Gujarat Vidyapith; in the DES, S.V. Trivedi and H.R. Gandhi; in the Rural Development Department, Commissioner A. M. Tiwari; in the Planning Department, Z.G. Seikh; at the NABARD, Miss Kamakshi Pai and Sarda Nath. At Mumbai: Dr. A.M. Murudkar and Dr. Jayant S. Sawant at the University of Mumbai, University sub centre Ratnagiri. Dr. Md. S. Rahaman, Ahmedabad Textele Industries Research Association. At Kolkata, S.K. Bhattacharya of DGCIS (Commercial Library). R.R. Shinge and D.N. Gholap in the DES. At Pune: Mrs. Gadre and Dr. Srikant S. Kalamkar in the Gokhale Institute.

Above all is probably my debt to the North Bengal University, Siliguri, where I joined as a full Professor and Head of Department as early as 1981. Particularly valuable here was the excellent service I received from its Library. I express my deep gratitude to the staff of the library. Finally, no word is adequate to express the debt I owe to my wife, late Kalpana, without whose full cooperation and care the work would not have been possible.

Kalipada Deb
Siliguri

10th April, 2013

PART I: INTRODUCTION

1

NATURE OF GOVERNMENT AND THE PATTERN OF DEVELOPMENT IN INDIA

The pace and pattern of economic progress in a country is primarily determined by the quality of government available. It is not so much the question of the formal type, like monarchic, oligarchic, dictatorial or democratic, within each type there can be great variations in nature of operation. Even a monarchy may be better at looking after the welfare of the people than an apparently democratic regime. A democracy based on adult franchise may be manipulated with muscle power and other means, and may function only in the interest of a small segment at the top.

Right type of development — that is, one which looks after the interest of the majority, particularly to their basic needs — can be brought only by a government appropriately motivated in that direction. Whatever is the formal type, the government must have the ability and determination to bring the desired pattern of progress. In a backward country with the vast majority in semi-starving condition and steeped in ignorance, the task of development is indeed very challenging. All the available and potential resources have to be mobilised with a strong hand and deployed in the right direction. The human resources, available in plenty, have to be moulded to suit the needs of development. A socialist pattern of society cannot be built by men with feudal and capitalistic mentality.

THE INDIAN CONSTITUTION: DEFICIENCIES AND DISTORTIONS

The Constitution of India, which came into force in January 1951, is apparently in the right direction. The Preamble to the Constitution says: "resolved to constitute India into a Sovereign Socialist Secular Democratic Republic and to secure to all its citizens: JUSTICE, social, economic and political; LIBERTY of thought, expression, belief, faith and worship; EQUALITY of status and of opportunity; and to promote among them all FRATERNITY assuring the dignity of the individual and the unity and integrity of the Nation ...." The Directive Principles of State Policy, which are concerned with peoples' livelihood, include, among other things, the following important provisions:

Section 39 states: "The state shall, in particular, direct its policy towards securing—(a) that the citizens, men and women equally, have the right to an adequate means of livelihood; (b) that the ownership and control of the material resources of the community are so distributed as best to subserve the common good; (c) that the operation of the economic system does not result in the concentration of wealth and means of production to the common detriment; (d) that there is equal pay for equal work for both men and women; (e) that the health and strength of workers, ... and the tender age of children are not abused and that citizens are not forced by economic necessity to enter vocations unsuited to their age or strength; (f) that children are given opportunities and facilities to develop in a healthy manner ... and that children and youth are protected against exploitation and against moral and material abandonment ..."

Section 41 calls for making "effective provision for securing the right to work, to education and to public assistance in case of unemployment, old age, sickness and disablement, and other cases of undeserved want". Section 45 assures "to provide, within a period of ten years from the commencement of this Constitution, for free and compulsory education for all children until they complete the age of fourteen years". Special attention was to be given to "the educational and economic interests of the weaker sections of the people, and, in particular, of the Scheduled Castes and the Scheduled Tribes". (Section 46). The need for protecting the environment was also not neglected. Section 48a states: "The state shall endeavour to protect and improve the environment and to safeguard the forests and wild life of the country". The provisions under Directive Principles are, however, not justiciable. And this is indicative of a sinister motive of the framers of Constitution. The Constitution has turned out to be a propaganda material for vote catching and for creating a good impression to the outside world.

The Constitution also provides for many fundamental rights: The Right to Equality before law prohibits any discrimination on the ground of religion, race, caste, etc. The Right to Freedom provides for freedom of speech and expression, to form associations or unions, to move freely throughout the country and to reside anywhere, to carry on any occupation or business, and of protection of life and personal liberty. The Right Against Exploitation prohibits trafficking in human beings and forced labour, of employment of children in factories, etc. These rights are justiciable, but were largely violated, and proved meaningless for a vast majority.

Apparently the Constitution is of federal type, but the historical background made its makers swing towards a strong Centre. The Constitution guarantees the existence of states but the Central Parliament can create new ones, abolish existing ones, or alter the boundaries simply by majority vote. But the Constitution is silent on the subject of criteria. In 1956, after the reorganisation of the states, there were 14 states and eight union territories; presently, it is 28 and seven, respectively. The states are of extremely disparate size, both in terms of population and area.

The Constitution divides legislative powers into three groups: Union, State and Concurrent. The longest and most important is the first one, with 97 items. The State List has 66 items, of which 30 deal with ordinary police functions and 22 with taxation; the remaining 14 are on 'development'. Most of the powers are, however, hedged about with qualifications, and in certain circumstances the Centre may override state powers. The Concurrent List, containing 47 items, has 'economic and social planning and trade, but, where there is conflict, laws passed by the Central Parliament prevail over the state's. At the executive level also there are decided constitutional limits to provincial autonomy. The source of executive authority is the state governor, appointed by the President. This power is normally exercised by the provincial council of ministers but the governor has important discretionary powers. The actual administration of the state is in the hands of the all-India services, and the chief secretary, the most senior administrative officer in the state, may find himself subjected to a division of loyalties. The distribution of taxes also disadvantages the states.

The Finance Commission (FC), appointed by the President every five-year, is a quasi-judicial body, and recommends on how the centrally collected resources should be distributed between the government of India (GOI) and the states, how the states' share should be distributed among them, and what principles should govern the allocation of grants-in-aid to individual states. The commission's recommendations, which are usually accepted by the Centre, covers around one-third of all the resources transferred from the Centre to the states. The Planning Commission (PC) is a non-statutory body concerned with plan as opposed to revenue expenditure. In practice, this is an ambiguous distinction and has led to strained relations between the two commissions and much discontent in the states. The PC transfers resources to the states in two forms: central investment for projects of all-India significance and central assistance for approved local projects. The latter has been increasingly in the form of loans and dominates the total transfer of resources. Consequently, the states have run deeply into debt.

What the Constitution called the Union government is wrongly described as the Central government by officialdom and subsequently, all powers have been centralised. The Centre-state relations, however, varied from time to time and from state to state depending on many political factors, including the unity and standing of the central government and the bargaining strength of the state concerned.

The deficiencies in the Constitution became apparent soon after it came into operation. The first amendment was made in the first year itself, and by the year 1980 there were 45 amendments; in 2011, it reached 116. Some of the important amendments were: imposition of reasonable restrictions on the right of freedom of speech and expression in 1950; reorganisation of the states and introduction of union territories in 1956; power to enact any legislation for imposing reasonable restrictions in the exercise of fundamental rights in 1963; withdrawal of recognition to former rulers of princely states and abolition of the privy purses in 1971; making right to property not a fundamental one in 1978; curb on defection from one political party to another in 1985; strengthening of the panchayat system in 1993; and provision of free and compulsory education for all children by the state in 2002.

CHALLENGES TO GOVERNANCE

The Period of Jawaharlal Nehru

In the initial years of freedom, the ruling Congress Party faced many threats, both from within and from outside. It was without a unifying purpose. From West Bengal to Uttar Pradesh, along the Gangetic Valley, the Congress was split. In late 1949 Nehru and Patel had a major disagreement. A growing Hindu tint of the Congress had led to the departure of some of the most vocal leaders.

The first general elections were held in 1952 — i.e., five years after Independence — and it was a big challenge to Nehru. There were varied parties but all had one target: the ruling Congress. Nehru had to face many problems, which included angry refugees from East and West Pakistan, not yet settled in their new homes. The Andhras in the south and the Sikhs in the north were getting restive. The Kashmir question was still unresolved. Faced with wide-ranging opposition from outside, and with some dissidence within his own party, Jawaharlal Nehru took to the road and on occasion the plane and the train as well. However the Congress had won comfortably. The party had secured 364 out of 489 seats in Parliament and 2,247 out of 3,280 seats in the state assemblies.

Nehru ruled continuously for nearly 17 years, until his death on 27 May, 1964. In the following two elections, held in 1957 and 1962, also the Congress party was in good position. The party's vote share in the parliamentary elections were 47.8 and 44.5 per cent respectively, with the share of seats at 75.1 and 72.8 per cent. For state Assemblies, the vote shares were 45.5 and 44.0 per cent and in seats at 65.1 and 60.7 per cent, respectively. This strong position notwithstanding, the government had to face many challenges — particularly the problem arising from Partition of the country, securing of Kashmir, the tribal trouble, the linguistic division of the country, the Southern challenge, and the Chinese war. A brief idea is given below on the magnitude of each of these problems.

1. The Partition of the Country

On the problems arising out of Partition, it is necessary to note a few of the events leading to the Partition: The Congress formally accepted Partition on 3 June 1947. There was tension and political divide between the Congress and the Muslim League but entirely insufficient violence to justify the decision. The most controversial move in the Partition drama was, however, Mountbatten's decision to bring forward the date of Partition to mid-August instead of June, 1948. Only Nehru was informed of this pre-planning in advance and not other leaders and this had disastrous consequences for Punjab. (Nevile, Pran 2011). Personal ambition of Nehru and Jinnah probably played an important part in partitioning of the country.

India was partitioned first and the provinces, Punjab and Bengal, partitioned later. The Punjab assembly was divided between Muslim majority West Punjab and the Hindu-Sikh majority East Punjab to ascertain the view about partitioning Punjab from both sides. The Hindus and Sikhs knowing that Pakistan had already been accepted voted for partitioning Punjab in order to remain with India. The Muslims voted against partitioning Punjab. Punjab's foremost Muslim leader Sir Sikandar Hayat Khan before his death stated in 1942 that if the creation of Pakistan meant the partition of Punjab, he would not accept Pakistan.

2. The Kashmir Problem

On Kashmir, it has to be noted that of the princely states that joined the Indian Union, the most important was, and continues to be, the state of Jammu and Kashmir. The province of jammu, touching Punjab, had low hills and large areas of arable land. Before Partition the Muslims were in a slight majority, but with the wave of panic migration that year Jammu came to be dominated by Hindus. In contrast, the Valley of Kashmir had a substantial Muslim majority. The Maharaja of Kashmir in 1947 was Hari Singh.

In 1932, an All-Jammu Kashmir Muslim Conference was formed to give shape to the growing opposition to the Maharaja. Six years later, Abdullah took the lead in transforming the organisation into a 'National Conference', which would also include Hindus and Sikhs. The new body asked for representative government based on universal sufarge. At about this time Abdullah made acquaintance with Jawaharlal Nehru. Both had similar views — a commitment to Hindu-Muslim harmony and to socialism. The National Conference grew closer to the Indian National Congress, alienating some of its members, most notably Ghulam Abbas, who left the party and sought to organise Kashmiri Muslims on their own. This was the beginning of a bitter rivalry with Sheikh Abdullah. Abdullah had been in and out of jail since 1931, and in 1946 he was incarcerated once more after he asked the Dogra dynasty to 'quit Kashmir' and hand over power to the people. In the ensuing unrest more than twenty people died. The Maharaja declared martial law and had the Sheikh sentenced to three years imprisonment for 'sedition'. As it was clear by now that the British would soon leave the sub-continent, Hari Singh's prime minister, Ramchandra Kak, encouraged him to think of independence for his state. The idea of independence had taken strong hold over the Maharaja. Pakistan tried to occupy Kashmir desparetly.

Nehru was of the opinion that India must come to some 'rapid and more or less final decisions about Kashmir with the Pakistan Government'. He wrote to Maharaja Hari Singh, outlining the various forms a settlement could take. It could be a plebiscite for the whole state to decide which dominion it would join. Or the state could survive as an independent entity, with its defence guaranteed by both India and Pakistan. A third option was of a partition, with Jammu going to India and the rest of the state to Pakistan. A fourth option had Jammu and the Valley staying with India, with Poonch and beyond being ceded to Pakistan. Nehru himself was inclined to the last alternative. These four options he outlined in December 1947.

On January 1, 1948, on the advice of the governor general Mountbatten, India decided to take the Kashmir issue to the United Nations in order to get its help to clear the northern parts of what it said was an illegal occupation by groups loyal to Pakistan. Through January and February Security Council held several sittings on Kashmir. Pakistan now suggested the withdrawal of all armed forces in the state, and the holding of a plebiscite under an 'impartial interim administration'. A striking feature of the UN discussion on Kashmir was the partisanship of the British. By now, Nehru bitterly regretted going to the United Nations. By March 1948 Sheikh Abdullah was the most important man in the Valley. Kashmir remained quiet for a decade or two. But in 1989 — when V.P. Singh was Prime Minister — the Valley erupted again. (Joshi, Manoj 1999).

3. The Tribal Problems

Among the problems related to the tribals, the most worisome was the Naga problem. The early meetings of the NNC witnessed a vigorous debate between these factions which spilled over into the pages of the Naga Nation. Meanwhile, the moderate wing had begun negotiations with the Congress leadership. In July 1946 the NNC general secretary, T. Sakhrie, wrote to Jawaharlal Nehru, and in reply received an assurance that the Nagas would have full autonomy, but within the Indian Union. They could have their own judicial system, said Nehru, to save them from being swamped by people from other parts of the country. Sakhrie now declared that the Nagas would continue their connection with India, 'but as a distinct community . . . We shall enjoy home rule in our country but on broader issues connected with India.' (Chasie, Charles 1999). The radicals, however, still stood out for complete independence.

The Constituent Assembly recognised the vulnerability of the tribals, and decided to designate some 400 communities as 'scheduled tribes'. These constituted about seven per cent of the population, and had seats reserved for them in the legislature and in government departments. Schedule V of the Constitution pertained to the trilbes that lived in Central India; it allowed for the creation of tribal advisory councils and for curbs on moneylending and on the sale of tribal land to outsiders. Schedule VI was for the tribes of the north-east. It went further in the direction of local autonomy, constituting district and regional councils, protecting local rights in land, forests and waterways and instructed state governments to share mining revenues with the local council, a concession not granted anywhere else.

The Naga radicals were for an independent, sovereign state carved out of India and quite distinct from it. Among the Nagas this view was upheld most insistently by the Angamis and their leader was Angami Zapu Phizo, with whose name the Naga cause was to be identified for close to half a century. Botn in 1913, Phizo was educted by the Baptists.

There was also a major revolt in the Mizo Hills — a tribal district bordering East Pakistan (presently Bangladesh) with a population of mere 300,000. But, as in Nagaland, among them were some motivated young men determined to carve out a homeland of their own.

4. Linguistic Division of the Country

The division of the country on the basis of language was comtemplated very early. As early as 1917, the Congress party had committed itself to the creation of linguistic provinces in a free India. When Independence finally came Gandhi thought that the states should be defined on the basis of language. Nehru, however, was not in favour of linguistic division of the country. Towards the end of 1947 he said that the country had just been divided on the basis of religion: would not dividing it further on the basis of language merely encourage the break up of the Union. Nehru's view had the support of both Vallabhbhai Patel and C. Rajagopalachari. The latter insisted that 'further fissiparous forces' had to be checked forthwith. And Patel worked hard within the Constituent Assembly to reverse the official Congress position. The Assembly appointed a committee to report on the question. It concluded that in the prevailing unsettled conditions 'the first and last need of India at the present moment is that it should be made a nation . . . Everything which helps the growth of nationalism has to go forward and everything which throws obstacles in its way has to be rejected'. (Constituent Assembly, Report, 1948). The verdict caused dismay among large sections of the Assembly. It slowed things for a while, but in 1948 and 1949 there was a renewed movement for linguistic autonomy.

A campaign for Samyukta (Greater) Karnataka, aiming to unite Kannada speakers spread across the states of Madras, Mysore, Bombay and Hyderabad. Complementing this was the struggle for Samyukta Maharashtra to bring together Marathi speakers in a single political unit. The Malayalis wanted a state of their own, based on the merger of the princely states of Cochin and Travancore with Malabar. There was also a Mahagujarat movement, and the struggle for a Sikh state in the Punjab. The most vigorous movement for linguistic autonomy was, however, that of the Telugu speaker of the Andhra. Telugu was spoken by more people in India than any other language besides

Hindi. It had a rich literary history, and was associated with such symbols of Andhra glory as the Vijayanagara Empire. After Independence the speakers of Telugu asked the Congress to implement its old resolutions in favour of linguistic states.

After Nehru

On 27 May, 1964, two hours after the announcement of Nehru's death, Home Minister Gulzarilal Nanda was sworn in as acting prime minister. Almost immediately the search commenced for a more permanent successor. Lal Bahadur Shastri was elected as the successor.

Lal Bahadur Shastri as Prime Minister

During Shastr's Prime Ministership, the Indo-Pak border conflict threatened to become a full-fledged war. On September 1, 1965 the Pakistan army launched a major offensive in Chhamb. An infantry division with two regiments of American Patton tanks crossed the border. Catching the Indians by surprise, they occupied thirty square miles within 24 hours. Their aim was to capture the bridge at Akhnoor, thus to sever links between J&K and the state of Punjab. The defence now called in their airforce, with some thirty aircrafts raining down bombs on the enemy. The Indian vampires were answered by Pakistani Sabre jets. As the battle raged, the Chinese weighed in with words in support of the Pakistanis. On 4 September, Marshal Chen Yi, visiting Karachi, condemned 'Indian imperialism for violating the Cease-Fire Line', and endorsed the actions taken by the government of Pakistan. Four days later Chou En-lai stated that 'India's acts of aggression pose a threat to peace in this part of Asia'. The escalation of hostilities alarmed the superpowers, and on 6 September the United Nations Security Council met to discuss the matter. The UN secretary general, U. Thant, flew to the subcontinent, and after meeting leaders in both capitals got them to agree to a ceasefire.

After the war had ended, the Soviets offered their help in working out a peace settlement. In the first week of January, 1966, Shastri and Ayub khan met in Tashkent, with the Soviet prime minister Alexei Kosygin as the chief mediator. After a week of hard bargaining the two sides agreed to give up what they most prized - international arbitration of the Kashmir dispute for Pakistan, the retention of key posts captured during the war for India. After signing the agreement, on the night of the same date Shastri died in his sleep.

In the war of 1965, Prime Minister Shastri proved his mettle. One of Shastri's first acts as prime minister was to increase budget allocations to agriculture. He was deeply concerned about the shortfalls in food production in recent years.

Indira Gandhi's Period

The attitude autocratic nature of Mrs. Gandhi was perfectly reflected in the Emergency she imposed on the country from June 1975 to January 1977.

Within a week of the emergency, she offered a 'Twenty Point Programme for Economic Progress'. This promised reduction in prices of essential commodities, the speedy implementation of land reforms, the abolition of indebtedness and of bonded labour, higher wages for workers and lower taxes for the middle class. Soon she began the packing of the civil service, the judiciary and the Congress party with individuals committed to the prime minister.

The opposition MPs were put behind bars and a series of constitutional amendments were passed to prolong her rule. The 38th amendment, passed on 22 July 1975, barred judicial review of the emergency. The 39th amendment, two weeks later, stated that the election of the PM could not be challenged by the Supreme Court, but only by a body constituted by Parliament.

Among the casualties of the emergency was the freedom of the press. Within its first week the government had instituted a system of 'pre-censorship', whereby editors had to submit, for scrutiny and approval, material deemed to be critical of the government or its functionaries. Guidelines were issued on what did and did not constitute news. There could be no reports on processions or strikes, or of political opposition or of conditions in the jails. Even stories mildly critical of the administration were not permitted. The space had to be filled ; and it was, by the words of the prime minister or by stories in praise of her government. (Basu, Sajal 1978). The independent news agencies, the UNI and the PTI, were amalgamated with two lesser agencies into a single state-controlled news service called Samachar. The Press Council of India, an autonomous watch dog body, was abolished. The emergency was, however, widely welcomed by the middle class. The crime rate had come down and the trains ran on time. A good monsoon in 1975 meant that prices also fell.

Resistance to the emergency in the country was not much. The middle class was almost totally silent. There was hardly any official resigning in protest against the emergency. In the Parliament, however, some resistance was offered. On 23 July the House met to ratify the emergency. The Congress commanded a comfortable majoraity; and 34 MPs were in jail. Finally, there was resistance that was carried in underground. The key figure here was George Fernandes, the firebrand socialist.

Soon came the elevation of Indira Gandhi's son Sanjay Gandhi. He was given charge of the Congress's youth wing. Although in theory he was merely a member of the Executive Council, in practice the Youth Congress president took orders from him. By now Sanjay Gandhi had formulated a five point programme to complement his mother's twenty point. His programme dealt with, respectively, family planning, afforestation, abolition of dowry, the removal of illiteracy and slum clearance. Of these, the focus was on the first, nationally, and on the fifth in case of Delhi. Following the order of Sajay Gandhi the close aid Jagmohan demolished the poor colonies of Delhi.

Sanjay Gandhi expressed himself in favour of compulsory sterilisation, for which facilities should be provided 'right down to the village level'. Here was a

Herculean project, the solving of which, everyone acknowledged, was vital if the nation hoped to survive'. It, therefore, became 'the lynchpin of Sanjay's Emergency activities'. (Mehta 1978). In his tour around India, Sanjay Gandhi catalysed a competitive process between the states of the Union. Sanjay would tell one chief minister of what another had claimed to have done — '60,000 operations in two weeks' and encourage him to exceed it. These targets were passed down to district officials, who were rewarded if they met or exceeded them and transferred otherwise. The process led to widespread coercion.

On 19 January, leaders of four parties — the Jana Sang, the Bharatiya Lok Dal (a party principally of farmers led by the veteran Charan Singh), the socialist Party and Morarji Desai's Congres (O) — met at the residence of Morarji Desai in New Delhi and decided to fight the elections under a common symbol and common name. On the 23rd, the Janata (Peoples) Party was formally launched at a news conference in the presence of Jayaprakash Narayan. Afer ten days, Jagjiban Ram — a lifelong Congressman, a prominent minister in Nehru's and Indira Gandhi's Cabinets and the acknowledged leader of the Scheduled Castes who made up some 15 per cent of the electorate - announced that he was leaving the Union government. It was Ram who had moved the resolution in the Lok Sabha endorsing the emergency. His resignation came as a shock to the Congress. Ram formed a new Party, the Congress for Democracy (CFD), which collaborated with the Janata Party. The elections were held in the third week of March. The results started coming from the night of 20 March. Mrs. Gandhi was defeated in her previously safe seat of Rae Bareilli, and Sanjay Gandhi defeated in the adjoining Amethi constituency. Mrs. Gandhi had lost to her old foe and litigant Raj Narain; and Sanjay Gandhi to an obscure student leder. (Pillai, S. Devadas 1977).

These two defeats were part of a wider wash out of the Congress in Uttar Pradesh. They lost all 85 seats in the state, and all 54 seats in neighbouring Bihar, to the Jaanta - CFD alliance. In Rajasthan the Congress won one seat out of 25; in Madhya Pradesh one out of 40. These losses were partly offset by a robust performance in southern India, where the emergency had rested lightly. In Andhra Pradesh the Congrss won 41 seats out of 42; in Karnataka 26 out of 28; in Tamil Nadu, 14 out of 39. In the country as a whole the Congress won 153 seats in a house of 540. On the other side, as many as 298 Janata and CFD candidates were successful. (Prachand, SLM 1977). Two groups in particular — the Scheduled Castes and the Muslims — long considered to be loyal 'vote banks' of the ruling party, had this time deserted the Congress. The latter had suffered grievously at the hands of Sanjay's pet programmes. For the first time in the nation's thirty-year history, a non-Congress party came to power.

The Janata Party in Power

Unlike the Congress, the Janata Party had not fought the elections under a single leader. After the results were announced, a controversy arose as to who should be chosen prime minister. The contest was among Charan Singh, Jagjiban Ram and Morarji Desai. As regards the policies of the new government, the importance of Charan Singh signalled an anti-urban bias, and the Planning Commission was now dominated by economists who specialised in agriculture.

In foreign policy, the Janata government sought to mend fences with India's neighbours. In Novembe 1977 India and Bangladesh signed an agreement for the sharing of the Ganga waters, which gave the former 20,500 cubic feet of water during the lean season, and the latter 34,500 cubic feet. The greatest consensus of the Janata Party was on the new regime's treatment of the former prime minister. The Janata leaders were determined to make Mrs. Gandhi pay for having imposed the emergency. As many as eight Commissions of Enquiry were appointed, each headed by a retired judge. Several dealt with the corruption of Congress chief ministers, one with the treatment of J. P. in Jail. There was also a commission set up to enquire into the affairs of Sanjay Gandhi's Maruti company. The enquiry with the widest ambit was the Shah Commission, set up to punish those guilty of the excesses of the emergency. It was headed by a former chief justice of the Supreme Court, Justice J.C. Shah. It met in a court room of Patiala House in central Delhi. In its first few months the Commission examined scores of witnesses: bureaucrats, police officers, municipal officials, members of Mrs. Gandhi's Cabinet. But Indira Gandhi herself refused to testify. Three times she was called to the witness box; three times she came, and chose not to answer questions, claiming she was bound by the oath of Cabinet secrecy.' (Abbas, KA 1978).

The change of government at the Centre brought changes of regime in the provinces as well. The commercialisation of agriculture had benefited a significant section of farmers in rural India, and the economic gains had converted themselves into political ambition. By the 1970s they had made their presence felt in national politics. In the Janata dispensation the force of rural assertion was 'dramatically represented in the personality and ideology of Charan Singh'. But it ran deeper than this one man. After the 1977 Lok Sabha elections, 36 per cent of all MPs came from farming background. Their impact was felt in the rural orientation of the government's economic policies, as in the ever higher procurement price paid by states for wheat and rice. (Varshney, Ashutosh 1998).

The backward/forward divide and the caste conflict had sharpened in the Janata period. The second kind of caste conflict was that between the backwards and the SCs. This conflict too had a material basis; it was the former who mostly owned the land, and the latter who mostly laboured on it. Beyond disputes about wages and working conditions, this was also a dispute about dignity. The backwards slipped easily into the shoes of the forwards whose lands they had gained. Like them, they treated the SCs with disdain and often violated their women. At one time the lowest castes had no option but to suffer in silence. But th expansion of education, and the spaces opened up by political representation, meant that the younger Harijans were 'no longer ready to put up with contempt, abuse, beating and other forms of insult'. (Sachidananda 1979). Consequently, there had been a dramatic increase in the number of attacks on Harijans since the new government assumed power in New Delhi.

The dramitic situation made Indira Gandhi's image as a friend of the poor and the lowly. It also showed to the average member of the Congress Party that Indira Gandhi was a woman of action and she alone could be trusted to lead the fight back to power.' (Limaye, Madhu 1994). Mrs. Gandhi's revival was also helped by a less inspired initiative of the government in power. In the first week of October 1977 the home minister Charan Singh decided that he must arrest the former PM. Acting on his instructions, the CBI prepared a charge sheet accusing her of corruption. The police took her into custody. Their plan was to drive her to a rest house in the neighbouring state of Haryana. But because of some trouble in the way this could not be done and the police drove back to the capital. Mrs. Gandhi was kept overnight by the police, but when they produced her before a magistrate the next morning, he threw out the charge sheet as flimsy and insubstantial. The bungled 'arrest' redounded badly on the Janata government. She began making combative speeches against the new regime, singling out the increase in crime and inflation, and the profiteering of hoarders and blackmarketeers. The next month this party easily won state elections in Andhra Pradesh and Karnataka. The former prime minister had been the chief campaigner. The results showed, at least in the south her image as a saviour of the poor, the adivasi, the SCs and women was firmly in tact.

Janata's attempts to humiliate the former prime minister were seriously misjudged. The stoicism with which Mrs. Gandhi bore her sufferings was much admired, and the two brief arrests allowed her to acquire a halo of martyrdom. Admittedly, the men now in power had been victimised during the emergency, but that they chose to focus on taking revenge spoke of a certain narrowness of vision. Behind the attempts to arrest the former prime minister, however, lay personal rivalries within the Janata camp.

In October 1979 JP died a broken man. The editor of Opinion AD Gorwala paid tribute to Narayan as 'the great moral force of the country, the touchstone of right and wrong'. Beyond the fighting and squabbling, the Janata government made a notable contribution to Indian democracy, in repairing the Constitution from the emergency's depredations, in reviving open parliamentary practice through its consultatives style when rapairing the Constitution, and in restoring judiciary's independence'.

Although the Janata government failed to last its full term, the victory of the Janata Party was a watershed in Indian politics. For the first time since Independence a party other than the Congress came to govern at the Centre. In the states too the landscape of politics became more variegated. The late 1970s also witnessed the flowering of numerous 'new' social movements. In 1978 there was a major conference of 'socialist-feminist' in Bombay, which focused on the growing violation of women's rights. Campaigns were launched against dowry and rape, against male alcoholism, and for better working conditions for women.

Return of Indira Gandhi

Mrs. Gandhi returned to power agin in the election held in 1980. Her Congress Party won 353 seats in this elections. The Janata Party had thoroughly discredited itself. The rash of attacks on SCs turned this very numerous voting segment back towards the Congress. Sections of the Muslim 'vote bank' also returned to the Congress; Sanjay Gandhi had apologised to them for the excesses of the emergency. (Shakir, Moin 1980).

In this period, however, Indira Gandhi was in no mood to share power with any body except her son Sanjay, who was now both an MP and the general secretary of the Congress Party. Indira Gandhi persuaded her elder son, Rajiv, to fill the breach of Sanjay, who died in a plane crash. He had no previous political experience, working as a pilot in the Indian Airline. (India Today 1980). After nine months Rajiv Gandhi was elected as an MP from Amethi.

As Rajiv Gandhi took his first steps in Indian politics, Indira Gandhi was at work on the world stage to rebuild bridges torn down during the emergency. The movement for a tribal state state of Jharkhand had also taken new and more militant forms. The 1980s also saw a renewal of Naga militancy. During the emergency the government of India had been able to persuade many members of Phizo's Naga National Council to lay down their arms and come out of hiding. However, the accord on it was seen as a sell out by Naga radicals such as T. Muivah, trained in China. In 1980, Muivah and Isaak Swu set up the National Socialist Council of Nagaland and began building up links with other insurgency groups in India's North-east and in Burma.

There were movements for separate or new states within or outside the Union, and movements for greater autonomy within existing states. In the old Congress stronghold of Andhra Pradesh there was growing resentment at the centre's tendency to 'impose' chief ministers. Between 1978 and 1982 Mrs. Gandhi changed the state's chief minister no fewer than four times. Among those provoked into action was the great film star N.T. Rama Rao. He now formed a new regional party, Telugu Desam, which stood for 'the honour and self-respaect of the 60 million Telugu speaking people'. No longer, he said, would the great state of Andhra Pradesh be treated as a 'branch office' of the Congress Party. (Times of India, 30 March, 1982). A more serious movement took shape in Assam in late 1970s and early 1980s. The key organisation in this transformation was the All-Assam Students union (AASU). Its network extended throughout the state. Beginning in 1979 and carrying on over the next five years, the AASU led hundreds of strikes and processions intended to press the central government to clear their homeland of the infiltrators. The

AASU's more immediate demand was, however, for the deletion of immigrant from the voters list preparatory to their deportation from the state. This inevitably led to a polarisation on communal basis.

Contemporaneous with the Assam movement, there was a still more serious agitation for greater autonomy in the state of Punjab. It was still more serious because Punjab bordered Pakistan, a country with which India had fought three wars. Besides, the majority community of the state were not Hindus but Sikhs. As in Assam, the Punjab agitation also had causes both distant and proximate. A section of the Sikh intelligentsia hoped for the renewal, in some shape or form, of the Sikh state ruled by Maharaja Ranjit Singh in the first half of the 19th century. Others looked only as far back as Partition, and the tragedies and losses suffered by the community then. It had taken 20 years of almost ceaseless struggle to compel the Centre to constitute a Sikh majority province within India. In April 1978 there was a mass convention at Amritsar of a religious sect, the Nirankaris. They thought of themselves as Sikhs, but the faithful regarded them as heretics. Leading the opposition to the Nirankari meeting was a hitherto obscure preacher named Jarnail Singh Bhindranwale, who claimed that Sikhs 'were slaves in independent India' — discriminated against, by the Hindus. Bhindranwale wanted the Sikhs to purify themselves and return to the fundamentals of their faith. According to some accounts, Bhindranwale was built up by Sanjay Gandhi and the Union home minister Jail Singh - himself a former chief minister of Punjab — as a counter to the Akalis. While the Nirankari convention was in progress, Bhindranwale preached an angry sermon from the precincts of the Golden Temple. Moved by his words, a crowd of Sikhs descended upon the place where the heretics were meeting. The Nirankaris fought back; in the battle that ensued, 15 people died.

Sikhs pride took another blow in 1980, when the Akalis were dismissed and thc Congress returned to power in Punjab. In June of that year a group of students met at the Golden Temple and proclaimed the formation of an independent Sikh republic, named Khalistan. It had as president a Sikh politician based in London, named Jagjit Singh Chauhan. The announcement was made simultaneously in the UK, the United States, Canada and France. (Guha, Ramchandra 2007). The government of India's attention was focused on the Akalis, who, out of power, had chosen the path of confrontation. Through the early 1980s the politics of agitation co-existed uneasily with the politics of assassination. In April 1980 the Nirankari leader Baba Gurcharan Singh was shot dead in New Delhi. Then in September 1981 came the murder of Lala Jagat Narain, an influential editor who had polemicised vigorously against Sikh extremism. It was widely believed that Bhindranwale ws behind both the murders. His arrest provoked widespread violence and a dozen people died as a result. (IE, 21 September 1981) After three weeks he was released for lack of evidence. Bhindranwale's release transformed him 'from a murder suspect [into] a new political force'.

Throughout 1982 there were many rounds of negotiations between the centre and the Akalis. No agreement was reached, the sticking point being the areas Punjab would give up to Haryana in exchange for Chandigarh and the sharing of river waters. On 26 January 1983, Republic Day, the Akali legislators in the satate assembly resigned. The challenge of Bhindranwale was forcing them to become more extreme. On 22 April 1983 a high-ranking Sikh policeman, A.S. Atwal, was killed as he left the Golden Temple after prayers. Atwal's murder further demoralised Punjab police, itself overwhelmingly Sikh. A spate of bank robberies followed. Sections of the Hindu minority began fleeing the state. On 5 October 1983, terrorists stopped a bus on the highway, segregated the Hindu passengers and shot them. The next day President's Rule was imposed in the state. In the last weeks of 1983 Bhindranwale took residence in the Akal Takht, a building second in importance only to the Golden Temple. The next year the conflict in the Punjab assumed dangerous proportions. Then followed the Operation Bluedtsar.

In the evening of 6th May troops entered the building and found Shubeg Singh dead in the basement. Also found in the basement were the bodies of Bhindranwale and his devoted follower, Amrik Singh of the All India Sikh Students' Federtion. A reporter touring the Punjab countryside found a 'sullen and alienated community'. As one elderly Sikh put it, 'our inner self has been bruised. The base of our faith has been attacked, a whole tradition has been demolished.' The view from outside the Punjab was quite different. Many people commended Mrs. Gandhi for taking firm — if belated — action against terrorists claimed to be in the pay of Pakistan.

The prime minister herself was now prompted to move against elements in other states who were opposed to her. In Jammu and Kashmir she arranged for the dismissal of Farooq Abdullah's government. A month later a change of regime was effected in Andhra Pradesh also. Once more the governor, a former member of the Cngress Party, played a malevolent role. (The Week, 26 August 1984).

In the aftermath of Operation Bluestar the prime minister had been warned by intelligence agencies of a possible attempt on her life. She was advised to change the Sikh members of her personal bodyguard. Mrs. Gandhi rejected the suggestion, saying, 'Aren't we secular?' On the morning of 31 October, while walking from her home to her office next door, she was shot at point-blank range by two of her security guards, Satwant Singh and Beant Singh. They were both Sikhs who had recently returned from a visit home, and been provoked by the hurt and anger they witnessed to take revenge for Operation Bluestar. By the time the prime minister was admitted to hospital she was already dead.

The violence that began on the night of 31 October spread and intensified through the first two days of November. The first serious episodes occurred in south and central Delhi; later, the action moved east across the river Yamuna, to the resettlement colonies located there. Everywhere it was Sikhs alone were the target.

Mrs. Gandhi's impact on the history of India was definitive; as definitive, indeed, as her father Jawaharlal Nehru's When Indira Gandhi came to power in January 1966 'India was a coherent nation.' There was a set of socio-economic objectives aroud which it was united. The 'faith was still widely shared that the paraphernalia of the state was never intended — at least not consciously intended — to be put to use for advancing private interests'. But by the time of Indira Gandhi's death there had been 'a qualitative transformation. India is a divided nation.' There were now 'deep wounds and deep dissensions'. The five-year plans, once acknowledged as 'an earnest statement of hopes and aspirations', now 'do not mean a thing'. Now the 'apparatus of the state is all the time being manipulated for the sake of (the) fractional minority of the population at the top of the social hierarchy'. Now, the government at the centre is 'corrupt at the core and Indira Gandhi could not be absolved of direct responsibility for this state of affairs'. (*Ibid.*).

Rajiv Gandhi as PM

Against the bloody backdrop of violence by Hindus on Sikhs Rajiv Gandhi was sworn in as prime minister. A month after he took office the country witnessed a tragedy that claimed more lives than the anti-Sikh riots. In the early hours of December 3, 1984 white smoke began filling the air of Bhopal city, the capital of Madhya Pradesh. People asleep in their homes were woken up with fits of coughing , vomiting and burning sensation in the eyes. In panic they got out of bed and went out into the street, the gas cloud following them. By dawn, 'the main thoroughfares of the city were jammed with an unending stream of humanity, plodding its way in search of safer surroundings'. Many fell down in the streets, overcome by dizziness and exhaustion. Others found their way, somehow, to the city's few modern hospitals, whose beds were rapidly filled to capacity. (Times of India, December 4, 1984). The deadly gas was methyl isocyanate (MIC), and it came from a pesticide plant owned an run by an American firm, Union Carbide.

The Congress campaign presented Rajiv Gandhi as the logical heir to his mother's legacy, and the party itself as the only bulwark against the forces of secession. When the results came in, the Congress had swept the polls, capturing almost 80 per cent of the seats in Parliament. Under the leadership of a political novice, the Congress won 401 seats, far more than they ever had under Nehru or Indira Gandhi. The victory was, however, 'as much his late mother's as his own'. (Aiyar, Mani Shankar 1992).

With a comfortable majority, the prime minister immediately moved to make peace in the Punjab. The leaders of the Akali Dal were let out of jail and emissaries sent to talk to them. In July 1985 Sant Harcharan Singh Longowal and Rajiv Gandhi signed an accord, agreeing to transfer Chandigarh to Punjab within a specified time frame, assuring Punjab a fair share of waters and committing the government to a fresh review of centre-state relaions in general. President's Rule was to be revoked and state elections held. The government also signed an agreement with the All-Assam Students' Union on the infiltration issue. It was agreed that those who had arrived after 1 January 1966 but before 25 March 1971 (when the civil war in East Pakistan began) would be allowed to stay but not vote, while those who came later would be identified and deported. In Mizoram also the government of India signed a peace agreement with Laldenga, Leader of the Mizo National Front, in June 1986.

The first crisis of the new regime came from a lower court's decision. One Mahammed Ahmed Khan had appealed against the lower court's decision that he pay monthly maintenance to his divorced wife Shah Bano. Khan contended that he had fulfilled his duties by paying her an allowance for three months, the period specified — he claimed - under Islamic law. The Supreme Court rejected Khan's appeal invoking Section 125 of the Criminal Procedure Code (CPC), whereby a divorced woman was entitled to claim an allowance from her ex-husband if he had taken another wife, as Khan had, and if she had not remarried and could not otherwise maintain herself, as was the case with Shah Bano.

Towards the end of 1985, the Congress Party lost a number of by-elctions in northern India and it was attributed to the 'Shah Bano factor', with rivals of the Congress 'whipping up religious fervour' by attacking the Supreme Court in constituencies with large Muslim populations. (TST, In February 1986, the government introduced a 'Muslim Women's Bill in Parliament which sought to overturn the Supreme Court (SC) verdict, by taking Muslim personal law out of the purview of the CPC. The Bill placed the burden of supporting the divorced wife on her own relatives; all the husband was obliged to do was provide three months' maintenance. In May, the bill was passed into law, with the Congress issuing a whip to its members to vote for it. As a protest, Arif Mahammed Khan resigned, telling that with this new legislation 'Indian Muslim women will be the only women to be denied maintenance anywhere in the world'. (Eves weekly, 29 March - 4 April). This incident firmly proved that the country lacked a prime minister consistently committed to social reform. With 400 MPs supporting him at the time, a reform of Muslim personal law was very much within his reach.

Within a year of the SC verdict in the Shah Bano case, a judgement by a lower court provoked a more serious controversy. On February 1, 1986 the district judge of the town of Ayodhya, in UP, ordered that the locks be opened to permit worship at a small Hindu shrine, located inside a large mosque. The mosque was built in the sixteenth century by a general of the Mughal emperor Babur - hence it is known as the Babri Masjid. There appeared to be a strong connection between the Muslim Women's Bill and the Ayodhya verdict. It was said that Rajiv Gandhi opened the locks on the advice of his colleague Arun Nehru, who thought the Congress now needed to compensate the chauvinists on the other side. If one act was aimed at the 'Muslim' vote, this other one seemed to target the far larger 'Hindu' vote. A policy of appeasement of both communities began to be pursued by the government for electoral gains. (TST 1986: April 20, May 1).

On the economic front, Rajiv Gandhi's one of the daring departures was the appointment of Mr V.P. Singh from UP, a politician with reputation for integrity, as his finance minister. The government's first budget, introduced in March 1985, sought to remove some of the controls and checks in what was one of the most tightly regulated economies in the world. The trade regime was liberalised, with duties reduced on a variety of items and incentives provided for exports. The licensing system was simplified, and some key sectors deregulated. Curbs on assets of individual companies were partially lifted, and rates of corporate and personal income-tax reduced. In February 1985, the PM said in an interview that the Indian economy had got 'caught in a vicious circle of creating more and more controls. Controls really lead to all the corruption, to all the delays' (in Financial Express). Left-wing intellectuals rightly attacked the budget as pandering to the rich. Freeing the trade regime, they said, would make India excessively dependent on foreign capital. (Paranjape, H.K. 1985). The new policies were naturally welcomed by the business sector, and by the middle class. There was an expanding market for consumer durables. (India Today, 15 March and 15 April 1985; Ninan, TN 1985). These doings were not confined to the national capital; state ministers and chief ministers were alleged to be handing favours to industrialists in exchange for money.

By the end of his second year, Rajiv Gandhi was confronted with fresh challenges based on the claims of ethnicity, apart from the ongoing challenges based on religion and class. Some instances of conflict between different groups in the same state may be noted. In Assam, the Bodo tribals, led by the All-Bodo Students Union, revolted against the locally dominant Assamese, demanding a separate state to be carved out of Assam. In Tripura also around this time, tribal activists launched a struggle against the Bengalis who had migrated in large numbers to the state after Partition. In Punjab, the euphoria generated by the Rajiv Gandhi — Longowal accord proved to be short-lived. In Jammu and Kashmir also there was renewed trouble. Kashmir was quiet for a decade or two until 1989. But in 1989 — when V. P. Singh was Prime Minister — the Valley erupted again. (Joshi, Manoj 1999). On 8 December, a young woman doctor, Rubaiya Sayeed, was kidnapped in Srinagar by militants of the J&K Liberation Front. She was the daughter of Union home minister Mufti Mohammed Sayeed. The militants demanded that, in exchange for her release, five specified JKLF activists be freed from detention.

Although the Indian government had mixed success in containing secession at home, it went for an ambitious attempt to end ethnic strife in neighbouring Sri Lanka. Rajiv's decision on sending peace keeping forces to Sri Lanka brought a fatal consequence. The elections, held in November 1989, were a body blow to the Congress Party. They won only 197 seats, down more than 200 from their previous tally. The opposition also could not claim victory. The Janata Dal won 142 seats and the BJP 86. V.P. Singh was sworn in as head of a National Front govrnemnt, with the Left and the BJP choosing to support it from outside. The general election of 1989 was the first in which no single party won a majority. This election was the inauguration of an era of uncertainty. (Sanghvi, Vir 1989).

In November 1990, V.P. Singh had to resign, unable to sustain his minority government in the absence of BJP support. The Congress allowed Chandra Shekhar as a lame-duck prime minister to hold charge while they prepared for mid-term elections to be held in the summer of 1991. In the middle of the campaign Rajiv Gandhi was assassinated while speaking in a town in Tamil Nadu. The assassin, who was also blown up by the bomb she was carrying, was later revealed to be a representative of the LTTE. The killing was an act of vengeance, for the LTTE had not forgiven Rajiv Gandhi for sending troops against them in 1987. Notwithstanding the murder of Rajiv Gandhi, the elections were held on schedule. The sympathy generated by the killing allowd the Congress to win 244 seats. With support from independents they could form a government. P.V. Narasimha Rao, who had held important positions in Rajiv Gandhi's Cabinet, was sworn in as prime minister. Rao was the father of economic reforms, architect of India's 'Look East' foreign policy and the leader who brought peace to terror-ravaged Punjab. The economy was in a crisis at the time he took over with foreign currency reserves plummeting to around $ one billion.

In the elections of 1991, for the Parliament the BJP won 120 seats, up thirty-five from the last time. It also won the assembly elections in Uttar Pradesh, Madhya Pradesh, Rajasthan and Himachal Pradesh.

Rise of the BJP

In the eleventh general election, held in 1996, the BJP reaped the rewards. It won 161 seats, emerging as the largest single party in Parliament. The veteran BJP leader A.B. Vajpayee formed the government, but after two weeks he resigned, failing to cobble a majority. For the next two years the BJP sat in the opposition, while the country was governed by a coalition of regional parties calling itself the National Front. When a mid-term poll was held in 1998, the BJP improved its position further, winning 182 seats. This time, the support of smaller parties and independents gave it the numbers to govern. However, within a year it called a fresh election hoping to do better. A strong performance by its allies allowed the BJP to govern for a further period of five years.

In the elections of 1996, the Congress tally fell to 140 seats. P.V. Narasimha Rao resigned as prime minister and, shortly afterwards as party president. The party bosses now turned to Sonia Gandhi, the widow of Rajiv Gandhi. Sonia had no political ambition herself. In fact, in 1981 she had opposed the idea of Rajiv entering politics. (Kidwai, Rasheed 2003). Before the 1998 elections, however, she yielded to the pressure applied by old colleagues of her husband and mother-in-law, and joined the campaign. As the Party's performance in the election was very poor, the incumbent president, Sitaram Kesri, was replaced by Sonia Gandhi. A year later, mid-term elections were held, in which Congress tally dropped further to 114. However, she remained the president and campaigned energetically in a series of assembly elections. At one stage, as many as 15 state governments were headed by the Congress. (Khare, Harish 2003).

In early meetings held under Sonia Gandhi's leadership the Congress was against the idea of entering a wider alliance. But the realities on the ground compelled a change of orientation. Before the 2004 elections the Congress entered into alliances with a variety of other parties. In the event, the Congress won 145 seats, and their United Progressive Alliance (UPA) 222 in all. Since the BJP-led NDA had won only 189, the UPA formed the government with the support from outside of the communists. The fragmentation of the party system lies behind the rise of coalition governments.

Growth of Corruption

The evidence of political corruption is not easily available, for those who take or give commissions rarely leave a paper trail. However, in the 1990s the Central Bureau of Investigtion (CBI) laid charges against a number of prominent politicians for having assets 'disproportionate' to their position. The leaders so charged included the chief monister of Bihar, Lalu Prasad Yadav and of Tamil Nadu's J. Jayalalithaa. Each was accused of amassing huge wealth from the allocation of government contracts. It may also be noted that in the run-up to an election the Opposition makes a hue and cry about corruption in the ruling administration, but if it is elected it does not pursue cases against the previous regime, trusting that it will be similarly rewarded when it loses power. (Visvanathan, Shiv and Harsh Sethi (eds.) 1998). Indeed, politicians from different parties and different states often exchange favours. (Nagaraj, B.S. 2003).

Because being in power is so profitable, there is now an increasing trade in politicians. With corruption and criminalisation, Indian politics also increasingly became a victim to nepotism. The extent of deception in India's democracy is of incredible proportion. The use of money power for winning elections became common in the country. The ceilings on maximum permissible expenditure by a candidate are observed more in the breach. A newly elected legislator begins his tenure by willfully filing a false affidavit that the expenditure incurred did not exceed the laid down ceiling. And then, there is no ceiling on the expenditure that a party may incur on its candidates. Huge unaccounted expenditures are incurred by the parties. The State funding of legitimate election expenses was recommended by at least three committees since 1972, but none of them was acted upon.

On the behaviour of parliamentarians, the most shameful event was the purchase of MPs by the Congress party in 2008 - called cash-for-vote scam - to win a no-confidence motion. On 22 July, before the voting was to take place on the confidence motion, the opposition MPs had waved wads of currency notes in Lok Sabha. The MPs' irresponsible behaviour is endless. After a 300 per cent rise in their basic salary in 2001, in 2006 again, it was hiked by 33 per cent — raising their basic salary to Rs. 16,000 — costing the exchequer no less than Rs. 62 crore.

The parliamentarians take every opportunity to enjoy a lavish life style, and some times even in a period of austerity drive. The situation at the state level naturally could not be better. What happened in two of the states in recent times may be noted briefly. With such a profile of our legislators, probably it is too much to expect the bureaucrats to be honest and sincere.

This resulted in rampant corruption everywhere. It was reported in 2004 that Rs. 21,000 crore were exchanged as bribe. Corruption in public services is pervasive and a way of life. Barring exceptions, greasing babus palms is almost mandatory in government circles. In 2005, Transparency International revealed that 62 per cent of the people interviewed admitted that they had paid bribes. Approximately Rs. 2,106 crore change hands every year. Even people below poverty-line are compelled to pay bribes. (TST 2011x).

Among the government organisations, according to the Central Vigilance Commission, in 2011 the Railways topped the list with regard to the number of complaints of corruption received. It was as many as 8,805, followed by 8,430 agaisnt bank employees and 5,026 agaisnt Income Tax officials. (TST 2012z 101). In the Railways, corruption involving hundreds of croıe of rupees are particularly visible in traffic and in the system of procurement. In traffic, the rates for exported ore were deliberately left unchanged during the boom right up to May 2008.

The most horrifying scam in recent times is probably in the Central Telecom Department. In the allocation of 2G spectrum licences, even Prime Minister Dr. Manmohan Singh and Mr. P. Chidambaram — at that time finance minister have been caught in the wrong foot, although its kingpin was A. Raja, the minister in charge of the department until recently.

Corruption in private corporate sector is also not small. In 2009, Satyam Computers, the country's fourth largest IT firm, was caught in the biggest ever corporate fraud, involving Rs. 14,000 crore. This could happen despite the various high sounding regulatory bodies and the government departments meant for supervising working of the corporate sector. The government's reluctance to check corruption is evident everywhere. The CBI cannot prosecute any bureaucrat without prior permission from the government.

There are instances where the Prime Minister's office asked the CBI not to proceed against top IAS officers. Even the Lok Ayukta in states is sometimes not allowed to proceed with his work.

First, the Bofors case which has been hanging for a long period. It came to light in 1987 that nearly Rs. 64 crore were paid in kickbacks to the Congress party and the Rajiv Gandhi government for the multi-billion dollar Bofors howitzer deal. The scandal shook the nation and Rajiv Gandhi lost his two-thirds majority in the post-Bofors election two years later. After much dilly-dallying, on October 3, 2009, the CBI applied to a court in Delhi to quash all charges against Ottavio Quattrocchi, the Italian agent involved, from the Bofors payoff, saying the case cannot be kept pending for ever as attempts to extradite him have failed in the past. (TST 2009 z 39: 8). Recently, former Swedish police chief Sten Lindstorm - who led the investigation in Sweden - said that there was no evidence to suggest that Rajiv Gandhi had taken a bribe in the Bofors deal but that he did nothing to prevent the cover-up that followed in both India and Sweden to protect Quattrocchi, against whom there was "conclusive evidence". Quattrocchi, an Italian businessman, had disclosed in an interview his friendship with Sonia Gandhi. That he was a security-cleared visitor to the Prime Minister's residence was a well-known secret at the time. (Mustafa, Seema 2012a).

In the Jain Hawala case, diaries — actually books of accounts — seized in May 1991 contained names of leading politicians cutting across party lines who received Hawala money from S.K. Jain. The accounts revealed Rs. 64 crore received from abroad and their disbursement in India. The money distributed to political leaders was in most cases for use in an imminent general election. The Koda scam, dubbed the "great Jharkhand robbery", was a mining scam and its kingpin was Madhu Koda, a former chief minister of Jharkhand. In the mega sporting extravaganza Common Wealth Games, held in Delhi from three to 14 October, 2010, thousands of crore of rupees were swindled, and the sports minister Suresh Kalmadi — who was the organising committe chairman— was jailed after much hesitation. The Hasan Ali case relates to the black money of Indian citizens stashed in foreign banks.

The technique of delay is commonly used by the government for not punishing the corrupt officials. The CBI had a backlog of 9,000 cases in September 2009 awaiting dispensation of justice. A quarter of them were before various courts for more than 10 years and no fewer than 244 for more than 20 years. Including the subordinate courts, the total backlog of criminal cases reached a staggering 3.5 crore in January 2009. In case of government officials, even the granting of sanction is often greatly delayed. The Chief justice of India, Mr. K.G. Balakrishnan, has stated that the prosecution becomes ineffective if the sanction is granted after 6-7 years. Before the latest SC directions on the subject, in January 2012, the delay ran into several years and in more than 98 per cent of the cases at the higher or highest levels the sanctions were hardly ever given. (TST 2009b, z23; 2012 z56).

On the corruption at high places, the government's reluctance to act is evident also from the fact that in October 2004, the Union Cabinet failed to decide on the draft Lokpal bill for the ninth time since 1968. Recently, in 2011, a determined attempt was made by the civil society groups, led by Mr. Anna Hazare, to bring a comprehensive, effective Lokpal bill. The Jan Lokpal bill prepared by them proposed to bring all ministers, including the prime minister, the judiciary, conduct of MPs in parliament and the entire bureaucracy. Mr. Hazare resorted to fast four times to force the bringing of an effective Lokpal institution but he failed. The Lokpal Bill 2011 presented to the Parliament on August 4, had kept outside its purview the prime minister, the higher judiciary and conduct of MPs inside Parliament. The Bill was strongly objected to by Mr. Hazare and a modified Bill was presented on 22 December, 2011. This Bill was pssed by the Lok Sabha but failed in the Rajya Sabha. The Bill was referred to the Select Committee. (TST 2011m, z, z46; Nayar, Kuldip 2012a). This government will never allow a strong Lokpal Bill to be passed for the entire government machinery encourages corruption. (Sen, Sankar 2005; Rajappa, Sam 2012c). A strong Lokpal will put many of its own ministers in jail. The team Anna had demanded the setting up of a Special Investigtion Team to probe corruption allegations against 15 Union ministers, including PM Manmohan Singh and Mr. Pranab Mukherjee. To delay the passing of the Lokpal Bill, the government has resorted to devious tactics. (TST 2012 r, s, z41, z89).

To curb corruption at high places, there is actually no need for new legislation. All that is required is to make the CBI a constitutional body unshackled from the cabinet's control. At the same time, the President of India must be allowed to exercise the powers assigned to the office by our written Constitution. The President has immense power to set everything right. He is the singular office bearer - with the federal mandate of Parliament and all the states of the Union - in the entire nation who is under oath to "preserve and protect the Constitution and law". The President has been reduced to a rubber stamp of the Union Cabinet. All the flawed conventions that have no basis in the written Constituion should be removed and his power retrieved. If such a step cannot be taken, there is no point in spending crores of Rupees year-after-year on the maintenance of this useless office. It may be noted that the sprawling Rashtrapati Bhavan has 340 rooms and a huge amount is also spent on ornamental purposes. And this is being done in a country with at least a third of the population in semi-starving condition.

Absence of accountability in the administration is a prime reason behind the corruption in government offices. The Right to Information Act 2005, which could be a great help in reducing corruption, also fell disgracefully short of its ideal. There is a growing frustration with long delays in getting information. In Rajasthan, as many as 9,500 appeals were pending with the state Information Commission in November 2012. It took 8-12 months to get a date for hearing and upto two years for a decision. Moreover, a study by two NGOs had found that over 40 per cent of rural and 15 per cent of urban respondents faced "harassment and threats" from information officials. It was also found that even in cases where the commissioner had ordered passing of the desired information, only 39 per cent of the orders were complied with.

The functioning of the judiciary is also very poor. Number of pending court cases runs into millions. In October 2009, there were around 2.7 crore cases pending with the trial courts, over 40 lakh cases in High Courts and 53,000 pending before the Supreme Court. At the end of October 2011, number of pending cases in the SC rose to 56,383; and in the HCs to 42,17,903. In the lower judiciary, the total number of such cases stood at 2,79,53,070 at the end of March 2011. (TST 2009 z41, 2011 z49). Invoking the law for getting justice generally means only wasted years, a heavy financial burden and emotional and physical trauma. Prolonged delays in criminal cases result in a hgh rate of acquittals—as high as 93.02 per cent. When the victims are unable to get justice from the courts, they take the law into their own hands to settle scores. (Sharma, RD 2012). Corruption is rampant in the judiciary. There is urgent need for radical changes in many spheres.

PLANNING AND DEVELOPMENT

Given the quality of political leadership, economic planning as the situation demanded could not come. In fact, there were some inherent contradictions between the objectives and the means adopted. A socialist pattern of society could not be established by a government dominated by the bourgeois class, interested only in ostentatious living and self aggrandizement, ignoring its consequences. Naturally, the resource mobilisation remained low, and its deployment rarely for improving the living condition of the masses.

The level of savings and investment remained extremely low, and the domain of the public sector was far below what was required. The plan expenditure was always far short of what was required. Corruption took a dangerous form particularly in the post-Nehruvian economic system. The politician-contractor-bureaucrat nexus started grabbing most of the plan expenditures. It has been estimated that only 15 paise out of a rupee reached the people. (TST 2009 z9). Inter-state, the level of plan expenditures varied greatly, and very little efforts were made to raise them in poorer states.

In the sectoral distribution of expenditure, certain basic amenities were totally neglected. In the formulation and implementation of the plans there were many deficiencies. The planning continued to be a top-down process, despite plenty of talks on decentralisation of power and peoples' participation. Even the state governments were not consulted adequately in plan formulation. The planning commission and the concerned central ministries had a dominating role until recently. (CMIE 1997). Below the state level there were hardly any planning exercise. Even after the 73rd amendment of the Constitution (1993), giving wider powers to the panchayat raj institutions, district planning remained far from adequate, not to talk of block-level planning.

Achievements

This pattern of economic planning naturally could not bring any appreciable growth in income, nor could it reduce much the level of absolute poverty or regional disparities in development. The politicians and bureaucrats incomes, covering both legal and illegal means, were also huge. Three-fourths of the country's population were, however, surviving on less than Rs. 20 per day. (TST 2009 z31). The pattern of growth followed led to a sharp increase in demand for energy.

The diversification in economic activities was far below what was needed and generally not in the appropriate directions. The share of agriculture, etc., in the GDP had declined to 45.2 per cent in 1973-74 from 58.9 in 1950-51, but for the secondary sector it increased by only 6.7 points, from 14.9 per cent to 21.6. In the following years, agriculture's share declined faster, being down to 20.2 per cent in 2004-05. Its place was largely taken over by the tertiary sector; the relative share rising to 53.7 per cent, from 33.2 in 1973-74. The indiscriminate push for industrialistion has caused immense harm to the environment, despite the existence of the Water Act, 1974, Air Act, 1981, the Forest (Conservation) Act, 1982, the Environmentatl Protection Act, 1986, and the Biological Divesity Act, 2002. The destruction of environment is inevitable so long as the obsession with growth in GDP - with focus on industrialisation - is not given up. No rigid policy on environmental screening will work. Whatever is the law, it will be largely nullified at the stage of implementation, given the qulity of governnance in the country. Environmental clearance had been given to 181 coal mines with a total capacity of 83 million tonnes per annum during the 11th plan period. In addition 113 coal mines had been granted permission to divert 26,000 hectares of forest land for industrial use. (TST 2012 z68).

The implementation of the Minimum Wages Act, 1948 continues to be very poor. Grinding poverty for a vast majority was natural in this situation. The proportion of population below the poverty line (BPL), based on calorie intake only, had declined from 54.88 per cent in 1973-74 to 44.48 in 1983, 35.97 in 1993-94 and 27.5 in 2004-05.

The measures for poverty alleviation were implemented very callously. The public distribution system was thoroughly vitiated by corruption, and the poor were largely deprived from its benefit. The employment schemes were also thoroughly mismanaged. Even the National Rural Employment Guarantee Act (NREGA), introduced with much fanfare in 2005, has proved largely a fraud on the people. The farm-debt waiver scheme 2008 was also thoroughly mismanaged.

Proper education which is of critcal importance for manpower development, was totally neglected by the government. The literacy situation continued to be grim. The question of children's education - although almost 42 per cent of India's total population is under age 18 - received no attention until recently. It was made a fundamental right only in 2002; and another seven years taken to pass the Right to Education (RTE) Act. And then, even at the end of 2011 the Act was a non-starter in as many as 15 states as they failed to implement the mandatory provision of opening primary schools in "neighbourhoods", and therefore could not avail central funds for the purpose. Violation of the Act's regulations is common across the country. In West Bengal, parents and children were being forced to pay school fees or screened. (TST 2011z23; 2012 z10, z78). The state governments have failed to provide the essential facilities in schools. Even in 2012 drinking water and toilet facilities were not available in all the schools in the country. The educational scenario at higher levels is also extremely disappointing. The Vocationalisation of education is given scant attention. India presently has only 5,500 vocational training centres, called ITIs, training about 1,00,000 persons every year. China, in contrast, has 5,00,000 vocational training centres, training over 80,00,000 per year. (TST 2009 z44).

Improvement in health condition of people was also utterly neglected. The health indicators continued to be in a very poor state. Percentage of children under age three suffering from anaemia was 79 in 2005-06, and the underweight children below five constituted as much as 42.5 per cent in 2007. (IIPS 2000; IIPS 2007; GOI 2008c). Improved health will require actions in several directions, covering both preventive and curative measures. The present situation is so distressingly poor that the provision of even certain basic facilities are non-existent for a vast population. The rural medical facilities continued to be extremely poor.

And then, there are reports of uncontrolled human drugs trials in the country. Recently, on 3 January, 2013, the Supreme Court slammed the Centre saying uncontrolled clinical trial of drugs on humans by multinational companies was creating 'havoc' in the country. It pilloried the government after it was told that various committees have been set up to look into the issue. Earlier, on 8 October last year, in response to a PIL by an NGO, the Court had sought the replies of the Centre and various state governments to the allegation that human beings were being used as guinea pigs for clinical trials by drug companies. (TST 2013 d).

The control over population growth - a prerequisite for any development effort - was almost a total failure. The decadal growth in population increased from 21.51 per cent in 1951-61 to 24.80 in 1961-71. In the following decades, it declined to 21.54 per cent during 1991-2001 and 17.64 in 2001-2011. Over the entire period of six decades - 1951 to 2011 - the population had a 3.35-fold rise, from 36.11 crore to 121.02 crore. Even the lowest growth of the last decade added 18.15 crore to the country's population. A much sharper reduction in population growth is urgently necessary.

Inter-state, there were wide variations in every aspect of development. In the social sector, the female literacy rate in 1981 was at the lowest 13.6 per cent in Bihar as against the highest of 65.7 in Kerala.

It needs to be noted that the extent of involvement in the globalised world should depend on how far the world order itself changes to one based on equity and justice. The present efforts at globalisation has a sinister purpose - to strengthen the existing domination of the developed economies over the developing ones. The emphasis is on market creation for giant corporations, and shifting the environment-polluting industries to developing countries. The government of India's policies are overwhelmingly for benefiting the giant corporations, often ignoring even the national interests. It has signed bilateral investment agreements with 82 countries whose basic feature is that India cannot put any condition on foreign investors which are not applicable to domestic investors. Recently, on 13 September, 2012 despite vehement country-wide protests, the government decided to allow foreign direct investment in multi-brand retail outlets, besides relaxing FDI norms for civil aviation and broadcasting sector. In the next month, the Cabinet approved legislative changes that will allow up to 49 per cent foreign equity in the pension sector and hike the present limit in the insurance sector to 49 per cent from 26 per cent. The American companies spent billions of dollars in recent years on lobbying for Indian business interests. (TST 2012 z66, z100).

The government gradually proved to be an oppressor of the masses, for serving a small segment at the top. Such an exploitative system of development naturally ultimately gave rise to violent protests in many places, particularly in tribal dominated areas. The government hardly took any measures to alleviate the distressing poverty of the tribals. It is all a story of deprivation, administrative corruption and ill-treatment, mostly of poor tribals, by the local administration and political leaders. This is the pattern of development that came over the last six decades. Was this the development for which the freedom fighters gave their lives? Did the Father of the Nation, Mahatma Gandhi, envisage such a development?

It is necessary to note here the bare truth that the government has an undisclosed policy of exploiting the masses to the hilt. The rural economy forms the base of its exploitation, and the main instrument used for this is low prices for agricultural commodities. The share of agriculture etc. in the GDP declined from about 67 per cent in 1947 to 17 per cent in 2008. Even if only 30 per cent is considered as its legitimate share, the sector was being defrauded to the extent of 13 per cent of GDP - which amounted to about Rs. seven lakh crore, the GDP that year being around Rs. 54 lakh crore. In this defrauding, starvation level wages to agricultural labour is an important factor. In 2009, an agricultural labour was getting less than Rs. 100 per day as against Rs. 300-400 for an industrial worker. There is urgent need for a sharp increase in agricultural prices. And at the same time appropriate measures taken so that the actual farmers - that is, those who toil in the field - are really benefited, and not grabbed by the middlemen.

Behind this pattern of development, one basic reason is that the nation from the beginning itself, fell into the hands of people addicted to things foreign. Jawaharlal Nehru, the first Prime Minister, was schooled and educated in Britain. And the political party he belonged to, Indian National Congress, was founded by a Briton, Alan Octavian Hume, in 1885. The far-sighted British planned early a peaceful transfer of power to a class of Indians educated and culturally influenced by them. After Nehru, except for a brief period, his daughter Indira Gandhi ruled and her actions were also mostly anti-national. (Puri, Rajinder 2011d). Then came her son, Rajiv Gandhi, western-educated and married to Sonia Gandhi, an Italian, to head the Congress party. Presently this party is headed by Sonia Gandhi.

References

- In British India, the princely states were so many that there was even disagreement as to their number. However, by any count they were more than 500, and they varied very widely in terms of size and status. At one end of the scale were the massive states of Kashmir and Hyderabad, each of the size of a large European country; at the other end, tiny fiefdoms or jagirs of a dozen or less villages. The larger native states had their own railway, currency and stamps. After Independence the states merged. The Fazal Ali Commission, set up in 1953, however, did not follow it. For example, it recommended Telangana and Vidarbha as independent states. It preferred making Bombay a Central Territory and not a part of Maharashtra. Its recommendations were largely ignored by the government for narrow political advantage. The linguistic identities became more and more assertive and demands were made for state reorganisation on linguistic basis. An ad hoc, arbitrary approach to the creation of new states followed, generally under duress of agitations. No wonder several issues remained unresolved.
- Just one instance of how much damage is being caused to the environment by mining activites may be noted here. In Andhra Pradesh, bauxite mining is playing havoc with the environment. In the Visakhapatnam district, the government acquired environmental clearance to mine 27 hills in the Araku Valley despite strong opposition and without consent from the Gram Sabhas. The project will affect at least 270 villages. The deposits are part of reserve forests and has a rich biodiversity. The cost of setting up the aluminium industry is

immeasurably high. The bauxite mining would require clearing of large forest cover and blasting off the hilltops upto a depth of 100 feet. Its impact on the sensitive ecosystem of the Eastern Ghats will be irreversible. At least six rivers flowing across the hills may dry up or be reduced to a trickle. This will affect major reservoirs that are the only source of irrigation and drinking water for Visakhapatnam and Vizianagaram districts.

- The main factor behind the delay and resultant backlog is the shortage of judges. In proportion to its population, India has only 13.05 judges per million people, against Australia's 58, Canada's 75, the UK's 100 and the USA's 130 per million. In 2002, the Supreme Court had directed the Centre to raise the judge/population ratio to 50 per million in a phased manner. Vacancies are not promptly filled. In October 2011, the Supreme Court had only 26 judges against the sanctioned strength of 31. The vacancies in the 21 High Courts together was 291 posts of judges for a long time, against the sanctioned strength of 895. In the subordinate courts 3,170 posts of district judges were vacant agaisnt the sanctioned strength of 17,151. (Sharma, RD 2012).
- Mahatma Gandhi had dreamt of an independent local self-government equipped with its very own local arbitration body at panchayat or village level. This made a beginning only in 2009, i.e., after around six decades, when 10 gram Nyayalayas began functioning. Each of these courts has its own Nyayadhikari, a first class judicial magistrate. (TST, 2009z35: 3).
- The need for a truly federal structure forces itself clearly if we look at the number of major secessionist and extremist movements in the country since 1947: 1. Kashmir separatists, since 1989 to the present; 2. Naga separatists, episodically from 1947 to the present; 3. Mizo separatists, 1965-1985; 4. Sikkim separatists, 1980-84; 5. Communist revolutionaries, 1947-51; 6. Maoist revolutionaries, episodically from 1967 to the present. The demand for furthr division of the existing states are also too many. Recently several chief ministers voiced their demand for federalism after the Union government tried to enforce a National Counter Terrorism Centre without consulting the state governments even though law and order is a State subject. The verdicts from recent Assembly elections in five of the states - where national parties were losing space to those in states that represented local aspirations - also point to the need for a genuine federalism in the country. (TST 2012 x).
- The norms used in calculating the BPL population are 2,400 kilo calories per day in the rural, and 2,100 kilo in urban areas. It is argued that although the poverty line income ensured the consumption of the

normative calorie intake in 1973-74, it no longer does so because of the fall in rupee value. The all-India official poverty line gave only 1800 calories, not the norm of 2,400. On this basis, the proportion of BPL population rose to 87 per cent. The Supreme Court has questioned the Tendulkar Committee's definition of poverty according to which, a person can be treated as poor, as on 2004-05, if his monthly income is les than Rs. 446.68 in rural areas and Rs. 578.80 in urban areas. The Court asked how a person will be able to consume 2400 calories in rural areas and 2100 calories in urban areas with such low incomes. (TST 2011 u).

- An idea may be given here of how the National Development Council meetings are held. The Statesman editor wrote about the 57th NDC meeting in New Delhi on 30 December, 2012 that the chief ministers are 'treated like school children and are expected to stop whe the bell rings'. A time-limit of 10 minutes was given to chief ministers who came for solution to problems faced by their states. The Centre made it a fruitless exercise and invited the wrath of most non-Congress CMs. (TST 2012, z103).
- To look into the state-wise situation in 2009-10: Percentage of functional girls' toilets in Andhra Pradesh was only 27.55, in Orissa 44.06, Bihar 50.53, Jharkhand 53.21, Meghalaya 46.58, Nagaland 29.76, Odisha 44.06, Jammu & Kashmir 16, Madhya Pradesh 32.81, West Bengal 47.99, Chhattisgarh 33.92, Manipur 11, Meghalaya 21.56, and Gujarat 54.64. Nearly 71 per cent of government-run schools lack boys' toilets. Percentage of schools with boys' toilets below 10 are in four states - Andhra Pradesh, Jammu and Kashmir, Manipur and Rajasthan. A senior official of the HRD ministry said that money is not a problem. Even the budget sanctioned for school infrastructure is not fully utilised. States lack the motivation to do the work. (TST 2011, z15).
- The situation in China is worth noting here. In 2007, the contribluton of the three sectors there were: Agriculture 11 per cent, Manufacturing 49 and services 40 per cent. In the USA, it was roughly 2, 27 and 71 per cent, respectively. It appears that India has bypassed the economic stage where manufacturing dominates. It is often asserted that China and India opted for different growth strategies when they adopted economic liberalisation policies, in late 1970's and early 1990's, respectively. China concentrated on low-end manufacturing, while India focused on services, specifically in the IT related areas. This perception is flawed, as far as India's planning is concerned. India's IT related services "grew by night", catchin the government off-guard.
- In 2001, India had 1.26 crore economically active children in the age group of 5-14 years. The Child Labour (Prohibition and Regulation)

Act, 1986 allows employment of children in industries that are not categorised as hazardous. Further, the provision that "children working as part of family labour are exempt from the purview of the Act" is being widely abused by employers who pass of all sorts of child labour as family labour. Work is being given to workers at home, that is inevitably shared by children and goes unaccounted for. Moreover, the Act does not cover agriculture and allied activities where nearly 70 per cent of child labourers are engaged. It may also be noted that the practise of bonded labour continues to be rampant in many industries. On 15 October, 2012, the Supreme Court directed all states and UTs to enhance the rehabilitation package for freed bonded labourers. (TST 2012z71).

- To improve the power situation, the 12th Plan (2012-17) has targeted a capacity-addition of .88,000 MW. But land-acquisition for power projects as well as the transmission infrastructure is posing a big problem. There is also problem in fuel supply. In the absence of gas supply, 4,000 MW of power capacity was lying idle. The supply of coal is also inadequate. The gap between demand for coal and domestic production increased to 156.09 million tonnes in 2011-12. The problem of finance is also quite serious. Inability to charge consumers right price for the electricity consumed has led to losses. (TST, 2012 z48). On the availability of oil and gas - constituting around 45 per cent of total energy consumption - also the situation is very difficult. The dependence on import of petroleum and its products continues to be around 80 per cent of total oil consumption. In the indigenous production, the share of ONGC is 70 per cent, and its financial situation is not good.
- As regards the situation in states, the Election Watch Committees, on the basis of affidavits filed by candidates in five state elections held in 2002-03, found that the major political parties had between 15 and 20 per cent of candidates with criminal records. A detailed study of Rajasthan's 2003 Vidhan Sabha election showed that as mny as 124 candidates had criminal records, of which 40 per cent had been charged with serious crimes. (Khera, Reetika 2004).
- To look after the quality of higher education, in addition to the existing National Board of Accreditation, a new agency Indian Board of Accreditation has been set up recently. Presently, only about 15 per cent of higher education institutions in India are accredited. (TST, 2013k). There is actually an open encouragement to low quality education in most of the states. A patent example on this is provided by West Bengal. Here, at the Madhyamik (Secondary) level there has been a conscious decision to reduce the standard. Under the Left

Front, the minimum benchmark of success was a ridiculous score of 25 per cent. Under its successor Trinamul Congress, examiners were instructed to be generous in the award of grace marks. Across party lines, the overriding anxiety is to jackup the success rate. (TST, 2012 z27; 2013 r).

- Mr. Vadra reportedly made some Rs. 700 crore through the deals. Now, to save him the Central government is ready to go to any extent. Mr. Ashok Kemka, a senior Haryana IAS officer was shunted out from his post for he had cancelled the mutation of 3.5 acre plot of land in Manesar-Shikohpur Mr. Vadra had sold to DLF on the ground that the mutation violated the Consolidation Act and was done by an officer not authorised to do so. A few days earlier, Mr. Khemka had also ordered an inquiry into the "alleged undervaluation" of some properties registered by Mr. Vadra or his companies. For his uprightness and exposing the scam, Mr. Khemka has been punished by transferring him to a post which was last under an officer 12 years his junior. Mr. Khemka's habit of exposing corruption led to 44 transfers in his 21-year-long carreer, being a 1991-batch IAS officer. (TST 2012 z72; 2013z2).

- Misuse of funds for school eduation is also rampant in many states. In the tiny North-Eastern states, there are a large number of what is called "ghost schools", where the government continues to pay salaries and maintenance to non-existent institutions. And even in schools that do exist, the teachers are all political appointees. To cite an example from Meghalaya: In 2010, the Eduation Department here held an examination for recruiting teachers for the elementary schools. But after the selection board had done its job, the list of appointees was tampered with by none other than the education minister. She accommodated the names of several candidates recommended by sundry legislators from the ruling Congress-led Meghalaya United Alliance. (Mukhim, Patricia 2012). (TST 2013 s, z1).

- The agreement was signed in 1985, but over the last nearly three decades the identification and deportation of the Bangladeshis from Assam could not be completed. Not only this, the infiltration to Assam and the neighbouring states has become a continuing precess. The Indo-Bangla border is largely porous, and once inside the country they can move to virtually any state they like to. Obtaining a ration card or any other proof of permanent resident of West Bengal, Tripura or Assam is not very difficult. Bangladesh is faced with a deepening crisis. The country is made up of the deltas of the Ganga, Teesata and Meghna. The construction of the Tehri dam and the Farakka barrage on the Ganga has deprived Bangladesh of sufficient river water. The silt gets deposited instead of being carried to the sea. River beds have risen and floods have wrought havoc to the country. In the struggle for survival, the people of Bangladesh have no option but to migrate. The deepening crisis in Bangladesh may lead to demand for 'Grater Bangladesh'. Sheikh Mujibur Rahman had once observed: "Because Eastern Pakistan must have sufficient land for its expansion and because Assam has abundant forests and mineral resources, Eastern Pakistan must include Assam to be financially and economically strong."

- The scope for mobilising larger resources was ample. Over the past two decades, several thousand crore rupees have accumulated in tax appeals, under the exaggerated assessment of taxes. The two major reasons are illegal gratification and tortuous judicial process. The CAG shows 42,402 cases involving a duty of Rs. 30,423 crore pending for adjudication/recovery as on 31 March 2008. Number of pending cases increased by over 23 per cent in 2007-08 over the preceding year.
- It may also be noted that the Indian rich are now one of the lowest taxed segments of the global rich, thanks to the abolition of the estate duty, the long-term capital gains tax, and a tax rate on individuals and companies which shows very little progressivity. This measure, among other things distorted the incentive structures in such a way that it has become increasingly difficult to recruit talented persons for service in the public sector. Realising that paying astronomical salaries to business executives or administrators elsewhere has damaged equity, growth and transparency in governance, some of the best economists had called for a tax rate of 80 per cent on top salaries. (TST 2013 m).
- A basic reason behind this depressing situation is that a market driven aspirational change now defines our middle class. They have started believing that "greed is good" and are after wealth and creature comforts. This "maximalist" lifestyle is a breeding ground for corruption. When every one wants to be rich in a poor country, the competition is so intense that values and ethics are thrown out of the window. Very recently, however, the situation has improved considerably in some of the states, for example, in Karnataka. (Sharma, Tyagaraj 2012).
- In the existing situation, it appears almost impossible to curb official corruption. Recently, an attempt was made to revamp public procurement — considered mother of all official corruption — but it encountered stiff resistance from bureaucrats. The Committee on Public Procurement had recommended a procurement law, a national policy on public procurement to minimise corruption and the establishment of a Department of Procurement to monitor purchase procedures. After nearly a year, on 14 May, 2012 the Public Procurement

Bill 2012 was introduced in the Lok Sabha in a diluted form. (TST 2011 r, s; 2012 z20)

- The formula used for HDI calculation considers three factors: health, education and prosperity. The indicator for health is the life expectancy at birth; for education, the years of schooling; and for prosperity, the per capita national income, normalised against the dollar by purchasing power. There is much controversy on the validity of this method of ranking. The question of sustainable development which the world and the UN now frequently speak for is in practice given no importance at all. The per capita carbon consumption in the developed countries was of the order of 15 to 50 tonnes in 2008. In comparison, India's was 1.4 tonnes and only a tenth of a tonne in Pakistan and some African countries. With the burning of fossil fuels and industrialisation rapidly polluting the earth's resources and environment, the high standard of living in the developed world is clearly at the cost of others. HDI by taking into consideration the per capita carbon footprint gave a totally different grading. The USA's rank became 28 up from 4 earlier and Australia's to 26 from 2. Norway remained 1in both the ranking and for Sweden it declined from 10 to 2. (quoted in, Ananthanarayanan, S 2011).
- The entrance of FDI in the retail sector was approved by the Parliament in the first week of December 2012, and it was obtained through a manipulated majority - "by armtwisting the BSP and the SP with the CBI handle". There are also allegations of bribery by the giant retail outlet Walmart to acquire legal rights to enter the Indian market. (TST 2012 z61, z97, z99).
- Sometimes, in order to reduce the burden of disposing RTI queries, or for not disclosing information that may affect high level government functionaries, the relevant files are even burnt out.
- It may be noted here that even Dr. Manmohan Singh took recourse to electoral fraud. He was holding the offices of minister and prime minister since 1991 as a member of the Rajya Sabha from Assam. His claim that he is a Guwahati man because he has a ration card, a rented house, electricity and telephone connections is a total negation of the truth. The Upper House gradually degenerated into a chamber mostly of defeated and discredited politicians and he had no difficulty in getting elected uncontested every time. (TST 2007; 2009 z40).
- Another scandal similar to Bofors came to light recently. It relates to the 3,546-crore deal for 12 Augusta-Westland helicopters from Italian manufacturer Finmeccanica. The Italian authorities have confirmed the payment of kickbacks - to the extent of a total of 51 million euros - to key individuals to ensure that the deal could be swung. It has also

been reported that Congress President Sonia Gandhi's two sisters in Italy have acquired half the kickback amount On 27 Febraury 2013, the government got a 30-member JPC formed to probe the VVIP chopper deal amidst strong protests from opposition parties. The opposition's contention is that the decision is meant to put the issue on the bckburner. That an attempt to cover up the scam has already started is evident also from the fact that the FIR filed by the CBI on 13 March, has booked the former air chief Marshall S.P. Tyagi (Rtd), his cousins and nine others in this helicopter scam. Mr. Tyagi and his relatives have been named for having received 2 lakh Euros. Italian prosecution claims that ten times this amount was paid to "the family" in India. (TST 2013 m, 2013 x, y).

- It is now wll-known that the Army has been ravaged by politicians and rampant corruption over decades. Seema Mustafa wrote in 2012: "The pride within the service has been replaced by a certain demoralisation and unprecedented levels of shame due to interference by unscrupulous politicians, a relentless bureaucracy and, of course, corrupt defence officers". (TST 2013 u).
- The 26 th Report on panchayati raj of the Parliamentary Standing Committee has stated that "almost all the constitutional provisions related to Panchayats have not been implemented in letter and spirit". The report states that as against the ministry's plans to provide training to 30 lakh elected representatives each year, it could be provided to only 3.5 lakh in 2009-10 and 11.65 lakh in 2010-11. The other shortcomings noted included mismatch of official figures of training with ground realities, absence of physical verification of training, absence of accountability of funds given for training, and delay in releases of funds for training.
- The exploitation of the forest dwellers, in fact, began from the mid-nineteenth century when the jungles of Chhotanagpur plateau—spread over 30,000 sq km in Odisha, Jharkhand and West Bengal—drew the attention of the British colonists. To support the need for timber for laying Railway lines, particularly sleepers made of Sal trees, large-scale extraction of timber began in 1891-92. The Indian Forest Act of 1878 empowered the colonists to have absolute control over these valuable forest resources. Vast forest areas were declared the country's first reserved forests in 1884. The British seized the ownership rights after suspending all rights and concessions enjoyed until then by the forest-dwelling people.
- Even 60 years after Independence, the mindset of forest authorities carry the legacy of their British predecessors and continue to treat the forests as their fief. The forest policy of Independent India and its

management are still governed by the Indian Forest Act of 1927. The first forest-related legislation of free India was enacted in 1950 and it withdrew the occupancy and subsistence rights of forest-dwelling people, making them homeless and destitute. The government of India has always treated the forest-dwellers as nothing but impediments in national development initiatives. Chhotanagpur plateau is the country's biggest repository of iron ore and chromite ore. The National Mineral Policy of 1993 mooted the idea of encouraging private investment in exploratic.ı and mining of several strategically-important natural resources. It also allowed extraction and export even by commodity traders. Prospects of making enormous profits encouraged proliferation of illegal mines. The margin of profit to be made by the traders was incredibly high. The cost of extraction and transportation to the point of exports ranged between Rs. 250 and Rs. 325 per tonne (in 2007), against the prevailing selling price of around Rs. 4,000 per tonne. (Chaudhuri, Kisor 2012).

- In 2001, the seven tiny states together had a population of 12.397 million, which was not even half of Assam's. Assam's per capita budgetary expendityre was, naturally, much smaller than in any of the other states. Among the small states also it varied greatly. For example, in 1996-99, the per capita revenue expenditure in Sikkim was as much as 25,312 whereas Tripura had only Rs. 3,037. In relation to All-states' average (Rs. 2,041) Sikkim's was around 13 times higher. Total plan expenditure of the small states also varied greatly. The per capita total in this period came to only Rs. 1,439 in Megalaya as against Rs. 4,766 in Arunachal. (Deb, Kalipada 2006, Vol. 2).
- One reason behind this situation confusion over the roles of two Central agencies entrusted with the region's development: the North Eastern Council (NEC) and the Ministry of Development of North Eastern Region (MDNER). The former was constituted in 1972 by a Central Act to supervise development of the region, and latter in 2001 to coordinate infrastructure projects within the states. This marked the beginning of the confusion and the resulting clash between the two agencies. The situation became worse, when in 2002 the Centre amended the NEC Act and made it a planning body under the MDoNER. The ministry, with its headquarters in New Delhi, virtually controls all the decision-making powers of the NEC although it is oblivious to the ground realities. (TST 2013 g)
- Rampant corruption is another factor behind the lack of development. Patricia Mukhim (2013) wrote recently that all the money pushed in by the government of India to develop the North-east is actually "invested in private bank accounts of the political and bureaucratic class and

their partners in crime, the business lobby". One of the great bnefits that the STs enjoy is income-tax exemption. Members of the political and business class and even government employed engineers and bureaucrats in the N-E states have amassed wealth beyond any of their known sources of income. At the time of elections, politicians worth crores of rupees declare their assets in a few lakh rupees only "when everyone around them knows how many prime properties they own not only in their own states but also in the metros. The wealth they have earned is in direct proportion to the ramshackle public buildings and roads they construct which require annual repairs. "It is all a money making racket. And they get away because they are tribals!" Even the RTI does not tell much. For instance, in Meghalaya a government contracator was found from RTI documents to have misappropriated Rs. 9 crore by way of claiming payment for CGI sheets not supplied to the government. "But the contractor is sitting pretty" because the government will not take action and nor will the Central Vigilance officer, "for the government is always in cahoots with contractors and businessmen/women".

- The 8th Annual Status of Education Report (Rural) of the HDR ministry states that almost half the children in the 6-7 age group studying in class I cannot write a single letter in any language and almost 40 per cent cannot recognise numbers between 1 and 9. It has also highlighted that the number of standard V kids able to read standard II textbooks has dipped from 53.7 per cent in 2010 to 46.8 per cent in 2012. The proportion of standard III students who could read standard I textbooks, too, has gone down from about 50 per cent in 2008 to 30 in 2012. TST 2013 h).

2

CENTRAL AND WEST INDIAN ECONOMIES: AN OVERVIEW OF PERFORMANCE

The central and western regions of India presently comprise of six states, four in the former, viz, Uttar Pradesh, Madhya Pradesh, Chhattisgarh and Uttaranchal, and two in the latter, viz, Maharashtra and Gujarat. The Central India accounts for 24.9 per cent of the country's population, and Western India 14.3 per cent; that is, the two together 39.2 per cent. Their share in the country's geographical area is also similar, being 39.4 per cent, with the former having 24.1 per cent. The situation of each of the states with regard to resource endowment and nature of development over the years is looked into below; the newly created ones are not discussed separately.

UTTAR PRADESH

Uttar Pradesh has always been the largest state in terms of population, and in geographical area also it was so until the separation of Uttarakhand region. UP's population in 2001 was 166 million, constituting 16.2 per cent of all-India total (the estimate for 2006-07 was 185 million); in 1991, the undivided state had 139 million and 16.4 per cent. In relation to the smallest state Sikkim, it is still 308 times larger. UP's area is presently 294 thousand sq. km, constituting 8.9 per cent of A-I total, and is the fourth largest. Uttarakhand, created in November 2000, had a population of only 8.48 million in 2001, with the area at 53.57 thousand sq. km.

Physical Resources

Physically and geologically Uttar Pradesh can be divided into three distinct regions, viz, the Himalayan mountains, the Indo-Gangetic plain, and the hills and plateaus in the south. The Himalayan region can again be divided into three zones: the great Himalaya, the lesser Himalaya, and the sub-Himalaya or the foot hills. The first one is high peaked and mostly ice-capped throughout the year. The highest peak is Nanda Devi, measuring 7,698 metres. The snow-clad peaks have given rise to several rivers which carry silt to the plains rendering the land below fertile for agriculture. These rivers provide a perennial source of irrigation, sites for generating hydel power, serve as means of transport, and promote fisheries. The lower Himalayan zone is of moderate height, and is thinly populated. Owing to the stony nature of the land, cultivation is possible only in the river valleys and terraced hill slopes. This zone has several minerals and a large part of it is under forest. The sub-Himalayan zone has two distinct parts. The first, a strip of land called the bhabar, has a large portion covered with forests. Below this, a wider strip called the Tarai, is damp and marshy, and for the most part covered with thick jungles and tall grasses.

Climatically, the entire state falls in tropical monsoon, but there are great variations due to differences in altitude. The Himalayan region has cold climate except in the valleys.

Income Growth, Assets

The development efforts in Uttar Pradesh had very poor results. The state's relative share in all-India total income declined from 15.7 per cent in 1958-61 to 10.3 in 1994-97 and further to only 5.82 per cent in 2002-05, including Uttaranchal. (CMIE 2007). The per capita income also moved similarly. In relation to the national average, UP's declined from 80 per cent in 1960-63 to 60.4 per cent in 1994-97. Post-bifurcation, the situation worsened further. In 2003-06 it averaged 52.0 per cent of the national per capita; for Uttaranchal, it was 95.1 per cent. In 2008-09, UP's per capita income stood at only 46.6 per cent of all-India's; for Uttarakhand at 91.4. (GOI 2011). The states share of All-India GDP in 2009-10 came to only 8.5 pr cent, with the amount at Rs. 519,899 crore; for Uttarakhand it was 1.01 per cent and Rs. 62,214 crore. (CMIE 2011a).

The asset situation of the state was, however, quite good. The possession of land was, however, extremely low for a large proportion of population. The economic diversification in UP was insignificant over the years. Post-bifurcation, in the annual average GSDP of Rs. 251,155 crore in UP in 2003-06, the primary sector had contributed 31.3 per cent, the secondary 22.0 and the balance of 46.7 by the tertiary; for all-India, it was respectively 19.7, 27,7 and 52.6 per cent. As regards the distribution of workers among different sectors, the proportion non-agricultural in rural workforce not only remained below the national average, the disparity widened over the years. In 1991, at 15.9 per cent, it was 4.3 percentage points below the latter's; in 1961, at 12.8 per cent, it was 1.5 points lower.

Poverty and Consumption Level

This nature of economic growth naturally implied a high level of unemployment and absolute poverty. The work participation rate in UP continued to be very low, and declined from 39.12 per cent in 1961 to 32.20 in 1991; at the national level, the fall was from 43.00 and 37.46 per cent. The situation of asset-holding by the households was also not good. The level of consumer expenditures was naturally low. Percentage of households with MPCE of less than Rs. 125 in 1987-88 was 45.1, which was higher than in four of the states.

The proportion of BPL population continued to be very high in UP, and the relative position worsened in recent years. In 2004-05, it rose to 33.25 per cent from 31.15 in 1999-00. The latest was higher than the national average by 4.98 points; in 1973-74, it was higher by only 2.2 points. If price adjustments are made for the calorie intake, the BPL population presently will be no less than 80 per cent.

Trend in Social Indicators

On the most important variable, the educational attainment, UP continued to be in a very poor situation. The health condition of the people was also very poor. The life expectancy at birth continued to be below the national average. In 2002-06, at 60, it was 3.5 points lower. The hygienic condition in UP continued to be distressingly poor. The provision of economic infrastructure in the state progressed very slowly. The accessibility of some of the essential facilities to the village people continued to be very difficult in UP. The situation of Uttaranchal, a hilly region, was much worse.

Intra-State Disparities

The regional disparity in development continued to be very high in Uttar Pradesh, despite the objective of reducing the imbalance. Until the bifurcation, the state comprised of five regions: Uttarakhand, Western, Central, Bundelkhand and the Eastern region. The last one has always been the most backward. On certain other indicators also Uttarakhand had the best performance. It always had the highest literacy rate, and the eastern region's the lowest. District-wise, there were wide variations even within a region.

In the social sector, the variation in literacy rate was very high, particularly with regard to females. The consumption of electricity also varied greatly. On the overall development, many of the districts continued to be very backward. Behind this depressing performance, the quality of government was primarily responsible. The political leadership has been abominably poor. Their only concern was somehow to grab the offices, and for this they did not hesitate to encourage the mafias and criminal elements. Hardened criminals joined politics and sometimes became ministers. Instability of the government became a key factor. In August 2003, when Mulayam Singh Yadav became the chief minister for the third time, it was the ninth chief ministerial change in around a decade. Governance and development continued to take the back-seat, while number games, coalition management and vote-bank politics came to the forefront. (Narayan, H 2003; Diwakar, D M 2009).

There is little hope of the situation getting improved in near future. In this situation of criminals becoming ministers, corruption became rampant in the government. A strong nexus between powerful politicians and big construction companies thrived. For the horrifying backwardness of UP its mammoth size is also partly responsible. If UP were a country, even after the creation of

Uttarakhand, it would be the ninth most populous in the world. There is an urgent need for further division of the state. In fact, chief minister Mayawati herself had been suggesting a division of UP since 2007. Recently, in November 2011, she got a resolution passed by the Assembly to split the state into four parts - Purvanchal, Paschimanchal, Awadh Pradesh and Bundelkhand. (TST, 2009 z62, 2011 z36).

MADHYA PRADESH

Until recently, Madhya Pradesh was the largest state in the country in terms of area, and sixth in population. With an area of 443,446 sq. km. it accounted for 13.49 per cent of all-India total; and in population 7.82 per cent, with 66.18 million (1991). After the bifurcation in November 2000, its area was reduced to 308,144 sq. km. which is 9.37 per cent of A-I total and the second largest. The population in 2001 was 60.39 million, the seventh largest; in Chhattisgarh, it was 20.80 million, and lower than in as many as 15 states. In 2006-07, the population was estimated at 67.1 million and 23.1 million, respectively and constituted 5.98 and 2.06 per cent of A-I total.

On the basis of physical features, the pre-bifurcation MP was divided into five regions - viz, the Gird, the Malwa plateau, the Narbada Valley, the Satpura range and the Chhattisgarh plains. The main river systems are the Chambal, the Betwa, the Sone, the Narbada, the Tapti, the Mahanadi and the Indrawati. The annual rainfall in the state varies from 30 to 60 inches in Mahakoshal, 30-40 in Malwa, 30-35 in Vindhya Pradesh and 30-50 in Bhopal. The state has a large hydro-power potential - estimated at 4,070 thousand kW - and is rich in mineral resources. (GOMP 1957).

Income Growth, Assets

Despite having ample natural resources, the economic performance of Madhya Pradesh was very poor. The asset situation of the households was also very poor. On the possession of land, MP's situation was relatively good. In 2004-05, 54 per cent of rural persons had 1 ha and above as against only 29 per cent at the national level. The diversification in economic activities was low. The workers were overwhelmingly engaged in the low-productive agriculture.

Poverty and Consumption Level

This pattern of change could not create the needed employment opportunities. In this situation, the consumption level of the population could not but be very low. The proportion of population below the poverty-line naturally remained very high. Even in 2004-05 it was as much as 37.21 per cent (including Chhattisgarh) as against 28.27 at the national level. Earlier, the relative position was significantly better. The proportion rises noticeably if the minimum private expenditure on health and education are included. For rural

MP in 2004-05, it increased from 37.7 to 45.2 per cent, and in Chhattisgarh from 41.4 to 50.4 per cent. (Mahendra Dev, S et al 2008). The availability of certain basic amenities was also extremely low.

Social Indicators

In the social sector, even after five decades of efforts, the literacy rate could not reach the national average. At 64.1 per cent in 2001, it was 1.3 points below the latter's; in 1981, at only 27.9 per cent, it was 8.4 points lower. On female literacy, even in 1991, at 28.8 per cent, it was 10.5 points below the national average. Only in the following decade a significant improvement came - the proportion reached 50.3 per cent in 2001.

The health situation was extremely poor here. The life expectancy at birth for 2001-06 were the lowest for both males and females. The IMR stood at as much as 70 per thousand even in 2005, which was 13 points higher than the national average. The mortality rate for under-5 was 94 as against 74 in the latter. The hygienic condition remained distressingly poor even in recent years. On the provision of economic infrastructure also the situation was similar.

MAHARASHTRA

The state of Maharashtra came into existence in 1960, after the bifurcation of the erstwhile Bombay state. With an area of 307,713 sq. km. it is the third largest state, after Rajasthan and Madhya Pradesh. In population also its position was third, until the year 2000; in 2001, with 96.9 million, it was next to Uttar Pradesh (the estimate for 2006-07 was 105.7 million). The state's share in all-India total area is 9.36 per cent and in population 9.42 per cent. Historically, Maharashtra is divided into three regions: Western Maharashtra consisting of 13 districts, Vidarbha with eight districts and Marathwada with five. Agro-climatically, it is divided into nine zones, of which the scarcity zone covers a large area while areas with assured and well distributed rainfall are limited. In the total geographical area of the state, forests constituted 14.5 per cent in the late fifties. The state has a substantial reserve of mineral resources like manganese ore, coal, lime stone, salt, bauxite and iron ore. It has a coastal length of 720 sq. km. (GOB 1958; GOM 1961).

Income Growth, Assets

On State Domestic Product, Maharashtra's relative position worsened noticeably over the years. The sectoral composition of the income changed noticeably. The contribution of primary sector declined from 34 per cent in 1960-61 to 15 in 2000-01; the secondary sector's share rose to 30 per cent from 26, and for the tertiary increased from 40 to 55 per cent. In employment, however, agriculture continued to bear the main burden.

Poverty and Consumption Level

The employment situation was relatively good here. The proportion of non-workers stood at only 57.0 per cent in 1991 as against 62.5 per cent at the national level. The annual growth in workforce (main workers) during 1991-01 was by 1.41 per cent as against 0.81 in all-India. The current daily status unemployment rate stood at 6.50 per cent in 1999-00, substantially below the national average (GOI 2002c). In recent years also the situation was quite good. In 2004, number of working persons per thousand stood at 508 in rural areas as against 431 in all-India; for urban areas, it was respectively 381 and 354. The asset-holding situation of workers was, however, very poor. The level of consumer expenditure in the state was low. In this situation, it is no surprise that the proportion of BPL population was high in Maharashtra. In 2004-05, at 29.95 per cent, it was not only higher than at the national level, among the selected states also higher than in most of them.

Social Indicators

On the social indicators of development, Maharashtra's position was not bad. The literacy rate was always much above the national average. It rose to 76.9 per cent in 2001, with females at 67.0 per cent, from 47.2 and 34.8, respectively, in 1981. In relation to all-India's, the latest was 12.1 points higher for persons and 13.3 for females. At higher levels also the situation was similar. In 1995-96, the proportion with middle school and above constituted 44.8 per cent, 12.8 points higher than in all-India. The rural-urban disparity was, however, very wide.

On the health indicators also the state's position was similar. The life expectancy at birth was estimated at 66.75 for males and 69.76 for females in 2001-06; the former was lower than in three of the states and the latter the second highest. The IMR improved noticeably over the years, and in 2005, at 38 per thousand, it was the lowest among the states. On the provision of certain hygienic facilities the state's performance was very poor. The index of overall human development of the state was not in good position. In 2001, it was placed fourth among the 15 major states, declining from third in 1981, and continued to be in the same position in 2007-08, with the score at 0.572 as against the highest of 0.79 for Kerala. Its score on the Health Index in the latest year was 0.650 and on the Education index at 0.715; Kerala with the highest index had, respectively, 0.817 and 0.924.

The provision of economic infrastructure was relatively good. Maharashtra's biggest failure was in reducing the regional and inter-district imbalance in development. The sectoral diversification of income also varied greatly. In 2002-03, the secondary sector's share in total income was at the highest 45.7 per cent in Raigad and the lowest at 13.4 in Amravati and Buldhana, with 25.8 per cent at the state level. In the provision of employment, the sector-wise inter-district variation was much higher. On the agricultural situation also there were great variations. In the social sector, the literacy rate in 1991 was below 50 per cent in five of the districts as against the state average of 64.9. On female literacy, three districts—Jalna, Gadchiroli and Parbhani—had below 30 per cent in 1991, with the state average at 52.3. As regards health situation, the IMR in 1991 was as much as 106 in Gadchiroli as against the lowest of 34 in Mumbai, with the state average at 58. The under-five mortality also varied similarly.

In overall term also, the inter-district disparities in development were very high. A composite index, based on 13 parameters, prepared by the IIPS for 2002-04, gave the highest of 0.832 to Mumbai and the lowest 0.503 to Gadchiroli; for five of the districts—Ahmednagar, Nanded, Hingoli, Nandurbar and Gadchiroli—it was below 0.60 while 13 had above 0.71, with three at above 0.80. (GOI 2006).

For this poor situation of Maharashtra corruption in government offices is largely responsible. Mr. Vilasrao Deshmukh—who was Union minister until his death on 14 August 2012—was involved in other land scams also.

GUJARAT

The state of Gujarat came into existence in 1960, with the separation of the predominantly Gujarati speaking areas from the erstwhile Bombay state. It had a population of 50.60 million in 2001 (the estimate for 2006-07 was 55.5 million) and constituted 4.94 per cent of all-India total, the tenth largest among the states. In area, with 196,024 sq km, its position is seventh. The state comprises of three geographical regions: (i) the peninsula, traditionally known as Saurashtra, essentially a hilly track sprinkled with low mountains; (ii) Kutch on the north-east, which is barren and rocky and contains the famous Rann (desert) of Kutch; (iii) the mainland, extending from the Rann of Kutch and the Aravalli hills to the river Damanganga, is on the whole a level plain of alluvial soil.

Agro-climatically, the land is predominantly characterised by semi-arid conditions with a large proportion of area facing frequent drought. Only the southern districts, covering three per cent of the net sown area, generally receive high rainfall. The northern districts, with 66 per cent of the NSA, receive scanty and irregular rainfall; and the irrigation facility is still very insufficient. As regards temperature, as the Tropic of Cancer passes through the northern border of the state, Gujarat has an intensely hot or cold climate. This is, however, softened by the existence of the Arabian sea and the Gulf of Cambay in the west and the forests in the east. The plains of Gujarat are watered by big rivers like Sabarmati, Mahi, Narmada and Tapti.

The state has rich fishery resources. Besides rivers, canals, reservoirs, etc., it has the longest coast-line of over 1600 km. As regards mineral resources, Gujarat has an abundance of non-metallic minerals. The important ones are lime-stone, manganese, bauxite, lignite, gypsum, fireclay, fluorspar, dolomite, glass and sand. The state leads in production of salt—supplying about half the country's production. It is second in calcite and third in production of china-clay. Extensive oil and gas structures have also been struck at Ankleshwar and other places in Gujarat.

Income Growth, Assets

Gujarat's performance on the growth of income has not been good. The asset situation of the households was also similar. The diversification in economic activities was appreciable in Gujarat. As regards the sectoral distribution of employment, percentage of non-agricultural workers in rural workforce rose to 23.3 in 1991, from 11.8 in 1961; at the national level, it was from 14.3 to 20.2 per cent. The relative share of industry was trebled over the period, and at 15.8 per cent in 1991, it was the second highest among the states. In recent years, the situation appears to have worsened. In 2004, per thousand usually working persons in rural areas, the primary sector contributed 766 and the secondary sector only 121; at the national level, the latter was 136.

Poverty and Consumption Level

In reducing absolute poverty, Gujarat's performance was quite good. The proportion of BPL population had declined to 14.1 per cent in 1999-00 from 48.1 in 1973-74; the latest was 12 points below the national average; the rural proportion this year was lower by around 15 points. In 2004-05, however, the proportion of BPL population increased to 16.75 per cent, with rural areas at 19.76; the former was 11.5 points below the national average and the latter 9.4 points. On the availability of certain basic amenities, the state's position was fairly good. The underlying factors were quite good. The work participation rate in Gujarat was generally higher than the national average.The level of MPCE in Gujarat was always noticeably higher than at the national level. In 1999-00, for rural areas stood at Rs. 551 as against Rs. 486 in all-India; Gujarat's was the second highest among the states. The bottom 40 per cent of rural population had an MPCE of as much as Rs. 348 as against Rs. 293 in all-India. In recent years also the situation was good. In 2004, the proportion with MPCE of below Rs. 380 was only 18.2 per cent, which was lower than in most of the states. The proportion of expenditure going to food items was relatively high here.

Trend in Social Indicators

On most of the social indicators Gujarat's situation was not good. As regards the health condition of people, on the whole, the situation was not good. The life expectancy at birth in 2001-06 was only 63 years for males and 64 for females; both were below the national average. The hygienic condition in Gujarat was not good. As regards the provision of economic infrastructure, percentage of villages electrified by 1973-74 was only 31, lower than in six of the major states.

SUMMING UP

While the central region is incomparably backward than the western, intra-region, state-wise, also the disparity continued to be wide. In the central region, on the whole, Madhya Pradesh is in a better position than Uttar Pradesh. On the human development scale, the former's position was just above the latter's, respectively 12th and 13th among the 15 major states in 2001. In the western region, on the whole, Maharashtra is in a better position, but on certain critical aspects it lags behind Gujarat. To look into some of the state-wise details:

UP, the largest state, always had a very low per capita income, being the second lowest, above Bihar only. The economic diversification was extremely low; only 20.7 per cent of state income came from secondary sector in 2004-05. The absolute poverty remained very high. Even in 2004-05, the proportion of BPL population was five percentage points higher than the all-India average. In the social sector, the literacy rate stood at only 57 per cent in 2001, second lowest among the states; in relation to MP, it was seven points lower. The health condition of the people is also very poor, and the birth rate is highest among the states. The inter-regional and inter-district disparities are very high.

MP's performance was also very poor. The per capita income remained much below the national average. The diversification in economic activities was, however, better. The secondary sector's contribution to state income stood at 30.7 per cent in 1999-02, five points higher than in all-India. The proportion of BPL population continued to be very high. In 2004-05, it was six point higher than in UP. In the social sector, on literacy rate, its performance was better than UP's, but on health it was much worse. The birth rate had, however, declined faster than in UP. Intra-state disparities in development are very high. Percentage of urban population was less than 10 in a number of districts.

In the Western region, Maharashtra's overall performance has not been good. The proportion of BPL population became substantially higher than the national average in recent year. The situation of per capita income also worsened. The economic diversification was however high, with the tertiary sector accounting for more than half the state income in recent years. In the social sector, its literacy rate was next only to Kerala. On health, the IMR was low and the life expectancy quite high. The birth rate declined significantly over the years. On the HDI, however, the state's position was fourth in 2001. The regional imbalance in development continued to be extremely high.

Gujarat's performance was also on the whole not good. On the HDI, its position declined to sixth in 2001 from fourth in 1981. The literacy situation worsened significantly, and on health, the life expectancy went below the national average. The birth rate continued to be relatively high. On per capita income, the state's latest was fourth among the states. The economic diversification was, however, appreciably high, with industry's contribution rising to 41 per cent in 2002-05. On absolute poverty, the situation was not bad. The proportion of BPL population in 2004-05 was much below the national average. The regional imbalance in development, however, continued to be very high.

For better governance of the states, an essential step required is decentralisation of power on a much greater scale, and at the earliest. It has to start with division of each of the states into smaller ones. This is particularly necessary for Uttar Pradesh. Smaller states are bound to be more effective in reducing regional imbalance in development. The administrative cost will go up only if the present extravagant ways of the government continue. Along with creation of smaller states, much greater power needs to be given to the district level administration and below. The Panchayat Raj system should become more effective, so that people's participation in development efforts becomes a reality.

NOTE

- A recent study by the Association of Local Governance of India has brought out a growing role of violence and crime in UP's Panchayats. The reports from Sultanpur, Moradabad, Bijnore, Barabanki, Sant Kabir Nagar, Gazipur and Mainpuri districts reveal a grim picture. The study found that the growing corruption in the panchayat raj system was also related to violence. With the availability of more funds to Panchayats, many candidates are also likely to spend more on elections and, having spent a lot, they are more ready than before to resort to violence. Due to ineffective action against them for their previous crimes, they grew more reckless about resorting to violence, even murder to influence panchayat election results. (Dogra, Bharat 2011).

PART II: THE ECONOMY OF UTTAR PRADESH

3

RESOURCE MOBILISATION AND DEPLOYMENT

Probably the most difficult task for any government in a planned development effort is the raising of resources. Taxing heavily the richer section of population — generally enjoying a strong bargaining power because of their proximity to the ruling class is virtually impossible. There is also the need for making everybody work harder. The plentiful supply of labour in a backward economy is an important resource waiting to be utilised. But it requires a motivational change through their proper educational and skill development. Deployment of the collected resources to appropriate places is also not an easy job due to the operation of vested interests. In a multi-party democracy of our type, there is a strict limit to how far the government can go.

The analysis of resource mobilisation here is focused primarily on the budgetary resources of the state government, and only briefly on the mobilisation and deployment of banking resources. The first part deals with budgetary resources and addresses the questions like: Did the government make utmost efforts to utilise all the tax and non-tax sources of revenue? What was the role of Central transfers in augmenting the resources? Were the expenditures adequately development-oriented and for the benefit of the poor majority in particular? What was the extent of self-reliance of the government? At every point, UP's relative position among the states has been looked into.

PART I

THE GOVERNMENT BUDGET

The government of Uttar Pradesh had a very poor performance in resource mobilisation. The fiscal deficit had risen continuously, reaching an average of Rs. 13401 crore in 2000-03, from Rs. 2931 crore in 1988-91. As percentage to GSDP, it reached 6.27 in 1996-99 from 4.21 in 1987-90. In recent years also it was in a similar situation, being at 6.02 per cent in 2002-05. Only in 2009-10, the proportion came down to 3.60 per cent. The per capita GFD this year was Rs. 954 as against Rs. 1699 for allstates.

Resource Mobilisation

Over a period of nearly four decades, between 1965-68 and 2000-03, the total budgetary receipts of the state had risen by only 90.5 times at current prices. UP's relative position among the states was very poor. Its rate of growth was lower than in all but two of the states. The composition of the receipts changed adversely over the years. In the revenue receipts, the share of central transfers rose to 51.5 per cent in 1988-91, from 37.3 in 1965-68, but declined again to 48.4 per cent in 1997-00; each of these was higher than the A-S average. The per capita transfer was, however, always below the latter's. After the state's bifurcation, in 2002-05, the central transfer constituted 49.4 per cent of total revenue in UP, which was 13.3 points higher than in A-S. The per capita transfer, however, remained below the latter's.

Revenue Receipts

In the revenue receipts, tax revenue had a very low growth. Over the entire period of nearly four decades, 1965-68 to 2000-03, it was by only 135 times, below that in all states. Sub-period-wise, the growth was much faster during 1975-78 to 1988-91. In non-tax revenue also UP's performance was not good. The growth in collection was very low and its relative share in total revenue declined to 17.9 per cent in 2000-03, from 31.8 in 1988-91; the latest was far below the A-S average.

Capital Receipts

The growth in capital receipts was also very low here. The composition of capital receipts changed noticeably over the years. Among other items, deposits and advances, although fluctuated widely, generally provided the largest share till the end of eighties, contributing 14.6 per cent in 1988-91. In recent years, it stood at only 7.6 per cent in 2000-03. Despite low growth in capital receipts, the state's debt burden was not low.

Expenditure

With the resource mobilisation remaining low, the growth in expenditure could not be high. The per capita total expenditure in UP was always much below the A-S average. In the state's total expenditure, the revenue expenditure had a rapid growth. Between 1975-78 and 2000-03, it had multiplied 36.7 times as against only 14.7 times for capital expenditure. The relative share of the former rose to 82 per cent in 2000-03, from 64 in 1975-78. The per capita expenditure was, however, only Rs. 1,971 in 2000-03, which was 63.9 per cent of the A-S average. On capital expenditure, it was Rs. 438 and 64.1 per cent of that in A-S. A large portion of the capital receipts was generally preempted by revenue account deficit. In 2000-03, it was to the extent of 42.6 per cent. In recent years the situation has changed somewhat. In 2009-10, the share of revenue in the toal came to 73.8 per cent as against 78.1 for A-S. The per capita revenue expenditure was only Rs. 4,564-65.2 per cent of the A-S average. In Ukh, the per capita came to Rs. 10,941 and constituted 156.4 per cent of that in

A-S. (*ibid.*). Below, a detailed look is given into the pattern growth in revenue and capital expenditure.

Revenue Expenditure

In the revenue expenditure, the development expenditure had a very low growth. Between 1975-78 and 1997-00, it had risen by only 21.3 times, and the relative share declined from 66.7 per cent to 51.8. At the level of A-S, the latest was 59.4 per cent. In the development expenditure, social services naturally accounted for the largest share; and increased to 62.8 per cent in 1997-00 from 53.0 in 1975-78. In 2000-03 also the proportion was similar, but the per capita expenditure came to only Rs. 606.53 - 57.1 per cent of the A-S average. Earlier, in 1975-78, the situation was better. As regards recent situation, the per capita in 2009-10 came to only Rs. 1,637, which was 60.2 per cent of that in A-S. In Uttarakhand, however, it was as much as Rs. 5,113 - 188 per cent of the latter's.

In social services, although education etc. always received more than 60 per cent, the per capita expenditure continued to be much below the A-S average. Economic services, the other group, had a very low growth. Between 1975-78 and 2000-03, it was by only 21.3 times. The growth in expenditure was highest in soil and water conservation, and its relative share rose to 17.0 per cent from only 3.0. Forestry also had a high growth, and its share rose to 16.8 per cent from 5.15. Irrigation and flood control came next with a share of 23.9 per cent in 200-03, declining from 28.8 in 1988-91. Major and medium projects accounted for the overwhelming bulk here. The share of transport, etc., stood at 10.3 per cent in 2000-03, rising from 7.1 in 1988-91. Industry and minerals was largely neglected; the per capita expenditure in 2000-03 came to only Rs. 9.62 as against Rs. 24.55 at the level of A-S. (*ibid.*).

The non-development expenditure had a rapid growth in UP. Administrative services came next, with a share of 22.0 per cent in 1997-00, declining from 30.6 in 1988-91. Within it, police accounted for as much as 62.5 per cent in 2000-03, declining from 64.3 in 1975-78; at the level of A-S, the latest was 61.3 per cent. The expenditure on compensation and assignments to local bodies, etc., had also risen rapidly. Over the entire period, it was by 122.7 times, which however, came mainly in recent years.

Capital Expenditure

In the capital disbursements also the proportion of developmental was very low. In the development expenditure, economic services always accounted for an overwhelming proportion. Social services hardly received any attention till mid-eighties. Its relative share had risen from 4.2 per cent in 1975-78 to 10.6 in 1988-91 and 15.1 in 1997-00. In social services, medical and public health generally received the highest share, followed by education. In recent years, the situation of capital disbursements improved considerably. In 2002-05, the relative share in total expenditure rose to 25.1 per cent as against 11.07 per cent in A-S. The per capita expenditure was, however, still only Rs. 816 as against Rs. 1215 for A-S. In the total disbursements, economic services constituted 44.3 per cent, and social services only 3.44 per cent. In economic services, transport and communication accounted for 15.8 per cent, followed by irrigation, etc., 12.3 and agriculture and allied services 9.51. In Uttaranchal, the situation of capital disbursements was significantly better.

Plan Expenditure

The plan expenditure of Uttar Pradesh was relatively low. Among the major states, UP's was lower than in all but two. The plan expenditures of UP moreover had a very low level of capital expenditure. The plan revenue expenditure as percentage to the total increased from 53.26 during 1987-90 to 67.21 in 1996-99; the all-states' average was much lower throughout the nineties.

As regards the sectoral pattern of expenditure, over the entire period between 1951-52 to 2006-07, i.e., till the end of the Tenth Plan, economic infrastructure had received 45 per cent, with power receiving 19 per cent and irrigation and transport 13 per cent each. Social infrastructure received 17 per cent, with education at 8 per cent, medical and health 5 per cent and the balance for water supply and sanitation. Agriculture and allied sectors received 9 per cent and Rural development 10. The highest proportion for irrigation and energy was during 1966-85 at 56.9 per cent, rising from 37.7 per cent the first three plans. The per capita expenditure was much below the national average even in the period with the highest share, being respectively Rs. 562 and Rs. 868. (based on 1981 population). The share of agriculture and allied had a sharp fall after mid-sixties, declining from 27.6 per cent during 1951-65 to 11.3 in 1966-85. The per capita expenditure on agriculture came to Rs. 112.06 during 1966-85, which was only 48.0 per cent of the national average.

The apparent situations do not tell the whole story. Corruption and leakage of funds to unauthorised channels are rampant everywhere. Contractor-bureaucrat-politician nexus greatly reduces the real expenditure. The control system is extremely weak. Even if any thing wrong is detected by the CAG, these are not acted upon promptly or followed up properly. The punishment meted out is generally so insignificant that it does not act as a deterrent.

Delays in implementation of projects are very common, and this greatly nullifies the development efforts. Not only the people suffered due to non-availability of the services at the right time, the cost escalations were also huge. The budget allocations remaining unspent and being returned were also not uncommon. And then there are instances of expenditures on totally useless projects.

Local Bodies

Panchayat Raj Institutions

The implementation of the Act in UP was, however, very unsatisfactory. After a decade, in 2003, number of departments/subjects yet to be transferred to panchayats was as many as 17 with regard to funds, 16 on functions and 20 with regard to functionaries. The relative position of UP among the states was very poor; six of the states had transferred all the 29 functions required to be transferred. On devolution of funds, very little has been done in UP, as in most other states. As regards the latest situation, a devolution index prepared by the IIPA shows UP's at 41.73 and for Uttarakhand 28.92 in 2009 as against the national average of 45.04. UP's rank among the states in performance was 13th and Uttarakhand's 20th. Even the planning system remains far from what was envisaged. The DPCs rarely function properly, and many of their recommendations do not get reflected in the annual state plan and budget. Panchayats continue to be merely agencies for implementing schemes handed down from above. (Pal, Mahi 2004, GOI 2011a). Below, a brief look is given to the changes in the resource position and expenditures of the panchayats.

Revenue Receipts

The gram panchayats (GPs) of UP were in an extremely poor state until recent years. According to a report of the Commission on District Level Administration of the UP government, in 1986, 54.6 per cent of the GPs here had income of less than Rs. 250, with 20.5 per cent at below Rs. 100; only 11.3 per cent had income of above Rs. 1,000. (VANI 1995).

The revenues of panchayats for all tiers together had risen to the annual average of Rs. 743.5 crore in 1995-98 from Rs. 446.4 crore in 1990-93, i.e., a growth of only 66.6 per cent; at the level of all-states, it was by 112.5 per cent. At the village level, UP's situation was still worse. The scope for larger collection of revenue by the PRIs was not low. The per capita tax revenue of the PRIs in UP came to only Rs. 1.48 in 1995-98 as against the A-S average of Rs. 5.43. Between 1990-91 and 1997-98, the collection here had risen by only 39.1 per cent as against 58.0 per cent in the latter. In recent years, the situation worsened further. The village level situation was extremely poor.

Trend in Expenditure

With the revenue position so poor, the expenditure could not be high. The aggregate for all tiers combined annually averaged Rs. 766.0 crore during 1995-98, which was a mere 4.36 per cent of A-S total. The per capita expenditure came to Rs. 68.69, a quarter of that in A-S and lowest among the selected states. The revenue account deficit was also low here, being only 2.94 per cent as against the A-S average of 6.86 per cent. At village level, the situation was only slightly better. The per capita expenditure in 1995-98 came to Rs. 58 as against Rs. 75 for A-S. This was despite as much as 84.4 per cent of all-tiers' total being spent here as against only 26.9 per cent in A-S. The expenditures, moreover, were very little for the benefit of people. The proportion going for core services was only 3.4 per cent in 1995-98 as against 10.5 in A-S. In fact, until 1997-98 it was much lower; the average for 1994-97 being only 1.24 per cent. The per capita expenditure in 1995-98 came to only Rs. 1.95 as against the A-S average of Rs. 7.92. Apart from the expenditure being very low, it is a moot question whether the beneficiaries were the really needy. The gram sabhas are rarely held in a proper manner, and the money is largely misappropriated by the functionaries and contractors. The illiteracy and ignorance of an overwhelming majority are great obstacles in the way of proper functioning of the panchayats. The socio-economic situation in villages is such that even the elections cannot be held properly; these continue to be dominated by money and muscle power. (The Asian Age 2005:3).

Urban Local Bodies

The urban areas being more developed, their local bodies presented a much better picture than the rural ones. But here also, the relative position of UP among the states was very poor. Total revenue of the ULBs constituted only 5.39 per cent of A-S total during 1995-98. The per capita revenue was less than half that in the latter, being respectively Rs. 203 and Rs. 498. The growth in total revenue between 1990-91 and 1997-98 was by only 92 per cent as against 210 per cent for all-states; UP's was the lowest growth among the states. The situation of own revenue in it was still worse. In the own revenue, the contribution of tax revenue was very low. The revenue was low, but even this often could not be spent fully. The transfers to local governments were extremely low in UP.

PART II

The Banking System

Major Changes

Co-operative Credit Institutions

For two decades after Independence, co-operative credit was the only organised source of finance for rural activities, and afterwards also it generally remained the single most important source. But the operation of these institutions in UP continued to be far from satisfactory, and the people had to rely largely on the unorganised sources like money-lenders. For all types of societies together, the number of societies in UP had a sharp fall over the years. On the working capital, the situation was much worse. UP accounted for only 6.2 per cent all-India total in 1998, declining from 9.91 in 1982. The growth over the entire period of nearly three decades was by only 36 times as against 48 times in all-India. The working capital per society was always much below the latter's. The deposit mobilisation was very low. The growth between 1970 and 1998 was by only 89 times as against 101 times in all-India. Per society it came to only Rs. 50.20 lakh in 1998, which was 71 per cent of the latter's. The situation of paid-up capital was worse. The average per society came to only Rs. 4.23 lakh in 1998, 61 per cent of the A-I average. Among the societies, the most important are the ground level ones: primary agricultural (PACS) and non-agricultural societies (PNACS). A detailed look is given below to their operation.

Primary Agricultural Credit Societies

In the total number of co-operative credit societies, PACS constituted as much as 95.3 per cent in 1970 and around 85 per cent in the eighties onward. The number of societies declined in every state, but it was sharper here. Per million operational holdings, the state had only 77 societies in 1997 as against 121 in all-India. The membership per society was much higher here than in the latter; around mid-nineties, it was a fifth higher.

In recent years, the situation of PACS worsened further. In 2005, the total number of societies here constituted only 8.21 per cent of A-I total, and including Uttaranchal 8.62, as against 10.4 per cent in 1998. Average population per society came to 19 thousand, double that in all-India. The situation of membership worsened sharply; being down to only 2.16 per cent of A-I total, from 12.4 per cent earlier. As regards resources, the working capital per society came to only Rs. 14 lakh, a fifth of the A-I average. The deposit per society could not reach even Rs. one lakh as against the latter's Rs. 17 lakh. The reliance on borrowings increased further to 77.1 per cent of working capital as against the national average of 53.7 per cent. The lending activities remained extremely low. The amount outstanding per society in 2005 came to only Rs. 8.96 lakh, a quarter of that at the national level. The proportion of borrowing members was only 1.6 per cent as against 12.4 in the latter. The business per society and per staff were very low. For Uttaranchal also the situation was not good.

Primary Non-Agricultural Credit Societies

The PNACS were also not in a good position. The growth in number of societies was very low, and the relative share in all-India total declined from 8.4 per cent in 1970 to 4.1 in 1998. On membership, the situation was worse.The working capital of the societies was extremely low. Average per society came to only Rs. 3.19 lakh in 1998, which was a tenth of the all-India average. Earlier, the relative position was better. The growth in total working capital over the 28-year period was by only 471 per cent, a sixth of that in all-India. The contribution of deposit in it had on the whole declined. The deposit per society in 1998 came to only 14 per cent of the A-I average. The borrowings were also in a similar position.

Commercial Banks

The lower availability of bank offices, along with poor quality of services, had affected both the deposit mobilisation and credit deployment. Looking to credit first, the growth in credit outstanding over a period of thirty-six years, between 1971 and 2006, was by only 276.5 times here as against 299.7 times in All-India. The rural share of total credit is, however, relatively high here. On deposit mobilisation also the performance was not good. The per capita deposit was always much below the national average, and the relative position worsened over the years. As regrds the recent situation, the per capita deposit with SCBs in 2009-10 stood at Rs. 15,662 in UP and Rs. 42,486 in Uttarakhand as against Rs. 38,400 for All-India. UP's share in All-India total deposit stood at 6.85 per cent, declining from 7.92 in 2003-04; for Uttarakhand, the fall was from 1.18 per cent to 0.92. The rural share of total deposit in UP stood at 20.4 per cent in 2010, declining from 26.2 in 2004; for Uttarakhand, it increased from 21.7 to 22.9 per cent. At the national level, the proportion had declined from 12.9 to 9.22 per cent. (CMIE 2011b). The efficiency level of the bank offices here was apparently low.

Regional Rural Banks

The RRBs, catering primarily to the weaker sections, had a much better performance. In the all-India total deposit from RRBs, UP's share stood at 21.3 per cent in March 2010, declining from 23.9 in 2006 and 27.0 per cent in 1989. On the provision of credit, the situation was not so good. The C-D ratio was very low here, being always much below the A-I average. Overall, the role of institutional agencies in providing credit to UP was not good. Their relative share in total outstanding cash debt in rural areas increased from 23 per cent in 1971 to 69 in 1991, but declined again to 56 in 2002; the latest was only 1 point higher than the A-I average as against 5 points higher in 1991.

4

HUMAN RESOURCE DEVELOPMENT

Education

In the area of education, UP's performance was extremely poor. This gloomy situation was mainly due to the utter inadequacy of schooling facilities. Even the availability of schools in rural areas continued to be very poor. The state's share in all-India total number of primary schools rose to 18.8 per cent in 2005, from 14.5 in 200-01, and on middle school from 10.7 per cent to 14.8; for secondary schools, the growth was much faster, rising from 4.38 per cent to 9.62. As regards the management-wise distribution of schools, the proportion under government management was very low here, and this probably had affected the quality of service provided. In 2004-05, not a single primary school in UP was under government management as against 43.33 per cent in all-India; on middle school, it was a negligible 0.59 and 42.96 per cent, respectively; on high schools, 4.96 and 31.66 per cent; and on Pre-degree/ HS schools, 3.90 and 36.08 per cent. The proportion of unaided private schools was very high, except at the Primary stage. In Pre-degree/ HS schools, it was as much as 58.67 per cent as against 31.79 in all-India; in High schools, 56.22 and 28.52 per cent, respectively; and on Middle schools, 30.91 and 21.39 per cent. The primary schools were under local bodies to the extent of as much as 90.47 per cent and in middle schools at 58.02 per cent; at the national level, it was respectively 46.87 and 29.24 per cent. In Uttarakhand, the proportion of government schools were high at High and Higher Secondary levels, respectively 70.38 and 67.74 per cent. In the other two stages, local bodies predominated; 79.82 per cent at Primary and 69.75 in Middle schools. (GOI 2007a).

The enrolment ratio in the state continued to be very poor. The net attendance ratio was very low. The lack of facilities in schools continued to hamper progress. The growth in number of teachers was very low at every stage. The quality of teaching continues to be very depressing in general. The efforts to improve the quality of teacher education started only in late 'eighties, after the introduction of the National Policy on Education 1986. A centrally sponsored Scheme of Restructuring and Reorganisation of Teacher Education was launched in 1987 for providing pre-service and in-service training of elementary and secondary school teachers. The measures for attracting poor students to schools were also utterly inadequate.

In recent years, however, the situation improved noticeably after a Supreme Court order in September 2004 made the provision of mid-day meal obligatory. The recent improvement in the situation of elementary education is primarily a product of the Sarva Shiksha Abhiyan, launched in 2001-02 for universalisation of elementary education. But here also the relative position of UP is very poor. An Educational Development Index on the SSA—calculated by taking into account 22 variables related to the broad parameters of access, infrastructure, teacher related indicators and outcomes—gave Uttar Pradesh the rank of 31st among 35 States and UTs, and for Uttarakhand 15th in 2005-06. (GOI 2007b: 47).

Intra-State Disparities

The schooling facilities varied greatly inter-regionally. At the senior basic stage, the situation was much worse. District-wise, the highest availability of primary schools in 1999-00 was in Garhwal, at 228 per lakh population, and the lowest 26 in Ghaziabad; in the plains, the highest was 105 in Kanpur Rural. Two decades earlier, in 1978-79, the highest was 222 in Uttar Kashi and the lowest at 49 in Azamgarh; in the plains, the highest was 130 in Lalitpur. On senior basic schools, the disparity was much higher. In 1999-00, the highest was twenty-one times the lowest, being respectively 63 in Tehri Garhwal and 3 in Mirzapur; in the plains, the highest was 30 in Kanpur Rural. Over the period, the number had declined in 12 of the districts.

As regards the pupil-teacher ratio, in 1999-00, at the junior stage, the highest was 64 in Faizabad and the lowest at 23 in Ambedkarnagar. A decade earlier, in 1990-91, the highest and the lowest were respectively 82 in Lalitpur and 23 in Uttar Kashi. The ratio declined in most of the districts, but seven districts showed increases. A number of districts with very low ratio also recorded declines. In the latest year, 19 districts had less than 25. (*ibid.*).

Adult Education

Adult education was of critical importance for a meaningful democratic government. It needed to be pursued on war-footing. But there was virtually a total neglect of it. The lackadaisical attitude of the government is evident from the fact that it was proposed to be developed as "extension activities" from the educational institutions, particularly village schools, in collaboration with panchayats and cooperatives and voluntary organisations. (GOI 1961: 599). There was total absence of any compulsion. The National Board of Adult Education was set up to advice the government on the Programme and to enlist the cooperation of different agencies. Naturally, nothing tangible came out of these efforts.

In 1978, a National Adult Education Programme was launched. But this also could not be successful largely due to being based on honorarium. After another decade, towards the end of eighties some bold steps were initiated. The National Literacy mission was launched in May 1988, and for the educationally backward districts and those with high concentration of SC/ST population the Total Literacy Campaigns in 1989. It was aimed to cover all the illiterates in the age-group 15-35 by 1990 through a mass movement involving social institutions, voluntary organisations, students, etc. A brief look is given below on how the programmes performed in UP.

District-wise, there was great variation in the achievement. In the literacy phase, only 12 districts had more than 60 per cent achievement in relation to the target. In the post-literacy phase also UP's performance was very poor. In the Tenth Plan (2002-07), the scope of the AEP was expanded significantly. It was revised to give an integrated approach to literacy by amalgamating the literacy and post-literacy phases. A strict system of quality control and enforcement of accountability are very necessary.

Higher Education

At the post-school level also UP's situation was not good. On degree standard and above, the number of institutions was large, constituting 27.4 per cent of A-I total this year; but in enrolment the relative share was only 12.0 per cent. In the total number of institutions, a distinctive feature of UP is the low share of general degree colleges; being only 21.7 per cent of total as against 56.4 per cent in all-India. The highest proportion of institutions here was in Oriental studies, being 74.7 per cent. In enrolment, the picture was quite different. Over the following two decades also no noticeable improvement came. The state accounted for only 7.34 per cent of all-India total. The pupil-teacher ratio came to as much as 48 in UP and 38 in Uttaranchal as against 25 in all-India. As regards the distribution of enrolment over different areas, the situation of polytechnic institutes worsened further. UP and Uttaranchal together accounted for only 5.49 per cent of all-India total in 2004-05, with the number at 21,342; the share of Tamil Nadu alone was 21.3 per cent. At the degree level and above, engineering etc. accounted for only 1.42 per cent and medicine 0.74 as against 3.34 and 4.70 per cent in all-India. The proportion for general education, which is largely unproductive, was very high. At the PG level, the state's share in A-I total came to 25.1 per cent; and within it Arts accounted for as much as 71.2 per cent as against 59.4 in all-India. (*ibid.*).

Health and Family Welfare

The nutritional status of children was very poor. An important reason behind this situation is that the MCH activities were at a very low level. Children aged 12-23 months fully immunised in 2005-06 was only 23 per cent, around half the national average. Earlier also it was in a similar position. On the timely complementary feeding of infants, the coverage was only 17.3 per cent in 1999, around half the national average. Percentage of children registered for paediatric care was only 26.6 in 1995-96. The maternal healthcare was also similarly placed. Percentage of pregnant women registered for pre-natal care was only 19.2 in 1995-96 as against 45.5 in all-India. In recent years, in 2004, per 1000 women, antenatal care was availed by only 544 here as against 698 at the national level. Percentage of births attended by health professionals stood at only 29.2 in 2005-06 as against 48.3 in the latter; the institutional deliveries constituted respectively 22.0 and 41.0.

Infrastructural Situation

The health infrastructure was extremely poor in UP. Even the lowest level facility, the availability of sub-centres, was very low. The progress in setting up rural health centres was very slow. As regards medical personnel, number of doctors per lakh population increased from 14.6 in 1971 to 23.9 in 1991; the latest was less than half the national average. In rural areas, the situation was much worse. At the level of PHCs, average number of doctors per PHC came to only 0.59 in 1997, around half the national average. There is a large body of "registered medical practitioners", substantial portion of which is complete quacks and others having some medical experience. The first category continues to flourish despite a ban on it due to the system of illegal registration. (Mehrotra, Santosh 2008a).

The situation of health workers was still worse; the number available being only 5.57, lower than in all but three of the states. On other personnel also the situation was not good. After the introduction of the National Rural Health Mission in 2005, the quality of service in rural areas improved somewhat. The NRHM had laid down the following norms to be achieved throughout the country: At the village level, there was to be at least one accredited social health activist (ASHA), anganwadi worker, village health drug day kit for 1,000 population; sub-primary health centre for five to six villages for population with telephone link; PHC for 30-40 villages with round the clock services; and a block level hospital for 100 villages or 100,000 population. Execution of the NRHM was severely affected by corruption.

Indigenous Systems of Medicine

The allopathic system of medicine is more costly and is known to have adverse side effects, but until recently there was virtually no attempt to develop the alternative systems. Apart from certain initiatives from the government of India, very few states took any concrete step. How scanty the efforts were may be gauged from the fact that in the first two five-year plans, a total of only around Rs. 4 crore were spent on promoting research in the indigenous systems. There were many suggestions from the Planning Commission on their development but these were not given any serious attention. (GOI 1961a: 670-01). A brief look is given below on the situation of the alternative systems in UP. Region-wise, the availability of indigenous systems varied greatly. The neglect of the indigenous systems and over-emphasis on the allopathic is an important reason behind the failure of the policy of 'Health for all by 2000 AD'. Large amount of funds were preempted by the latter, and naturally the other systems of medicine, supply of drinking water, environmental sanitation and hygiene, nutrition, etc., could not get the necessary attention. And then, the total expenditure on health itself was low in UP, as will be evident later.

Family Planning

Small family is an essential key to family welfare. It is also necessary from the macro angle, for development implies substitution of man by machinery, and the earth's carrying capacity is not unlimited. The crude birth rate (per thousand population) was to come down to 21.0 from 33.3 in 1978. (GOI 1981a: 368). These targets are, however, yet to be reached nationally, and UP is far behind the national average also. In 1997, the NRR here stood at 2.32 as against 1.42 for all-India.

Causal Factors: This poor performance in birth control was largely because the government did not take it seriously due to the vote-bank politics and vested interests of the richer sections being involved. A serious attention to it would have required actions in a variety of directions, for the poverty itself is greatly responsible for the high birth rate. And given the nature of the government, it could neither put much pressure on the people to reduce the family size, nor had the will to spend the necessary money. The long-term consequences of rapid population growth was beyond their concern.

The variables affecting the birth rate were, therefore, in a very poor state. The use of contraceptives was very low in UP. Behind this situation, illiteracy among women was an important factor. There are many reports of hardship and even death of women who came for tubectomies. The Dalit women were always at the receiving end of the callously managed family planning programme.

Intra-State Disparities: Within the state, inter-regionally, there were wide differences on all the aspects of family planning. The variation in use of contraceptive was very high even in recent years. The rural-urban disparity in performance was very high. In 1998-99, the actual TFR in urban areas was only 2.88 as against 4.31 in rural areas. The difference in standard of living also had a great impact. The above analysis points to the need for vigorous actions in a number of directions. But the actions will not come unless there is the necessary political will. And the latter will not come easily because of its class-character— i.e., it is a government primarily for the benefit of the richer section of population. The rich are not interested in lowering the birth rate, Poverty or illiteracy of the masses, for these make the exploitation of the poor easier. But, if somehow the government realises the dangers from high birth rate, it will be forced to attack poverty and illiteracy. Poverty is both a cause and an effect of population growth. Combined and concerted actions with much larger resources than provided so far are urgently called for. The urgency is evident from the fact that by the year 2050, India is projected to be the most populous country in the world, with a population of 165.8 crore. (TST 2008 k). Providing food and all the basic necessities to such a huge population will be impossible; and there is bound to be violent protests.

Pattern of Expenditure: The expenditure on healthcare in India comes largely from private households, estimated at 75 per cent of total. State governments contribute 15.2 per cent, the Centre 5.2, and third-party insurance and employers provide 3.3 per cent. (Bhat, Ramesh et al 2006). Given the extent of poverty of the overwhelming proportion of population, in this situation, the health care is bound to be in a very poor state. There is urgent need for a manifold increase in public health care expenditure.

The per capita revenue expenditure on health, including family planning, was always below the all-states average. As regards the distribution over different heads, hospitals and dispensaries naturally accounted for the largest share, declining from 39.4 per cent in 1980-81 to 30.1 in 1992-93. As the share of RHS increased greatly, naturally that for other heads declined. For making any noticeable improvement, two things are vitally necessary: (i) a much larger allocation of funds for them, and (ii) greater control over fund utilisation so that leakages to unauthorised uses are totally stopped. These changes can come only if they are forced on the government by the combined strength of the masses. More funds can flow only if these sectors get the right priority, and all unnecessary expenditures at every level of the government are drastically cut. The critical importance of cent per cent literacy and bringing down the net reproduction rate to less than one must be brought home to the government by all people concerned with the nation's well-being.

5

AGRICULTURAL GROWTH AND TRANSFORMATION

The growth in agricultural production is of critical importance for more than one reason. Agriculture is a source of food and raw materials for the economy. It is also a source of income and employment, and thus contributes to economic growth by providing a demand base for other sectors. The importance of the sector was, however, much greater in UP than in most other states. The analysis here is divided into two parts: the first dealing with crop farming, and the next with the allied activities. The focus is on the resource base and their utilisation, and the growth in use of inputs and production.

I. CROP FARMING

Growth in Production

The state's performance in agricultural production has been on the whole very poor. The rate of growth was generally below the national verage. The yield per hectare was, however, always higher than the national average.

Food-grains

Among the crops, the situation of food-grains as a whole was not bad. The latest yield rate was 26.6 per cent higher than in the latter. In the following three years, 2003-06, however, the situation worsened somewhat. The production averaged 42507 thousand tonnes, and the relative share in A-I total declined to 20.6 per cent; the yield rate at 2052 kg., was only 20.8 per cent higher than the A-I average. Individual crop-wise, in terms of area, the most important crop in UP was wheat, and the area under it had increased noticeably over the years. In rice, the second important crop, the growth in production over the period of three-and-half decades was by 237 per cent, more than double that in all-India. The state's share in all-India production rose to 13.6 per cent in 2000-03 from 8.3 in 1968-71. In the state's food-grains production, the share of rice rose to 26.8 per cent from 19.0. The yield rate which was below the A-I average, became higher by early 1990s. The area under rice had risen by 26.5 per cent, much higher than in all-India. In 2003-06, the situation worsened somewhat. The yield rate, at 1994 kg., was below the A-I average. The production averaged 11813 thousand tonnes, and constituted 13 per cent of A-I total.

All the other foodgrains had recorded continuous fall in area. In pulses, gram continued to be the dominating crop, despite a sharp fall in area. The production had a sharp fall, and the relative share in A-I total declined from 32.3 per cent in 1968-71 to 12.7 in 1997-00. In recent years, however, the situation improved noticeably. During 2002-05, the yield rate came to 946 kg, which was 21.1 per cent higher than the national average. Arhar came next with an area around half that in gram. Here also the performance was not good. Both the area and the yield rate declined.

Non-Foodgrains

UP has a very low proportion of cropped area under non-foodgrains. In oilseeds, rapeseed and mustard had a sharp fall in acreage since the late 'eighties, after a rise by 128 per cent between 1950-1 and 1980-83. The growth in yield rate was also not high. In groundnut also the area declined, and in 1997-00 stood at around a third of that in 1968-71. In other oilseeds also the situation was not good. The situation in Uttaranchal was significantly better. The acreage under it averaged 14.1 thousand ha in 2001-04, with the yield rate at 1043 kg. (CMIE 2009). It may be noted that in oilseeds as a whole, UP accounted for only 5.10 per cent of A-I total in 2000-03, declining from 6.30 in 1990-93 (in value term). (GOI 2006a).

Tobacco, with a relatively small acreage, had a good performance. In fruits and vegetables, UP had a very poor performance. The value of output had risen from an annual average of Rs. 3174.70 crore in 1990-93 to Rs. 6264.45 crore (at constant 1993-94 prices) in 2000-03; the relative share in A-I total rising from 9.11 per cent to 10.67. In vegetables, the most important crop is potato, and its performance was quite good. In onion, UP's performance has not been good, although the yield rate was always significantly higher than at the national level. The production declined from 305 thousand tonnes in 1997-00 to 241 thousand in 2002-05, with the area declining from 25.1 thousand ha to 21.0 thousand and the yield rate from 12103 kg to 11496 kg. UP's share in A-I production came to only 4.03 per cent in 2002-05. On garlic, the production had risen noticeably in recent years, to 151.2 thousand tonnes in 2003-06 from only 30.0 thousand in 1999-00. Thus, there was hardly any diversification of agricultural production in Uttar Pradesh.

Reasons Behind

This poor situation of UP's agriculture is due to both natural and man-made factors. The state has maximum agro-climatic and economic diversity. There are nine agro-climatic zones (excluding Uttaranchal) ranging from temperate to dry and hot rain-fed semi-arid condition in Bundelkhand, plateau area in Mirzapur and Allahabad and water logged/high ground water area in the eastern part. A detailed look is given below on the situation of different parameters affecting agricultural growth.

Resource Endowment

The undivided UP accounted for only 9.7 per cent of the country's total reporting area (RA), which was lower than in three of the states. In the total area, however, the proportion of NCA in 1999-00, stood at 59.0 per cent as against 46.6 per cent in all-India. After the bifurcation, in 2005-06, UP's proportion increased to 68.9 per cent; Uttaranchal's was only 13.5 per cent. Among the states, UP's NCA continues to be third highest. In terms of population, the situation was very poor. Per thousand, it was only 101 ha in 2000-01, the second lowest among the states. Post-bifurcation, it declined to 93.3 ha in UP in 2005-06 (based on estimated population of 2004-05). The utilisation of even this low level of NCA was far from satisfactory. The ratio of GCA to NCA increased from 1.28 in 1962-65 to 1.48 in 1992-95 and in 2005-06, it was 1.50 for UP and 1.65 in Uttaranchal. UP's latest was lower than in three of the states. The total GCA this year constituted 13.0 per cent of A-I total. Per thousand population, it came to only 140 ha. As regards inter-district disparities in resource endowment, the reporting area itself varied greatly.

Man-made Factors

For raising the productivity of land, the first essential requirement is the right motivation of the farmers. The actual farmer must have the urge to make the best possible use of the resources at his disposal. The motivation is, however, dependent on certain objective factors like the pattern of land-holding, availability of the required inputs at the right time and at right prices, extension services, marketing facility and remunerative prices for the produce. Below, a brief look is given into the situation of UP on these factors.

Land-Holding System

The land reform measures in UP met the same fate as in most other states. The Zamindari Abolition and Land Reform Act (ZALRA) was passed in January 1950 but the Act could not be enforced till July 1952 as the zamindars challenged the Act in the High Court and Supreme Court. Moreover, the Act had no provision for land distribution. However, even the provisions like not allowing landowners to evict the tenants for personal cultivation could not be enforced properly. In the period when the case was pending before the court, the zamindars had evicted tenants on a large scale and executed 'pattas' of land to influential and 'favourite' people after collecting 'nazrana'.

The Ceiling, Surplus Distribution, etc.

The ceiling on land-holdings came only in 1960, and then the limit was fixed at as much as 40 to 128 acres, depending on the quality of land, for a family of five members. An extra eight acres were provided to larger families. There were also a large number of exemptions, and these were utilised fraudulently. Large land-holders planted trees on the excess land as all grove land was exempted. Similarly, land was transferred to fake cooperative societies as the latter was exempted. Land was also donated to Bhoodan Yojana committee although for all practical purposes it remained with the owner. Large scale transfers had actually started in late fifties itself with the beginning of a talk of ceiling on land-holdings. Consequent on all these, only two lakh acres of land could be declared surplus.

The pro-zamindar attitude of the ruling class becomes transparent from the report of the Zamindari Abolition Committee, headed by G.B. Pant. He was opposed to any form of land redistribution despite being aware of the huge concentration of land-ownership. The committee noted: "......we do not think that the results achieved would be commensurate with the discontent and hardship resulting from it. We, therefore, recommend that no limits be placed on the maximum area held in cultivation". It observed further that the land redistribution would "increase the difficulty of zamindars in adjusting them to changed condition". These were stated after mentioning that "a bare 1.49 per cent of the bigger landlords own nearly 57.77 per cent of the land". (Quoted in Shankar, Kripa 1991: 1086).

In the following years, the situation instead of improving, worsened. This distribution of surplus land could not bring any improvement in the land ownership situation. This poor performance was due to the pro-landlord and anti-poor attitude of the government. There were large scale evictions of the allottees in the second half of the seventies, particularly following the allotments under the 20-point programme. The performance in reducing the incidence of tenancy was also very poor. As regards the trend in terms of lease, UP's situation was somewhat different than in most other states.

Land Records

It was found that in many cases the land is recorded in the name of a person who died long ago and whose legal successors are now the owners but their names are not in the record. Similar is the situation with regard to transfer of lands by acts of parties; mutation in the records do not take place. This section may be concluded by citing a bizarre instance of the extent of fraudulent activities carried out in the district of Azamgarh due to the acute scarcity of land. This heinous crime could be perpetrated because of a corrupt system in which land records officials can be bribed to get any work done.

Irrigation Facility

Proper irrigation facility is an essential prerequisite for agricultural growth, and UP's performance on it has not been bad. The proportion of net sown area irrigated reached 67.2 per cent by 1991-2, from 40.4 in 1971-2; in the following years, it reached 73.5 per cent in 1998-01. Post-bifurcation, in 2005-06, UP had 79.0 per cent and Uttarakhand 45.0; both were much higher than in all-India. In terms of gross cropped area, however, it was not so good.

Crop-wise, food-grains as a whole had a coverage of 64 per cent of the area in 1995-6, rising from 35 per cent in 1973-4; both were much higher than at the national level. Among non-foodgrains, the major beneficiaries were rapeseed and mustard, cotton and sugarcane. On the source of irrigation water, some significant changes came. The importance of wells increased greatly while that of canals and tanks declined. From the angle of the state's irrigation potential, this was not a very good performance. The provision of free electricity to farmers has resulted in over-exploitation of groundwater, mostly for irrigation, causing the water table to plummet. The government should realise groundwater is public property, not private, and its exploitation should be regulated.

Use of Different Inputs

Fertiliser Consumption

On the use of fertilisers for crop growth, UP's relative position was not bad. But it was a heavy dependence on chemical fertilisers. A disconcerting aspect of the fertiliser consumption in UP is its unbalanced use. The soil quality varies greatly from place to place, but in general because of being cultivated for a long time, they lack micro-nutrients particularly and also organic matter. The health of the soil needs a much greater attention than given hitherto. (TST 2007k). A particularly weak spot in UP is the quality of extension work available. The extension personnel's advice also often could not be followed properly due to lack of timely availability of credit, fertilisers, etc. Number of fertiliser depots and sale points were relatively high, but these proved inadequate due to lack of proper communication facility.

On the use of fertilisers, particular attention needs to be given to increased use of organic and microbes fertilisers, for indiscriminate use of chemical fertilisers ultimately results in drastic reduction of crop yield. Chemical fertilisers affect the water supply to crops during the growth period, and salt and acid in the soil are also increased. Soil erosion as well as pollution of under ground water are the other major consequences. (TST 2006). For retaining the productivity of soil, there is an urgent need for adopting the Integrated Nutrient Management system everywhere. Presently it is being introduced in only 32 of the districts.

Implements and Machinery

The use of implements and machinery in UP's agriculture could not but be small, given the tiny size of holdings for an overwhelming proportion of farmers. District-wise, there were great variations in mechanisation of agriculture. For the optimum use of different inputs in agriculture, while certain objective factors are vitally important, proper education of the farmers is probably more important than most others. But here UP's situation was pathetically poor. In 2003, percentage of farmer households having a literate male member was only 60 as against 65 in all-India; among the selected states, it was lower than in all but three. The situation of female members was still worse; being at 19 per cent as against 31 in all-India. Among males, percentage with secondary and above was only 9.

Provision of Bank Credit

Timely availability of credit is an essential prerequisite for agricultural growth, particularly in a situation where marginal and sub-marginal farmers predominate. But the role of the organised sector of banking in providing credit was extremely poor in UP. The relative position of UP among the states was also very poor. In the provision of credit to agriculture, the cooperative credit system plays the leading role in UP. A redeeming feature of the credit flow from PACS is, however, that a relatively large share of the total was going to marginal farmers. The performance of scheduled commercial banks was better. The marginal farmers were in a very poor situation here.

As regards the RRBs, sponsored by commercial banks, UP's relative position was quite good. At the end of March 1996, their agricultural advances outstanding constituting 21.1 per cent of A-I total. Per hectare credit came to Rs. 285, which was 52 per cent higher than the national average. Earlier also the relative position was not bad.

Marketing Facilities

The provision of proper marketing facility is an essential requirement for inducing the farmers to raise the productivity of land. On the storage facility, the state's situation continued to be very poor until recently. Only recently the situation improved noticeably. In 2005, the cold storage capacity stood at 36.7 per cent of the total production of fruits and vegetables in the state, which was three times the national average.

The availability of markets was very low. The problem was further accentuated by the absence of proper communication facility. As regards cooperative marketing facility, it was virtually non-existent. The price support system through the government's procurement machinery also did not prove very effective in providing remunerative prices. First, the coverage of commodities itself was low, and then the operations suffered from many deficiencies. There were transportation, storage and other problems with the FCI. The price fixation itself was rarely fair, being influenced by non-economic considerations, and did not take into account the individual state's peculiarities or the intra-state variations in costs and prices. For better price realisation, there was need for a greatly improved market intervention system from the government. Probably a Price Risk Mitigation Fund on a state basis needs to be created so that there is quick response to collapsing prices of locally important crops. (GOI 2007c).

The existing scheme of crop insurance is also of little use in mitigating crop production risk. In assessing yields and losses for compensation, average yield in a "block" is used, but there are huge variations in the yields and practices within a block. Unusual delay in settlement is also against the interest of farmers. The scheme is run by the Agriculture Insurance Company, with virtually no risk sharing, and the annual cost to the government comes to well over Rs. 1,000 crore, with a coverage of only about 10 per cent of the cropped area. (*ibid.*). What is needed is hundreds of weather insurance products based on local requirements for different parts of the country.

Finally, a mention is necessary of the situation in agricultural education, which is of critical importance for promoting the growth of agriculture. There are 46 agricultural universities and one central farm university in the country, but they are in shambles almost every where. The primary objective of these institutions is to impart agricultural education at the graduate and post-graduate levels, provide practical training in respect of field problems, integrate research, teaching and extension work for development. But with some exceptions, the progress of these institutions has been far from satisfactory because of the utter chaos that prevails in them. There is little or no accountability in these universities. Many of them are plagued by intrigue and infighting. This has affected both farm education and academic standard as a whole. Casteism, in particular, has wrought havoc. There have been frequent agitations over the removal of vice-chancellors. (Gupta, YP 2011). The decline in farm education is also attributed to the faulty system of internal evaluation.

II. ALLIED SECTORS

Animal Husbandry

Animal husbandry plays a pivotal role in the rural economy of Uttar Pradesh. Over 70 per cent of rural households own livestock and it is an important source of income to the poor. It supplies a significant portion of the draught power for farming and rural transportation, and dairy products are a major source of nutritious food. The growth in livestock population was very low here; being by only 51.5 per cent between 1956 and 1992—from 427.6 lakh to 648.0 lakh—as against 53.6 per cent in all-India; UP's share in the latter's total came to 13.8 per cent in 1992. In the composition of the livestock, cattle constituted 39.6 per cent in 1992 and buffalo 31.0; at the national level, it was respectively 43.4 and 17.9 per cent. Among other livestock, goat, sheep and pig were important. As regards the recent situation, in 2003, per thousand hhs, rural UP had 366 cattle, 443 buffaloes, 531 sheep and goat, 31 pigs and 137 poultry; at the national level, it was lower in the first two but higher in the remaining three. The situation of Uttaranchal was noticeably better.

Cattle and Buffalo

The cattle population of UP increased nominally over the years. Between 1972 and 1992, it was by only 26 per cent as against 60 per cent at the national level. In the all-India total number of cattle, the state's share declined from 15.9 per cent to 12.5 over the period, and further to 10.0 in 2003. The proportion of cross-bred in the total declined to only 8.8 per cent in 2003 from 9.74 in 1992; at the national level, the latest was 13.3 per cent. The low proportion of C-Bs might be due to the poverty of the farmers as its feed requirement is higher than that of the local cattle. The mortality rate among the C-B calves is also reported to be higher. (Rajapurohit, A R 1979). A more disturbing aspect is the low growth in female population, largely determining the milk output. On the buffalo population, UP's situation was significantly better.

Milk Production

In the production of milk, UP's performance was not good. The relative share in all-India total had declined from as much as 29.2 per cent in 1961 to 19.1 in 1971-72 and only 17.7 in 1994-95. The growth in production over the entire period was by only 84.9 per cent as against 204.8 per cent in all-India. In 1999-02, UP's share increased to 18.6 per cent. The per capita production, however, continued to be higher than in all-India. It may be noted that the Operation Flood, managd with foreign assistance, had very poor performance here. Over the entire period of July 1970 to March 1996, the annual growth came to only 3.74 per cent as against 4.84 in all-India. Within the state, inter-district, the milk production varied greatly, as may be inferred from the number of milch animals in different districts.

Smaller Livestock

In minor livestock, goat is the most important, primarily because of its role as provider of meat. However, UP's performance in meat production has been very poor. UP's production was always the highest among the states, and constituted 24.3 per cent of A-I total in 1994-5. The goat population here had risen by 98 per cent between 1972-1992 as against 67 per cent in all-India. In the preceding period of 16 years, however, it was by only 5.6 per cent as against 22 per cent in the latter. On sheep, maintained for both meat and wool, the state's position was very poor. As regards pigs, it is a preserve of certain communities only, and therefore, the production is very low. However, UP's relative position among the states was quite good. In 1992, it accounted for 22.7 per cent of A-I total number. Pigs are reared mainly for meat production, and in 2001-02 it stood at 89.48 lakh kg. (GOUP 2004: II).

Poultry

Traditionally poultry rearing was confined to certain communities, and was done primarily on a household basis. But in recent years there has been considerable expansion as a commercial activity. The development of poultry is, however, still very low in UP, and it can be explained only partly by the food habits of the people. The state accounted for only 2.80 per cent of all-India total number of poultry in 2003, declining from 3.51 in 1992; the growth over the period was by only 27.0 per cent as against 59.2 in all-India. District-wise, there was great variation in poultry rearing. In 1993, the highest number reared per thousand population was 237 in Nainital as against the lowest of 18.7 in Mathura, with the state average at 77.6; there were 18 districts with less than 50 poultry.

As animal husbandry is broadly related to the extent of crop farming by a household, a brief look may be given to the pattern of livestock-owning by the size of operational holding. In smaller livestock, on sheep and goat, while the numbers reared by marginal and sub-marginal holdings were relatively large, for larger holdings it was extremely low; in fact, in the highest two sizes there was absolutely no rearing. At the national level in contrast, the 10-20 ha had as many as 253 per thousand hhs and for the highest class at 194. With proper promotional measures, easily their rearing could be greatly increased in the upper sizes.

Facilities Available

Behind this poor situation of animal husbandry in UP, a number of factors like the utter inadequacy of veterinary facilities, scarcity of feed and fodder, a large number of infertile cows and buffaloes, lack of proper extension services and marketing facility were responsible. A brief look is given below into how the situation changed over the years.

The growth in number of vet. hospitals and dispensaries was very low. Among other facilities, number of sheep wool extension centres had risen from 55 in 1960-1 to 202 in 1980; but over the following nearly two decades, it could reach only 263 in 1998-9. Number of poultry breeding farms increased from 33 in 1960-1 to 42 in 1980-1; and in the following years, the maximum reached was 46. Pig breeding farm began to be established only in 1984-5, and it was static at 9 since 1987-8. The progress in improved breeding was very low. The proportion of breedable livestock reached only 23.5 per cent in late nineties. As regards the availability of green fodder, the gap between availability and requirement was estimated at 23.5 per cent in 2001-02.

In the area of marketing of products, the role of cooperatives was far from satisfactory. Number of milk producers' unions per lakh of milch animals stood at 107 in 1998, rising from 78 in 1990-1. The district-wise situation on every facility varied greatly. The availability of cooperative milk producers' union also varied greatly. Behind the poor facilities, low level of plan expenditure was an important reason. During the first two five-year plans, a total of Rs. 312 lakh was spent on animal husbandry and in the Third plan Rs. 462 lakh (GOUP 1968:50). The outlays increased significantly only in the Eighth Plan, rising to Rs. 13,100 lakh, nearly four times the preceding plan's. In the following two plans again the growth was low—the Ninth Plan had Rs. 14,000 lakh and the Tenth Rs. 17,500 lakh. The actual expenditure almost always fell short of the outlay. In the Third Plan, for instance, it was 69.4 per cent of the target, and in the Ninth Plan a mere 45.4 per cent. (GOUP 2004: I: 74).

Development of Fishery

Although Uttar Pradesh is without marine water resource, there is a vast potential for developing the inland fishery. The resources are varied and extensive, covering large perennial rivers, tributaries, alpine streams, irrigation canals, natural lakes, reservoirs and numerous small ponds and tanks. The total water area is around 12 lakh hectares, constituting four per cent of the state's total area. The relative position among the states was also not bad.

But all these resources remained largely unexploited. Production of fish in a planned way did not get any attention until recent years.The pace of progress in utilisation of the water was very slow. The overall productivity was very low even in 1998-99. The critical input in aquaculture is high quality fish seed, but its production remained very low. Proper disposal of fish is another problem area. The marketing system is very unsatisfactory, and the poor fishermen are deprived from getting the right price due to exploitation by middlemen. The fishermen are under the clutches of middlemen. The latter advances loans to the former on various social occasions, and also provide the boats and gear for fishing. The efforts to correct the situation were utterly inadequate. There are only a few marketing units with necessary infrastructure at identified places in Ghaziabad, Bareilly, Allahabad and Gorakhpur districts. An important reason behind this situation is the low level of plan expenditure on fishery.

Forest Management

The forests are of immense value to a region. They perform at least three sets of function: (i) ecological security, (ii) provision of fuel and fodder, and (iii) raw materials to industries. The forests act as gene pool for scores of plants and wildlife species; they are home to more than half the terrestrial species. Forests also serve as sink for environmental pollution. They help sustain the quality and availability of freshwater supplies. In fact, more than three-quarters of the world's accessible freshwater comes from forested catchments. Water quality declines with a decrease in forest condition and cover. Forests also help decrease the impact of storms and floods, whilst helping to control erosion.

To get these services properly on a continuing basis, adequate attention needs to be given to the maintenance and development of forests. The National Forest Policy of 1952 had expected the forests to constitute at least a third of the land area. But Uttar Pradesh, including Uttarakhand, had only 17.5 per cent in 1998-99. The per capita forest area here came to only 32.44 ha, less than half that in all-India. The total forest area had declined from 41.469 lakh hectares in 1960-1 to 37.247 lakh in mid-sixties and in the following years gradually increased to 51.663 lakh ha in 1997.

The forest areas were largely confined to the Himalayan region, to the extent of 55.2 per cent in 1972. The Tarai and Bhabar and Vindhya regions had respectively 24.5 and 17.0 per cent, and only the balance of 3.3 per cent was in the Gangetic plain. (GOUP 1973). This situation is primarily a result of the mindless exploitation of the forests with hardly any efforts to regenerate them. There was the pressure of increasing population on one side, and then the rising consumerism of the richer section. The large-scale pursuing of monocropping, especially of conifers, for commercial purposes had interfered with the natural process of water supply. The chir-pine was extended aggressively over all types of broad leaved species, especially oak and rhododendron, which have a water retaining and soil stabilising capacity. The population pressure brought more land under plough and upset the balance between field and forest. Over-grazing of land by cattle, and collection of fuel wood and fodder also added to the destruction.

The government's expenditure on maintenance of the forests was very low. In this situation, the yield from the forests had very low growth. All these were largely due to some significant changes in the forest policy. The social forestry scheme was launched in the Sixth plan to provide fuel, fodder and small timber, etc., to the rural people. And then, a new National Forest Policy came in 1988, which significantly changed the priorities and pattern of management. The emphasis now was on the restoration of ecological balance, preservation of protected areas and maintenance of forest for their sustained use. The main thrust areas became increasing the forest cover, forest productivity and conservation of soil and water. In the implementation of programmes, people's participation was introduced for the first time.

Naturally, the pattern of fund allocation changed noticeably in the last two decades. However, the quality of planning also became abominably poor. As regards physical achievements, the growth in plantation decelerated noticeably in recent years. The progress in adopting the participatory system of management was very slow. If the forests are to be saved on a sustainable basis for the purposes assigned to it, the root causes behind the dismal situation has to be tackled firmly. Over-population in relation to poor land productivity has resulted in land degradation and deforestation. There is an urgent need for stabilizing the population size, along with a greatly improved management of the land and livestock. The acute scarcity of land may be gauged from the fact that for every hectare of cultivated land about five ha of uncultivated land is necessary to maintain supplies of organic inputs for crop yields. In many villages this proportion has been lost, and to restore it some land may have to be taken out of cultivation. This may necessitate substituting high value cash crops for foodgrains. Land used for grazing has also to be substituted by grass-lands. In the context of small hill villages, numbering some 13,000, general schemes of improved land management have to be adapted to each village's specific conditions. There are enormous variations in topography, soil types, attitude belts, etc., and these have to be given due consideration.

While conservation of the forests is vitally necessary, the conservation laws are increasingly becoming an impediment to development of the infrastructure and cultivation.

NOTES

- It may be noted that although the most dangerous Persistent Organic Pollutants have been banned from use, production or import, somehow they continue to be used in the country. (Sahara Times 2005. November 12). Trade in spurious pesticides is carried out on a large scale. The size of this market at farmers' level was estimates at about Rs. 1500 crore in 2006. (TST 2006; 2009 z55).
- For this situation of fertilizer consumption in UP, the government's fertliser policy was greatly responsible. A recent CAG report has stated that while subsidy costs have galloped, production has not increased in step with demand even as systemic flaws exist in assessing total fertiliser requirement. Despite the Rs. 270,648 crore spending on fertiliser subsidy during 2003-10, annual production of fertiliser increased only marginally from 248 million tonnes in 2003-04 to 298 mts in 2008-09.

6

INDUSTRIAL GROWTH AND STRUCTURAL CHANGE

FACTORY SECTOR

In industrial output, the factories registered under the Factories Act, 1948 account for the largest share in every major state. UP's relative position in it is very poor. In the national total of output from the sector, the state's share stood at only 7.13 per cent in 2004-05, declining from 6.90 in 1977-8 and 9.72 in 1955. The per capita output had declined from 55.5 per cent of the national average in 1955 to 42.9 in 1977-78 and further to 41.4 per cent in the latest year. The situation of net value added to output was very poor. As regards provision of employment, after a continuous rise till 1990-1, in recent years it recorded an absolute fall. In 2004-05, at only 4.88 lakh, it was 62 per cent of that in 1990-91 and constituted 7.4 per cent of A-I total. The productivity of the employees was very low; being generally below the national average. And this was despite a relatively high level of fixed capital per employee until recently. The capital/output ratio was also similarly placed. Even after decreasing to 0.61 in 1999-00, it was higher than in all but two of the states. In 2004-05, however, at 0.28, it was lower than in all but two. The NVA/FC ratio was always below the national average. (*ibid.*). The total factor productivity itself was low in UP.

Structural Change

The industrial structure of Uttar Pradesh changed noticeably in the nineties. In 1989-90, six industries—food products, electricity, basic chemicals, machinery and equipment, rubber, plastic, etc., and metal and alloys—together accounted for 75.5 per cent of the factory sector's total output. In 1999-00, their share declined to 61.9 per cent. The combined growth for the six industries over the period was 23.8 times, from Rs. 1671.5 crore to Rs. 39756 crore, compared with 29.0 times for all industries—from Rs. 2212 crore to Rs. 64189 crore.

Among these industries, while food products had a growth of 36.67 times, for electricity and gas it was only 4.24 times. The share of the former in total output rose to 24.4 per cent in 1999-00 from 19.3 in 1989-90; for the latter, on the other hand, it dropped to 1.7 per cent from 11.6. The only other industry, among the six, to raise the share is metal and alloys—from 8.7 to 9.1 per cent. The share of machinery and equipment declined from 13.5 per cent to 10.9, and of rubber, plastic etc. from 10.8 to 5.7 per cent over the period.

Among other industries, the important ones in 1989-90 were transport equipment, cotton textile, beverages and tobacco, paper, etc., non-metallic mineral products, metal products and wool, silk etc. They together accounted for 21.4 per cent of total output. Thus, a total of 14 industries contributed 97 per cent. The importance of the second group as a whole increased noticeably over the years. Among the products showing high growth, the highest was in textile products, a 442-fold rise over the decade, and the relative share rose to 13.3 per cent from less than one per cent. This was followed by metal products with 112.6-fold, the relative share rising to 9.12 per cent from 2.35. For transport equipment, with 66-fold rise, it was from 4.14 to 9.42 per cent.

The capital intensity of a number of industries increased greatly by the end of 'nineties. The efficiency in use of fixed capital varied greatly, and for a number of industries the C/O ratio increased greatly over the period. In basic chemicals—with the highest amount of fixed capital—it was from 0.65 to 0.78, in metal products from 0.16 to 0.84, and paper etc. from 0.33 to 0.88. Among the industries showing declines, a notable one was electricity and gas, from 2.42 to 0.38, and in transport equipment, from 0.35 to 0.10.

SMALL-SCALE INDUSTRIES

On the small-scale industries (SSI), no data are available on a comprehensive basis from any single source, and there is considerable overlapping among the sources. Even the annual survey of industries by the CSO includes part of the SSI sector, and till early seventies it was the only source on the modern sector—i.e., the units registered with the Small Industries Development Organisation (SIDO).[1] In 1972, for the first time, a census of SSI units was undertaken, and that too covering only the SIDO units. There were as many as 22 types of units, including handlooms and power looms and khadi and village industries, not covered by the census. A similar second census was carried out in 1990 for the units registered up to March 1988. A brief look is given below on their findings in Uttar Pradesh.

Modern Sector

Both the censuses found the situation in UP very unsatisfactory. On the provision of employment also the situation was similar. The number employed constituted only 9.5 per cent of all-India total in 1987-88, a nominal rise over 1972. The productivity of the employees continued to be very low; among the major states, the latest was lower than in all but three. From the angle of dispersed development, UP's situation was very poor. A very small proportion of the units were located in the rural areas; being at only 32.3 per cent in 1987-8 compared with 42.1 per cent at the national level. Similar was the situation of backward districts.

Structural Change

As in the factory sector, in SSIs also the importance of different industries changed noticeably over the years. Industry-wise, UP's relative among the states on some of the technical co-efficient was very poor. An important reason behind this situation is the low capacity utilisation. In food products, UP had only 48.3 per cent utilisation in 1987-8 as against 69 per cent in Maharashtra.

The Unorganised Sector

The unorganised manufacturing and repairing enterprises are in large numbers in every state. The productivity of workers in UP was very low. The low productivity might have been at least partly due to the low level of fixed assets, and plant and machinery in particular. The enterprises in UP faced a variety of problems. The growth status of the enterprises in UP was very poor. Over the period of three years preceding the survey, only 10.6 per cent of enterprises had reported expanding as against 15.6 per cent at the national level. The proportion contracting was 17.7 per cent and 12.3 per cent respectively. The relative position of Uttaranchal was worse. Only 3.5 per cent of enterprises had reported expanding. The proportion of enterprises stagnant was as much as 64.3 per cent in Uttaranchal and 59.2 in Uttar Pradesh.

Inter-District Disparities

It is not only that UP's performance among the states was poor, within the state also there were wide differences in the industrial situation. Region-wise, Bundelkhand was the least developed, followed by Uttarakhand. In 1976-7, that is, two-and-half decades after economic planning began, the contribution of the manufacturing sector to total net output was only 6.38 per cent in the former and 9.66 in the latter as against 15.3 per cent at the state level. The per capita value of industrial output in Bundelkhand was only Rs. 9.22 lakh in 1992-3 as against the highest of Rs. 37.18 lakh in Uttarakhand and in the plains, Rs. 16.96 lakh in the Central region. District-wise, many of the districts continued to have a negligible industrial sector. The disparity in productivity of the workers increased greatly over the years. On the small-scale industries exclusively, also the inter-district disparity was wide.

CAUSAL FACTORS

The industrial growth of a state is determined by a variety of factors like availability of infrastructure, raw materials, skilled manpower, the labour situation, general work culture, the availability of entrepreneurs, institutional finance, and above all the attitude and policies of the government. All these factors together determine what is called the investment climate (IC) in a state. A recent study on this, using six variables, placed Uttar Pradesh in a very low position. Percentage of total factor productivity lost in the registered manufacturing sector due to adverse IC was found to be as much as 18.68, which was higher than in all but three of the major states. (Veeramani, C et. al. 2005). We give a brief look below on UP's situation in some of the factors influencing industrial growth.

INFRASTRUCTURE

Adequate availability of infrastructural facility is an essential requirement for industrial growth. But UP's situation on this was very poor. On the provision of power, the state's position was extremely poor. The low industrial consumption of electricity was also due to slow progress in rural electrification. This again was only a notional figure, the real situation was far worse; a village is considered electrified, if there is just one point. This situation was largely due to an extremely low growth in installed capacity and its poor utilisation. The capacity utilisation was very low. The non-utilities sector was substantial in recent years. As regards transportation facility, although the road length in the state was relatively good, the quality of roads was very poor. Moreover, the growth came quite late. District-wise, the road availability varied greatly.

INSTITUTIONAL FINANCE

On the provision of short-term capital, commercial banks are the leading institutions, followed at a great distance by cooperative credit and the regional rural banks. For long-term credit, until recently, there were 14 institutions—six all-India development banks, three investment institutions, three specialised financial institutions, and two state-level institutions. First, the trend in provision of working capital to the sector is looked into, concentrating only on the commercial banks; the other two groups play an insignificant role, providing finance only to the small and tiny units.

Commercial Banks

In commercial banks, as noted in chapter 3, scheduled banks account for the overwhelming proportion of business. However, their role in providing industrial credit to UP was very poor. The number of accounts under industrial credit had a sharp fall in recent years. In the provision of credit to the industrial sector, the small-scale industries did not get the due attention. District-wise, the provision of industrial credit naturally varied greatly.

Long-Term Finance

The institutional structure for providing long-term finance to industry changed considerably over the years. The apex institution, Industrial Development Bank of India (IDBI), was set up only in July 1964 to provide various facilities to the medium and large industries. A similar institution, the Small Industries Development Bank of India (SIDBI), came up after nearly three decades, in April 1990, for the growth of small-scale industries. The earliest institution for providing industrial finance was, however, the Industrial Finance Corporation of India, set up in 1948, followed by the ICICI in 1955; both of them were for large and medium industries. The Industrial Reconstruction Bank of India came up in 1985, as the principal agency for assisting reconstruction and rehabilitation of sick and closed units. Among other major changes was the setting up of the Technology Development and Information Company of India Ltd. in 1988 to provide venture capital to the small and medium scale projects. The investment institution, the Life Insurance Corporation of India was set up in 1956, the Unit Trust of India in 1964 and the General Insurance Corporation of India in 1973. The provision of term loans by the UTI, however, started only in 1986.

The state-level institutions set up were the State Financial Corporations (SFCs) in the 'fifties and the State Industrial Development Corporations (SIDCs) in the sixties and early seventies. The objective of the former was to promote dispersal of industries by assisting the growth of small and medium enterprises. The SIDCs were meant for promoting the development of medium and large industries. In the provision of finance by all these institutions, there was hardly any attention to reducing the inter-state or intra-state disparities in development. The state level institutions in UP also provided a very small amount.

COST OF INDUSTRIALISATION

The cost of even the low level of industrial growth that UP had was quite high. First, an example may be given of the extent of exploitation of the weaker sections by industries. In the lock industry of Aligarh, around mid-eighties, children below the age of 14 years, numbering 7,000-10,000, were working at Rs. 5-10 a day and often had to work more than 20 hours at a stretch. Some of the work done by them—like those in polishing, electroplating, spray painting and in hand-presses—were extremely hazardous. The work of polishing was probably the most dangerous, and here more than 60 per cent of workers were below 14. Even children 8-9 years were working very late at night. The workers inhaled the emery powder and metal dust, and the polishers got covered from head to toe by the powder. (Burra, Neera 1987). And these were going on despite being prohibited under the Factories Act and the Child Labour Act. The recent situation of the workers in lock industry was also no better, as the era of globalisation has brought higher competition.

Pollution and Environmental Destruction

At a broader level, the industrial pollution is causing havoc in many places. The air and water pollutions have increased manifold over the years. I may note here how the people of Singrauli—located on the border of UP and

MP—are facing the ill effects of coal mining for the last 35 years. The pollution of river waters due to industrialisation is also very high, and it has severely affected the aquatic life in many of the rivers in UP. The industries have not complied with the condition mentioned in the no-objection certificate. There was commitment to set up a common effluent treatment plant by 1989 but this has not happened. Untreated municipal waste from two nearby towns is also discharged into the river. In the process of environmental destruction, the construction of dams over rivers, and even construction of roads in hill areas, play a major role. Over the past few decades, ill-conceived, mismanaged, unrestrained and unplanned construction work have resulted in large scale cutting of the mountain surface, and consequent landslides. Tehri dam is one of the highest dams in the world and it harnesses the waters of two important Himalayan rivers—Bhagirathi and Bhilangana. The project was conceived in 1949 but the work on it began only in 1978. The dam is finally to be 260.5 metre high. The reservoir is likely to irrigate 2,70,000 hects of land, and generate 346 MW of hydel power. The dam's submergence area is the Tehri town and 23 villages in the vicinity; 72 other villages are partially submerged. Nearly 5,200 hects of land is lost to the reservoir. About 85,000 persons were fully or partially displaced. Despite adverse reports from officially constituted committees and severe opposition to the project, and Chamoli earthquake of 1999, work on the dam continued in spurts.

Despite the below capacity performance of earlier projects and the massive distress and hazards caused by them, the government is bent on a course of speeding up dam-construction work. With none to check the arbitrary and ruthless exercise of powers in favour of these projects, a many-sided threat to the Ganga and its tributaries has emerged.

NOTE

1. The definition of the organised sector of SSI changed significantly over the years. In 1966-67, the investment limit for it was Rs. 0.75 million in plant and machinery, and for ancillary units Rs. 1.00 million. Gradually, it increased to Rs. 3.50 and 4.50 million, respectively in 1985-86, Rs. 6 and 7.50 million in 1991-92 and Rs. 30 million for both in 1997-98. In 1999-00, however, it was reduced to only Rs. 10 million. (SIDBI 2002).

7

ABSOLUTE POVERTY AND THE MEASURES

The poverty situation in Uttar Pradesh continued to be very depressing, as has been noted in Chapter 2. Even in 2004-05, the proportion of BPL population—based on unadjusted price—stood at as much as 32.9 per cent in rural areas, which was 4.6 points higher than at the national level; the adjusted one will be not less than 80 per cent. Here, first we look at some of the details of poverty, particularly the variation in terms of socio-economic categories and the inter-district disparities; and then into the nature of implementation of the poverty alleviation measures.

Social class-wise, the situation of the scheduled castes—constituting around a quarter of UP's total population in 2004-05—was very depressing. Their consumer expenditure continued to be extremely low. To look at some of the underlying factors: The proportion of SCs in self-employment was as much as 41.1 per cent here in 1999-00 as against 28.4 per cent in all-India. The size of land cultivated was, however, extremely small; for as much as 71.8 per cent it was less than 0.40 ha. The credit available from formal sourced had also declined sharply, from 73 per cent of total debt in 1992 to only 47 per cent in 2002. On literacy, the SCs were in the worst position. In 1999-00, per thousand hhs as many as 471 were without a literate adult male member and 856 without a literate adult female. The STs were in a much better position both on the size of land cultivated and on literacy. (*ibid.*).

On the inter-district disparities, only the situation of consumer expenditure and the proportion of BPL population may be looked into. The proportion of BPL population varied to a much greater extent. The poverty reduction is crucially dependent on pro-poor rural economic growth. But agriculture, the main stay of the rural economy, did not do well in UP, as noted in chapter 5. In recent years also the state's situation was very poor. The share of agriculture in total employment declined from 68.4 per cent in 1993-94 to 60.6 in 2004-05; the latest was 3.6 points higher than at the national level. The growth in labour productivity in the sector was by only 14.7 per cent as against 18.3 in the latter. In the manufacturing sector, the situation was still worse. The labour productivity here had an absolute fall by 23 per cent as against a 13.8 per cent rise in all-India. At Rs. 16,393 in 2004-05, it was the lowest among the states. The sector's share in total employment increased from 8.7 per cent to 12.3 over the period; both were below the national average.

WAGE EMPLOYMENT PROGRAMMES

The importance of wage employment increased greatly over the years. The proportion of labour households in rural UP increased from 16.0 per cent in 1964-65 to 19.0 in 1974-75 and 25.6 in 1987-88. The first employment scheme, Crash Scheme for Rural Employment (CSRE), was launched in 1971 by the Central government, and it aimed to create 2.5 lakh person-days (lpds) in each of the districts of UP. After the CSRE, for three years there was no national programme. In 1977, the Food for Work Programme (FWP) was launched and it continued till September 1980, when the National Rural Employment Programme (NREP) replaced it. The implementation of the NREP in the state was also not satisfactory. On the employment guarantee programme (RLEGP), launched in 1983, also the performance was similar. The fund utilisation was lower than the target but on employment creation it was significantly higher. The utilisation foodgrains was very low; at the average of 71.9 per cent of the quantum released during 1985-89, it was 15 percentage points below the national average. The employment created was 26 per cent higher than the target set, and constituted 18.4 per cent of all-India total. (*ibid.*). This speaks of the low quality of planning and implementation.

Jawahar Rozgar Yojana (JRY)

The performance of the JRY/JGSY in UP has been very poor. The expenditure on the programme always fell short of that available. The performance of the sub-schemes were also very poor, particularly of the MWS. The operation of the JRY in UP suffered from many deficiencies. The selection of works was found to be largely guided by the convenience of making money by the functionaries. In all the panchayats, the laying of bricks in the pathways constituted more than 50 per cent of the total expenditure as the scope for leakage was much larger here. The first item in the guideline, social forestry, on the other hand, received less than 3 per cent of total. The importance of irrigation through open dug wells to SC and ST farmers was recognised by the government, and for this 20 per cent of the JRY fund was earmarked. Corruption in the implementation of the JRY was ingrained in the system.

Employment Assurance Scheme

The performance of the EAS was also not good in UP. The overall position of employment creation in rural UP continued to be very poor. As the existing employment schemes proved very inadequate, a new scheme, Sampoorna Grameen Rozgar Yojana was introduced in November 2001, by merging the JGSY and the EAS. Under it, among the beneficiaries, preference was to be given to the poorest among the poor, the SCs/STs and parents of child labour withdrawn from hazardous occupations.

The NREGA

In the first year, 2006-07, number of person-days created per hh. in UP came to 32.0, in the next year 33.1 and in 2008-09 at 54 as against the A-I average of 43.1, 41.8 and 48, respectively. Percentage of hhs. completing 100 days of employment in the first two years were respectively 6.0 and 10.9; at the national level, it was 10.2 and 10.8 per cent. This failure was primarily because of rampant corruption and inefficiencies in the panchayats. A significant number of the unemployed could not obtain the job card even—the basic document required for demanding the employment—due to procedural complexities and inadequate cooperation from the panchayats. The women's participation was low partly due to non-provision of the mandatory crèche facility. The provision for social audit under the Act also remained unimplemented.

Trend in Wage Rates, etc.

An important reason behind the high rural poverty is low wage rates. The wage rates in UP continued to be very low. In recent years also UP's relative position was very poor. For labourers in general, however, the situation improved noticeably in recent years. In 2004, the average daily wages of casual workers in rural UP stood at Rs. 56.22 as against Rs. 50.70 at the national level. In urban areas, however, it was significantly below the latter's. The situation of regular salaried/wage employees was also similar. If the government was serious about raising the BPL population above the poverty-line income, the wage rates in agriculture should have risen at a much faster rate, and be equal to the minimum a worker in the organised sector gets. The wage rates, however, continued to be much below the poverty-line income. Not only this, even the rates fixed are rarely implemented. The situation of wage rates would have improved greatly if the labourers were properly organised.

SELF-EMPLOYMENT PROGRAMMES

The IRDP

The performance of the IRDP in UP was relatively good. After the restructuring of the programme, immediately the situation worsened sharply. As regards the type of assets distributed, UP's was quite different from that in most other states. A very disturbing feature of the IRDP's operation in UP is that the lower income groups did not receive the due attention. This quantitative picture does not reflect the whole situation. Corruption was rampant in the implementation of the IRDP in UP. In the initial years when the poor were not aware of the existence of the scheme, better-off farmers were taking the asset (buffaloes) in the name of their servants by just asking them to affix their signature/thumb impression on the application form. There were also cases of lower functionaries at the block level misappropriating the loan on the basis of fake applications. When the racket assumed a serious proportion, it became mandatory to attach a photograph of the applicant but this could not end the mischief. Now the corrupt officials began paying a small sum to the poor person for signing the application form. The loan amount would be withdrawn and paid back to the bank after some time, while the subsidy pocketed. (Kripa Shankar 1991: 2339).

The Sub-Schemes

As regards the sub-schemes, the number trained under the TRYSEM was quite good. The performance in the DWCRA, was very poor. The scheme for supply of improved tools appears to have had a relatively good performance.

NOTES

- With regard to the SC-ST categorisation and reservations for them, it may be noted that constitutionally it was intended for only a daecade. Six decades have passed but no improvement in anti-Dalit atrocities has come. Over the decades, this sort of categorisation was extened to other communities also with a view to make political gains out of them. Recently, on December 22, 2011, the government decided to carve out a sub-quota of 4.5 per cent for minorities within the 27 per cent reservation for OBCs, a move which comes ahead of the UP Assembly elections. Muslims, Sikhs, Christians, Budhists and Zoroastrians (Parsis) are notified as minority communities under the National Commission for Minorities Act, 1992. This decision would pave the way for reservation in government jobs and educational institutions for these communities. This is blatantly a distortion of the Constitution—Clause 2 of Article 16. Rajinder Puri (2011e) rightly says: "By not following the Constitution, politicians have fragmented society into innumerable warring castes and communities." Affirmative action including reservation quotas on the basis of economic criteria would have allowed a judicious representation to genuinely backward classes regardless of caste or community.
- On the naming of different schemes, institutions and projects in the country, it may be noted that no effort is spared to put the name of a Prime Minister from the Nehru family. Although the list is almost endless, I may name here some of them to give an idea of the extent of spread. The list includes Indira Gandhi Medical College (Shimla), Jawaharlal Nehru Medical College (Raipur), Rajiv Gandhi College of Nursing (Bangalore), Indira Gandhi Institute of Child Health (Bangalore), Rajiv Gandhi Institute of Pharmacy (Kerala), Rajiv Ratna Awas Yojana (Delhi), dozens of officially named Jawahar Nagar, Indira Colonies or Rajiv Chowks across the country, Indira Awas Yojana, Rajiv Gandhi Grameen Vidyuti Karan Yojana, Jawaharlal Nehru Urban Renewal

Mission, and Rajiv Gandhi National Drinking Water Mission throughout the country. It is not only the naming of projects and institutions, a huge expenditure is also incurred on print advertisements on the birth and death anniversaries of the three former Prime Ministers from the Nehru-Gandhi family. In 2011-12, for example, the total cost of print advertisement for the death anniversary of Indira Gandhi on 31 October came to Rs. 6,44,53,146 while the same for the death anniversary of her son Rajiv Gandhi on 21 May was Rs. 3.08 crore. The birth anniversary of Rajiv Gandhi on 21 August had cost Rs. 4.75 crore while that on his mother was Rs. 2.55 crore. (TST 2011 z37).

PART III: THE ECONOMY OF MADHYA PRADESH

8

RESOURCE MOBILISATION AND DEPLOYMENT

I: THE GOVERNMENT BUDGET

The fiscal situation of Madhya Pradesh government worsened noticeably over the years. The gross fiscal deficit as percentage to GSDP rose to as much as 6.25 in 2002-05 as against the All-States average of 3.94. In the entire nineties, the highest reached was 5.18 in 1998-99 and generally remained below 3. The situation of revenue deficit also worsened sharply. It averaged Rs. 3,368 crore in 2001-04, from only Rs. 68.9 crore in 1991-94. The index of self-reliance declined to 0.97 in 2000-03 from 1.07 in 1990-93, taking All-States at 1.00; among the 14 major states, the latest was lower than in eight. The composite index, based on eight indicators, also declined from 63.81 in 1990-95 to 44.13 in 2000-03.(CMIE 2006a; Dholakia, Archana 2005). If we analyse the trend in budgetary position of the state over a period of nearly four decades we see that between 1965-68 and 1975-78, the fiscal deficit had risen by only 126 per cent but in the following period, ending in 1988-91, it was by 704 per cent, and by 2001-04 another 671 per cent. The revenue account was in surplus to the extent of Rs. 99.6 crore in 1975-78 but by 1988-91 it was a deficit of Rs. 83.1 crore. In the following years, it reached Rs. 3,368 crore in 2001-04. The recent situation, however, appears relatively good. In 2009-10, the per capita gross fiscal deflicit of MP stood at Rs. 881 and for Chhattisgarh at Rs. 719 as against the All-States average of Rs. 1,699. The gross revenue deficit was in surplus to the extent of (-) 5497.8 crore in MP and (-) Rs. 888.2 crore in Chhattisgarh; for All-States together, there was a deficit of as much as Rs. 28,634 crore. (CMIE 2011c). A detailed look is given below to the situation of different componenets.

RESOURCE MOBILISATION

In raising resources MP's performance was very poor. The per capita total receipt averaged only Rs. 2,801 in 2000-03 as against Rs. 3,861 at the level of All-States— i.e., the former 72.5 per cent of the latter. Earlier, in 1975-78, the situation was better, being 82.9 per cent. The per capita receipt in 2000-03 came to only Rs. 751, a mere 56.6 per cent of the latter's. In recent years, the situation improved somewhat. In 2009-10, the total budgetary receipts of MP was Rs. 48,829.7 crore and constituted 4.60 per cent of All-States'. The per capita receipt came to Rs. 6,918 as against Rs. 9,100 for A-S—i.e., the former 76 per cent of the latter. In the total receipts, the revenue receipts constituted 84.8 per cent as against 74.2 per cent in A-S. The per capita receipt was, however, below the latter's—being respectively Rs. 5,865 and Rs. 6,750. The situation of Chhattisgarh was noticeably better. The per capita total receipt came to Rs. 8,715, which was 95.8 per cent of All-States'. The share of revenue receipts in the total was 85.0 per cent. The per capita receipt came to Rs. 7,410—i.e., 9.8 per cent higher than in A-S. (CMIE 2011c).

REVENUE RECEIPTS

In the revenue receipts, the relative share of tax revenue increased noticeably over the years—from 58 per cent in 1965-68 to 74.3 in 2000-03. The per capita receipt, however, remained very low; being only Rs. 1,569 in 2000-03 as against the A-S average of Rs. 1,794. The per capita OTR came to only Rs. 913 in 2000-03 as against Rs. 1,281 for A-S, i.e., the former 71 per cent of the latter. The recent situation was also similar. In 2009-10, the per capita tax revenue for MP came to Rs. 4,017 and of Chhattisgarh (Chg) at Rs. 4,695; the A-S average was Rs. 4,637. On the OTR in it, both the states had poor performance; the per capitas being respectively Rs. 2,447, Rs. 2,907 and Rs. 3,224. The situation of NTR was much worse.

Composition of OTR

The scope for larger collection of tax revenue in MP was not low, as will be evident from a look at the contribution from different sources. The reliance on only one of the sources, taxes on commodities and services, was too heavy; providing as much as 91.3 per cent of total in 1993-96, rising from 84.4 in 1975-78. In recent years also it stood at 87.9 per cent in 2000-03 (including Chg). In taxes on commodities and services, sales tax generally provided half or more, with the state sales tax contributing the lion's share. In 2000-03, the collection from sales tax annually averaged Rs. 3085.4 crore, and in it state sales tax provided 83.5 per cent; in 1975-78, it was 76.5 per cent. In the taxes on property and capital transactions, the contribution of land revenue had a sharp fall—being down to 0.74 per cent in 2000-03, from around nine per cent in 1975-78; for All-States, the latest was 1.25 per cent.

Composition of ONTR

The situation of ONTR was much worse. Most of the items had very low growth, and only one source, the economic services, had provided an overwhelming proportion of collection. In the 'nineties, it provided nearly 80 per cent and in 2000-03 also it contributed 75.3 per cent. In economic services, industries provided 50.7 per cent of total in 1997-00, rising from 20.0 in 1988-91. Among other groups, the contribution from social services was down to only 3.02 per cent in 1993-96, from 5.80 in 1975-78, and then recovered to 4.33 in 2000-03; at the level of A-S, the latest was 7.73 per cent. In recent years, the situation appears to have improved. In 2009-10, the per capita collection from it came to Rs. 120 as against Rs. 78 for A-S; in Chhattisgarh, however, it was only Rs. 18. In social services, education, etc., had provided a fifth of total in 1997-00, and medical etc 17.9 per cent. The contribution from interest receipts was very low, and had declined from 17.8 per cent in 1988-91 to 10.0 in 1997-00 and further to 8.83 in 2000-03; at the level of All-States, the latest was as much as 30.3 per cent. The general services had also provided only 11.0 per cent in 2000-03 as against 22.9 in A-S. The most depressing was the collection from dividend and profit.

CAPITAL RECEIPTS

The composition of capital receipts changed noticeably over the years. While the contribution of internal debt had a rapid growth, the recovery of loans and advances recorded a sharp fall. In the post-bifurcation period, the share of internal debt rose further to 39.3 per cent in 2002-05 (for the two states combined); in MP, it was 40.1 per cent. Recovery of loans and advances became negligible; providing only 0.56 per cent. The contribution from Central loans also had a sharp fall, to only 21.2 per cent; however, it remained higher than in all-states, being at 15.1 per cent. As regard the recent situation, in 2009-10, the per capita Central loans to MP came to Rs. 190 and for Chg at Rs. 91, with A-S aveage at Rs. 87. (CMIE 2006a; 2011c). The debt burden of the state remained relatively low. The relative share of central loans declined from 63.2 per cent in 1981 to 37.7 in 2003, whereas for internal debt it increased from 14.3 to 39.2 per cent. At the level of All-States, the latest were respectively, 35.4 and 48.2 per cent.

TREND IN EXPENDITURE

Given the level of resource mobilisation, the budgetary expenditure could not be high. The per capita total expenditure in 2000-03 came to only Rs. 2761 as against Rs. 3768 in the latter, i.e., the former 73 per cent of the latter. Earlier, the relative position was better; at Rs. 820 in 1988-91, it was 84 per cent of the A-S average. In recent years, the situation has improved. In 2009-10, the per capita total expenditure came to Rs. 7089 in MP and Rs. 8799 for Chhattisgarh as against the A-S average of Rs. 8,952. In the total expenditure, the proportion of revenue had a sharp rise. During 2000-03, it constituted as much as 83.2 per cent as against 65.2 in 1975-78; for A-S, the rise was from 67.3 per cent to 81.9. In recent years, however, it has declined. In 2009-10, revenue expenditure constituted 71.7 per cent in MP and 80.1 in Chg; with the A-S average at 78.1 per cent.

Revenue Expenditure

In the revenue expenditure, the proportion of developmental had a noticeable fall over the years. The per capita expenditure on social services came to only Rs. 839 in 2000-03 as against Rs. 1062 in A-S. In recent years also the situation was similar. In 2009-10, MP had a per capita of only Rs. 1,836 as against Rs. 2,719 in A-S; Chhattisgarh, however, had as much as Rs. 3,275. In social services, the highest share always went to education, etc., although it declined from 52.9 per cent in 1975-78 to 43.3 in 2000-03. The per capita expenditure on it came to only Rs. 363 in 2000-03 compared with Rs. 599 at the level of A-S. In 2009-10 also it was below the latter's; MP had only Rs. 888 and Chg Rs. 1,295 as against Rs. 1,334 in A-S. The expenditure on medical and public health was also low.

In economic services, the growth in expenditure was very low; and the relative share declined to 39.8 per cent in 2000-03 from 42.8 in 1988-91. The per capita expenditure in 2000-03 came to only Rs. 575 as against Rs. 652 for all-states. In 2009-10 also there was no noticeable improvement. Agriculture, etc., include many important areas, but the most important, at least since early eighties, has been forestry and wildlife. Although its relative share declined from 46 per cent in 1997-00 to 41.0 in 2000-03, the per capita expenditure on it came to Rs. 82 in 2000-03 as against only Rs. 35 in A-S.

Capital Expenditure

In the capital disbursements in MP, the proportion of capital outlay was relatively high, being at 59.9 per cent in 1997-00, declining from 62.1 in 1988-91; at the level of All-States, the latest was 50.7 per cent. The per capita outlay, however, came to only Rs. 159 in 1997-00 as against Rs. 253 in A-S—i.e., the former only 62.8 per cent of the latter. The capital outlays were almost entirely for development purposes.

The most neglected was the critical sector of water supply, etc., recording a sharp absolute fall. In recent years also it was extremely low. The per capita in 2009-10 came to only Rs. 15.51 in Chg and Rs. 89 in MP as against Rs. 109 in A-S. On economic services, although the state spent the overwhelming proportion, the per capita expenditure in 1997-00 came to only Rs. 131 as against Rs. 2005 at the level of A-S, i.e., the former a mere 6.5 per cent of the latter. In economic services, the highest proportion always went to irrigation and flood control, followed by energy in recent years. The relative share of the former stood at 41.1 per cent in 1997-00, declining from 65.6 in 1988-91; and of the latter, rose to 36.4 per cent from only 8.1. In 2000-03, however, while the expenditure on irrigation etc. was more than doubled, on energy it was only a 25 per cent rise. Among the other categories of disbursements, the largest was generally on loans and advances. Its share had risen from 15.9 per cent in 1988-91 to 44.4 in 2000-03; in 1975-78, however, it was 39.7 per cent.

PLAN EXPENDITURE

The plan expenditures in Madhya Pradesh continued to be very low. The low plan expenditures were at least partly due to inappropriate policies of the

Centre. The Seventh through Ninth plan, however, provided a relatively low share, and the average for all the plans together came to 45.3 per cent. Transport received a very low share, declining from around six per cent till the end of Sixth Plan to half this level in the following Plans. The allocation for other sectors naturally could not be high.

LOCAL BODIES

Panchayat Raj Institutions

Revenue

On the revenue collection by the PRIs, the relative position of MP was on the whole quite good. Their total revenue had risen noticeably since the early 'nineties. Between 1990-1 and 1997-8, it was by 661 per cent, and the relative share in All-states' total rose to 9.19 per cent from 3.53; on three-yearly average basis, it came to 6.04 per cent in 1995-98. The high growth notwithstanding, the per capita revenue remained very low. At Rs. 194.56 in 1995-98, it was much below the A-S average and among the selected states lower than in all but two. At the village level, however, the situation was much better. The per capita revenue in 1995-98 came to Rs. 100.21, higher than in most of the states. The growth in total revenue was 208 per cent over the eight-year period as against 181 per cent for A-S. MP's share in the latter's total increased from 11.4 per cent to 12.5.

In the total revenue, however, the contribution of own collection was very low. In the own revenue, the contribution by tax revenue was very low. At the village level—contributing the overwhelming proportion of total revenue—the situation was worse. In recent years, the PRIs here made a noticeable progress. Their share in the total of own tax revenue (PRI+ state) during 2001-03 averaged 2.52 per cent compared with only 0.64 per cent in A-S.

Expenditure

The expenditure level of the PRIs was quite low. At the village level, although the growth in expenditure was low—being by only 222 per cent over the eight-year period—the relative position among the states was significantly better. The progress in reforming the PRIs was very slow. Consequent on the 73rd amendment of the Constitution, number of departments/subjects transferred in 2003 was only 10 with regard to fund, 23 on functions and nine on functionaries; the numbers yet to be transferred were 19, 6 and 20, respectively. The state finance commission could be set up only in mid-nineties, and the report submitted did not suggest any effective mechanism for PRIs generating their own revenue. The spending responsibilities were also not clearly delineated. (Pal, Mahi 2004). As regards the latest situation, a devolution index prepared by the IIPA shows MP with 59.78 in 2009 and for Chattisgarh 34.24, with the national average at 45.04; their ranks among the states are respectively 6th and 18th. (GOI 2011a).

URBAN LOCAL BODIES

The proportion of urban population in Madhya Pradesh is very low. At 23.2 per cent in 1991, it was below all-India's. There were 370 urban locations, with the population varying between the lowest of 2,412 in Hoshangabad and the highest at 11,09,056 in Indore. The ULBs had a very poor performance in raising their own revenue. In the own revenue, the proportion of tax revenue was very low until recent years. The situation of ULBs' expenditures was much worse. Behind the low level of expenditures by the PRIs and ULBs, an important reason was the extremely low transfers from the state government.

II: THE BANKING SYSTEM

Cooperative Credit Institutions

Although this is the oldest formal institution for providing credit, it continued to be in a very poor shape in Madhya Pradesh.The situation of working capital was, however, very poor.

Primary Agricultural Credit Societies

Among the credit societies, PACS, the most important category, were in a very poor situation. The availability of PACS was very low here. The working capital of the societies was very low. Per society, it averaged only Rs. 17.13 lakh in 1998, which was 54 per cent of the A-I average. Earlier, in 1970, it was 59.6 per cent higher than in the latter. When the working capital was so low, naturally the lending activities could not be high. In recent years, however, the situation improved considerably. At the end of March 2005, the working capital per society in MP came to Rs. 76 lakh, which was higher than at the national level. The reliance on borrowings, however, continued to be high, and the deposit per society remained low. The lending activities increased considerably, but the amount outstanding per society still could not cross the A-I average. The loan recovery continued to be a matter of concern, and percentage of societies in loss stood at 59.2. The situation of Chhattisgarh is much worse.

Primary Non-agricultural Credit Societies

On the non-agricultural societies also the state's performance was not good. Even the number of societies was very low. The situation of working capital of the societies was distressingly poor. Given the low level of working capital, lending activities could not be high. Between 1970 and 1998, the loans outstanding had risen by only around 11 times as against 26 times at the national level. MP's share in all-India total LO declined from 1.39 per cent in

1982 to a mere 0.41 in 1998. The LO per society came to only Rs. 3.37 lakh in the latest year, around a sixth of the all-India average. The loan recovery position was relatively poor. Overdue as percentage to LO constituted 11.1 per cent in 1998 as against 8.6 at the national level. Earlier, in 1982, the situation was still worse, being respectively 14.4 and 4.8 per cent.

COMMERCIAL BANKS

The performance of Commercial Banks in Madhya Pradesh has not been good. The population per bank office had declined from 1.74 lakh in 1960 to 58 thousand in 1972 and further to 17.3 thousand in 1983, but in 2006 it increased to 18.9 thousand; all these were higher than the national average. A good aspect is, however, that the rural share of offices was relatively high here, and increased from 22.5 per cent in 1960 to 67.9 in 1983 and then declined to 51.8 in 2006; even the latest was much higher than the national average.

The deposit mobilisation continued to be very low. On credit deployment, the situation was worse. A good aspect of the credit deployment here is that the proportion going to small borrowers was much larger than at the national level. This was mainly because the rural share of total credit was relatively high. Although it had declined from 22.9 per cent in 1993 to 18.1 in 2006, still the latest was more than double that at the national level. The C-D ratio for rural areas had declined from 66.0 per cent in 1977 to 43.0 in 2003, and then recovered to 61.2 in 2006; each of these was nonetheless higher than in all-India. The investment activities of the banks in MP appear to be relatively large. The efficiency level of the banks was very low here.

Regional Rural Banks

The RRBs also had a very poor performance here. The loans outstanding per branch came to only Rs. 81.3 lakh in March 2002, which was a mere 62.7 per cent of all-India average. In the A-I total of loans outstanding from RRBs, the state's share stood at 7.1 per cent in 2002, with the share in number of accounts at only 5.4 per cent. The C-D ratio had a sharp fall over the years; down to as low as 33 per cent in 2002 from 93 in 1989 and 126 in 1981. In recent years, however, the situation improved considerably. In 2006 the state accounted for 8.62 per cent of A-I total loans outstanding, and the amount per branch was nearly trebled in relation to 2004; however, it remained below the national average. The C-D ratio increased to 45.9 per cent, but was still 6 points below the latter's.

On deposit mobilisation, the situation was much better. The operation of the RRBs here was plagued by many deficiencies. The loan recovery situation was extremely poor. The recovery as percentage to demand stood at only 63 in 2001 as against the all-India average of 71; among the selected states, it was lower than in all but Bihar.

Inter-RRB Variations

Bank-wise, there was great variation in performance. The variation in credit deployment was much higher. In 2002, the credit outstanding per branch was at the highest Rs. 246 lakh in Vidisha-Bhopal and the lowest at Rs. 49.2 lakh in Mahakaushal—i.e., the former 5 times the latter—with Rs. 100.7 lakh at the state level. In 1989, the highest was 6.5 times the lowest—being respectively Rs. 28.76 lakh in Bundelkhand RRB and Rs. 4.37 lakh in Gwalior-Datia, with all banks' average at Rs. 15.27 lakh. The growth in per-branch credit over the period was at the highest 33 times in Vidisha-Bhopal and the lowest at 2.15 times in Bundelkhand; the average for all banks was 6.6 times in MP and only 3.8 times in Chhattisgarh.

The efficiency level of banks differed widely. The productivity of the employees was very low in many of the banks. In 2002, the volume of business per employee was below Rs. 70 lakh in five of the banks and only six had above Rs. one crore; the lowest was Rs. 54 lakh in Mahakaushal and the highest at Rs. 182 lakh in Vidisha-Bhopal, i.e., the latter 3.37 times the former. Earlier, in 1989, the highest was 4.60 times the lowest—being respectively Rs. 12.66 lakh in Rewa-Sidhi GB and Rs. 2.75 lakh in Gwalior-Datia—with Rs. 8.75 lakh at the state level. Overall, the role of institutional agencies in providing credit was relatively good in Madhya Pradesh. In the total outstanding cash debt, their share had risen from 32 per cent in 1971 to 73 in 1991 and then declined to 59 in 2002; the latest was 2 points higher than at the national level as against nine points higher in 1991. The incidence of indebtedness of rural households was 15.2 per cent institutional as on 30.6.02 as against 13.4 at the national level. (NSSO 2005c).

District-wise Disparity

On the inter-district variation in availability of banking services, only the situation of the scheduled commercial banks is looked into. Even the number of banks was very low in many districts. Nearly three decades after Independence, in 1974, one bank office had to serve a population of as much as 1.33 lakh in Surguja as against the lowest of 0.14 lakh in Indore, with state average at 0.51 lakh; ten districts had more than 80 thousand. After another two-and-half decades, in 1999, at the highest it was 40 thousand in Sheopur and the lowest at 9.5 thousand in Bhopal; 15 districts had more than 20 thousand.

This disparity in availability of banks was reflected in the deposit mobilisation and credit deployment. On credit deployment, even in 1999, the highest per capita credit was as much as 28.5 times the lowest, being respectively Rs. 8,530 in Bhopal and Rs. 299 in Dindori; 25 districts had below Rs. 1,000. The growth in credit outstanding over 1977 was less than 20 times in six of the districts, with the lowest at 11 times in Shahdol. The C-D ratio continued to be very low in many districts. In 1977, it was below 50 per cent for 22 districts; only nine districts had above 80.

NOTE

- This distressing situation notwithstanding, the government is extravagant in spending money. To cite a recent instance: For the MP foundation day function in Bhopal on November 1, the government spent Rs. 7 crore for invitation cards only. More than 5.5 lakh cards were distributed although the Lal Parade Grounds' capacity is merely one lakh. The show was highlighted by renowned musician A R Rahman's performance. The objective behind distributing so many cards was stated as invoking pride towards the state in maximum number of people. (TST 2012 z98).

9

HUMAN RESOURCE DEVELOPMENT: EDUCATION AND HEALTH

The educational scenario in Madhya Pradesh continues to be very poor, despite some noticeable improvement in recent years. Level of education-wise, the situation was extremely poor. The growth in number of schools was, however, quite high here. The state's share in all-India total number of secondary schools stood at only 7.22 per cent in 2005, rising from 5.75 in 2000-01.

As regards the pattern of management of the schools, percentage of government schools was high here. Purely private schools were relatively high in High and HS levels; this year, it was at 36 per cent of total in both. (GOI 2007a). The enrolment ratio in schools continued to be extremely low until recently. On the attendance also the pattern was similar. The net attendance ratio in 1995-96 stood at only 63 per cent for primary stage and 35 at the middle level; in rural areas, the latter's was only 28 per cent. The drop-out rate was also very high. The high drop-out rate was mainly due to lack of facilities in the schools. The pupil-teacher ratio at the primary level increased to 43 in 2000-01, from 37 in 1980-81, and in 2004-05 also it was at the same level. At the middle and high school levels, however, the situation was significantly better. Average number of teachers per elementary school in 2005 was only 3.4 in MP and 2.7 in Chhattisgarh. Percentage of single teacher school in the two states were respectively 20.2 and 21.9. Another negative aspect was that the proportion of female teachers was very low at every stage. The physical facilities were also in general very poor. Even the number of rooms for instructional purpose was very low. The schools were also mostly without drinking water facility.

Intra-state, district-wise, the availability of facilities varied extremely. In 1988-89, number of primary and sub-schools per lakh population was 291 in Mandla as against only 10.0 in Shajapur, with the state average at 102.3; 11 districts had below 90 (excluding Chhattisgarh region). The availability of middle schools also varied greatly. This year, per lakh population, there were only 14.9 schools in Datia and 16.4 in Sagar, with the state average at 21.16. The direct measures for attracting students to schools were also very inadequate. In recent years, however, the situation improved noticeably. In 2002, out of 313 blocks in the state, cooked meals were provided in 89 tribal blocks and in the remaining ones food-grains were given to the students. In view of the critical importance of this item, a more detailed look is given to it below.

The Mid-day Meal Scheme

MP was one of the first states to introduce Mid-day Meal scheme. But after a pilot beginning in a few blocks, the programme was discontinued in 1997 in non-tribal blocks. Even in tribal areas, it remained only on paper till 2002; in most schools raw grains were provided. The scheme was reintroduced only after the Supreme Court ordered the central government in April 2004, to make provision for construction of kitchen sheds and allocate funds for meeting the cost of providing cooked mid-day meals. The directive insisted on better infrastructure, improved facilities, closer monitoring and regular inspection. In drought-affected areas, mid-day meals were to be supplied even during summer vacation. The deficiencies not withstanding, enrolment in class I had increased by 36 per cent after its introduction and for girls by 38 per cent. For SC/ST it was still better, being by 43 and 41 per cent respectively. The Sarva Shiksha Abhiyan, launched in 2001-02, had a very poor performance here. An Educational Development Index on it—based on four broad parameters of access, infrastructure, teacher related indicators and outcomes—gave the state the 29th rank and Chhattisgarh 22nd in 2005-06 among all the States and UTs. (GOI 2007b).

Adult Literacy

As regards adult literacy, it hardly received any attention in Madhya Pradesh. Even under the NLM, launched in 1988, the performance continued to be very poor. In recent years, as noted in Chapter 4, the scope of activities under the adult education programme was expanded greatly, and its organisational structure strengthened. The scheme of Jan Shiksha Sansthans—looking after the vocational development of the weaker groups—has been extended to rural areas. The continuing education programme also now includes a variety of activities, like providing facilities of library, learning centres, sports and curriculum centres and other individual interest promotion programme. The State Literacy Mission Authority has been suitably strengthened for this. The role of the NGOs has been greatly expanded in every sphere. The success of the new initiatives are, however, unlikely to be appreciable, given the socio-economic situation in rural areas.

Higher Education

The facilities for higher education in the state were also not good. After two decades, in 2000-01, MP's relative position worsened. In the A-I total enrolment in polytechnique, the state's share was down to 4.1 per cent. At the degree level, the share of engineering declined to 7.5 per cent and of MBBs to 3.8. Total number of degree colleges, however, increased significantly. The growth was mainly in general education; its relative share rising to as much as 81.1 per cent compared with 67.4 in all-India.

In recent years also general education received an undue importance. Its relative share in total number of institutions no doubt declined to 73.3 per cent in 2004-05 and further to 66.2 in 2006-07 (including Chhattisgarh), but even the latest was higher than at the national level, being 58.8 per cent. The proportion in professional education was only 20.7 per cent as against 27.7 in the latter. The enrolment in engineering declined further to 4.31 per cent of total in 2004-05 as against 5.91 at the national level; in medicine, it was respectively 1.02 and 2.18 per cent. District-wise, the facility for higher education varied greatly.

Pattern of Expenditure

An important reason behind this poor state of affairs in education is the extremely low level of government expenditure. The total budgetary expenditure on education in MP had an annual growth of only 10.6 per cent between 1979-82 and 1994-97, which was below that in seven of the major states. As regards the patter of per pupil expenditure, in elementary education, it was always below the A-S average. In recent years, some significant changes have come in the pattern of expenditure on education.

Health and Family Welfare

The health situation of the people of MP continued to be very poor, as has been noted in chapter 2. To look into some more parameters: The incidence of certain diseases were very high. The health condition of children in Madhya Pradesh continued to be very poor. Malnutrition was widespread. The mortality rate for every category of infant and children was very high here. Severe malnutrition, leading to various deadly diseases like pneumonia, diarrhea, measles and others, killed 21,409 children aged below 6 years, between January and December 2012.[1] The health situation of women was also not good. Percentage of women suffering from any anaemia stood at 56.0 in 2005-06, higher than in all but three of the states. The preventive measures taken were very inadequate in most areas. The proportion of children fully immunised in 1999 stood at only 22.4 per cent, around half that for all-India. After six years, in 2005-06, the coverage increased to 40.3 per cent, but remained below the latter's. On timely complementary feeding of infants also the situation was poor. In 1998-99, the coverage was only 27.3 per cent as against 33.5 in all-India. The maternal health care was in a worse position. Percentage of pregnant women registered for pre-natal care had risen from 41.7 in 1995-6 to 57.4 in 2004; the latest at the national level was 69.8 per cent. The situation of post-natal care was also similar. As regards the provision of drinking water, the situation continued to be extremely poor. The situation of the sanitation facility was also extremely poor; in 1998, it was absent in 92.3 per cent of the hhs. (IIPS 2001b; NSSO 2006; GOI 2005a).

Infrastructure

The infrastructure for providing medical care continued to be very poor in MP. The Plan targets on setting up health centres failed miserably. On the para-medical personnel also the situation was not good. In this situation, naturally the people's reliance on government health facilities continued to be very low. Percentage of treated ailments receiving non-hospitalised treatment from government sources in rural areas stood at only 23 in 2004, the same as that in 1995-96. These were nonetheless higher than at the national level.

Family Welfare

Small family is essential for family welfare. But MP's performance in birth control was very poor. Behind this poor situation many factors had operated. The mean age at effective marriage continued to be relatively low. Some of the underlying factors were very unfavourable here. Illiteracy among married women was very high. In 1998-99, it stood at 58.5 per cent as against the national average of 49.1. The exposure to media was also very low. The proportion of married women having regular exposure to any media this year was only 54.8 per cent, 4.9 points below the national average. Earlier, in 1992-93, at 41.0 per cent, it was 11.7 points lower. (*ibid.*). The quality of services available from the family welfare centres were also very poor. In 2005-06, the proportion with unmet need was 11.8 per cent, higher than in five of the states. The FP centres here were also less successful with the illiterate women. Percentage of illiterates using any contraceptive in 1992-93 was only 33.6, below that in most of the states. Poor service is evident also from the fact that percentage of safe delivery in 1998-99 stood at only 30.1 here as against 42.3 in all-India.

Pattern of Expenditure

Behind this poor situation, an important reason is the low level of expenditure. As regards recent years, in 2000-03, the annual average of expenditure on health and FW in MP came to Rs. 1127.7 crore, giving a per capita of Rs. 186.75 as against Rs. 210.27 for all-States. In the total expenditure, the share of medical and public health was 49.1 per cent, of family welfare 8.81 and the balance for water supply and sanitation. The per capita expenditures on them were respectively Rs. 91.74, Rs. 16.44 and Rs. 61.99 as against Rs. 132.37, 23.42 and 54.47 in all-States. For Chhattisgarh, the situation was much worse. The per capita total in this period came to only Rs. 147.10. In the total expenditure, the share of medical and public health was 53.4 per cent, of water supply etc. 40.1 and the balance on family welfare. The per capita expenditures were respectively Rs. 78.51, 58.99 and 9.62. A look at the plan-wise situation also does not present any better picture. In the small First five-year plan, medical and public health received Rs. 162 lakh and constituted 12.0 per cent of the grand total. In the recent plans, the expenditure on health, etc., increased noticeably. The Seventh plan provided a total of Rs. 457.0 crore, which was 21 times the Third plan's; the relative share in grand total, however, came to only 6.9 per cent.

NOTES

1. For this distressing situation, various reasons like lacunae in state government health schemes, improper utilisation of funds, poor implementation of schemes at the ground level and lack of awareness in people are cited by experts on the subject. "It is imperative to improve the situation from the aanganwadi level and in households, as they are the two most crucial points where children can be provided the basic health nutrients, opined Mrs. Usha Chaturvedi. In 16 districts of the state malnourishment in kids is reported to be stark. Another expert, Sachin Jain says presently 500 calories of food nutrients is being provided to a malnourished child, whereas they need 1400-1600 calories per day. It is also stated that Rs. 4 per child per day should be spent on providing nutrition whereas merely Rs. 2;88 is being spent at present. (TST 2013 m).

10

AGRICULTURAL GROWTH AND TRANSFORMATION

Madhya Pradesh is highly dependent on agriculture, as noted in Chapter 2. In 1960-61, 79.3 per cent of the workforce were in the agricultural sector , and 57.9 per cent of the NSDP came from it. After three decades, in 1991 also 75.3 per cent were found to be in agriculture as against 65 per cent at the national level. Post-bifurcation, in 2005, MP had 73.1 per cent of rural households in agriculture, with the share of labour hhs at 27.7 per cent. In Chhattisgarh, it was as much as 82.0 and 37.6 per cent, respectively. In this situation, if the development process is to be meaningful for the masses, it is imperative that agriculture gets the highest priority. However, in 2003-06, the contribution of agriculture etc to MP's GSDP came to only 28.1 per cent, and for Chhattisgarh at 21.4; at the national level, it was 19.6 per cent. These low shares naturally implied low level of income. But this is mainly a product of the exploitative nature of the society. Below, a detailed look is given into the pattern of growth in agriculture etc over the years.

I: CROP FARMING

Growth in Production

Overall, the state's performance in crop farming was very poor. The annual growth in production was generally below the national average.

Food-grains

Among the agricultural products, food-grains, accounting for the lion's share of cropped area, had a very poor performance. The growth in production over the entire period of three-and-half decades, between 1968-71 and 2000-03, was by only 48.9 times as against 93.1 times at the national level. The relative share in A-I production declined to 7.7 per cent from 10.0; in the cropped area, the state's share in 2000-03 was 13.1 per cent. The yield rate declined from 73.0 per cent of the A-I average to 58.8 per cent over the period. The per capita production of food-grains became lower than in the latter, from significantly higher earlier. In 2003-06, however, the situation improved noticeably. The production averaged 20177 thousand tonnes—with the share of Chhattisgarh at 28.4 per cent—and constituted 9.76 per cent of A-I total. The per capita production became 231 kg as against 190 kg in all-India. The yield rate, at 1151 kg, was now 67.8 per cent of the A-I average.

Among food-grains, rice accounted for the largest acreage; rising to 34.0 per cent of total in 2000-03 from 26.0 in 1968-71. In production, however, its share stood at only 32.1 per cent in 2000-03. In wheat, the next important crop, the situation was better. The growth in production over the entire period was by 121.0 per cent, i.e., more than two-and-half times that in rice. In the all-India production, however, the state's share declined to 7.26 per cent in 2000-03 from 11.11 in 1997-00. The yield rate remained much below the national average. The situation of other cereals was also not good. The next important crop jowar had an acreage of 669 thousand ha in 2002-05, declining from as much as 2046 thousand in 1972-75. The yield rate remained almost static over the years, but it was generally much higher than the national average; during 2002-05, it was respectively, 1106 and 756 kg. The production dropped sharply from 1511 thousand tonnes to 749 thousand over the period, and the relative share in A-I total from 17.1 per cent to 10.7. In bajra also the area under the crop had declined. In 2002-05, at 162 thousand ha, it was 61 per cent of that in 1968-71. The yield rate increased noticeably, and was always much higher than at the national level. In 2002-05, it was respectively 1247 kg and 914 kg. The state's share in A-I production, however, continued to be insignificant. Among pulses, gram was the most important crop and its performance was very good.

Non-Food Grains

Until recently, the area under NFG was quite low in MP. It averaged 7510 thousand ha in 1995-98 and constituted 29.8 per cent of total GCA; at the national level, it was 34.5 per cent. After one decade, in 2005-06, however, it increased to 8531 thousand ha (including Chhattishgarh), and constituted 40.4 per cent as against 36.9 in the latter In the all-India total area under NFG, the state's share came to 12.0 per cent.

Among the crops, the largest area in recent years was under soyabean. During 2003-06, it averaged 4349 thousand ha, constituting more than half the total under NFG. The growth in production between 1968-73 and 2000-03 was 21.5-fold, and the state's share in A-I total rose to 61.8 per cent; in 2003-06, however, with 4330 thousand tonnes, it declined to 56.6 per cent. In cotton, the next important crop, acreage declined noticeably. The growth in rapeseed and mustard was on the whole significant. The performance in linseed was very poor. Both the area and production had sharp fall.The areas under sesamum also declined; in 2000-03, it was less than half that in 1968-71. The growth in yield rate was substantial but remained below the national average. In most other NFGs, MP's performance was poor. Sugarcane, the most important among them, had very low yield rate. Over the entire period of nearly four decades, 1968-71 to 2003-06, it had risen by only 48.6 per cent; and the latest at 38369 kg/ha, was only 60 per cent of the national average. In fruits, banana had good performance.

Causal Factors

Land Resource and Utilisation

In terms of geographical area, the undivided MP was a very large state, accounting for 14.5 per cent of the country's total and highest among the states. The proportion available for cultivation was also as much as 90.5 per cent as against the national average of 86.4. After the bifurcation, in 2005-06, it was 89.0 per cent in MP and 92.8 in Chhattishgarh. The net cropped area, however, constituted only 48.7 per cent of the total in MP this year and 34.5 in Chhattishgarh; even the former was lower than in most of the states. In the national total of NCA, MP's share was 14.1 per cent in 1999-00; in 2005-06, it came to 10.6 per cent in MP and 3.36 in Chhattishgarh. In terms of population, the situation was very good. In 2000-01, per thousand population, it came to 239 ha, which was second highest among the states. In 2005-06, it was 230 ha in MP and 214 ha in Chhattishgarh as against the national average of 130 ha (based on the population of 2004-05). The cropping intensity was, however, very low here. The scope for bringing more land under cultivation was substantial. District-wise, the resource endowment and level of land utilisation varied greatly.

Land Tenure System

The land-holding system in MP did not have any radical change over the years. The measures taken faced the same type of problems as in most other states. The land ownership continued to be highly skewed. The distribution of surplus land to the landless was very small. The amount distributed by June 2005 constituted only 2.72 per cent of A-I total, declining from 3.58 per cent in September 1999 and as much as 14.8 per cent in 1982. The relative share in number of beneficiaries was much worse; declining from 5.63 per cent of A-I total in 1982 to only 0.88 per cent in 2005. The quantum distributed per beneficiary was, however, much higher here. Social class-wise, among the beneficiaries, the SCs constituted only 34.2 per cent as at June-end 2005 as against 46.7 per cent at the national level. For STs, however, it was respectively 39.0 and 15.7 per cent. District-wise, the distribution of surplus land varied extremely. The slow progress was mainly because of the legal battles that the government had to fight in taking possession of the surplus land. The quantitative distribution of surplus land, however, does not tell the whole story. In many cases, the land distributed could not be taken possession by the beneficiary. Wherever the ceiling land belonged to influential local people, the poor beneficiary could not dare to approach him for taking the possession. The progress in restoration of land to tribals was also very poor. On the prevalence of tenancy, MP's position was relatively good. The proportion of tenant holdings in 1981-82 stood at only 8.0 per cent, which was around half the national average. As regards the size of operational holdings, which has an impact on the productive efficiency, MP's situation was relatively good. On the fragmentation of holdings, although the required legal provisions were there since 1959, the state's situation was not good.

Irrigation Facility

The critical importance of irrigation facility in MP is evident from the fact that the state accounts for 19 per cent of the total dry-land area in the country; also, 89 per cent of its districts, covering 81 per cent of the area, are dry land. The irrigation facility, however, continued to be very poor. The source of irrigation water—which influences productivity considerably—changed noticeably over the years. The share of canals in total NIA declined from 43.3 per cent in 1973-74 to 17.7 in 1999-00; at the national level, the latest was as much as 31.4. For tanks, there was a sharp fall, from 13 per cent in 1960-61 to 2.3 in the nineties. The use of ground water increased greatly. Crop-wise, for food-grains as a whole, even in 1995-96, the proportion of area irrigated stood at only 29.3 per cent, rising from 8.5 in 1973-74; at the national level, the latest was 40.5 per cent. In wheat, the coverage was 68.1 per cent in 1995-96 as against 86.8 in the latter. In recent years, the situation improved noticeably, but remained below the national average; the coverage in 2005-06, being respectively 80.0 and 89.8 per cent. Agro-ecological region-wise[1], which focuses the need for irrigation more clearly, the distribution continued to be very uneven. The regions with lowest rainfall, Gird, Malwa and Nimar, receiving only 800-1000 mm/year, had the GIA/GCA of respectively 39, 28 and 19 per cent in 2002. The irrigation potential of the state was, however, not low. The ultimate potential in major and medium irrigation constituted 10.3 per cent of all-India total, and in minor irrigation 14.7 per cent. The potential created, however, remained very low even in recent years. In MMI, the relative share in all-India total rose to 7.0 per cent in 1997 from 4.8 in 1969.

Provision of Inputs

On the use of different productivity promoting inputs, the state's situation was very poor. The consumption of fertilisers no doubt increased greatly over the years, but then also the per hectare consumption remained way behind the national average. District-wise, even in recent years the consumption varied greatly. The low consumption was not only due to inadequate irrigation facility. The availability of fertiliser itself was poor in many areas. The use of non-chemical plant nutrients was also low. On the use of high yielding seeds, the state's position was very poor. The low spread of HYV seeds is due to a number of reasons. At the first instance, there is the poverty of the farmers—ninety per cent being small and marginal—which discourage them from taking risks. Use of HYVs increases the plants vulnerability to pests and diseases, needs chemical fertilisers, insecticides and assured irrigation water, and has to buy seeds every year. Non-availability of appropriate seeds was also not an significant factor.

On the plant protection measures, data are available only on the use of pesticides. Its application appears to have declined considerably in recent years, probably due to the harmful effects reported from time to time. As regards the use of implements and machinery in agriculture, from the angle of consumption of electricity in agriculture, the situation appears quite good. In 2002-03, per farmer hh, it came to Rs. 88.79 in MP and Rs. 83.30 in Chhattisgarh as against the national average of Rs. 63.81. To look at the use of some of the specific implements and machinery: Number of pump sets per 100 hhs, came to only 11.85 in 1992 as against 12.78 in all-India. The indigenous water lifting equipments were used to a much larger extent here; numbering 62.2 as against 38.4 in the latter. Among others, the use of carts, seed drill and sprayer were relatively high. Carts numbered 13.23 as against only 5.84 in all-India. Minor implements were also used to a relatively large extent here. In the way of optimum use of different inputs, along with other factors, illiteracy of the farmers was a big obstacle. In 2003, in the farmer hhs, only 59 per cent of males and 22 per cent of females were literate as against 65 and 31, respectively in all-India. Among the literate males again, only 6 per cent were with secondary and above.

Bank Credit

Easy availability of credit is an essential requirement for the growth of agricultural production. But the role of banking system here was far from satisfactory. In the all-India total flow of credit from all agencies, the state (including Chhattisgarh) accounted for only 6.16 per cent in 2002-03, which was lower than in all but three of the states. The credit per hectare came to only Rs. 375, around a quarter of the national average. In the provision of credit, the most important institution here is co-operative credit; always accounting for more than half of total, and increased from 50.8 per cent in 1986 to 60 in 2002-03. In recent years also the situation was poor. The credit per hectare in 2002-03 came to Rs. 1135, less than half the national average. The beneficiaries from PACS' credit were primarily the large and medium holdings. In the distribution of credit, here also the marginal holdings were benefited to a very small extent. The situation of the RRBs was also not good. Their share in the total credit to agriculture stood at only 5 per cent in 1996-97 and increased to 8.8 in 2002-03. MP's proportion, however, became lower than the national average from higher earlier.

Marketing Facilities

The storage facility continued to be very poor. In 1993, as percentage to total food-grains production, it stood at only 19.5, which was lower than in most of the major states. In recent years also the situation was not good. Number of markets available in the state was very low. Per 100 sq. km. of area, there were only 1.4 markets in 1993 compared with 2.4 at the national level. The regulated markets were rare. In March 1982, it was only 0.07, less than half that in the latter. And then, even the regulated markets were rarely regulated properly. Unauthorised deductions and price riggings were common phenomenon. The problem of marketing was further accentuated by the lack of proper road communication from the villages. As regards the co-operative marketing facility, its situation was very poor. Number of societies was large but their coverage and activities were very low.

II: ALLIED ACTIVITIES

Animal Husbandry

The animal husbandry sector in MP was in a very poor state. The growth in number of livestock was very low here. Over a period of nearly four decades, between 1956 and 1992, the total population had risen by only 35.7 per cent, from 344.5 lakh to 467.5 lakh, as against 53.6 per cent at the national level. The state's share in the latter's total declined from 11.24 per cent to 9.93. In poultry, the performance was still worse. The relative share in A-I total number declined from 5.69 per cent to 3.84 over the same period. In recent years, the situation worsened further. In 2003, including Chhattisgarh, the total number of livestock came to only 213 lakh, 45.6 per cent of that in 1992; the relative share in A-I total declined to 4.39 per cent. In poultry, the situation improved somewhat; the share in A-I total rising to 4.07 per cent. Below, the pattern of growth in important categories are looked into.

On the cattle and buffalo, the most important category in livestock, MP's situation was on the whole good. In cattle, the growth in number, until recently, was not bad. In the cattle, the proportion of cross-bred was very low. The proportion of milch cattle in females was not bad, being higher than in most of the states in 1992; but that in milk was very low. The situation of cross-bred in them was extremely poor; both the proportions were around a tenth of the national average. In 2003 also it was not much better. Number of adult female cross-breds in milk per thousand hhs in rural areas stood at only 8 as against 33 at the national level. For other categories of cattle, however, the number was much higher than in the latter. Number of adult males was very high in MP; being at as much as 670 per thousand hhs in rural MP in 2003 and 858 in Chhattisgarh as against the national average of 367. On buffaloes, the state's situation was much worse. In recent years also the situation was not much better. In 2003, number of buffaloes per thousand hhs came to 580 in rural MP and 370 in Chhattisgarh as against 514 at the national level. Number of females in them were respectively 343, 76 and 294. All these changes were not much conducive to increased milk production. Consequently, the per capita production in 1994-95 stood at only 72.2 kg, nominally higher than in all-India.

In minor livestock, goat is the most important animal in Madhya Pradesh, providing a substantial amount of meat and also some milk. The growth in number of goats was relatively low until recently. On sheep, the situation was much worse. An important reason behind this poor performance is the unfavourable composition of sheep. MP's situation on pig production was also not good.

Poultry Rearing

In poultry also, if Chhattisgarh is excluded, MP was in a very poor situation. In 2003, per 100 hhs, MP had only 40.7 poultry compared with 280.7 in Chhattisgarh and 123.2 at the national level. In the all-India total number of poultry this year, MP's share was only 2.39 per cent and of Chhattisgarh's 1.67—i.e., a combined total of 4.06 per cent. It had declined from 6.11 per cent in 1956 to 4.85 in 1972. The growth in egg production was relatively good. This poor situation was due to a number of reasons. The composition of poultry here was very unfavourable. While the proportion of fowl was high, the share of deshi variety in them was also high. In 1992, fowls constituted as much as 98.6 per cent of total as against 92.5 at the national level. But the proportion of deshi in it was as much as 76.7 per cent compared with 65.2 in the latter. Moreover, the share of ducks was only 0.40 per cent as against 3.45 in all-India. As the animal husbandry is largely related to the level of crop farming, a look may be given to the rearing pattern in terms of size of operational holdings, in order to find out whether there was scope for any increase in the number reared. On cattle, every size-class in MP had a larger number than at the national level. But the number of cross-breds in them was very low; under every size, it was much less than in the latter. There should have been measures by the government to induce the farmers to substitute the non-descript cattle by cross-breds.

Causal Factors

Behind the slow growth of the animal husbandry sector, both natural and man-made factors were responsible. The fact that 76 per cent of the state's geographical area is in semi-arid and dry sub-humid agro-ecological regions was a great natural obstacle. Inadequacy of fodder was a serious problem in many parts of the state. But, probably a greater obstacle was the poverty of the people and the government's lack of initiative in providing the necessary facilities. A brief look is given below on how the veterinary facilities changed over the years. Number of vet hospitals in the state increased from 279 in 1960-61 to 509 in 1965-66, but in the following years it could reach only 627 in 1979-80; and then dropped to 563 in March 2000. The growth in number of dispensaries was also not much. The extent of service provided was very low.

Forest Management

The forest areas are distributed very unevenly in the state. In the management of forests, the dominating aim until recently was optimising of revenue, although the National Forest Policy, 1952 had focused on the multiple benefits of forests. The management was expected to take care of the development of forest. For this purpose, the forests in MP were divided into three categories: (i) Protection forests (for soil and water conservation), 5.40 per cent of total; (ii) Production forests, 85.2 per cent; and (iii) the balance for national parks and sanctuaries. In the production forests, tree forests (industrial and commercial wood) constituted 30.2 per cent and the balance minor forests. Between 1960-61 and 1997, the proportion of reserved forest increased from 45.7 per cent to 53.5 in 1997, but the protected forests declined from 46.8 per cent to 43.2; at the national level, the former was around the same as that in MP, but the latter much lower, being only 29.2 per cent in 1997. (*ibid.*).

This classification could not save the forests. The deforestation increased enormously over the years due to increased pressure from livestock and human population. There were other reasons also. Forests received low priority in the state's resource allocations. The expenditure on forestry increased from Rs. 431 lakh in the Third Five-year Plan to Rs. 5,051 lakh in the Sixth, i.e., a growth of 11.7 times as against 13.8 times in the grand total; the relative share declining from 1.51 per cent to 1.28. In the following plans, the growth was faster; rising to Rs. 400.95 crore in the Ninth Plan, which was 2.80 per cent of the grand total. Even the latest was very low on per hectare basis; rising from Rs. 1.80 in 1960-61 to Rs. 442 in 1999-00 as against from Rs. 3.52 to Rs. 539 at the national level.

The system of forest management itself was not conducive for the protection and development of forests. The demand-supply gap in fuel wood and grazing had increased enormously over the years. Behind the degeneration of the forests, above all was probably the role of the people in authority. A powerful nexus between politicians, forest mafia and government officials was wreaking havoc in the state's forests. Apart from illegal felling of teak trees in staggering numbers, there were also many instances of illegal mining, poaching, various forms of encroachments and illegal grant of pattas. In these nefarious activities, at one time, the "kingpin" was reported to be the forest minister (Ratnesh Solomon) himself. He was involved in illegal felling of thousands of teak trees, and was also responsible for encroaching upon protected forest land. (Pervez, Md. Shahid 2000). The Supreme Court had ruled in December 1999 that there shall be no felling of any tree in the state of MP and no movement of any timber without further orders of this court.

Forest Policy and Implementation

This policy deprived millions of poor of the livelihood goods they used to get from mixed forests. No measures were also taken to meet tribal demands for fruits, medicinal herbs etc. from forest lands. The scheme of social forestry was launched in 1981-82 in 21 of the districts in MP. Plantations were raised over 41,875 ha of village common lands, and 2,328 ha were brought under pasture development. The scheme proved almost a total failure as the revenue and community wastelands were not made available to the forest department on time. Fodder trees were generally ignored. The problems of the poor forest-fringe dwellers were exacerbated also by the industrial plantations. The rights of a huge section of society were wiped out in many places in order to benefit a few industrialists. For instance, the Orient Paper Mills was promised a lakh ton of bamboo per year from four districts of the state. The process of deforestation remained unchecked. The failure of the policies followed till late eighties, brought a new forest policy in 1988. Now higher priority was to be given to environmental stability than to earning of revenue. It discouraged monoculture and preferred mixed forests. The system of participatory forest management was introduced in 1992 as it became clear to the government that it alone cannot effectively protect and manage the forests. Consequent on these changes, the collection of forest produces declined noticeably. The plan targets on different forestry projects often remained unachieved.

Development of Fishery

Although Madhya Pradesh is, like UP, without any marine water resource, on inland water the state is one of the richest. The level of resource utilisation remained low, and it was primarily due to the low plan expenditure on fishery. Poor utilisation of the water areas was due to a variety of factors like low level of seed production of genetically improved variety, high rate of mortality of fish seed in rearing, and inefficiencies in the operation of Fish Farmers Development Agencies. The role of the fisheries department, concerned with development of reservoirs with capacity varying between 200 and 2,000 ha, and of the State Fisheries Development Corporation with above 2,000 ha, were far from satisfactory. The performance of the panchayats, entrusted with water areas up to 200 hects, was also very poor.

The decrease in fish production under the MPFDC was due to its bungling with the dropping of fingerlings. There were large variations in the number dropped each year. The lowest was 4.20 lakh in 1986-87 and the highest at 34.33 lakh in 1990-91. The fishermen had also doubted the number dropped. This was based on the fact that in the first four years of its working, the MPFDC had dropped 18.38 lakhs per annum and obtained 669 tonnes of fish per annum, but in the last four years, 1988-92, it was respectively 21.8 lakh and 547.3 tonnes. Moreover, the corporation had resisted the fishermen's genuine demand for presence of their representative at the time of dropping.

The economic condition of the fisherfolk had worsened under the MPFDC. Earlier, they were the producers and sellers of fish. But now they became mere labourers; earning piece-meal wages. On an average, Rs. 22.42 lakh per annum were distributed as wages to fisherfolk during 1979- 92, giving them an average income of Rs. 169.7 per month, with wide fluctuations. Their share in the sale proceeds also declined. This poor situation of the fisherfolk was due to the very high wage bill of the employees.

The chapter may be closed by giving an idea about the trend in capital formation in agriculture etc. as a whole. The per hectare capital formation in MP had declined from the average of Rs. 339.56 in 1980-83 to Rs. 298.05 in 1998-01, and averaged Rs. 332.51 for the entire period since 1980-81; for All-states, on the other hand, it increased from Rs. 521.75 to Rs. 748.84, and averaged Rs. 584.18. MP's latest was thus only 39.8 per cent of All-states', and the average for entire period at 56.9 per cent. In this capital formation, the share of public investment was relatively high. Among the five time-points considered, the highest was 42.14 per cent in 1988-91 and the lowest at 30.69 in 2001-04; both were significantly higher than the A-S average.

NOTES

- Madhya Pradesh is divided into nine agro-ecological sub-regions—namely, Gird, Malwa, Nimar, Vindhyachal, Satpura, Baghelkhand, Wainganga, Chhattisgarh plains and Chhattisgarh hills—on the basis of uniformity in physiography, climate, length of growing period, soil character, etc. The smallest region is Satpura with five per cent of the state's area, and the largest Chattisgarh hills with 17 per cent.
- Under the nistar, the state has accepted the responsibility of meeting the village requirements of forest product and grazing from the protected forests. Every villager was entitled to 250 bamboos per year at low prices, except in Bastar where it was free. Traditional bamboo workers or basod, cultivators of pan and orchard owners, and agarbatti manufacturers were given concessions. Fuel wood supply was free, except for a fee for extraction by bullock cart. Poles and round logs for construction were also supplied at highly concessional rates, except in Bastar where they were free. For encouraging the villagers to raise trees on their marginal lands and achieve self-reliance in forest produce requirements, the government had declared a new nistar policy in 1994, under which the nistar facility was restricted to villages located within 5 km of forest boundary.

11

INDUSTRIAL GROWTH AND STRUCTURAL CHANGE

Madhya Pradesh, despite having large natural resources and a central location in the country, had very low industrial base at the time of Independence. In 1949, the state accounted for only 2.95 per cent of the all-India total output value from manufacturing industries. Number of persons employed in the sector was 56,807, constituting 3.37 per cent of A-I total. The productivity per employee came to only Rs. 5,065, the second lowest among the states. (GOI 1954).

The growth of the industrial sector since then was quite rapid. The contribution of the manufacturing sector to the NSDP (at 1960-61 prices) increased from 12.7 per cent in 1960-61 to 20.3 in 1974-75, with a growth in value of output by 119.9 per cent as against only 37.3 for the state income. In the following 15 years, ending in 1988-89, however, the growth was below that in the latter, and the relative share declined to 13.0 per cent. In the nineties again the situation improved; the relative share reaching 16.9 per cent in 2001-02 from 14.6 in 1993-94. (at 1993-94 prices). As regards recent years, during 2003-06, the contribution of manufacturing to the state GSDP stood at 10.27 per cent and for industry as a whole 25.1 per cent; in Chhattisgarh, the situation was much better—for industry as a whole it was 41.9 per cent. At the national level, the share of manufacturing was 15.7 per cent, and for industry as a whole 27.8 per cent.

Factory Sector

The factory sector is the primary determinant of the industrial situation of a state. But in MP this sector was in a very poor state. The total value of output from it in 2004-05 stood at only Rs. 74,769 crore (including Chhattisgarh), and constituted 4.47 per cent of all-India total; in 1999-00, it was 6.35 per cent. The per capita output in 2004-05 came to only Rs. 8,517, and constituted 55.5 per cent of A-I average. In the pre-bifurcation period, the situation was not so bad; being at 80.4 per cent in 1999-00, rising from 56.3 in 1977-78 and 32.9 in 1955. The growth in total output between 1955 and 1999-00 was by 1,699 times compared with 637 times in all-India. The NVA to output ratio was very low until recently; being below the A-I average. In 2004-05, however, it went above the latter's.

On the provision of employment, the situation was very poor. Between 1990-91 and 2004-05, the number employed had declined from 4.17 lakh to 2.42 lakh; the relative share in A-I total dropped to 3.67 per cent from 5.11. The productivity of the employees, however, increased significantly, and became higher than the national average. Over the entire period between 1977-78 and 2004-05, it had risen by 54.8 times as against 46.2 times in all-India. This was, however, aided by a very high level of fixed capital per employee. In 2004-05, at Rs. 12.30 lakh, it was 58.5 per cent higher than the national average. The emolument per employee was also high. (ibid.). The capital-output ratio was also high in MP, being always higher than in all-India, although it had declined from 0.72 in 1977-78 to 0.40 in 2004-05. The NVA/FC ratio was also similarly placed, although increased from 0.29 in 1990-91 to 0.48 in 2004-05.

The average size of factories in MP was much higher than at the national level. In terms of invested capital, it had risen from Rs. 47.4 lakh in 1977-78 to Rs. 926 lakh in 2004-05; at the national level, it was from Rs. 35.0 lakh to Rs. 556 lakh. This higher size, however, did not give much benefit in terms of economies of scale. According to a recent study, the total factor productivity here remained below that in most of the major states. In relation to Maharashtra, the state's index had risen from the average of 71.1 (taking Maharashtra's value-added function in 1981-82 as 100) during 1980-91 to 85.4 in 1992-00; even the latest was lower than in all but two of the states. (Veeramani, C et al 2005)

Structural Change

The industrial structure of MP changed noticeably in the reform period, i.e., since 1991. The relative share of the seven most important industries—viz, metal and alloy, food products, non-metallic mineral products, electricity, machinery and equipment, wool, silk and man-made textiles and basic chemicals—together, in the total output rose to 83.7 per cent in 1993-94 from 55.5 in 1989-90, with the output rising by 204 and 101.3 per cent, respectively. Among them, the highest growth was in basic chemicals, by 252.0 per cent, and the lowest at 61.4 per cent in non-metallic mineral products. Metal and alloys continued to be the largest industry, although its relative share declined from 28.3 per cent to 25.6, with the growth in output by only 82.2 per cent; Food products came next with a share of 16.3 per cent in 1993-94, rising from 13.6; the growth in output was by 140.6 per cent. The electricity industry raised its share to 12.0 per cent from 9.10, with a 165.4 per cent rise in output. For basic chemicals, with highest growth, the relative share rose to 8.97 per cent from 5.13. On non-metallic mineral products, it declined to 8.40 per cent from 10.5.

Another group of seven industries, viz, beverages and tobacco, transport equipment, rubber, plastic etc., cotton textiles, paper etc., gas and steam and metal products, together contributed 14.6 per cent in 1993-94, a nominal fall from 1989-90. Among them gas and steam had the highest growth, a 17-fold rise, but still it accounted for only 1.39 per cent of total output. Beverages and tobacco accounted for 3.06 per cent, with a growth of 103.7 per cent. As regards the provision of employment, as many as seven industries—viz., electricity, beverages and tobacco, cotton textile, paper etc., metal products, leather etc. and wood and its produce—had recorded an absolute fall. The sharpest fall was in cotton textiles, from 47,709 to 32,692, and the share in all industries' total declined from 11.4 per cent to 7.19. For metal and alloy, the growth was by 27.8 per cent as against 8.93 per cent for all industries; its relative share rose to 19.0 per cent, from 16.2, and became the largest employer.

The inter-industry variation in productivity of the employees was very high. The output per employee in 1993-94 was as much as Rs. 25.22 lakh in gas and steam, rising from Rs. 3.78 lakh in 1989-90; the latest was nearly five times the average for all industries (Rs. 5.40 lakh). Among the seven most important industries, the highest in 1993-94 was in basic chemicals, at Rs. 9.10 lakh, followed by food products Rs. 8.89 lakh, wool silk, etc., Rs. 7.71 lakh and metal and alloys Rs. 7.27 lakh. The growth over the five-year period was highest in electricity, by 172.3 per cent, but the output per employee remained the lowest, at Rs. 3.73 lakh. The lowest growth was in metal and alloy, by only 42.5 per cent.

The data for recent years are not comparable with the earlier ones due to the change in industrial classification. However, to look into the situation of some of them: In 1999-00, the highest output on 3-digit classification basis was in food products (151, 152, 153 and 154), at Rs. 10077.44 crore, and it accounted for 22.9 per cent of total output. This was a 152.3 per cent rise over 1993-94 as against only 79.5 per cent for all industries. The growth in fixed capital in the industry was by 105.7 per cent, and the relative share in all industries' FC rose to 6.28 per cent from 3.16. The NVA/output ratio was very low, declining from 0.095 to 0.060; for all industries, it increased from 0.219 to 1.28.

Electricity and gas combined (401 and 402) accounted for 13.2 per cent of total output in 1999-00, with the amount rising by only 76.5 per cent in the seven year period. The NVA/output ratio had declined sharply from 0.384 to 0.090. The amount of FC in the industry also had a sharp fall. Basic iron and steel (271) came next with a share of 11.2 per cent of total output. The NVA/output ratio was very low, being only 0.041. The textiles (171 and 172) provided 8.50 per cent of total output and non-metallic mineral products (261 and 269) 6.30. Rubber and plastic (251 and 252) had a noticeable growth in output, by as much as 231.0 per cent over the period, but the relative share in total output was still only 4.19 per cent. Leather and its products had a very high growth, but the relative share was still only 0.66 per cent.

Small-Scale Industries

Modern Sector

The situation of the modern sector of SSI in MP has not been good. The number of units had risen quite rapidly but the production, despite a significant growth, remained low. On the provision of employment also the situation was not good. Over the 16-year period, it had risen by only 166 per cent, lower than in four of the states. The relative share in A-I total employment increased from 3.61 per cent to 4.33; the latest was the third lowest among the states. A good aspect of the situation here is, however, that a large proportion of the employees were in rural enterprises; as much as 47.2 per cent in 1987-88 compared with 33.3 per cent at the national level. The rural share in number of enterprises was 64.4 per cent, far higher than in any other state. The productivity of the employees was relatively low.

There was ample scope for raising the production level. The capacity utilisation in 1987-88 was only 46.3 per cent, which was below the national average. The level of mechanisation was also very low. The proportion of units consuming energy in 1987-88 was only 47.8 per cent, lowest among the states. The consumption of energy per unit averaged Rs. 14,000 this year as against the A-I average of Rs. 24,000. The proportion of closed units in the state was also not low. At 32.4 per cent in 1987-88, it was higher than in four of the states.

Structural Change

The industrial composition of the sector in MP changed considerably over the years. In 1972, seven industries, viz, metal products, wood and wood products, chemicals, mineral products, basic metal and alloy, machinery and parts and food products together accounted for 77.3 per cent of the total output. After 16 years, in 1987-88, it was down to 49.5 per cent. Within them, the share of metal products had declined from 19.3 per cent of total to only 7.54, of wood etc. from 14.5 to 8.45, chemicals from 14.1 to 6.0, mineral products from 9.37 to 6.75 and machinery and parts from 5.95 to 2.70. On the other hand, basic metal and alloy raised its share to 14.8 per cent from 8.22, repair services from 1.01 to 6.72 and rubber and plastic from 3.77 to 6.41. In terms of number of units, the highest share in 1972 was of metal products, at 26.7 per cent, but in 1987-88 it was only 8.04 per cent. On the other hand, metal products raised its share to 17.8 per cent from only 5.58 and food products to 17.1 per cent from 6.90. For wood products, with the second largest number in 1972, the proportion declined from 16.0 per cent to 11.6. (GOI 1976, 1990).

In recent years, the SIDO has not undertaken any census. The data available from the state directorate of industries presents a very gloomy situation. During 1992-93 to 2004-05, the number of SSI units had recorded a sharp fall; declining from as many as 29,075 in 1992-93 to 4,297 in 2002-03 and then recovering to 15,873 in 2004-05. On three-yearly average basis, the fall was from 27,921 in 1990-93 to 11,843 in 2002-05. As regards investment, it increased from the average of Rs. 63.00 crore in 1990-93 to Rs. 95.24 crore in 2002-05. The per unit investment increased from Rs. 22.6 thousand to Rs. 93.0 thousand. The employment had, however, recorded a sharp fall; declining from the annual average of 67.9 thousand in 1990-93 to 30.9 thousand in 2002-05. (GOMP 1999, 2002, 2006).

Within the state, inter-district, the distribution of SSI units was very uneven, and it became more skewed in recent years. In 1997-98, 10 districts—viz, Khargone, Khandwa, Gwalior, Morena, Ujjain, Indore, Hoshangabad, Bhopal, Ratlam and Sagar—together accounted for 28.9 per cent of total employment, 16,496 out of 57094. In 2001-02, each of these districts recorded sharp fall, and the total provision by them came to 13,174; the relative share, however, increased to 37.4 per cent. The largest employer in 1997-98, Khargone, with 3,556, could provide only 385 in 2000-01 and no employment at all in 2001-02. The second largest, Khandwa, had provided 290 in 2000-01 as against 2137 in 1997-98. For Ratlam the fall was from 1119 to 162, and Indore from 1961 to 755.

Unorganised Sector

MP's situation was very poor here also. The NSSO survey in 1994-95 found the state having only 4.5 per cent of A-I total number of enterprises, which was lower than in most of the states. Moreover, the enterprises were of very small size. The OAMEs, which do not employ any hired worker generally, constituted 88.0 per cent of total as against 84.5 per cent in all-India. Another deficiency was that the rural share of enterprises was only 69.3 per cent compared with 72.4 per cent in all-India. Also, OAMEs constituted as much as 94.6 per cent of total in rural areas.

In this situation, the production in the unorganised sector could not be high. The state accounted for only 4.56 per cent of A-I total GVA in 1994-95, lower than in most of the states. The rural share of production came to only 32.6 per cent as against 41.0 in all-India. The GVA per rural OAME was, however, relatively high. The situation of employment was worse. In the A-I total employment, MP's share came to only 4.0 per cent, the third lowest. The rural share of employment again was only 63.2 per cent as against 66.6 in all-India. The productivity of the workers was, however, relatively good. Five years earlier, in 1989-90, the production situation was worse but in employment it was better; the former being only 3.35 per cent of A-I total as against the latter at 4.06 per cent. The rural share was much higher in both GVA and employment, being respectively 55.7 and 74.5 per cent. (*ibid.*).

As regards the survey in 2000-01, it found the relative share in number of enterprises and in employment to have improved considerably, but on the GVA it is worse; the proportions (including Chhattisgarh) being respectively 5.8, 5.22 and 3.42 per cent. The rural share of the GVA was 46.3 per cent in MP and 58.8 in Chhattisgarh as against the national average of 44.3 per cent. In employment, it was respectively 67.4, 72.5 and 64.7 per cent.

The size-wise composition of the enterprises worsened. The proportion of OAMEs increased to 92 per cent as against 86 per cent in all-India; and for NDMEs it was respectively 5.6 and 10.1 per cent. In rural areas, the share of OAMEs became 97 per cent and of NDMEs only 2.0 per cent; at the national level, it was respectively 93 and 5.3 per cent. This change naturally influenced the GVA per enterprise. In 2000-01, it averaged only Rs. 21,780 in MP and Rs. 18,131 in Chhattisgarh as against the A-I average of Rs. 35,357. For rural areas, it was respectively Rs. 14,135, 13,953 and Rs. 22,348. Enterprise type-wise, the OAMEs in MP had only Rs. 13,905 as against Rs. 17,352 at the national level.

The productivity of workers worsened. Annual GVA per worker in MP averaged only Rs. 11,200 for rural-urban combined, which was the lowest among the states; in Chhattisgarh, it was still lower, only Rs. 9,100. The rural-urban disparity was very high. In MP, rural areas had only Rs. 7,700, mere 42 per cent of that in urban areas. Enterprise type-wise, in OAMEs, MP had Rs. 8,200 and Chhattisgarh Rs. 7,000 as against Rs. 10,200 in all-India. The emolument of workers was also very low. Annually, for NDMEs and DMEs combined, per hired worker it averaged only Rs. 13,228 in MP and Rs. 12,572 in Chhattisgarh compared with Rs. 18,488 in all-India. In rural areas, the situation was much worse. MP had only Rs. 4,406 and Chhattisgarh Rs. 6,897 as against Rs. 13,082 in rural India.

The low productivity of workers was at least partly due to the low level of fixed assets. Fixed assets to employment ratio in the rural OAMEs of MP stood at only 9062.50 in 2000-01 and in Chhattisgarh at 7797.79 as against the national average of 10184. The value of fixed assets per enterprise (rural+urban) averaged only Rs. 37,500 in MP and Rs. 27,400 in Chhattisgarh as against Rs. 60,500 in all-India. In OAMEs, it was respectively Rs. 22,400, 16,100 and 25,400. In rural MP, for all enterprise types together, it came to only Rs. 18,100 compared with 27,600 in rural India. The situation of plant and machinery in it again was extremely low. For rural-urban combined, per enterprise it averaged Rs. 6,071 in MP and Rs. 5,149 in Chhattisgarh compared with Rs. 10,030 at the national level.

The enterprises in Madhya Pradesh had to face a variety of problems, like power cut, non-availability of raw materials, shortage of capital, etc. The survey in 2000-01 found that 26.1 per cent of the enterprises had difficulties in getting the raw materials; the second highest proportion among the states. As much as 40.4 per cent of rural enterprises had no source agency for purchase of basic input; for all-India, it was 32.7 per cent. Power cut was reported by 18.2 per cent, which was significantly higher than in all-India. The shortage of capital was faced by as much as 41.0 per cent. Apart from these, 22.5 per cent of enterprises had local problems, 13.4 per cent competition from larger units and 11.3 per cent reported non-recovery of service charges/fees/credit. In this situation, the growth status of the enterprises in MP was very poor. As much as 68.2 per cent of rural enterprises had reported stagnant over the last three years.

Causal Factors

Infrastructural Situation

Trend in Power Situation

Among the infrastructural items, the power situation was relatively good until recent years. The installed capacity had risen by 44.5 times between 1957-58 and 1998-99 as against only 28.9 times in all-India. The state's share in A-I total capacity rose to 4.4 per cent from 2.9; in 1980-81, however, it stood at 5.40 per cent. The energy generation also had a similar trend. The growth over the entire period was nearly three times the national average. The capacity utilisation was very low until the late 'nineties; in 1980-81, it stood at only 41.7 per cent. In 1997-98, however, it reached 59.3 per cent, 5.4 points higher than in all-India.

After the state's bifurcation, MP faced severe power shortage. In 2003, the installed capacity stood at only 31 thousand kw, constituting 2.9 per cent of A-I total. The power shortage during 2000-02 was 13.9 per cent as against 7.65 per cent for all-India, and in the next year it reached 27.5 per cent. To overcome the problem, the government allowed setting up of captive power plants by industry. The power shortage became an important reason behind the fall of the 10-year old congress regime in December 2003. (Sharma, Sanjay 2005).

As regards the recent situation, the installed electricity generating capacity (utilities) as on March 2009 was 3,901 MW in MP and 2,917 MW in Chhattisgarh. The gross generation in 2008-09 came to 19,744 mkwh in MP, 77.4 per cent of which was thermal and 20 per cent hydro. In Chhattisgarh, the generation was 20,564 mkwh, with 95 per cent from thermal. The T&D losses did not show any noticeable fall. During 2006-09, it averaged 37.7 per cent in MP; in 1997-2000 it was 25.3 per cent .The generation from renewable sources in 2008-09 was 520 mkwh in MP and 723 mkwh in Chhattisgrh. Both were lower than in most of the states. In non-utilities, the installed capacity in 2007-08 stood at 1575 MW in MP and 1522 in Chhattisgarh; both were higher than in all but five of the states. The gross generation from non-utilities in 2008-09 was as much as 12,825 mkwh in Chhattisgarh, which was the second highest mong the states, next only to Gujarat. In MP it was only 3,863 mkwh, lower than in most of the states. (CMIE 2011). The industrial consumption of power in Madhya Pradesh had a sharp fall over the years.

MPSEB and Power Sector Reform

Since the early 1990s, MPEB started facing a variety of problems. The dependence on power purchase from the central sector generating stations (CGS) started increasing, and it inflated the total expenses. Since 1992, the Board could never achieve the minimum return of 3 per cent over net fixed assets as stipulated by the Electricity Supply Act, 1948. The revenue subsidy from the state government rose to Rs. 1,697 crore in 1999 from Rs. 380 crore in

1993. The worsening financial situation made it difficult to raise funds for investments in generation and T & D, which further aggravated the poor condition. To face this grave power situation, the government started the power sector reform in early 1990s, as in most other states. In November 2000, with the state's bifurcation, the MPEB was split into two Boards, one for MP and the other for Chhattisgarh. In the apportionment of assets and liabilities, the former assumed nearly 79 per cent of the long-term debt but only 67 per cent of the revenue base and 94 per cent of agricultural consumers. (GOMP 2003). This not only skewed the power availability, but also impacted MPSEB finances.

The installed capacity of MPSEB stood at 3058 MW in 2002, and in the following two years at 3108 MW. The firm allocations from CGS averaged 1339 MW in 2002-2004 and purchase from other sources at 316.7 MW. The gross own generation averaged only 15235 MU, and the power purchase at 13574 MU. The sales increased from 13960 MU in 2002 to 16006 in 2004. The peak shortage rose to the average of 28.7 per cent in 2002-2004, from 23.1 per cent in the undivided state in 1998-2000. The T &D losses also rose sharply to 47.6 per cent, from 28.0 per cent. The average cost of power supply increased from Rs. 2.48 per kWh to Rs. 4.37, while the realisation from Rs. 1.72 to Rs. 2.82.

In the operating expenses of MPSEB, the highest proportion went for power purchases, followed by employee costs and interest and finance charges. The expenditure on the first item rose to Rs. 2680 crore in 2004 from Rs. 719 crore in 1993, and averaged Rs. 2507 crore during 1999-2004, constituting 40.9 per cent of total. In recent years, nearly 50 per cent of the power demand was met by power purchase. The employee cost had a sharp rise and accounted for about 16 per cent of total expenses in 2004; per unit of electricity sold it came to more than 60p as against 24 p in Maharashtra.

The grave financial situation of MPSEB was also due to the poor performance in power generation. Almost all generating plants of MPSEB are very old; average age of thermal plants being 20 years. The plant Load Factor and secondary oil consumption of the plants had improved, but the station heat rate, which is a measure of the plant efficiency, remained way below the norm. This was largely due to poor R and M activities, which in turn was mainly due to paucity of funds. But the R &M cost in the state was also high. Another factor was the defective system of calculating agricultural consumption. Nearly 80 per cent of agricultural connections in MP were not metered, and the estimated consumption often appeared unrealistically high.

The bungling in power planning was also greatly responsible for the crises. In early nineties, the MP government had started signing MOUs with independent power producers (IPP). Agreements were signed with 22 private generation companies for a proposed capacity addition of about 8,235 MW. These agreements were not based on even elementary power system planning like demand forecasts and evaluation of least cost plans. Only 13 of the MOUs could receive the techno-economic clearance from the CEA. None of the IPPs in the state could reach commercial operation.

Even after the experience of filing two tariff proposals, the MPSEB failed to submit the proposal for FY2004 in December 2002. And after many rounds of submissions and rejections by the commission, finally the proposals for FY2004 and FY2005 were submitted together in August 2004. Revision of tariff was requested only for FY 2005. T & D loss reduction were proposed at only 2.1 per cent and 1.5 per cent for the two FYs, respectively. The commission allowed an overall tariff hike of 14 per cent and approved the T & D loss reduction of about three per cent for each FY.

The regulatory process brought a reduction in the level of cross-subsidisation and tariffs began to approach the cost of supply. But all tariff hikes by MPERC were highly skewed. The tariff for domestic and agricultural consumers (LT) in 2005 was more than three times that in 2001, whereas for industrial consumers it was by only 1.2 times. It may be noted that the Draft National Tariff Policy 2005 had wanted the tariffs for all categories to be at least 80 per cent of the average cost of supply (ACoS) by 2011-12. At the tariff level of the FY 2005 tariff order, all consumers in the state were charged above 80 per cent of ACoS, except agricultural who were charged at 60 per cent.

On reducing the T & D loss, the performance was very poor. The MPERC's target, set in the very first tariff order, was to bring it down to 37.0 per cent by 2003 and 28.0 by 2005, from 51.0 per cent in 2001. But the actual in 2003 was 44.2 per cent and in 2005 at 43.1. The ADB's investment loan thus failed to realise the objective of reducing the T&D losses. Eighty per cent of the loss was, however, due to theft and the commission did not take any strict action against the MPSEB for its failure to check it. (MPERC 2001).

Transportation System

On the transportation facility, as noted in the preceding chapter, MP's situation was very poor. The road length per thousand sq. km. of area stood at only 662.9 km. in 1998-99, which was much below the all-India average. The proportion of unsurfaced roads was also very high, and it increased from 45.3 per cent in 1990-91 to 54.8 in 1998-99. The situation of railways was also not much better. Route length per thousand sq. km. of area stood at only 15.6 km. in 2000-01, which was much below the national average and second lowest among the states. Earlier, in 1992-93, at 19.4 km., it was slightly higher than at the national level.

On the availability of motor vehicles also the state's situation was very poor. The density per sq. km. of area was always below the national average; in 1990-91, it was respectively 3.29 and 6.50, and improved to 11.24 and 14.74 in 1999-00. Number of goods vehicles in them was also very low. In 2003, in the total number of vehicles at 31.73 lakh, goods vehicles constituted only 3.06 per cent as against 5.17 per cent at the national level. Earlier, in 1975, the situation was much better; being 15.7 and 13.5 per cent, respectively.

Institutional Finance

Commercial Banks

The provision of industrial credit from the commercial banks was very low here. The amount outstanding in 2004-05 stood at only Rs. 7737.1 crore in MP and Rs. 3257.5 crore in Chhattisgarh; the two together constituted 2.46 per cent of A-I total, with the former at 1.73 per cent. Earlier, in 1995-96, the situation was much better; the relative share being 3.25 per cent, with the amount at Rs. 3967.9 crore. The growth over the period was by only 177.1 per cent compared with 265.5 per cent in all-India. In the total for industrial sector, the share of manufacturing and processing in 2002-05 averaged 89.1 per cent in MP and 85.4 in Chhattisgarh as against 77.7 per cent in all-India.

As regards the SSI sector, the growth in credit till early eighties was quite high. The amount outstanding had multiplied 34 times between 1968 and 1983 as against 28 times in all-India. In the following years till March 2004, it was by only 11.8 times, nominally higher than in the latter. MP's share (including Chhattisgarh) in A-I total credit came to only 2.96 per cent in 2004, which was lower than in all but two of the states. In terms of number of accounts also the situation was similar. The growth in the first period was by as much as 81 times as against a mere 25 per cent in the following one. The average amount per account was very low.

Within the state, inter-district, the provision of industrial credit varied greatly. On March-end 2001, in Chhattisgarh, the amount outstanding stood at only Rs. 94.69 lakh in Kawardha as against the highest of Rs. 110970 lakh in Durg—i.e., the latter 1172 times the former; the related number of accounts stood at 808 and 14,671, respectively. In Madhya Pradesh, while the highest was Rs. 222843 lakh in Indore, for Neemuch it was only Rs. 272.5 lakh—i.e., the former 817.8 times the latter; the number of accounts were respectively 6,220 and 1,284. There were 17 districts with below Rs. 10 crore (covering both the states). Earlier, in December 1977, the situation was much worse. The highest amount outstanding was Rs. 3988 lakh in Indore and the lowest at Rs. 1.21 lakh in Panna; number of accounts were 2,707 and 50, respectively. For 22 districts the amount was below Rs. 50 lakh, with 8 at below Rs. 10 lakh. (RBI 2002a, 1979).

Long-Term Finance

On the provision of long-term finance also MP's situation was very poor. In the all-India cumulative total of assistance by all the institutions together till March 2001, the share of MP came to only 3.70 per cent, declining from 4.91 in that till 1990. On per capita basis, it was always far below the national average. The cumulative total till March 2001 came to only Rs. 2,258, which was 46.8 per cent of the latter's; in the period till March 1990, it was respectively Rs. 423 and 64.1 per cent. Among the major states, the latest was lower than in all but three.

In the provision of term finance, the state-level FIs played an insignificant role. In the cumulative total till March 2001, their share came to only 1.5 per cent, declining from 7.1 in that till March 1990; for all SFIs, it was from 9.8 to 5.0 per cent. Among the all-India FIs, the IDBI played the dominant role; providing 41.8 per cent of the cumulative total till March 2001, declining from 58.8 per cent in March 1990. Even the latest was much higher than at the national level. The per capita assistance, however, came to only Rs. 929 in 2001, a mere 65.1 per cent of the A-I average. Of the state-level FIs, the oldest one, State Financial Corporation, had a very poor performance here. The per capita assistance from it came to only Rs. 113.60 in 2001, which was a mere 39.8 per cent of all SFCs' average.

As regards the provision to small-scale industries, they were largely neglected by the term-financing institutions. The only institution at the state level providing finance to them, the SFC, had provided a relatively low share here. The proportion going to them declined from 72.4 per cent in 1990 to 67.5 in 2001; both were substantially below the A-I average. The cumulative total of assistance to SSIs constituted only 2.71 per cent of the grand total in 2001, declining from 4.16 in March 1990. The national level institution for SSIs, the SIDBI, also provided a very low amount. The per capita cumulative total to MP in 2001 came to only Rs. 187, which was 57.1 per cent of the A-I average.

The country's industrial policy had an objective of bringing balanced regional development, but it was not reflected in the provision of finance by the FIs to the backward states. Till March 2001, Maharashtra had received a per capita cumulative assistance from the IDBI of more than double the national average. The backward MP on other hand received only 31.8 per cent of Maharashtra's. The provision from the SIDBI was also similar. (*ibid.*).

Special Steps

Since early eighties, the government of MP began taking some special steps for promoting industrial growth. The MPSIDC had set up five Audyogic Kendra Vikas Nigam (AKVN) in the 1980s, with their nucleus centres at Indore, Bhopal, Jabalpur and Gwalior to cover the regions of Malwa, Narmada, Mahakaushal and Vindhya and Bundelkhand, respectively. These were basically infrastructure development corporations for creating infrastructure in the growth centres totalling 19. The performance of these corporations were far from satisfactory. As on March 2002, out of 6,400 hectares of land acquired, only approximately 2,770 ha could be allotted. Number of SSI units set up totalled 1103 and of large/medium units at 244 in the 19 growth centres. The investments generated in them were of Rs. 12,250 crore and the employment at over one lakh. The growth centres were suffering from inadequate development and organisational problems. They lacked specialised infrastructure like CETP, warehousing, training centres, testing laboratories, etc., Inordinate delays in processing the applications, in obtaining clearances, etc., were hampering the growth.

The government had also introduced a number of incentives and concessions for attracting industries to the state. The capital subsidy of 10-15 per cent, up to a maximum of Rs. 5 lakh, was introduced in 1994; and for units in agro and urban waste processing, a special state subsidy of 25 per cent of the cost or Rs. 25 lakh, whichever is lower. There was also provision for interest subsidy of Rs. 10 - 40 lakh depending on the extent of backwardness. For promoting the SSIs, there were many measures like reservation, price preference, etc., operating for a long time. The government had also started District Industries Centres for providing all the services and support facilities under a single roof.

All these and other measures, however, proved very little effective, particularly in the backward areas. Number of development blocks with 'no industries' continued to be very high. In 2003, 206 DBs, out of the total number at 318, were with 'no industries'. In the Rewa region, it was 29 out of 37; in Jabalpur, 44 out of 64; in Sagar 27 out of 37; in Gwalior, 21 out of 30; and in Chambal region 8 out of 10. District-wise, in Sheopur, all the three blocks remained 'no industries'; in Dindori, all the seven blocks; in Chhatarpur, all the eight blocks; and in Shahdol eight out of nine. (GOMP 2003a).

The Bhopal Disaster

While industrialisation is necessary up to a point, the extent of environmental pollution it inflicts on people has always to be borne in mind. The people of Madhya Pradesh have not yet forgotten the Bhopal tragedy—the world's worst industrial disaster—nearly three decades ago, on December 2-3, 1984. It killed at least 20,000 people and left generations of Indians afflicted. Out of 56 wards in Bhopal then, 36 with 62.6 per cent of population were affected by the tragedy.[1] The Union Carbide factory, established in 1969, was manufacturing fatal and deadly pesticides and was dumping toxic effluents in a pit adjacent to the factory. Thousands of tonnes of poison seeped inside the soil and water, and now thousands of Bhopal residents are drinking the poisonous groundwater. (Singh, Shiv Karan 2009a).

The initial victims of the disaster were paid a meagre compensation of Rs. 12,410 each as one-time relief. The total compensation received from the Union Carbide was Rs. 750 crore—which with interest increased to Rs. 3,000 crore. Number of people awarded compensation was 574,366, and the amount disbursed by March 2009 at Rs. 1,548.93 crore. Medical expenditure on the victims till this date was Rs. 512.09 crore. Health of survivours has not improved and the second-generation ailments are often even more debilitating. Thousands of victims are living a pathetic life and visiting hospitals for treatment every day for the past 27 years (ibid.; Down To Earth: 24-26; Dogra, Bharat 2012a).

To prevent future Bhopals, the government did not take any tough stand. Successive governments handled this sensitive case very carelessly and casually. The main accused, Warren Anderson, CEC of the Union Carbide during the disaster, was arrested on 7 December 1984, but was bailed out within hours, flown to Delhi in a state government plane and allowed to flee the country. The Indian government took almost 20 years after the disaster to send its first extradition request to the US. On the disposal of the 350 tonnes of toxic wastes lying in the defunct UCIL plant (now represented by Dow Chemical) for the last 28 years, the Supreme Court was compelled on 28 May, 2012 to pull up the Centre asking it to take a final decision on it soon. (TST 2012 Z59) The government's nature of actions on the Bhopal disaster have shown the world what corporations producing unsafe products can get a way with.

In this situation, it is no surprise that in the winter of 2009, the government tried to pass two bills, the National Green Tribunal Bill and the Nuclear Civil Liabilities Bill, which hardly provide any protection to the people from industrial pollution. Both the bills entail forcing the people to bear the cost of acute and chronic toxicity caused by polluting technology. In the first bill, when dealing with civil cases of "substantial questions related to the environment" affecting the "community at large", the proposed tribunal will not entertain any application "unless it is made within a period of six months from the date on which the cause of action first arose, or given "sufficient cause" allow another 60 days. For granting any compensation or relief, no application will be accepted "unless it is made within a period of five years" with a similar grace of 60 days for "sufficient cause". This time frame is grossly insufficient in cases of chronic toxicity, effect of which might manifest themselves over decades.

NOTE

1. It may be noted that even after 27 years a consensus between the government and the NGOs on the number of victims of the Bhopal gas disaster is elusive. The MP government has put the death toll at 5,295 in an affidavit filed in the Supreme Court. But in another criminal petition filed in the apex court, government put the death toll at 15,248. (TST 2011 z40).

12

ABSOLUTE POVERTY AND THE MEASURES

The poverty situation in Madhya Pradesh continued to be very depressing, as noted in Chapter 2. The proportion of BPL population was always much higher than at the national level; in 2004-05, at 37.21 per cent, it was higher by nine points. The rural population with MPCE of below Rs. 380 in 2004 was as much as 42.1 per cent, more than double that at the national level. The proportion of population with calorie undernourishment in 2008 stood at 23.4 per cent as against the national average of 20.0 per cent.

The inter-district disparity in the poverty situation was very high. The MPCE in rural MP stood at only Rs. 278 in Dindori in 2004-05 as against the highest of Rs. 749 in Dewas, with the state average at Rs. 439; for 19 districts, it was below Rs. 400 while only two had above Rs. 600. In Chhattisgarh, the highest was Rs. 627 in Korba and the lowest at Rs. 21 in Dantewada, with Rs. 425 at the state level. In urban areas, MP had the highest of Rs. 1,648 in Indore and the lowest at Rs. 479 in Shivpuri, with state average at Rs. 904. In Chhattisgarh, the highest was Rs. 1,934 in Rajnandgaon and the lowest at Rs. 418 in Dantewada, with Rs. 990 at the state level.

The proportion of BPL population also varied similarly. In 2004-05, in rural MP, the highest was 76.4 per cent in Umaria and the lowest at 0.2 in Neemuch, with 36.8 per cent at the state level; as many as 13 districts had above 50 per cent—with three at above 70. In urban areas, the highest was 77.4 per cent in Shivpuri and the lowest at 12.6 in Shahdol, with 55.5 per cent at the state level. In Chhattisgarh, rural areas had the highest of 88.2 per cent in Dantewada and the lowest at 16.9 in Kawardha, with 40.8 at the state level. In urban areas, the highest was 84 per cent in Dantewada and the lowest at 15.7 in Surguja, with 42.2 per cent at state level. (ibid.).

Social class-wise, the situation of scheduled tribes—constituting around a quarter of the total population—continued to be very depressing. In 2004-05, in rural areas, they had MPCE of only Rs. 343 as against Rs. 426 at the national level. Earlier, in 1987-88, it was respectively Rs. 106 and Rs. 123. Among the STs, agricultural labour households constituted as much as 44.7 per cent in 1999-00 as against 39.7 per cent in all-India. The proportion in self-employment this year was 40.0 per cent, with those in non-agriculture at 3.3; at the national level, it was respectively 41.4 and 5.2 per cent. The land-holding situation was relatively good. The proportion with less than 0.40 ha was 35.4 per cent as against 46.3 at the national level. The literacy situation of STs was very poor. As much as 56.1 per cent of hhs were without a literate adult male member in 1999-00 as against 47.6 per cent in all-India.

The SCs were also in similar situation. In rural areas, they had MPCE of Rs. 384 in 2004-05 as against the national average of Rs. 475. In 1999-00, it was respectively Rs. 375 and Rs. 419. Occupation-wise, the proportion of labour households was relatively low. In 1999-00, it stood at 52.7 per cent as against 61.4 in all-India. The proportion in self-employment was respectively 39.5 and 28.4 per cent. The land-holding situation was relatively good. The availability of institutional finance, however, had a sharp fall. In rural areas, in 2002, only 50 per cent of total debt was with the formal sources, declining from 70 per cent in 1992. The literacy situation was also not good. (ibid.).

Wage Employment Programmes

The employment situation in MP was relatively good. In 1972-73, the rural unemployment rate stood at 3.4 per cent as against the all-India average of 7.7. Income of the labour households, however, remained very low. Per agricultural labour hh, it came to only Rs. 928.65 in 1970-71 as against Rs. 1131.25 in all-India. The daily wage rate continued to be very low. In 1971-72, at Rs. 2.25, it was the lowest among the states; the growth over 1956-57 was a negligible two per cent. The proportion of agricultural labourers with land was also only 50.4 per cent here as against 61.4 per cent in all-India. In the following years, the situation worsened much. The proportion of labour households rose to 35.4 per cent in 1987-88, from 22.4 in 1964-65. The daily earnings of male agricultural labourers in 1983 was only Rs. 3.96, which was the lowest among the states. Despite this worsening, the employment programmes did not get the attention it deserved, as will be evident from the analysis below.

CSRE and FWP

Under the first rural employment scheme, the CSRE, during 1971-74, a total of 396.88 lakh persondays (lpd) were created in MP, constituting 13.7 per cent of A-I total and the highest among the states. The wage rate paid was, however, very low. The programme suffered from lack of proper planning both at higher levels and on-the-spot. The distribution of fund did not take into account the varied situation of districts and it was distributed equally among them. The inter-block allocation in a district also followed the same procedure. The CSRE works were actually listed and identified after the sanction of funds and without reference to the block/panchayat agencies' readiness to carry them through.

The scheme was discontinued after three years, and in 1977 the Food for Work Programme (FWP) was launched. This also lasted for only three years, till September 1980, when it was replaced by the National Rural Employment Programme. The implementation of the FWP was also far from satisfactory. An evaluation study in 1979 of two districts, one good (Indore) and another average (Raisen), found that even in the good district only two beneficiaries, out of the 38 interviewed, reporting the wages to be sufficient for meeting daily requirements. The increase in total wages received following the implementation of the scheme was only 16.4 per cent in Indore, and in Raisen at 57.0 per cent. Even after the higher rise, the average per family in Raisen came to only Rs. 1,689 in 1978-79 as against Rs. 2,718 in Indore. Total number of persondays created increased by 58.5 per cent in Raisen as against 19.2 per cent in Indore. The average number per family was still only 373.2 in the former as against 632.8 in the latter.

The total expenditure, including the value of food-grains, came to only Rs. 3,606 in Raisen in 1978-79 as against Rs. 2,42,491 in Indore. The entire expenditure in the former was on construction of additional room to Panchayat Bhavan and on construction of Monoranjan Kendra. In Indore, however, a substantial portion went for construction/repair of school building, roads, drainage, dispensary and latrines.

NREP and EGS

Implementation of the NREP also suffered from many deficiencies. To look into its operation for a period of four years: Total number of person-days created during 1985-89 constituted 10.13 per cent of all-India total, with the share in expenditure at 9.07 per cent. The cost per Pd averaged only Rs. 17.81 as against Rs. 19.90 at the national level. The utilisation of available fund and of foodgrains was relatively good. Poor planning and implementation were reflected in the fact that while the expenditure fell short of the amount released, the target on employment was over-fulfilled by as much as 26.6 per cent.

The Employment Guarantee Scheme, launched in 1983, had worse performance. The total of Pds created in the state during 1985-89 constituted 8.79 per cent of A-I total, with the share in expenditure at 7.31 per cent. The cost per Pd came to only Rs. 17.38, which was lower than in most of the states. The expenditure, in relation to the amount released, came to only 80.4 per cent, lowest among the states. The situation of foodgrains utilisation was, however, much better. The target on employment creation remained unachieved to a large extent.

Jawahar Rozgar Yojana

In the last year of the 'eighties, in 1989-90, the NREP and the RLEGP were merged to form the JRY and the mode of operation altered radically, as noted in Chapter 7. The scheme provided a substantial employment opportunity in the initial years. In the all-India total of Pds created during 1989-95, the state's share stood at 9.9 per cent, with that in expenditure at 10.0 per cent. The cost per Pd rose to an average of Rs. 34.79, higher than the national average. In the provision of employment, the share of SC/ST in this six-year period averaged as much as 65.7 per cent compared with 55.6 per cent at the national level. The situation of landless workers was, however, very poor.

Towards the end of 'nineties, the employment provided by the JRY declined sharply, and this was largely due to a major change in the objectives of the programme. In April 1999, the scheme's name was changed and creation of village infrastructure substituted employment creation as the primary objective. During 1997-00, the annual average of Pds created came to only 311 lpd as against 830 lpd in 1989-95, i.e., a fall by 62.5 per cent. The state's share in A-I total employment created declined to 9.0 per cent. The fall in expenditure was much less, and the cost per Pd became more than double the earlier level. In the employment created, the share of SC/ST declined and that for landless recorded a nominal rise. The former was, however, still 9.4 points higher than at the national level.

Under the stream of Intensive JRY—created in 1993-94 and ran for three years only—the performance in the first year was very poor. Against the fund available at Rs. 14507 lakh, only Rs. 3918 lakh, i.e., 27.0 per cent, could be spent. The employment generated was 79.99 lpd, constituting 10.9 per cent of A-I total. In the next year, 1994-95, the situation improved significantly. The fund utilisation rose to 74.6 per cent as against 67.9 per cent in all-India. The employment created was 39.8 per cent higher than the target; and constituted 19.8 per cent of A-I total.

As regards the sub-schemes of the JRY, the Million Well Scheme had a noticeably good performance here. Number of wells constructed during 1988-95 constituted 18.41 per cent of all-India total, the second highest among the states. The expenditure per well, however, averaged only Rs. 20 thousand as against Rs. 35 thousand at the national level. In the following four years, the situation improved further. The number constructed rose to 20.7 per cent of A-I total, highest among the states. The cost per well declined further, and became only 44.2 per cent of that at the national level. The quality of the wells here was probably poor.

On the IAY, the performance was not so good. The operation of the JRY suffered from many deficiencies. A very serious aspect of the operation was, however, the extremely low participation of the poorer groups in the employment created. The attitude of the bureaucracy towards the implementation of the JRY was far from congenial.

Employment Assurance Scheme (EAS)

The EAS, created in 1993-94, was merged into the JGSY in November 2001 to constitute the Sampoorna Grameen Rozgar Yojana (SGRY). The performance of the EAS was similar to the JRY. Between 1993-94 and 1999-00, a total of 2348 Lpds were created, constituting 10.5 per cent of all-India total, with the share in expenditure at 11.1 per cent. The utilisation of available fund was very poor, being an average of 73.4 per cent in this period. Even this was, however, the second highest among the major states. From the employment created, the landless were benefited to a very small extent; constituting only 32.2 per cent of total as against 39.0 per cent at the national level.

The overall situation of employment creation in rural MP was relatively good. In terms of households, the number participating in 1999-00 stood at 32 per thousand hhs, declining from 81 in 1993-94; at the national level, it was respectively 29 and 59. Among the beneficiaries, the lower income groups had very low representation. In 1999-00, for the MPCE class below Rs. 255, per thousand hhs, it was only 53 as against the national average of 72. For the class Rs. 775 and above, however, it was respectively 63 and 41. Social group-wise, the STs numbered 46 and SCs 31 as against 51 and 32 respectively in all-India. As regard recent years, in 2004-05, a total of 581.39 Lpds, constituting 7.11 per cent of A-I total, were created, and it was higher than in all but three of the states. The representation of landless improved but it was still below the national average, being respectively 37.5 and 39.9 per cent.

The NREGP, launched in 2006, had a relatively good performance here. The employment provided per hh. came to 68.9 Pds in 2006-07 and 63.3 the next year; both were the second highest among the states. The proportion of hhs. completing 100 days of employment was 18.5 and 21.0 per cent in the two years respectively, which were the highest among the states. In 2008-09, although only 57 days of work were provided per hh, it was the highest among the states. In the All-India total number of man-days of work created this year, MP's share was 14 per cent. The situation of Chhattisgarh was also good. The pds provided per hh in the three years of 2006-09 were respectively 55.6, 57.6 and 57 as against 43.1, 41.8 and 48 in all-India. The wage cost per pd was, however, low. In 2006-07, it was Rs. 59 in MP and 63 in Chhattisgarh as against Rs. 65 in All-India. The share of wages in total expenditure were respectively 63, 65 and 66 per cent. The statutory wage rate itself was low here. (GOI 2008, 2008a, 2006c, 2011a). This relatively good position in MP does not seem to have benefited the poor much.

Self-Employment Programmes

The IRDP

The scheme's performance in MP has not been good. The Plan expenditure on it had risen quite fast in the initial plans, but in recent years it was very low. From Rs. 76.27 crore in the Sixth plan, it increased to Rs. 137.14 crore in the Seventh and Rs. 301.08 crore in the Eighth Plan, i.e., a 295 per cent rise over the three Plans. In the total for rural development, its share declined to only 25.4 per cent in the Eighth plan, from 39.7 in the preceding plan. In the Ninth Plan, the expenditure had an absolute fall, being around Rs. 300 crore.

As regards the physical achievements, the number of beneficiary families had declined continuously from 17.66 lakh in the Seventh plan to 10.16 lakh in the Eighth, and then to only 5.10 lakh in the Ninth plan. Annually, the number had reached the highest of 242.67 thousand in 1993-94 and then declined continuously to 61.08 thousand in 2001-02. (GOMP 1992, 203b). The relative position among the states worsened noticeably over the years. In the A-I total number of families assisted, MP's share declined to 8.10 per cent in 1996-99, from 9.3 in 1992-95. In terms of households, the coverage per thousand had declined from 92 in 1993-94 to 51 in 1999-00.

As regards the sub-schemes like the TRYSEM and the DWCRA, which were merged with the IRDP after the restructuring, the situation in a few of the pre-merger years may be looked into. The TRYSEM had a relatively good performance. The total number trained during 1992-93 to 1998-99 constituted 13 9 per cent of all-India total, with the share in expenditure at 9.01 per cent. Naturally, the expenditure per trainee was very low. At the average of Rs. 2113, it was 64.8 per cent of the national average and lowest among the states. The low expenditure notwithstanding, the settlement of the youths was very good. During 1992-96, 72.3 per cent of the trained youths were settled here as against only 49.0 per cent at the national level. On the DWCRA, launched in 1982, the performance was not good.

Public Distribution System

The importance of a properly targeted PDS for the poor has been noted in chapter 7. But in MP the scheme itself came as late as March 1981; and then, as in other states, it was not aimed specifically towards the poor. The targeting of the PDS towards the poor came only at the end of 'nineties. A brief look is given below on how the system operated here.

In terms of rural sector's share of total PDS purchases, MP's situation was relatively good. In 1986-87, for example, on wheat, the most important cereal, it was 69 per cent as against 56 per cent at the national level. On edible oil and kerosene also the situation was similar; being respectively 78 per cent and 59 per cent in MP as against 69 and 55 per cent in the latter. On rice and sugar, however, the state's position was very poor. In terms of market dependent, the situation of PDS purchases was much worse. On rice, at 0.346 kg, it was less than a third of the national average; and on wheat, at 0.587 and 0.761 kg., respectively. For edible oil, kerosene and sugar also it was not good.

A look at the situation over a long period also presents a gloomy picture. The per capita PDS of total foodgrains in the state varied between the highest of 21 kg per annum in 1980 and the lowest at five kg in 1974 among the seven time-points considered. Even the highest was lower than in four of the states. Only towards the end of 1990s, a number of steps was taken to improve the situation of the poor. The targeted PDS was launched in 1997 and separate blue cards were issued for them. In 2002, such cards numbered 47.96 lakh and covered a population of around 40 per cent of total. Including the Antyodaya Anna Yojana, the total coverage rises to 271 lakh, 45 per cent of the population. (GOMP 2002c: 106). Under the AAY, very poor families were provided 35 kg of foodgrains a month at the rate of Rs. 2.0 per kg for wheat and Rs. 3.0 for rice. The Annapurna Yojana, introduced by the Centre for the homeless destitute above the age of 65, had a coverage of 5.74 lakh in 2002.

To facilitate the distribution, there are presently 39 base depots of the FCI in Madhya Pradesh and 179 supply centres of the state Civil Supplies Corporation (SCSC). Number of fair price shops in the state totalled 18,688 at the end of March 2002, 82.3 per cent of which were in rural areas. For the tribal areas, the government started a system of moving fair price shops from April 1999 to strengthen the TPDS. Under it, the essential commodities were reached to the 1,872 weekly hats through the moving transports. In 2002, there were 85 such vehicles, and each served around 12 thousand persons a week. A special system was also introduced in 2000-01 for reaching around 3,179 PD centres, serving 10,600 inaccessible villages. For constructing godowns, there is a scheme of godowns grid.

Consequent on all these measures, the situation improved noticeably in recent years. Percentage of rural hhs reporting consumption of wheat from the PDS in 2004-05 stood at 20.3 and in urban areas at 10.3 as against 11.0 and 5.8 per cent, respectively, at the national level. In rice, however, the situation was very poor. The proportion reporting consumption from PDS was only 17.9 per cent in rural areas and 8.7 in urban areas as against 24.4 and 13.1 per cent in all-India. The relative share of PDS in the consumption was, however, significantly higher here than in all-India in both the commodities. In wheat, for all hhs in rural areas it was 11.97 per cent and for the poor 32.12 as against 7.32 and 28.16 per cent at the national level. In urban areas, the situation was still better. (*ibid.*).

Inefficiencies and Corruption

The government's inefficiencies in running the PDS are a legion. To note just one instance: In 2001-02, the government could lift only 59 per cent of the allotted quota of foodgrains, 5.82 lakh tonnes out of 9.9 lakh, earmarked for the BPL families. The per capita off-take came to only 19.5 kg this year as against the A-I average of 38.5 kg; MP's was the second lowest among the states. Under the scheme of 25 kg per BPL family per month, the monthly off-take came to only 8 kg per family of 5 persons. (*Hindustan Times* 2003: 4).

Corrupt practices in running the PDS were every where. The diversion of PDS foodgrains—percentage of grain offtake from the FCI that did not reach households—came to as much as 46.9 in 1999-2000 against 23.9 per cent at the national level. In recent years, however, it declined noticeably, being at 16.2 per cent in 2007-08. The existence of ghost ration cards in the state was found to be to the extent of 12.58 lakh. There has also been large scale issuance of AAY cards to the rich. (Ahluwalia, MS 2011; GOI 2008b).

Although there are many schemes to help the poor and an abundance of funds, rural poor in general are deprived of basic facilities like healthcare, sanitiation, education, nutrition and means of earning. The main reason is corrupt and insensitive officials and ineffective people's representatives. Since 2003, however, the introduction of gramdoot—a volunteer who works for the village—by the National Institute of Women, Child and Youth Development (NIWCD), a Nagpur-based non-profit organisation, has improved the situation in many villages. Started with only 450 volunteers in four tribal districts of Madhya Pradesh—Dindori, Mandla, Baitul and Chhindwada—the number has now incrased to 10,000 in 1,000 villages in the tribal and rural parts of Maharashtra, Madhrya Pradesh and Chhattisgarh. The gramdoots have now mobilised communities, initiated dialogue with government agencies over rights and livelihood issues, improved the midday meal scheme and services at public health centres, ensured fair identification of beneficiaries under BPL schemes and regularised work and payments under the NREGA. They have also encouraged people, particularly women, to participate in village and panchayat level decision-making. (TST 2012 z75).

Plight of the Tribal Population

The scheduled tribes constitute around a quarter of the state's population (1991), and their living condition in general continues to be distressingly poor. The entire population is divided into 46 groups, some of which are primitive and living in most backward conditions. The proportion of BPL population in STs in 1993-94 stood at as much as 56.7 per cent in rural areas and 65.3 per cent in urban areas; in all-India, it was respectively 51.9 and 41.1 per cent. The literacy rate for them in 1991 was 21.54 per cent, with females at 10.73; both were much below the national average.

An idea about where the STs stood at the beginning of the planning era may be obtained from an NCAER study. The survey found their average annual income varying between Rs. 1132 in Bilaspur and the lowest at Rs. 316 in Raigarh. It was less than Rs. 500 in six of the districts, viz, Betul, Balaghat (East), Raisen (West), Chindwara (North) and Mandla (East), apart from Raigarh. Average indebtedness per capita per indebted household varied between Rs. 1254 in Ratlam and Rs. 28 in Durg. It was above Rs. 100 for 10 districts, out of the 15 studied. The high indebtedness was considerably due to a heavy expenditure on festivals etc., liquor and tobacco. (NCAER 1960: 166, 172, 39).

Even now, after five decades of development efforts, the STs remain deeply poverty stricken. The social position of some of the tribes like the Baigas, Pahari Korbas, Abuj Madias and Birhors is extremely low. They are not even enrolled as voters in most parts. Literacy among the Pahari Korbas is two per cent and non-existent among the Baigas of Kawardha and Bilaspur. Some of the tribes, particularly the Abuj Madias and Baigas, are still cut off from rest of the world due to lack of infrastructure. The Abuj Mad region covers an area of 6,000 sq. km. (Mishra, A 2006).

There are many reasons behind this situation, but the most important one is the government's inaction[1] and continuing exploitation of the tribals by traders and moneylenders who take full advantage of their illiteracy and barter habit. The technique followed is to induce the tribals to borrow from them on terms which are left unsettled and unwritten, and then put pressure on them to part with their property or to incur fresh debts to repay the old ones. The NCAER survey had concluded: "In the course of nearly hundred years of their contact with the tribal areas of the state, they have played havoc, appropriating large chunks of tribal lands and reducing a large number of the tribals to virtual serfdom." A brief look is given below on the situation in Bastar, a district with huge tribal populations.[2]

Bastar has an abundance of forest resources, and the forests are a major source of livelihood for the tribals. They collect a variety of forest produces like, saal-seeds, chironge, tendu leaf, harra, mahua flower/seed, torah, mango kernels, bamboo, gums, etc., and do not pursue other economic activities like poultry or dairying. They almost never go to a 'mandi' to sell goods due to the long distance and the small quantities of FPs collected. Sometimes they walk long distances to reach even a 'haat'. The villagers are generally illiterate and do not clearly understand the currency system, metric measures, and commodity pricing. The dominant features of the major tribes in Bastar, namely, the gonds, the halba, the madia, the muria, dhurva, the dorla, and the bhatra, are their unchanged ways of life. Living in small groups, they have so far somehow stayed away from official development efforts.

In the absence of any organisation of their own, the tribals are subjected to exploitation by the traders on forest produce. The district administration had initiated an 'Imli Andolan' in 1999 to protect the tribals from exploitation and provide a remunerative market largely through administrative directives and official arrangement with the TRIFED. The administration came down heavily on traders to enforce various statutes and to set up alternative marketing system. The provisions of the Krishi Upaj Mandi Act 1972 bar commercial transactions in regulated produce like mahua, tamarind, chironge, baheda, aowanla, honey, etc., outside the precincts of the mandi/up-mandi. Movement of tamarind was closely monitored to control clandestine sales outside the mandi. However, only some 50 cases could be registered for violation of the Act. Actions initiated for checking foul practices in weighment, price and calculation also did not prove much of a success. (Ganguly, B K et al 2003: 2988).

The exploitation by traders still continue, particularly in the haats, numbering 111 in new Bastar. Number of villages covered by a haat varies between the highest of 21 in Narayanpur and the lowest at eight in Kondagaon among the five tehsils. In the haats, small traders, known as 'koochiyas', move from one weekly haat to another, and taking advantage of the innocence of the tribals, buy on their own terms and outwit them in pricing, grading, weighing etc. The magnitude of the exchanges involved and the extent of exploitation is not easily realised. On a typical haat day, a tribal (many among them women) carries a head load of FPs from the village to the haat, sells them and buys her needs for the next week and carries them back home before dusk. This pressure on her time facilitates foul play. Tribals are unaware of the benefits they could derive from transacting with the LAMPS and other organisations. The koochiyas, after buying FPs from a village haat, sell them to the traders at the mandi or up-mandi who stores them (primarily mahua and tamarind) in a cold storage and later, in the lean season, sells them to bigger traders in large cities. The margin of a 'koochiya' is generally 50 per cent and of the mandi-trader as high as 100 per cent. (ibid).

The traders also exploit the tribals as money-lenders. The latter need large sums for fulfilling such obligations as payment of bride price or organising community feast on the death of a family member. This provides an opportunity to the trader to establish his foothold in tribal society by offering loans to the tribals in urgent need of cash. The rates of interest charged are some times as high as 120 per cent annually and often with a lien on the future supply of FPs.

Apart from these problems, there is the unfortunate situation that the tribals who have lived in the forests for centuries, are becoming encroachers in their own land. As the forests got depleted, the tribals had to shift to new locations for survival. In the areas cleared by them for cultivation, they became encroachers in the eyes of the forest department. According to one estimate, the amount of forest land encroached upon between 1956 and 1989 was 1.6 million ha, more than 10 per cent of the state's total forest land. (Baviskar, Amita 1994).

The growth in plan expenditure on the tribals was very low. The utilisation of available fund was very low in some of the areas. On economic upliftment, against a provision of Rs. 140 lakh only Rs. 96.92 lakh could be spent. In the Sixth Plan, the outlay was raised to Rs. 40 crore but only Rs. 29.23 crore were spent, and the relative share declined to 0.74 per cent. In the Eighth Plan, the expenditure came to as much as Rs. 230.42 crore, but the relative share was still only 1.88 per cent.

The state governors were given wide powers under Schedule V of the Constitution to protect the tribals. Agency and excluded areas in central India were termed scheduled areas spread across nine states where, though the executive powers of the state began to prevail, direct supervision came under the Union, with the Governor holding legislative powers therein. In an inversion of the pre-Independence practice, all the laws of Centre and states began to be applied in scheduled areas unless the Governor used his or her discretion to repeal or amend them. Furthermore, the Governor was given wide ranging powers to make any manner of legislations to cater to the needs of particular tribes in scheduled areas. The Constitution makers had expected that the Governors would be sensitive enough to make particular regulations to protect their needs, and save them from money-lenders and non-tribals in the grand total. In the last 60 years, the window offered by Schedule V was shut by Governors. The third report of the Planning Commission's Standing Committee on inter-sectoral issues relating to tribal development (2009d), states: "all laws now cover scheduled areas in routine...there is no realisation that a great damage has been done when general laws first flooded tribal areas in 1950 with no mechanism for their review. It is a continuing problem, which is not even acknowledged : There is a need to stop this practice and to consciously adapt the laws to the scheduled areas." Over the period of six decades, the Governors not even for once used their discretionary powers to withdraw or amend any law in scheduled areas. Their annual reports on scheduled areas to the President, on the basis of which the Union is supposed to give direction on governance, proved useless. The above-mentioned committee has stated: "For more than half a century now, there has not been a single case where the union may have deemed it necessary to issue a direction on any crucial point raised in a governor's report." Along with this short shrift given to schedule V, the Article 339—which requires the President to appoint a scheduled areas and scheduled tribes commission to report on the administration of these areas and welfare of its scheduled tribes—was also grievously violated. The first commission was duly formed in 1960. But in the following four decades, there was no such commission. In 2002, the second commission was constituted, but its report has not still reached the Parliament. As a result, the Centre has no idea about the realities in scheduled areas.

In this situation, it is no surprise that the Bastar region spread over 40,000 sq km area has become the seat of Maoist insurgency in Chhattisgarh, where cadres of the banned CPI-Maoist have run parallel government since late 1980s; up to 25,000 sq km is intensively mined. Trouble broke out after the government signed several MOUs with different companies allowing them to extract minerals since 2003. To implement these MOUs, tribals were being evicted from their land subsequently driving them to revolt. Maoists started paying Rs. 3,000 to each of their cadre as salary and a cut of the extraction money. The extremists extorted money to the tune of Rs. 1,400 crore annually as they operated in mineral rich areas. The situation is so terrifying that the allocated fund of about Rs. 3,000 crore for road construction in the interior could no be invested because no one is ready to partaicipate in tenders for certain projects. Even the Border Roads Organisation has backed out of road projects in Maoist areas. (TST 2010 s, t, z45).

Project Affected People

The displacements by mines and dams without proper rehabilitation also exacerbated the problem of encroachment. Although the MP government's rehabilitation policy, 1987 made it mandatory to provide land-for-land to the project affected adivasi and dalit families, it was often violated. Even if land was provided, it was rarely of the quality from which they were displaced.

Monetary compensations—generally frittered away in different ways—too were not paid properly. Any forced displacement—virtually all uprooting by mega projects is involuntary and brutal—leaves a trail for generations of human suffering, and ultimately a majority of them are compelled to become encroachers for a living. A brief look is given below into how the people displaced by two of the big dams were treated.

The construction of the Gandhi Sagar dam was started in 1954 and completed in 1960. The reservoir, storing 85 per cent of the harnessed Chambal water, is one of the biggest in the country, spread over 225 sq miles. It affected 228 villages in Mandsaur and Neemuch districts. Of these, 59 villages were fully submerged and the rest partially. Number of people displaced by it was counted by the government as 51,514; of which, 31,514 were from fully submerged villages. (Gupta, Ram Pratap 2002). These included only the title holders; many others lost their sources of livelihood.

The lands of the oustees were classified into three categories: the best type was paid Rs. 375 per acre for irrigated land, Rs. 125 for unirrigated and Rs. 90 on fallow land; for medium quality, it was between Rs. 70 and Rs. 350; and on those with low fertility, Rs. 60—325. Most of the submerged land on both sides of the river was very fertile and the price of Rs. 375 for irrigated land was far below the market price. The under-payment in cases where the exact amount of compensation could be calculated were as follows: The amount actually paid on wells was Rs. 20.54 lakh against that due at Rs. 52.88 lakh; on trees, Rs. 1.43 lakh and Rs. 3.90 lakh respectively; and on house sites, Rs. 5.08 lakh and Rs. 16.69 lakh. Thus, on these three types of property together the underpayment was to the extent of 63 per cent. Even of this meagre amount paid to the oustees, a substantial part had gone to the officials as graft. (*ibid.*).

Before ousting the affected people, the government made all sorts of promises about their resettlement and rehabilitation. It was declared that the oustees would be rehabilitated properly and that they would be better-off as a result. The then government of Madhya Bharat declared that, land for land to the cultivators who desired such arrangement would be the policy. It was announced that nearly 26,500 acres of forest land and 25,500 acres of revenue land had been set aside for the displaced persons. Due to such assurances, the displaced persons did not resist being displaced. But once they gave their consent and accepted the compensation, it was declared that much of the land set aside was not suitable for farming; and only 16,000 acres would be distributed among them. Even of this 16,000 acres, the oustees accepted only 12,000, since the remaining land was barren and unsuitable for cultivation. Those who accepted this land, complain that even after 40 years of efforts, they could not make it suitable for cultivation. (*ibid.*).

It was also promised by the government that all civic amenities would be provided at the newly settled villages and partially submerged villages. The amenities promised included : (i) construction of at least one drinking water well for every 500 displaced persons, subject to a minimum of one for every new village; (ii) small storage tanks in the forest area; (iii) provision of amenities as that existed in the submerged villages; and (iv) restoration of communications by constructing roads, bridges, telephone lines. All these promises remained largely unfulfilled. Three hundred public irrigation wells and bawris were submerged in the reservoir, but not a single new public irrigation well was provided in the newly settled villages. Number of tanks submerged was 90, and in place of them only three were constructed and 4 old tanks were repaired. On drinking water wells, against the promise of 104 wells for the 52,000 displaced persons, only 41 were constructed. The submerged settlements had 67 public institutions like schools, dispensaries etc against which only 43 were provided. As regards communication facility, it was reported in 1997 that 18 approach roads involving a total distance of 160 kms and periphery roads of 159 kms still remained to be constructed. That the government had no intention of rehabilitating the displaced people properly, became evident also from the fact that the R & R office was closed down in 1963. The total expenditure on the resettlement and rehabilitation came to only Rs. 64.70 lakh, 3.2 per cent of the total project cost, low by any standard. (ibid.).

The struggle for proper rehabilitation thus did not yield much result. After so much of sufferings by the project affected people at different places, in 2007 the government tried to amend the Land Acquisition Act, 1874 to straighten the R & R policy. But even in 2012 an appropriate Bill was yet to be passed. The Land Acquisition Amendment Bill and the Resettlement and Rehabilitation Bill 2007 were combined into one in 2011 and presented to the Parliament. The Bill continued to have many deficiencies. For example, while providing for compensation, the bill states that these shall apply only when (a) the government acquires the land partly or wholly for a public or private project; and (b) if a private party acquires 100 acres or more on its own. They do not apply when the private player buys the entire tract and if it is less than 100 acres. Thus, the farmers will not get compensation if the land is below 100 acres. This will affect particularly the states where the land-holding of farmers is generally small. In urban areas, the compensation will be twice the market value of land; and for rural areas, not less than six times that value. In view of the spiraling land prices, the compensation should be much higher both in urban and rural areas. A member of a dispossessed family is to be entitled to a job or a one-time compensation of Rs. two lakh. If only one of the two things are to be provided, then the cash compensation should be at least ten times higher. Another deficiency is that the draft defines "public purpose" as strategic projects, related to defence establishments, infrastructure and industries that benefit the people. In UP, the land acquired in the name of public purpose for developing infrastructure was actually given to promoters. Since the promoters had built houses for the public, can this be called a public purpose? The High Court has turned down such an interpretation.

Whatever provisions are made in the legislation to safeguard the interest of the displaced, it is equally important that a foolproof implementation of the provisions are ensured. But in the Bill itself there is scope for a marked degree of flexibility on the ground that local compulsions can differ from state to state. The government's motive itself is suspect on bringing a proper land acquisition legislation at the earliest. Passing of the Bill is already much delayed, and the government will try its utmost to delay it further so that the poor farmers can be deprived of their invaluable asset land as much as possible to benefit the richer section of population. In November 2011, the Supreme Court was compelled to ask the Centre to bring a 'fair, reasonable' Land Act at the earliest. (TST, 2011 z25). There is urgent need to work out a satisfactory package for displaced farmers. But even in the states where good packages have been offered, such as Uttar Pradesh and Gujarat, there are reports of widespread discontent. Therefore, efforts need to be made to minimise the extent of displacement and land acquisition. There is ample scope for this, provided the acquisitions are strictly need-based. Fairly extensive acquisition is taking place to feed the limitless demand for minerals and industrial goods for a global market; and for the production of luxury goods and services. Further, due to the pressure of profiteers and speculators, often the land acquired is much in excess of need.

Finally, with regard to MP and Chhattisgarh, it may be noted that the poor as a whole has very little hope of their situation improving remarkably in near future. The government is contemptuous about the role of popular movements. Any serious challenge to the actions of the state is construed as 'anti-national', 'anti-development' and are ruthlessly suppressed. The repression let loose in the Narmada valley for two and half years against the anti-dam movement were only the tip of the iceberg. A large number of atrocities and repression on people's movements go unreported. The draconian Chhattisgarh Special Public Security Act 2005 allows arbitrary detention of persons suspected of belonging to an unlawful Organisation.[3] The government even began secretly funding and arming a counter-insurgency group called Salwa Judum—to give a respectability to them, they were called Special Police Officers—as a ground clearance force.[4] This instead of containing the conflict exacerbated it and increased the miseries of people.

NOTES

1. What has happened to the Forest (Conservation) Act 1982 may be noted briefly. The Act, as it was originally, had the assurance of reversing the alarming trend of declining forest cover in the country. The populace was asked to believe that restrictions on the commercial utilisation of forests would ensure survival of forest dwellers and wildlife. But soon, considering the needs of the rich and powerful, an appendage—Section 2—was added that obscured the clauses compatible to conservation ideals. This Section renders endless

power to the Union ministry of environment and forests, which includes the right to denotify protected areas for non-forest activities like the setting up of ecologically unsustainable industries, even by private individuals. As per the Act, it is mandatory that prior to the denotification of any protected area, a study on the impact of any proposed industrial activity, on forests and their wildlife, along with dependent human communities, should be undertaken. However, experts are appointed by promoters of such industries to assess the probable impact and prepare an Environmental Management Plan to mitigate adverse impact, if any. (Chaudhury, Kisor 2011).

2. In May 1998, Bastar was divided into three districts: Bastar, Kanker and Dantewada. The new Bastar has 36 per cent of the land in old Bastar and 46 per cent of the households. Percentage of ST population in the new district is 72.

3. A recent example is the detention of Dr. Binayak Sen—a renowned paediatrician and human rights activists. He was detained for two years in jail, beginning from 14 the May, 2007 on the unproven charge of links with the Maoists. He was repeatedly denied bail. (TST 2009v).

4. In July 2011, the Supreme Court declared the deployment of youth as SPOs as illegal and unconstitutional. The Court came down heavily on the government for arming the youths "who have passed only fifth standard and conferring on them the powers of the police." The police remained in the background while the youngsters were positioned as 'canon fodder'. (TST 2011h, z34).

PART IV: THE ECONOMY OF MAHARASHTRA

13

RESOURCE MOBILISATION AND DEVELOPMENT

I: THE GOVERNMENT BUDGET

Maharashtra being a relatively developed state, the resource mobilisation here is expected to be better than in most other states. But as its mode of operation is influenced by Central policies and practices and the vested interests operating within the state, the results may not be much different than in other states. Nonetheless, the raising of resources by the government and its deployment reflect the quality of governance in the state. The questions addressed to here are more or less the same as those in the relevant preceding chapters: Did the government make utmost efforts to raise resources through all possible means? Were the spendings adequately spread out inter-regionally and for the benefit of the poor masses? What was the situation of finances at the level of PRIs and local bodies? How far the state was self-reliant with regard to its finances?

Looking to the last question first, Maharashtra's relative position on the budgetary self-reliance had worsened noticeably in the 'nineties onward. The gross fiscal deficit (GFD) as percentage to GSDP increased from the average of 2.53 in 1990-93 to 4.03 in 1998-01 and 5.08 in 2002-05; the latest was higher than that in All-States by as much as 2.14 points as against lower earlier. The per capita GFD in 2000-03 came to Rs. 1177 as against Rs. 940 for A-S., i.e., the former 125 per cent of the latter. In recent years, the situation worsened further. In 2009-10, the per capita GFD came to Rs. 2,369, which was 138 per cent of that in A-S (Rs 1,699). The ratio of own revenue receipts to own revenue expenditure had declined from 0.836 in 1990-93 to 0.675 in 2000-03; the latest was still the second highest among the states. However, the revenue deficit as percentage to fiscal deficit stood at as much as 75.0 in 2000-03 as against only 62.0 for A-S. As regard the recent situation, in 2009-10, the gross revenue deficit stood at as much a Rs. 8005.7 crore—giving a per capita of Rs. 725; at the level of A-S, it was Rs. 245. A more comprehensive index, based on eight indicators, had declined from 72.80 in 1990-95 to 50.06 in 2000-03; the latest was lower than in three of the states. (CMIE 2006, 2011c; GOI 2004; Dholakia, Archana). A detailed look is given below to the pattern of changes.

Resource Mobilisation

The growth in resource mobilisation was very low in Maharashtra. Between 1975-78 and 2000-03, the total receipts had risen by only 29 times as against 33 times for All-States; the relative share in the latter's total declined from 12.82 per cent to 11.24. The per capita receipt in 2000-03 came to Rs. 4534, which was only 17.4 per cent higher than in A-S as against 37.2 per cent higher earlier. In recent years, the situation worsened further. In 2009-10, the per capita receipt came to Rs. 10,616, which was only 16.7 per cent higher than in A-S.

In the total receipts, the share of revenue account had decline from 77.7 per cent in 1975-78 to 69.0 in 2000-03; the latest was still higher than the A-S average. The per capita receipt was Rs. 3,127 in 2000-03, which was only 23.3 per cent higher than in the latter; in 1975-78, it was 40.9 per cent higher. In recent years, the situation deteriorated further. In 2009-10, although the share of revenue receipts in total receipts increased to 74.1 per cent, the per capita receipt, at Rs. 7,866, was only 16.5 per cent higher than in A-S (Rs. 6,750). The growth in capital receipts was also low. Over the entire period of 1975-78 to 2000-03, it had risen by only 40.1 times as against 46.3 times for A-S; the relative share in the latter's total declining from 11.7 per cent to 10.2. The per capita capital receipts in 2000-03 came to Rs. 1,407, which was only six per cent higher than in A-S. In 2009-10, the situation improved somewhat. The per capita capital receipt came to Rs. 2750, which was 17.0 per cent higher than in A-S.

Revenue Receipts

In the revenue receipts of Maharashtra, the contribution of tax revenue was always much higher than at the level of A-S. In 2000-03, at 78.6 per cent, it was 7.8 points higher, declining from 12.3 points higher in 1975-78. In recent years also it was in a similar position. In 2009-10, with the TR at Rs. 67,354 crore, it constituted 77.5 per cent of total revenue, 3.3 points higher than in A-S. The per capita tax revenue came to Rs. 2,458 in 2000-03 and Rs. 6,096 in 2009-10. These were, respectively, 37.0 per cent and 31.5 per cent higher than in A-S; in 1975-78, it was higher by 57.0 per cent. On the NTR, the growth was very low; between 1988-91 and 2000-03, it was by only 198 per cent as against 297 per cent for A-S. The contribution of NTR in total revenue was always below that in A-S. The per capita NTR in 2009-10 came to only Rs. 1,770 here as against Rs. 2,113 in A-S.

Tax Revenue

In the tax revenue, the proportion of own revenue had risen noticeably over the years; to 89.5 per cent in 2000-03 from 83.3 in 1988-91 and 77.4 in 1975-78. The latest was 18 points higher than at the level of A-S as against only 7.3 points higher in 1975-78. The proportion rose further to 87.8 per cent in 2009-10; at the level of A-S, it was 69.5 per cent. The per capita OTR in 2000-03 came to Rs. 2,200, which was 72 per cent higher than in A-S (1,281); in 2009-10, however, at Rs. 5,349, it was higher by only 65.9 per cent.

As regards the composition of the OTR, the highest amount always came from taxes on commodities and services, as in every other state. Its contribution had, however, declined from 91.5 per cent in 1975-78 to 89.7 in 1988-91 and 83.7 in 1997-00; at the level of All-States, the latest was 88.7 per cent. Naturally, the contribution from other groups were low. Taxes on property and capital transactions, coming next, had provided 12.4 per cent in 1997-00, rising from 6.0 per cent in 1975-78; for A-S, the latest was 9.73 per cent. The growth in collection over the entire period was by 47 times, more than double that for total OTR. The collection from taxes on income had also risen rapidly, but still its relative share was only 3.87 per cent, rising from 2.51 in 1975-78.

There has been considerable diversification in the intra-group composition. In the taxes on commodities and services, although the sales tax continued to provide the lion's share—as much as 69.8 per cent in 1997-00—within it the share of state sales tax had declined from 65.3 per cent in 1975-78 to 61.9, and of central sales tax from 24.4 to 16.2 per cent. On the other hand, the share of tax on motor spirit and lubricants was nearly quadrupled—rising from 5.89 to 20.7 per cent. The contribution from state excise had also risen from 6.84 to 13.9 per cent. For all other items, the relative share was very small. Taxes on vehicles had provided only 5.55 per cent in 1997-00. In the taxes on property etc, stamp and registration fees were almost the sole contributor; its share rising to 93.2 per cent in 1997-00 from 59.2 in 1975-78. The only other item in the group, land revenue, had a rise of only 7.9 times over the entire period, and the relative share declined to 6.81 per cent from as much as 40.8; for A-S, the latest was 12.02 per cent.

As regards the situation in recent years, in 2002-05, the contribution of taxes on commodities and services declined further to 81.5 per cent, with the amount annually averaging Rs. 21357.1 crore. Within it, the state sales tax provided 44.1 per cent, the central sales tax 10.14, and the state excise also a similar proportion; the taxes on vehicles provided 5.19 per cent, goods and passengers 1.41 and duties on electricity 5.39 per cent. The taxes on property etc provided an average of Rs. 3800.4 crore in this period, and raised the relative share to 14.51 per cent. Within it, the share of stamp and registration fees declined to 90.3 per cent. (CMIE 2006a).

Non-Tax Revenue

In the NTR, the proportion of own collection had declined sharply over the years; from 83.2 per cent in 1975-78 to 69.3 in 1988-91 and further to 65.3 in 2002-05. However, it continued to be much higher than at the level of A-S. The per capita ONTR came to Rs. 403 in 2002-05 as against Rs. 383 for A-S (based on 2003-04 population)—i.e., the former 5.2 per cent higher. Earlier, in 1988-91, the state's was 90 per cent higher than in A-S.

The composition of the ONTR changed noticeably over the years. The relative share of economic services declined from 55.8 per cent in 1975-78 to 42.6 in 1988-91 and then to 37.8 in 1997. Even the latest was much higher than at the level of A-S; the latter's had declined from 52.0 per cent to 19.0. In recent years, the relative share increased to 45.0 per cent in 2002-05, which was nominally higher than in A-S. In economic services, the contribution from forestry etc. had a sharp fall; to only 9.79 per cent in 1997-00 from 21.7 in 1988-91 and 24.0 in 1975-78. Industries which had contributed only 2.54 per cent even in 1988-91, became the highest contributor in 1997, with 18.8 per cent. Power projects came next with 5.26 per cent in 1997-00, declining from 8.26 in 1988-91. The irrigation projects, with substantial investment, provided only 3.49 per cent in 1997.

Among other groups, interest receipts had a rapid rise. With a 30-fold growth, its share rose to 45.5 per cent in 1997-00 from 19.4 in 1975-78; for A-S also the latest was 45.7 per cent. In recent years, however, its contribution declined to only 23.6 per cent in 2002-05. The most distressing situation was in the receipts from dividend and profit; providing a negligible 0.17 per cent in 1997, declining from 1.19 in 1975-78. In 2002-05, it provided 0.39 per cent. More recently, in 2009-10, the per capita collection from it came to Rs. 7.32, nominally higher than in A-S.

The collection from general services was also not good. Over the period of two-and-half decades, between 1975-78 and 1997, it had risen by only 10.3 times and the relative share declined to 9.28 per cent from 11.4. In 2002-05, however, there was a noticeable recovery; rising to 22.0 per cent, with the collection averaging Rs. 895.6 crore. Even the latest was below the A-S average, being 24.3 per cent. A substantial portion of the collection here came from state lotteries. The situation of social services was much worse. The relative share had declined from 12.1 per cent in 1975-78 to 7.26 in 1997; even the latest was, however, double that in A-S. In recent years also there was no noticeable recovery. During 2002-05, it contributed 9.01 per cent. In 2009-10, however, the per capita collection came to Rs. 97 in Maharashtra as against the A-S average of Rs. 78. In social services, the highest contributor was medical, public health, etc.; the relative share declining from 37.9 per cent in 1988-91 to 31.1 in 1997-00. The collection from education, etc., was extremely low, and the relative share declined from 22.4 per cent to 11.3 over the period. (*ibid;* CMIE 2011c).

Capital Receipts

The capital receipts in Maharashtra had a rapid rise particularly in the last one decade or so. Between 1975-78 and 1997, it had multiplied 27.6 times, which was lower than in A-S. But in the longer period till 2002-05, it was by 73.1 times as against 63.0 times in the latter. The state's share in A-S total was 13.6 per cent in 2002-05, with the amount at Rs. 24,768 crore. The per capita receipt came to

Rs. 2,460 as against Rs. 1,740 for A-S, i.e., the former 41.4 per cent higher. In 2009-10, however, with Rs. 2,750, it was only 17 per cent higher—the latter's being Rs. 2,350. Earlier, in 1988-91, it was respectively Rs. 286 and Rs. 244. In the state's total budgetary receipts, capital receipts constituted 41.1 per cent in 2002-05, rising from 29.5 in 1997-00, in 2009-10, however, it was only 25.8 per cent.

The composition of capital receipts changed noticeably over the years. The loans and advances from the Centre constituted a very high proportion until recent years; rising to as much as 47.7 per cent in 1997 from 31.6 in 1988-991, but in 2002-05 it was only 5.40 per cent; at the level of All-States, the latest was 15.1 per cent. In recent years also it was relatively low. The per capita in 2009-10 came to Rs. 68 as against the A-S average of Rs. 87. The loans were largely for non-plan purpose, being to the extent of 77.1 per cent in 1997-00. In the total loans, the state plan schemes constituted only 22.5 per cent in 1997-00, declining from 46.1 in 1975-78.

The internal debt came next, and its relative share rose to as much as 23.6 per cent in 2002-05, from 9.48 in 1997-00. At the level of A-S, however, it was still higher; rising from 19.4 per cent to 36.3 in this period. In internal debt, market loans had the dominating share; being at 75.4 per cent in 1997-00, rising from 65.0 in 1988-91. The contribution from recovery of loans and advances had a sharp fall; declining from 20.6 per cent in 1975-78 to only 2.54 in 1997-00, and then recovered to 4.03 per cent in 2002-05; for A-S, the latest was 5.37 per cent. The role of small savings etc was also very low. Of the three time points considered, the highest reached was 10.9 per cent in 1997-00; even this was much below the A-S average, being 14.4 per cent. (*ibid.*).

Consequent on this pattern of mobilising capital resources, the debt burden of Maharashtra increased noticeably. Between March 1981 and 2003, it was by 29.1 times, which was higher than in all but two of the states. The per capita debt, however, remained low; at Rs. 6568 in 2003, it was substantially below the A-S average. The debt as percentage to GSDP increased noticeably, but was still below the A-S average. During 2003-07, it averaged 32.0, rising from 27.3 in 1999-03 and at 12.7 in 1980-81; the latest at the level of A-S was 40.2.

As regards the composition of the debt, while the share of Central debt declined sharply, that of internal debt soared.

Trend in Expenditure

The expenditure situation of Maharashtra government worsened considerably over the years. The per capita total expenditure in 2000-03 averaged Rs. 4,544, which was only 20.6 per cent higher than in A-S; in 1975-78, it was higher by 36.6 per cent. In recent years, it worsened further. In 2009-10, the per capita came to Rs. 10,628, which was only 18.7 per cent higher (for A-S, Rs. 8,952). The growth in TE was by only 29.2 times between 1975-78 and 2000-03 as against 32.3 times in the latter. Furthermore, in the total, the proportion of developmental had declined from 66.2 per cent in 1988-91 to 56.9 in 1998-01; the latest was below that in A-S. As percentage to GSDP, the development expenditure constituted only 9.3 in 2006-07 as against 12.0 in A-S. The state in recent years was spending about 81 per cent of its revenue on salaries, allowances, travel and tour of ministers. (RBI 2009; CMIE 2011c; TST 2012 z98).

Between revenue and capital expenditure, the proportion of the former had risen fast, to as much as 88.1 per cent in 2000-03, from 68.1 in 1975-78; at the level of A-S, it was from 67.3 to 81.9 per cent. The per capita revenue expenditure in 2000-03 came to Rs. 3,959 as against Rs. 3,027 in the latter—i.e., the former 30.8 per cent higher. In recent years, the situation worsened somewhat. In 2009-10, Maharashtra's per capita stood at Rs. 8,590, which was only 22.8 per cent higher than in A-S (Ra 6,995). In capital disbursements, the state's situation was much worse. The per capita disbursement in 2000-03 came to only Rs. 537 as against Rs. 670 in A-S. The capital disbursements, however, fluctuated widely from year to year; and the per capita in 2002-05 was 25.6 per cent higher than in A-S, being respectively Rs. 1547 and Rs. 1232. In recent years, in 2009-10 again the state's per capita was nominally higher, being at Rs. 2,038 as against Rs. 1,957 in A-S. The low expenditure in 2000-03 was largely because a large portion of the capital receipts went to meet the revenue deficit, to the extent of 62.2 per cent as against the A-S average of 41.5. The changes in the composition of revenue and capital expenditures are looked into below.

Revenue Expenditure

In the revenue expenditure, the proportion of developmental had declined to 59.2 per cent in 1997-00 from 70.0 in 1988-91; for All-States, it was from 68.3 per cent to 59.4. The growth in development expenditure over the 12-year period was by only 185 per cent as against 215 per cent in A-S. In the development expenditure, social services always accounted for the highest proportion, and increased from 56.1 per cent in 1975-78 to 63.3 per cent in 1997. The per capita expenditure on it came to Rs. 1106 in 1997-00, which was 26.5 per cent higher than in A-S (Rs 874). In recent years, the relative position improved further. In 2002-05, the per capita came to Rs. 1,581, nearly double that in A-S (Rs. 823). In 2009-10, however, at Rs. 3711, it was higher by only 36.5 per cent—the amount for A-S being Rs. 2719.

In social services, the share education was generally more than half, and stood at 59.2 per cent In 2002-05; at the level of A-S, it was 76.0 per cent. The per capita expenditure came to Rs. 945, which was 51.2 per cent higher than in the latter; earlier, in 1997-00, it was higher by 34.1 per cent; the amount being respectively Rs. 660 and Rs. 492. The expenditure on medical etc was much lower. The per capita in 2002-05 was Rs. 161.42, rising from Rs. 136 in 1997-00; at the level of A-S, it was from Rs. 134 to Rs. 138. All the other items in social services naturally had very low shares. Water supply, etc., despite its high importance, received only 7.22 per cent in 1997-00, rising from 6.72 in 1988-91.

The per capita expenditure was, however, relatively high. In 1997, it came to Rs. 79.85 as against Rs. 54.10 in A-S, i.e., the former 47.6 per cent higher. In recent years, it improved further; being 60.1 per cent higher in 2002-05, with the amount at Rs. 95 and Rs. 59, respectively. On the welfare of SC. etc., the per capita expenditure came to Rs. 106.39 in 2002-05 as against Rs. 75.10 in A-S. More recently, in 2009-10, the situation of per capita expenditure in these items stood at follows: education, etc. Rs. 2010 as against Rs. 1334 in A-S—i.e., the former 50.7 per cent higher; on medical, etc., Rs. 297—nominally higher than in A-S (Rs. 296); on water supply, etc., it was only Rs. 64 as against Rs. 93 in A-S; and on the welfare of SC, etc., Rs. 375 and Rs. 181, respectively—i.e., the former more than double the latter. On family welfare, the per capita expenditure came to only Rs. 37 as against Rs. 48 in A-S.

In economic services, the growth in expenditure was very low and the relative share declined from 48.9 per cent in 1988-91 to 36.7 in 1997. The per capita expenditure on it came to Rs. 791 in 2002-05, which was only 7.5 per cent higher than in A-S (Rs 736). In 2009-10, however, at Rs. 1844, it was 25.4 per cent higher. In economic services, the share of agriculture, etc., had a sharp fall, from 65.5 per cent in 1975-78 to only 35.0 in 1988-91; in the following years, after rising to 40.5 per cent in 1997, it fell back to 35.7 in 2002-05. At the level of A-S, however, the proportions were much lower. The per capita expenditure on it was always higher than at the level of A-S. In 2009-10, at Rs. 585, it was higher by 52.7 per cent—the amount for the latter being Rs. 383.

In agriculture etc., dairy development received a high importance here; the relative share had declined from 47.0 per cent in 1975-78 to 31.5 in 2002-05. In the A-S total expenditure on it, Maharashtra's share came to as much as 79.1 per cent in 2002-05. For animal husbandry, however, the expenditure was not high. The per capita in 2009-10 came to only Rs. 42.54, nominally higher than in A-S (Rs. 42.24). The expenditure on crop husbandry had a significant growth; and the relative share rose to 19.3 per cent in 2002-05, from 14.4 per cent in 1997. Soil and water conservation had a noticeable growth in expenditure till 1997-00, but in the following years it declined sharply. The per capita in 2009-10 was only Rs. 2.35 as against Rs. 16 at the level of A-S. Forestry and wildlife also had a similar pattern, and the relative share stood at only 11.3 per cent in 2005. The per capita expenditure in 2009-10 was Rs. 67.25, nominally higher than in A-S (Rs. 66.24). On fisheries also the state spent only Rs. 10 this year, the same as in A-S.

The next important item in economic services was irrigation and flood control, and its relative share rose to 30.9 per cent in 1997 from 16.6 in 1975-78. In recent years, however, the expenditure had a sharp fall. The average for 2002-05 came to only Rs. 994 crore and constituted 57 per cent of that in 1997-00. The per capita expenditure declined to Rs. 98.74 from Rs. 198.06. In recent years, there was a significant improvement. The per capita in 2009-10 came to Rs. 212, which was 15.8 per cent higher than at the level of A-S. As regards rural development, the proportion going to it increased to 21.8 per cent in 2002-05, from 16.8 in 1988-91. The per capita expenditure in 2002-05 came to Rs. 172 as against Rs. 123.33 in A-S. In 2009-10, however, it was below the latter's—being respectively Rs. 183 and Rs. 246. The state also spent a substantial sum under rural employment, a new head created recently. In 2002-05, the expenditure on it averaged Rs. 989 crore, and constituted as much as a third of the All-States total.

Of the remaining items, transport etc and energy were important. The former had a 27-fold rise in expenditure between 1975-78 and 1997-00, and the relative share rose to 6.49 per cent, from 4.83. The per capita expenditure which is higher than the A-S average for most items, was lower here. In 2002-05, it came to Rs. 48.97 and Rs. 76.87, respectively. In 2009-10, however, at Rs. 292, it was higher by as much as 51.3 per cent. On energy also the pattern was similar very The per capita in 2002-05 was only Rs. 136 as against Rs. 205 in A-S. But in 2009-10, it was, respectively, Rs. 375 and Rs. 277—i.e., the former 35.4 per cent higher. (*ibid.*).

As regards non-development expenditure, it had a rapid rise over the years. Between 1975-78 and 1997-00, it was by 27.2 times, and the relative share rose to 39.6 per cent from 36.9; for A-S, the latest was 40.6 per cent. The per capita expenditure, however, came to as much as Rs. 1169 in 1997-00 as against Rs. 857 in the latter. In the N-D expenditure, interest payment had a rapid growth, and the relative share rose to 37.0 per cent in 1997, from 18.0 in 1975-78; at the level of A-S, however, the latest was as much as 42.8 per cent. In recent years, the expenditure on it increased further, and the per capita in 2009-10 became Rs. 1277 as against the A-S average of Rs. 992. In the interest payments, central government accounted for the lion's share.

Next came administrative services, with 25.0 per cent of total N-D expenditure in 1997-00, declining from 32.8 in 1988-91; at the level of A-S, the latest was 23.3 per cent. The per capita expenditure on it came to Rs. 292 in 1997, which was 36.4 per cent higher than in A-S. In 2002-05, at Rs. 342, it was 26.2 per cent higher than in the latter. In 2009-10 also it was similarly placed, with the amount at Rs. 740 and Rs. 587, respectively. In administrative services, police accounted for as much as 55.4 per cent in 1997; at the level of A-S, however, it was still higher, being 60.9 per cent. The per capita expenditure came to, respectively, Rs. 162 and Rs. 130—i.e., the former 24.6 per cent higher. In recent years it improved somewhat. At Rs. 190 in 2002-05, it was 13.1 per cent higher than in A-S (Rs. 168). In 2009-10, the per capita increased to Rs. 427 as against Rs. 355 in A-S. On district administration, the expenditure was very high here. The per capita in 1997-00 came to as much as Rs. 51 as against Rs. 21 in A-S. In recent years, the disparity widened further; being at Rs. 87 and 28, respectively in 2002-05, and Rs. 190 and 57 in 2009-10.

Among other items, payment on pension had a rapid growth, and the relative share rose to 11.5 per cent in 1997-00 from 5.35 in 1975-78; at the level of A-S, however, the latest was as much as 22.5 per cent. The per capita expenditure in 1997 came to Rs. 131 as against Rs. 179 for A-S; in 2002-05, it was respectively, Rs. 266 and Rs. 319; and in 2009-10 at Rs. 555 and Rs. 714. On the fiscal services, the state was spending a very large amount. The per capita in 1997 came to Rs. 218 as against Rs. 62 for A-S. In 2002-05, it was still worse; being respectively Rs. 458 and Rs. 98.

The last category in revenue expenditure, compensation and assignments to LBs and PRIs, also had a rapid growth, but the amount remained small. With a 60.7-fold rise over the 25-year period, its share rose to only 1.13 per cent of total in 1997. The per capita expenditure in 1997 came to only Rs. 33.28 as against Rs. 39.09 in All-States. In 2002-05, however, the situation improved noticeably. With the expenditure averaging Rs. 999 crore, the relative share rose to 2.23 per cent as against 1.89 in A-S. The per capita expenditure came to Rs. 99.24, which was 49 per cent higher than the A-S average (Rs. 66.57). In recent years, however, the situation worsened sharply. The per capita expenditure in 2009-10 came to only Rs. 37.66 as against Rs. 177.51 for A-S.

Capital Expenditure

In the capital disbursements, the proportion of developmental increased noticeably over the years. With a 17.3-fold rise between 1975-78 and 1997, its share rose to 54.9 per cent from 40.0; at the level of A-S, the latest was 48.7 per cent. The per capita development expenditure came to Rs. 376 in 1997-00, which was 54.9 per cent higher than in A-S. In the development expenditure, economic services always accounted for the overwhelming proportion. In 1997, it was to the extent of 92.2 per cent compared with 82.6 in A-S. The per capita expenditure in 1997 came to Rs. 354, which was 76.5 per cent higher than in the latter. In recent years, however, the situation worsened. In 2002-05, it was only 58.8 per cent higher, the amount being respectively, Rs. 808 and Rs. 509.

In economic services, the most important item was irrigation etc, accounting for 48.4 per cent of total in 1997, declining from 64.7 in 1988-91. In 2002-05, however, it increased to 59.9 per cent. The per capita expenditure was generally higher than in A-S. In 2009-10, it came to Rs. 726 as against Rs. 356 in the latter. The next important item was transport, etc., with a share of 25.8 per cent in 1997, rising from 14.5 in 1988-91. In 2002-05, however, it was only 9.46 per cent; and the per capita expenditure came to Rs. 76.38 as against Rs. 87.61 in A-S. In recent years, in 2009-10, the per capita was only Rs. 295 as against Rs. 328 in the latter. Agriculture, etc., was in a relatively good position. In 2002-05, the per capita expenditure came to Rs. 124.96, which was nearly five times the A-S average (Rs 26.88). All other items had very low level of expenditures. In energy, despite a significant growth, the relative share came to only 8.88 per cent in 1997; in 2002-05, however, it increased to 24.4 per cent. The per capita expenditure remained low. In 2009-10, it was only Rs. 181 as against Rs. 199 in A-S.

The expenditure on social services was very low. The per capita in 2002-05 came to only Rs. 46.12 as against Rs. 115.69 in A-S. Among the different items under it, the per capita expenditure in the latest period was higher than in A-S only in medical and public health and in welfare of SC, etc. In the former, it was respectively Rs. 11.49 and Rs. 9.23, and in the latter at Rs. 8.41 and Rs. 7.74. In education, etc., Maharashtra had only Rs. 2.88 as against Rs. 7.66 in A-S.

Of the remaining groups, the highest proportion generally went for loans and advances, although it declined from 39.7 per cent in 1975-78 to 29.7 in 1997-00. The proportion of these loans going for development purposes had declined from 95.8 per cent in 1988-91 to 53.4 in 1997. In the development loans, economic services accounted for the lion's share; declining from 84.9 per cent to 71.3 over the period. Most of it were for power projects and cooperation. In social services, housing accounted for around half. Loans for non-development purposes had a rapid rise, and constituted 46.6 per cent in 1997; at the level of A-S, it was only 13.1 per cent. The repayment of loans to the Centre fluctuated considerably. It constituted 12.1 per cent of total in 1997, declining from 14.0 in 1988-91, but in 2002-05 it jumped to 39.3 per cent; at the level of A-S, the latest was 37.2 per cent. In recent years, it declined again. In 2009-10, the per capita expenditure on it came to only Rs. 39 as against Rs. 86 in A-S. The payment on discharge of internal debt had risen from 2.15 per cent of total in 1997 to 4.83 in 2002-05.

Plan Expenditure

The plan expenditure in Maharashtra was quite high, but it was not in keeping with its economic strength. The per capita expenditure was always below 3-4. In relation to the A-S average, at the highest it was 44.6 per cent higher in the Sixth Plan and the lowest at 9.47 per cent higher in the Ninth Plan (outlay). For the entire period of 46 years, 1951-52 to 1996-97, the per capita plan expenditure here came to Rs. 8984, which was 21.1 per cent higher than in A-S; and among the major states, it was lower than in four.

As regards the sectoral pattern of expenditure, the relative share of agriculture etc had a sharp fall over the years. In the last three plans, Eighth to Tenth, it averaged only 5.69 per cent as against 17.1 in the Third through Fifth plans. For all the plans together, it cam to 6.1 per cent. Irrigation and flood control had the highest of 29.8 per cent in the Ninth plan and the lowest at 14.9 in the Third plan, with the average for all plans at 24.4 per cent. On power/energy, the average for all the plans came to 16.5 per cent, with the highest at 28.2 in the Fourth plan and the lowest at 3.94 in the next plan. The share of transport and communication varied between 9.27 per cent in the Ninth plan and the lowest at 5.30 in the Seventh, with average for all the plans at 8.02.

Industry and minerals always had the lowest share. Rural development received an average of 10.1 per cent. In social services as a whole, the average was 23.8 per cent, and varied between the highest of 28.9 per cent in the Tenth Plan and the lowest at 16.1 in the Fifth Plan.

Local Bodies

Panchayat Raj Institutions

The reform in the PRIs, following the 73rd Amendment of the constitution in 1993 was relatively good. The devolution of powers and responsibilities was substantial. A devolution index prepared by the IIPA gave Maharashtra 61.49 in 2009 as against the national average of 45.04 and Kerala's at as much as 74.73. Maharashtra's rank among the states was fifth. Component-wise, the devolution was very poor with regard to functionaries; the index being at 44.17 here as against the highest of 61.25 in Keral, with the national average at 37.40. (GOI 2011a). Maharashtra has 5,264 Gram panchayats, 314 Mandal parishads and 30 Zilla parishads. Below a brief look is given to the revenue situation and pattern of expenditure of the PRIs in Maharashtra.

The Revenue Situation

In the resource mobilisation by the PRIs in Maharashtra, the situation of village panchayats was not good. Between 1984-85 and 1997-98, the total revenue had risen by 12.5 times—from Rs. 4084 lakh to Rs. 51146 lakh. On per capita basis, it was by 9.6 times, from Rs. 6.05 to Rs. 57.94. As regards the relative position among the states, in the A-S total revenue from gram panchayats, Maharashtra's share came to only 9.38 per cent in 1997-98, rising from 8.86 in 1990-91. The per capita collection in 1995-98 came to Rs. 87.10, which was 15.6 per cent higher than in A-S. For all tiers together, the situation was much better. In 1997-98, the state accounted for 17.09 per cent of A-S total, rising from 15.80 in 1990-91. The per capita in 1995-98 was Rs. 597.58, more than double that in A-S.

In the total revenue, the proportion of own revenue was very low. For all tiers together, it was only 3.3 per cent in 1990-91 and 3.4 in 1997-98; both were below the A-S average. At the village level also the situation was not good. Although the proportion increased from 18.4 per cent in 1990-91 to 20.6 in 1997-98, the average for 1995-98 came to only 5.7 per cent; in all-States, it was as much as 12.4 per cent. The per capita own revenue was, however, much higher here. For all-tiers combined, it came to Rs. 19.59 in 1995-98 as against Rs. 9.66 in A-S; at the village level, it was respectively Rs. 18.11 and Rs. 8.07. In recent years, the situation improved further. During 2000-03, for all tiers it was more than three times that in A-S, being respectively Rs. 68.94 and Rs. 19.80.

As regards the composition of own revenue, at the village level, own tax had provided an average of 71.6 per cent in 1995-98 as against 62.5 per cent in A-S. The per capita collection was more than double that in A-S, being respectively Rs. 13 and Rs. 5. The growth in tax revenue between 1990-1 and 1997-8 was by 214 per cent as against only 47.8 per cent in A-S. The situation of ONTR was much worse. The growth over the period was by 280 and 141 per cent, respectively. Its contribution to own revenue was only 28.4 per cent in 1995-98 as against 37.5 in A-S.

For all-tiers together, the contribution of own tax had averaged 70.9 per cent in 1995-98, declining from 73.2 in 1990-93; at the level of A-S, the latest was only 56.2 per cent. The growth over the period was very high, and in the A-S total tax revenue, Maharashtra's share increased from 13.5 per cent to 19.7. The per capital tax revenue in 1995-98 came to Rs. 13.90, which was 156 per cent higher than in A-S. In recent years, the situation improved further. In 2000-03, it was more than four times the latter's, being respectively Rs. 48.07 and Rs. 10.98. The non-tax revenue also increased fast, and Maharashtra's share in the A-S total rose to 10.35 per cent in 1995-98 from 6.76 in 1990-93. The contribution to the state's OR, however, stood at only 29.1 per cent in 1995-98 as against 43.8 at the level of A-S. The per capita ONTR was still higher than in the latter; being respectively Rs. 5.69 and Rs. 4.25 in this period. Transfers to the PRIs were also high; at the per capita of Rs. 816 in 2002-03, it was three times that in A-S.

Expenditure

The situation of expenditure was naturally good. In 1995-98, the per capita expenditure for all tiers together came to Rs. 807, which was 189 per cent higher than in all-states. Earlier, in 1990-93, at Rs. 372, it was 179 per cent higher. The scope for raising the expenditure further, particularly at the village level, was however, not low. There was often a substantial surplus in revenue account at the village level. In 1995-98, it was to the extent of Rs. 20.84 crore as against Rs. 16.77 crore in all-States. In the other tiers, however, there were huge deficits. For all tiers combined, the deficit came to as much as Rs. 1015.89 crore in 1995-98, constituting 26.0 per cent of total expenditure.

The potential of raising the resources further was not low, as evident from a look at the district-wise variation in resource raising. At the village level, in 1985-86, the per capita collection of taxes and fees was at the highest Rs. 8.33 in Raigad as against the lowest of 47 paise in Osmanabad—i.e., the former 17.7 times the latter—with Rs. 4.05 at the state level. The variation in total income was also not low. The per capita this year was at the highest Rs. 22.11 in Jalgaon and the lowest at Rs. 3.60 in Osmanabad, with the state average at Rs. 14.51.

Even the income raised, remained hugely unspent in many of the districts. Only one district, Dhule, had a small deficit of Rs. 1.62 lakh in 1985-86; for most others, there were substantial surpluses. In Jalna, the expenditure was only 40 per cent of its income—being respectively Rs. 37.55 lakh and Rs. 93.68 lakh; the per capita expenditure came to only Rs. 4.27. The lowest expenditure was in Osmanabad, a per capita of Rs. 2.60 as against the state average of Rs. 10.58;

the income could be utilised to the extent of only 72.4 per cent here. The district with the highest per capita, Jalgaon (Rs 17.66), also had unutilised income to the extent of 20.1 per cent. In the preceding year, 1984-85, also the situation was similar. The expenditure was below the income in all but two of the districts—Amravati and Parbhani. The shortfall was very high in some of the districts. Beed could utilise its income to the extent of only 34.7 per cent; and the per capita expenditure came to Rs. 2.84. (GOM 1990).

Urban Local Bodies

Revenue

The ULBs' performance in resource mobilisation deteriorated noticeably in recent years. The per capita own revenue in 2002-03 was only Rs. 247, around half that in 1998-99. In relation to the all-States' average, Maharashtra's was 80.3 per cent higher in 1998-99 but in 2002-03 it was 5 per cent lower. The proportion of expenditure finance by own revenue had declined from 73.01 per cent to 49.7; at the level of A-S, the latest was 52.6 per cent. Earlier, in 1990-93, the situation was significantly better; own revenue had constituted 90.2 per cent of total revenue as against 69.6 per cent in A-S. The per capita own revenue came to as much as Rs. 569 as against Rs. 152 in the latter.

In the own revenue, own tax had contributed 83.3 per cent in 1995-98, rising from 73.8 in 1990-93. The per capita OTR in 1998-99 stood at Rs. 360, which was 97 per cent higher than in A-S. Earlier, in 1990-91, the situation was still better; the per capita being respectively Rs. 136.30 and Rs. 22.87—i.e., the former around six times higher. The worsening of the situation continued in recent years also. In 2002-03, Maharashtra's per capita OT was only 19.8 per cent higher than in A-S. On the ONTR, the state's position was very good. The per capita increased from Rs. 49.54 in 1990-91 to Rs. 134.11 in 1998-99; both were more than five times the A-S average—respectively Rs. 9.47 to Rs. 25.15.

The transfers to ULBs were relatively low in Maharashtra. The per capita transfer in 2002-03 came to Rs. 114.69 as against Rs. 152.10 in A-S. Including the transfers to PRIs, however, it was as much as Rs. 318.57 as against Rs. 238.04 in A-S. Transfers as percentage to the state revenue stood at 16.87 in 2002-03 as against the A-S average of 8.96.

A more detailed look into the ULBs' resource mobilisation may be given with reference to 2000-01. This year, out of the total receipts at Rs. 8685.25 crore, rates, taxes, etc., had contributed 48.6 per cent, followed by other income 25.6, government grants 14.43, deposits and loans 9.24 and commercial enterprises 2.14 per cent. In the total receipts, the share of municipal corporations was as much as 82.2 per cent, followed by municipal councils 16.9 per cent and the rest by cantonment boards. In the total for municipal councils, the share of A class was 45.3 per cent.

As regards the category-wise source of resources, in corporations, the share of rates, taxes etc was 55.06 per cent and in councils only 17.90 per cent.

Government grants had provided only 6.74 per cent of total in corporations as against 52.0 per cent in councils. Deposits and loans provided 8.03 per cent in corporations as against 14.9 per cent in councils; and commercial enterprises 2.30 and 0.50 per cent, respectively. The other income had provide as much as 27.9 per cent in corporations compared with only 14.6 per cent in councils.

Expenditure

The expenditures of the ULBs in Maharashtra increased noticeably over the years, ignoring the year to year fluctuations. Between 1990-91 and 1997-98, it had risen by 765 per cent, from Rs. 11,986.6 crore to Rs. 103,659.8 crore; the growth, however, came only during 1995-98. The per capita expenditure in 1995-98 came to Rs. 16924, which was 282 per cent higher than in A-S; in 1990-93, it was 164 per cent higher—the amount being respectively Rs. 3113 and Rs. 1177. The expenditures were far higher than their revenues. The average deficit during 1995-98 came to Rs. 47408.1 crore, the highest among the states and 57.7 per cent of the total for all-States.

In the expenditure, a high proportion generally went for core services. During 1995-98, it was to the extent of 75.5 per cent as against 57.8 per cent at the level of A-S; Maharashtra's was the highest among the states. The expenditure had multiplied 9.4 times between 1990-93 and 1995-98, from Rs. 4,162.8 crore to Rs. 39,042.0 crore. In the expenditure on core services, water supply accounted for the highest proportion, followed by drainage and sewerage. In 2000-01, for example, it was respectively 10.4 and 6.73 per cent. Most of these went to corporations. The street lighting received 2.36 per cent, and 79.2 per cent of it was by corporations. (GOM 2002).

II: THE BANKING SYSTEM

Co-operative Credit Institutions

The co-operative credit system in Maharashtra has been quite strong on the whole. Taking all the societies together, their total working capital had multiplied 36.6 times between 1960-61 and 1990-91; in 1999, however, there was an absolute fall. The working capital per society increased from Rs. 0.97 lakh in 1960-61 to Rs. 14.81 lakh in 1980-81 and Rs. 177.79 lakh in 1999-00, i.e., by 183 times over the entire period. In the total working capital, however, the share of PACS—critically important for rural areas—declined from 26.0 per cent in 1960-61 to 14.8 in 1980-81 and 7.8 in 1999-00; the growth over the entire period was by 99 times—from Rs. 5,812 crore to Rs. 575,303 crore. In total membership also their share declined from 65.1 per cent to 34.4. The gain was for PNACS; their share in working capital rising from 20.6 per cent in 1960-61 to 46.0 in 1999-00, with a 740-fold rise in the amount—from Rs. 4,593 crore to Rs. 3400,686 crore. The share in membership had risen from 32.6 per cent to 61.1. (GOM 2002).

As regards the lending activities, the loans outstanding for all societies together had multiplied 13.5 times in the first two decades and by 19.6 times in the following two; the amount rising from Rs. 16,687 crore in 1960-61 to Rs. 4406,515 crore in 1999. The share of PACS in the total had, however, declined from 28.7 per cent in 1960-61 to 17.0 in 1980-81 and 9.49 in 1999; the growth over the entire period being by only 87 times. The apex body's share had also declined, while the PNACS made a huge gain. The latter's share rose to 47.3 per cent in 1999 from 19.1 in 1960-61, with a 654-fold rise in the amount outstanding. (ibid.).

The relative position of Maharashtra among the states was quite good. For all types of societies together, the state's share in all-India total number increased from 12.7 per cent in 1970 to 28.4 per cent in 1998. On the membership of societies, however, the situation was not so good. The state's share had risen from 11.9 per cent to 18.8 over the period. The membership per society was very low. Despite this, the position of working capital was very good. Maharashtra accounted for 28.8 per cent of all-India total in 1998, rising from 23.5 in 1970. The situation of working capital per society had, however, worsened.

On deposit mobilisation, the co-operatives' performance was very good. The relative share in working capital had risen from 29.2 per cent in 1970 to 63.2 in 1998; at the national level, the latest was 50.9 per cent. In the A-I total deposit, the state's share rose to 35.7 per cent in 1998, from 28.4 in 1970. The deposit per society was the highest among the states. The situation of paid-up capital was also good, although the relative position had worsened.

Primary Agricultural Credit Societies

The performance of PACS in Maharashtra has not been good. The growth in number of societies was negligible. Even then, however, the state's relative share in A-I total increased from 12.3 per cent in 1970 to 21.5 in 1998. The accessibility to the PACS was apparently good. Average number of villages covered by a society was only two as against seven in all-India. In terms of operational holdings, per million numbers, Maharashtra had 379 PACS compared with 121 in the latter. The membership of the societies was, however, very low. Per society, it averaged only 536 in 1998, less than half that in all-India. In recent years, the situation was worse.

It was largely because of this, the situation of working capital was not good. The state's share in all-India total working capital declined from 20.1 per cent in 1970 to 13.3 in 1982 and in the following years also it was around the same level. The amount per society came to only Rs. 20.14 lakh in 1998, which was 63.5 per cent of all-India's. In recent years also the situation was similar; at Rs. 43 lakh in 2005, it was 62.3 per cent. The PACs were a miserable failure in mobilising deposits. Deposits' share in working capital declined from 2.19 per cent in 1970 to 1.33 in 1998; at the national level, it increased from 6.80 per cent to 21.05. The deposit per society in 1998 stood at only Rs. 26.8 thousand, a mere 4.01 per cent of A-I average. In recent years, it worsened further. The reliance on borrowings for working capital was very heavy. The relative share stood at 69.6 per cent in 1998 as against only 46.0 per cent at the national level. In 2005, it increased further to 77.3 and 53.4 per cent, respectively. In the A-I total borrowings by PACS, however, the state's share declined from 20.7 per cent in 1998 to 17.5 in 2005.

The lending activities remained very low. The loans outstanding had risen by only 20.6 times between 1970 and 1998 as against 26.3 times for all-India. The amount per society in 1998 came to only Rs. 14.49 lakh, which was 72.7 per cent of A-I average. In 2005 also it remained below the latter's. An important reason behind this situation was low loan recovery. Loans overdue as percentage to demand increased from 39.5 in 1998 to 43.2 in 2005; at the national level, the latest was 33.6.

Non-Agricultural Credit Societies

On PNACS, Maharashtra's position was the best among the states. The state accounted for 45.2 per cent of all-India total number of societies in 1998, rising from 18.9 in 1970. In membership, the situation was still better; being 55.1 per cent of A-I total in 1998, rising from 26.3 in 1982. The average membership per society had, however, declined sharply. On working capital, the situation was very good. The state's share in A-I total increased from 38.0 per cent in 1982 to 58.8 in 1998. The amount per society in 1998 was 30.3 per cent higher than in all-India. In the working capital, however, the share of deposits was very low. This year, at 30.9 per cent, it was lower than in all but Andhra among the selected states. The deposit per society was, however, still the second highest.

As regards lending activities, the total loans outstanding in 1998 constituted as much as 57.3 per cent of all-India total, rising from 39.5 in 1982 and 28.0 in 1970. The amount outstanding per society came to Rs. 23.90 lakh in 1998, which was 26.8 per cent higher than the national average and second highest among the states. The proportion of loans overdue had, however, risen rapidly, from 1.7 per cent in 1982 to 8.7 in 1998.

Commercial Banks

The commercial banks played a significant role in Maharashtra in mobilising deposits and deploying credit. The state's share in all-India total deposit mobilised by the SCBs stood at 26.35 per cent in March 2010, rising from 17.7 in 1993; earlier, in December 1971, however, it was 23.3 per cent. The per capita deposit in 2010 came to Rs. 1,07,280, which was 179 per cent higher than in all-India; in 1993, it was 143 per cent higher, and in 1971 at 153 per cent higher. The rural situation was, however, extremely poor. In the total deposit, the rural share came to only 1.94 per cent in 2010, declining from 2.21 in 2006 and 3.25 in

2003; for rural India, the fall was from 13.8 per cent to 9.2 over the period. The per capita deposit in 2003 came to only Rs. 852, half the national average. The rural deposit per office in Maharashtra stood at Rs. 10.75 crore in 2010 as against Rs. 13.01 crore in rural India.

On credit deployment, the situation was much better. The state accounted for 32.8 per cent of all-India total credit in 2006, rising from 24.4 in 1983. The per capita credit in 2006 was as much as Rs. 48,669, three-and-half times the national average; in 1983, it was only 166.2 per cent higher. In recent years, the relative position worsened. In 2010, at Rs. 81,324, it was 193 per cent higher than All-India's. The C-D ratio here averaged as much as 93.2 per cent in 2000-03 as against 59.4 at the national level. In 2006, it reached 102.2 and 72.4 per cent, respectively. The credit to GDP ratio stood at 58.3 per cent in 2002 as against 28.5 per cent for All-India. (ibid.).

The rural situation, as in rural deposit, was, however, very poor. In the state's total credit deployment, the rural share declined to 1.95 per cent in 2006 from 3.7 in 1993; at the national level, it was from 14.1 per cent tc 8.33. In the *A*-I total of rural credit, Maharashtra's share came to only 9.71 per cent in 2003, rising from 6.51 in 1993. The rural C-D ratio was much below that for rural-urban combined; and it declined from 71.5 per cent in 1977 to 62.1 in 1999 and then increased to 88.1 in 2003 and 90.4 in 2006. In the credit deployment in Maharashtra the small borrowers were largely neglected. In 2006, they accounted for only 5.8 per cent of total as against 16.4 at the national level.

Regional Rural Banks

It was not only that the SCBs had a distressingly poor performance in rural areas, the RRBs also played only a nominal role here. Number of RRB offices itself was very low. In the all-India total number, the state's share declined to 3.83 per cent in 2010 per cent from 4.04 in 2004. The deposit mobilisation was extremely low. At the end of March 2010, the amount outstanding stood at Rs. 4,109 crore and constituted only 2.89 per cent of A-I total; earlier, in 1981, it was still lower, being only 1.66 per cent. The deposit per office had risen from Rs. 2.73 crore in 2004 to Rs. 6.88 crore in 2010; both were much below the A-I average. The situation of credit deployment was also similar. In the all-India total credit outstanding with RRBs, the state's share increased from 2.03 per cent in 1981 to 3.47 in 2002, but declined again to 2.77 in 2006; the latest was second lowest among the states. The outstanding per branch in 2006 was only Rs. 175 lakh as against Rs. 251 lakh in all-India. The C-D ratio had a sharp fall over the years.

The efficiency level of the RRBs continued to be very low. The recovery as percentage to demand stood at only 69 in 2001, which was below the national average. Earlier, in 1987, at 78.1 per cent, it was 3.6 points higher than in the latter. Non-performing assets constituted as much as 17 per cent in 2002, higher than in five of the states. There was virtually no follow up of credit; and this was despite the banks being overstaffed. The business per staff came to only Rs. 8.84 lakh in 1989, which was lower than in all but two of the states. Salary and allowances to the staff, however, constituted as much as 35.34 per cent of total expenditure compared with 30.36 per cent in all-India. In recent years, there was further deterioration. The business per employee in 2002 was only Rs. 77 lakh, lowest among the states.

Among the RRBs in the state, the performance varied widely. In March 2002, the C-D ratio was only 12 per cent in Thane GB as against 93 per cent in Solapur GB, with the average for all banks (numbering 10) at 52. The recovery as percentage to demand varied between 60 in Thane and 76 in Buldhana GB. The business per employee also varied similarly. It was only Rs. 60 lakh in Marathwada GB as against Rs. 101 lakh in Buldhana. The accumulated losses, at the end of March 2002, was as much as Rs. 53.42 crore in Marathwada GB, constituting 46.4 per cent of the total for all banks. Earlier, in 1989, however, the variations were much higher. Recovery as percentage to demand was at the highest 78.47 in Thane GB as against the lowest of 22.26 in Akola, with the state average at 40.08. The C-D ratio was only 11.0 per cent in Thane while the highest was 253.3 in Nanded, with the state average at 132.3. The volume of business per staff varied between only Rs. 1.46 lakh in Buldhana as against the highest of Rs. 11.02 lakh in Aurangabad-Jalna, with Rs. 8.84 lakh at the state level. (NABARD 2003, 1990).

14

HUMAN RESOURCE DEVELOPMENT: EDUCATION AND HEALTH

Educational Situation

In the overall background of the Indian context, the educational situation in Maharashtra has been quite good, as noted earlier in Chapter two. After three decades of efforts, in 1981, the proportion literate here became the second highest among the major states. The gap with the most literate state Kerala, however, remained wide. The percentage literate in 2001 being respectively 76.88 and 90.86. Even in 2004, 31.4 per cent of rural persons (seven years and above) were not literate, with females at 42.1 per cent. At higher levels, the situation was much worse. This year, only 14.3 per cent of rural persons were with secondary and above, with females at 9.6; these were respectively 2.8 and 2.1 points higher than at the national level. Even the proportion with middle school complete was only 20.8 per cent for persons and 18.6 for females. Around a decade earlier, in 1995-96, percentage of persons, aged 15 years and above, with secondary and above constituted only 24.2, with rural areas at 14.0; for females, it was only 7.2 per cent. District-wise, there was great variation in the situation. In 1991, the literacy rate in rural areas varied between the highest of 74.8 per cent in Sindhudurg and the lowest at 40.2 in Gadchiroli, with the state average at 55.52. There were seven districts with the proportion at below 50 per cent while 11 had above 60. On the females, the disparity was much higher. The highest was 65.7 per cent in the same Sindhudurg and the lowest at 21.9 in Jalna, with the state average at 41.0; six districts had below 30. The situation for rural-urban combined has been noted in Chapter two.

Social group-wise, the STs were in a worse position than the SCs. In 1991, the proportion of STs literate varied between the highest of 64.62 per cent in Sindhudurg and the lowest at 23.71 in Dhule, with 36.79 at the state level; four districts had below 30 per cent. For SCs, the variation was significantly less. In the same year, the highest was 71.05 per cent in Nagpur and the lowest at 35.94 in Jalna, with the state average at 56.46.

Schooling Facilities

On the number of schools, the relative position of Maharashtra among the states worsened noticeably in recent years. In 2005, at the primary level, the state's share in all-India total number of schools stood at only 5.43 per cent, declining from 9.31 in 2000-01. Percentage of rural population with a primary school in the habitation stood at only 73.3 in 1994, which was below that in five of the states. On middle/senior basic schools, the coverage was only 61.1 per cent. Percentage of villages without an MS stood at 56.5 this year. The state's share in A-I total number declined to 9.57 per cent in 2005, from 11.7 in 2000-01 and 13.1 in 1980-81. On secondary schools, the situation continued to be very good. The share in A-I total number stood at 12.3 per cent in 2005, declining from 13.3 in 2000-01.

As regards the management-wise distribution of schools, at the Primary and Middle levels, local bodies accounted for the overwhelming proportion, respectively 88.60 and 85 per cent in 2004-05; at the national level, it was only 46.87 and 29.24 per cent. In the other two stages, private aided schools predominated; accounting for 63.12 per cent in High schools and 86.48 at HS level as against only 28.52 and 31.04 per cent respectively in all-India. The proportion under government management was a negligible 2.60 per cent in High schools and 2.38 in HSS compared with 31.66 and 36.08 in all-India. At the Primary and Middle levels, it was still lower; being respectively 0.40 and 1.00 per cent. Private schools were relatively high only in High schools, accounting for 29.19 per cent of total, nominally higher than in all-India. In Higher secondary, it constituted only 7.14 per cent, less than a quarter of that in all-India. At the Primary and Middle levels, the proportion was only five per cent in each. (GOI 2007a).

Number of rooms in the schools was very low. At the primary level, percentage with two rooms or less was as much as 72.5 in 1994, which was higher than in most of the states. Number of schools with no room for instruction was also high. In recent years also the situation was not good. In 2005, the proportion with single classroom was as much as 9.2 per cent. At upper primary, however, the situation was not so bad. Average number of rooms per school came to 5.6 in 1994, which was higher than in most of the states. On other physical facilities also the situation was not good. Drinking water was available in only 53.5 per cent of the primary schools in 1994, which was lower than in five of the states. At upper primary also it was similar. The urinal facility in the schools was extremely poor. Only 24.5 per cent of the primary schools had it this year. At upper primary, with 51.8 per cent coverage, it was lower than in all but three of the states. Separate urinal for girls was there in only 33.7 per cent of schools. The situation of lavatory facility was much worse. Even the quality of school building was not good in Maharashtra. In recent years also the situation was not good. In 2005, the drinking water facility covered 79.7 per cent of elementary schools, the common toilets covered 51.9 per cent and girls' toilets 43.2 per cent. (*ibid.*).

On the availability of teachers, on the whole, the situation was not bad. The pupil-teacher ratio at primary level declined from 39 in 1980-81 to 35 in

2000-01; the latest was 8 points below the A-I average. At the middle and high school levels, however, the ratio was higher than in the latter. After four years, in 2004-05, while the situation at primary level improved further, in the other two stages it continued to be worse than in All-India. Average number of teachers per elementary school became 5.8, but at the same time the proportion of single teacher school stood at 8.0 per cent. Among the teachers, number of females was very high. In 2004-05, per 100 males, there were 153 females as against only 64 in all-India. Maharashtra's situation continued to be far from satisfactory. In 2007-08, percentage of government elementary schools without head master was as much as 64.15. (*ibid.*; The Statesman 2009a).

The enrolment situation was quite good here. At the primary level, for girls the GER increased from 56.6 per cent in 1960-61 to 97.5 in 1979-80 and then to 107.8 in 2000-01. At upper primary, girls' ratio increased from 15.5 per cent in 1960-61 to 33.7 in 1979-80 and then to 80.5 in 2000-01; the latest was 30.6 points higher than in All-India. In recent years, it improved further to 110.4 per cent at the primary level in 2004-05 and at upper primary 98.1. At the secondary and higher secondary stage also the state was in a very good position. At 55.6 per cent for boys and girls combined in 2004-05, it was 15.7 points higher than in all-India. The attendance was also similarly placed. The net attendance ratio at the primary level stood at 85 per cent in rural areas in 1995-96, which was the highest among the states. For females also it was similar. At upper primary, however, the NAR was only 49 per cent. Taking all the stages together, percentage of persons aged 5-24 not attending any educational institution stood at only 41.6 in rural Maharashtra as against 53.9 in rural India; for females, it was respectively 46.9 and 61.9.

The drop-out rate in Maharashtra declined noticeably over the years. The provision of incentives for attracting students to schools were, however, not good. On the provision of mid-day meal, the situation was very poor. The coverage in 1995-96 was only 10.7 per cent of all students as against 17.9 in all-India. After five years, in 2000-01, the primary students were provided only 3 kg. of rice per month. The state's performance in implementing the Sarva Shiksha Abhiyan—introduced in 2001-02 for expediting the universalisation of elementary education—was very poor. The Educational Development Index, based on 22 variables, gave Maharashtra the 12th rank in 2005-06, among all the states and UTs. (GOI 2007b).

Inter-district, the provision of facilities varied considerably. Number of educational institutions per lakh population in 1998-99 was at the highest 326 in Gadchiroli and the lowest at 35 in G. Mumbai, with the state average at 133; six districts had below 100. This variation was, however, largely due to the difference in topographical features. Earlier the variation was much less. In 1987-88, the highest number per lakh population was only 141 and the lowest at 37, in the same districts respectively, with 94 at the state level; 14 districts had below 100. (GOM 1991, 2003).

The variation in pupil-teacher ratio was also significant. In 1987-88, at the primary stage, the highest was 50 in Jalna and the lowest at 26 in Sindhudurg, with the state average at 38; 13 districts had 40 or more. After around a decade, in 1998-99, while the highest was the same 50 per teacher, the lowest declined to 21, in the same districts respectively, with 39 for the state. On secondary schools, the variation increased considerably over the years. In 1987-88, the highest was 34 in two districts, Chandrapur and Wardha, and the lowest at 27 in Satara and Sindhudurg, with 32 at the state level. In 1998-99, the highest was 44 in Bhandara and the lowest at 27 in Sindhudurg, with 35 for the state.

Behind the non-enrolment, the NFHS-1998-99 found the most important reason to be 'not interested in studies' for males, and 'costs too high' for females; the proportion reporting these were respectively 23.9 per cent and 16.8 per cent. For females, 'required for household work' came next with 14.9 per cent. On the dropping out of school, 'not interested in studies' accounted for 39.7 per cent in case of males, and 21.6 per cent in females. The next reason for males was 'required for outside work for payment in cash or kind', and for females 'education not considered necessary'. Repeated failures was also an important reason for males, and 'got married' for females.

Adult Education

The adult illiteracy was quite high in Maharashtra. In 1981, the state had 73.49 lakh illiterates in the age-group 15-35. Under the National Literacy Mission (NLM), launched in May 1988, Maharashtra targeted to remove illiteracy in this age-group by 2000. The Seventh five-year plan provided for an outlay of Rs. 22.62 crore but only Rs. 12.56 crore could be spent. Even with this level of expenditure, however, the physical target was overreached; the coverage came to 24.37 lakh against the target of 20.5 lakh. The quality of work was probably very poor. By March 1998, total number made literate under the Total Literacy Campaign came to 53.99 lakh, out of 68.90 lakh adult illiterates in the state; the number enrolled was 64.69 lakh. (GOM 2002: 204). The situation of the post literacy programme was much worse. By this date, it could be completed in only 19 of the districts, out of 35.

The relative position of Maharashtra among the states was not bad. Total number made literate by March 1998 came to 8.4 per cent of A-I total, which was lower than in three of the states. The proportion under the TLC was only 65.1 per cent, lower than in most of the states. Phase-wise, the achievement on literacy was 59.4 per cent of the target, highest among the states. In relation to enrolment, it was 67.0 per cent compared with 54.3 per cent in all-India. In post-literacy, the achievement in relation to target came to 75.1 per cent, far higher than in any other state.

In recent years, the adult education programme has been considerably expanded, as noted in Chapter 4. The Tenth Plan (2002-07) revised the policy, and increased the scope of continuing education programme. The CECs are now expected to provide area-specific, need-based opportunities for basic literacy, upgradation of literary skills, pursuit of alternative educational programmes, vocational skills and also to promote social and occupational development. The State Literacy Mission Authority has been suitably strengthened for this purpose.

Higher Education

On the post-school level of education, Maharashtra's performance was quite good. Number of institutions had risen from 211 in 1960-61 to 739 in 1980-81 and 1541 (excluding medical and engineering) in 1999-00, i.e., a 7.3-fold rise over the entire period. The growth in enrolment in this period was 8.4 times, from 1.10 lakh to 9.28 lakh. The relative position among the states was not bad. In recent years also the situation was quite good. In 2003-04, per lakh population (18-23 years), there were 16.59 institutions as against 12.17 in All-India. (GOI 2006b).

Stage-wise, number of institutions offering diploma/certificate courses in Maharashtra in 1980-81 constituted 15.1 per cent of all-India total, which was the highest among the states. Among the institutions, general education predominated; numbering 147, it constituted 39.2 per cent of total. Engineering etc accounted for only 27.7 per cent of total compared with 35.7 per cent at the national level. On enrolment, the state's share in A-I total this year came to 14.1 per cent, higher than in all but West Bengal. In the distribution among different streams, education accounted for 21.5 per cent and engineering 50.5; at the national level, it was respectively 16.70 and 57.5 per cent.

On degree standard and above, the number of institutions was quite low. In 1980-81, Maharashtra accounted for only 9.8 per cent of A-I total. The situation of enrolment was, however, much better; being 14.06 per cent, and highest among the states. In the distribution among different streams, general education accounted for as much as 69.1 per cent of total number as against 56.4 per cent at the national level. In the A-I total number, the state's share was 12.0 per cent. In the enrolment this year, general education accounted for 86.8 per cent, higher than in five of the states.

The situation of professional education was also on the whole very good. In medicine, in the A-I total enrolment, Maharashtra accounted for 15.1 per cent in 1980-81, with the share in number of institutes at 12.05. In agriculture and forestry, the state was in the best position; the proportion being respectively 18.3 and 24.6 per cent. In education also the situation was quite good; accounting for 13.4 per cent of A-I total enrolment. The worst position was in engineering etc, having only 10.9 per cent of A-I total enrolment this year.

In the following two decades, Maharashtra's situation improved further. The state's share in all-India total enrolment in polytechnics in 2000-01 stood at as much as 21.2 per cent, much higher than in any other state. The situation of arts and crafts school was still better; the proportion being 28.3 per cent. At the degree level also the state was in a similar position. The total enrolment in engineering, etc., this year constituted 28.7 per cent of A-I total, more than double that in the second highest (Andhra Pradesh). In medical education also the state accounted for 24.4 per cent of A-I total, three times the second highest. In B.Ed./B.T., its share was 27.8 per cent. (*ibid.*).

As regards the recent situation, in 2004-05, Maharashtra accounted for 11.2 per cent of A-I total number of institutions in higher education, which was the third highest among the states. In the total number, general education accounted for 67.6 per cent as against 64.8 per cent in all-India. The GER in higher education stood at 13.24 per cent this year, which was the highest among the states. In the A-I total enrolment, the state's share came to 13.0 per cent. The enrolment in polytechnics had a sharp fall; the relative share in A-I total declined to only 10.5 per cent, with the number at 40,786. At the degree level and above, in engineering etc the state accounted for 19.1 per cent of A-I total this year, and in medicine. etc., at 16.3 per cent; the proportion of girls in the latter was as much as 48.7 per cent as against 34.7 in all-India. In B. ED./ B.T., Maharashtra's share in A-I total enrolment came to only 8.59 per cent, with the share of girls in it at only 29.4 per cent as against 43.8 in all-India. In the enrolment in general education, Arts accounted for as much as 64.9 per cent as against 59.4 in all-India. The P-T ratio in higher education was not high.

Pattern of Expenditure

The expenditure on education in Maharashtra has not been in keeping with its economic status. The proportion of total state budget going for it was generally below the average for All-states. For example, in 1985-86, it was respectively 17.6 and 20.5 per cent; in 1990-91, 19.9 and 21.1; and in 1995-96, 19.3 and 19.6. In recent years, however, it was higher than in the latter; being respectively, 15.80 and 13.26 per cent during 2002-05. On per capita basis, the expenditure was quite high. During 1994-97, at Rs. 119, it was 41.5 per cent higher than in all-states. In 2002-05, it improved further to Rs. 946 and 52.9 per cent. The budgetary revenue expenditure in 2004-05 (Centre/state) came to a per capita of Rs. 1,161 in Maharashtra, which was next only to Kerala.

In terms of pupil at different stages, the expenditure on education in Maharashtra was very low at least till mid-nineties. In elementary education, per pupil expenditure was below several of the states in each of the four time-points considered. In the secondary stage, of the three time-points, it was below the A-S average in two. At the university level also the expenditure was very low, and it declined from Rs. 431 in 1980-81 to Rs. 239 in 1995-96; the latest was only 67.9 per cent of the A-S average. In technical education, the relative position was still worse.

The recurring expenditure on education was, however, relatively high. In 1980-81, it constituted 13.36 per cent of all-India total, which was the highest among the states. The per capita expenditure came to as much as Rs. 73 as against Rs. 50 at the national level; Maharashtra's was higher than in all but Punjab. In the recurring expenditure, salary and allowances to academic staff accounted for the overwhelming bulk, to the extent of 72.4 per cent this year; at the national level, however, it was still higher. Non-teaching staff received a relatively high share here. At 11.7 per cent, it was higher than in most of the states. The worst situation was of stipends, scholarships, etc.; accounting for only 0.91 per cent of the total in 1980-81, less than a third of that at the national level. (GOI 1989).

Stage-wise, the recurring expenditure on higher education in Maharashtra was very high. It accounted for 20.3 per cent of total in 1980-81, which was the highest among the major states. The per capita expenditure came to Rs. 14.88, 69.5 per cent higher than in all-India. In the recurring expenditure, the proportion going for S and A of academic staff was only 55.0 per cent, which was below the national average and among the major states lower than in six. The non-teaching staff received 21.4 per cent, and it was higher than in most of the states. The proportion for stipend etc was only 2.03 per cent, the lowest among the major states.

HEALTH AND FAMILY WELFARE

Health Situation and Measures

The health condition of the people in Maharashtra has been relatively good, as noted earlier briefly in Chapter 2. We may look at some more details here. On the infant/children, the neo-natal mortality rate had declined by only 4.4 points between 1992-93 and 2005-06—from 36.4 per thousand to 32—as against by 9.6 points at the national level, from 48.6 to 39. In fact, in Maharashtra it did not decrease at all after 1998-99, and the relative position worsened. The under-5 mortality, however, had a sharp fall, to only 47 in 2005-06 from 70.3 in 1992-93; the latest was 27 points below the national average. The health condition of the children was, however, not good. The proportion with any anaemia stood at 72 per cent in 2005-06, only seven points below the national average. The under-weight constituted as much as 38 per cent this year, higher than in four of the states. The proportion with acute undernutrition stood at 15 per cent, declining from 21 in 1999; even the latest was higher than in three of the states. The situation of mother's health was also not good. Percentage of ever married women, ages 15-49, with anaemia remained virtually static in the last eight years; and at 48.4 in 2005-06, it was only 6.9 points below the A-I average. The general health condition of the people also does not appear good. In 2004, per 1000 persons, 93 had reported ailments in rural areas and 118 in urban areas as against the national average of 88 and 99, respectively.

There was, however, considerable variation socio-economic category-wise. The neo-natal mortality rate in 1999 was as much as 46.3 in rural areas compared with 24.6 in urban areas. The proportion of acutely under-nourished children (-3SD) in the former was more than double that in the latter, being respectively 22.0 and 10.9 per cent. The child mortality rate was, therefore, 22.1 and 10.3, respectively. Mother's education made a great difference to the situation. For those with middle school complete, the child mortality rate was only 7.7 as against 25.6 for illiterate mothers. The proportion of acutely under-nourished were respectively 14.5 and 25.0 per cent. Religion-wise, the neo-natal mortality was found to be as much as 41.3 in case of Hindus as against 19.3 in Muslims. Social class-wise, the STs had acutely under-nourished children to the extent of 35.4 per cent compared with 15.1 for SCs. (IIPS 2002).

The preventive measures taken were far behind what was necessary. On child health care, the coverage by full immunisation increased from 64.1 per cent in 1992-93 to 78.4 in 1998-99 but in 2005-06 it was only 59; the latest was only 15 points higher than in all-India as against much higher earlier. On the timely complementary feeding of infants, the coverage in 1999 was only 30.8 per cent, below the national average (33.5). On maternal health care also on the whole the situation was not good. Per 1000 women, number availing post-natal care in 2004 was only 609, which was below the national average. Around a decade earlier, in 1995-96, the relative position was better; the proportion registered being 51.8 per cent, nearly double that at the national level. Percentage of births attended by health professionals was also low until recently. The situation of ante-natal care was, however, relatively good.

Family Planning

On birth control, the progress in Maharashtra was not significant until recent years. Till late seventies, the TFR was higher than the national average; in 1971-76, it was respectively 4.86 and 4.45. In the following years also the progress was slow. Between 1990-92 and 2001, it declined from 3.0 to 2.6, that is, by only 0.4 as against by 0.5 at the national level, from 3.7 to 3.2. After four years, in 2005-06, it stood at 2.1, higher than in two of the states. The rural-urban difference in TFR has been substantial.

On the basis of socio-economic-religious criteria, there were noticeable variations. Education-wise, the illiterate women had a TFR of 3.12 in 1999 compared with 2.33 for those with M.S. completed. The mean number of children was 4.27 in the former as against 3.26 in the latter. On the distribution of birth by birth order, the illiterates had 31.3 per cent of the births in 4+ as against 14.7 per cent for those with MSC. The birth interval of 48+ months since the previous birth was found in only 15.4 per cent of births in case of illiterates as against 27.1 per cent in H.S. and above.

Religion-wise, the TFR for Muslims was found to be 3.30 as against 2.45 for Hindus. The mean number of children for them were respectively 4.58 and 3.69. On the birth order, Muslims had 26.3 per cent of births in 4+ while the Hindus only 16.9 per cent. The proportion wanting no more children after two (living children) were respectively 60.1 and 82.8 per cent. The difference on SC/ ST basis was also substantial. The birth interval of 48+ months was found to the extent of 16.5 per cent in the former as against 12.1 per cent in the latter percentage of currently married women who wanted no more children after two was 69.9 for STs as against 79.3 per cent in SCs. (IIPS 2002).

The government's efforts at reducing the birth rate began quite late. The effective couple protection rate due to all methods increased from 34.5 per cent in 1980 to 51.8 in 1985 and then declined to 50.7 in 1998; the latest was higher than the national average by only 5.3 points. The progress in use of contraceptive was very slow. In 1998-99, only 60.9 per cent of the couples were using any contraceptive, around the same as that in 1990. After seven years, in 2005-06, it increased to 66.9 per cent, 10.6 points higher than in all-India. The use of modern permanent methods, however, progressed faster. The cumulative number of sterilisation till March 2001 constituted 13.6 per cent of A-I total. The proportion of eligible couples unsterilised here in March 2004 was 47.8 per cent, the second lowest among the states.

Socio-economic-religious group-wise, there were significant variations in adoption of family planning methods.The mean age for females at effective marriage did not increase significantly in Maharashtra. After rising to 19.7 years in 1991, from 15.8 in 1961, it declined to 19.4 in 1996. Women ages 15-19 already mother/pregnant in 2005-06 was 13.8 per cent, higher than in four of the states. Percentage of women aged 20-24 married before age 18 had declined from 47.7 in 1996 to 38.8 in 2005-06; the latest was higher than in three of the states. This was the situation despite the proportion of illiterate married women being only 23.5 per cent here in 2005-06, lowest among the states.

One reason behind this might be a relatively low exposure to media. In 1992-93, the proportion of ever married women (ages 15-49) exposed to any media was found to be only 42.1 per cent as against 52.7 at the national level. In 1998-99, however, it increased to 79.2 per cent, which was higher than the national average by 19.5 points. The proportion in rural areas not regularly exposed to any media was as much as 43.1 per cent even in 1998-99. For the illiterates as a whole, it was 52.6 per cent this year. Hindu-Muslim difference was also very wide.

The services provided by the FP department were far from satisfactory. The proportion of ever married women's need for FP services satisfied had risen from 70.4 per cent in 1992-93 to 90.4 in 2005-06; but even the latest was lower than in four of the states. Religion-wise, the proportion satisfied in 1999 was only 69.1 per cent in case of Muslims; for the STs also it was only 76.1 per cent. This was despite their demand itself being low. The gap between wanted and actual fertility rate was very high for the illiterates and the Muslims. The former's actual was found to be 3.12 as against the desired 2.10, and for the latter 3.30 and 2.20 respectively. The proportion of ever married women who had at least one visit by a health/ FP worker was very low for certain groups.

For the illiterates, it was only 20.9 per cent as against 31.6 per cent for those with middle school completed. (*ibid.*; IIPS 2002). The quality of care given to sterilisation cases was also very low.

Pattern of Expenditure

Low level of expenditures are mainly responsible for this state of health and family welfare. The per capita revenue expenditure on health etc, stood at the annual average of only Rs. 197 in 1997, which was lower than in three of the states and a mere 14.8 per cent higher than the all-states' average. Earlier, in 1975-78 also it was in a similar position. The growth in expenditure was very low; and the per capita total in 2002-05 came to Rs. 195.05, which was lower than in three of the major states. As regards the distribution over different heads, hospitals and dispensaries naturally accounted for the largest share, although it declined from 38.5 per cent in 1960-61 to 28.3 in 1980-81 and 26.6 in 1992-93. Each of these was substantially below the national average. The per capita expenditure on hospitals and dispensaries was also low. In the latest year it was nominally higher than the national average and in 1980-81 below the latter's. Of the remaining heads, the per capita on national disease programme in 1992-93 came to only Rs. 8.76, which was below that in four of the states although higher than the national average by 20.8 per cent. Earlier, in 1980-81, the situation was much better, being 42.1 per cent higher. The expenditure on MCH was very low until early nineties. On family welfare also the state's expenditure remained low, despite a noticeable growth. The per capita expenditure went below the national average in 1992-93 from higher earlier. The latest was lower than in all but three of the states. The expenditure on medical education was, however, relatively high. The per capita expenditure was higher than the A-I average in each of the three time points, and among the major states higher than in most of them. (*ibid.*).

In recent years, during 2001-04, the revenue expenditure on medical and public health annually averaged Rs. 1570.3 crore, and constituted 11.3 per cent of all-states' total. The per capita came to Rs. 162 as against Rs. 137 for A-S—i.e., the former only 18.5 per cent higher. On family welfare, the state continued to spend a very low amount. The per capita in 2001-04 came to Rs. 17.08 as against Rs. 23.89 in the latter. On water supply and sanitation, it was relatively high; the per capita in this period came to Rs. 73.59, which was 26.6 per cent higher than the A-S average.

Plan-wise, the expenditure on health increased noticeably over the last two decades; rising from Rs. 156.44 crore in the Sixth plan to Rs. 1020 crore in the Ninth. The relative share in the grand total, however, remained low; rising to 2.78 per cent in the Eighth plan from 2.39 in the Sixth, and then declined to 2.21 in the Ninth. It needs to be noted that the actual expenditure often fell short of the proposed outlay. In these four five-year plans, while the Sixth plan overshoot the target by 75 per cent, in the remaining three it fell short; in the Seventh Plan, by as much as 23 per cent.

15

AGRICULTURAL GROWTH AND TRANSFORMATION

The growth in agricultural production is critically important to Maharashtra's economy. The proportion of total workers engaged in agriculture—as cultivators and labourers—constituted as much as 69.91 per cent in 1961, slightly higher than the national level. Out of this total, the proportion of agricultural labourers was as much as 23.80 per cent as against 16.71 in the latter. After a decade, in 1971, it rose to 28.98 and 25.76 per cent respectively. While the proportion of agricultural workers was large, the contribution of agriculture, etc., to the state's domestic product had declined noticeably. During 2003-06, in the GSDP at current prices, it contributed an average of only 12.69 per cent, declining from 18.7 in 1993-96; at the national level, the latest was 19.57 per cent. (CMIE 2008). Below, a detailed look is given to the pattern of growth in agriculture and allied activities over the years.

I. CROP FARMING

Growth in Production

Maharashtra's performance in agricultural production has been very poor. The compound annual growth rate over a period of more than three decades, between 1962-63 and 1994-95, was only 2.29 per cent, which was below the national average and among the selected states. However, sub-period-wise, the growth during 1968-82 was by as much as 4.48 per cent, more than double the national average. The situation worsened noticeably in the following years, and the state's share in A-I total value of agricultural output came to only 8.1 per cent in 1992-95, declining from 9.2 in 1962-65. In 2000-03, however, it increased to 10.0 per cent. The yield per hectare was always much below the national average.

Foodgrains

Food-grains account for the lion's share of the total cropped area in Maharashtra, generally above 60 per cent; in 2005-06, it was 64.5 per cent. The area had risen substantially till early nineties but in the following years it declined. On wheat, the next important crop, the situation was much worse. Among other foodgrains, jowar was the most important. In fact, until recently it had the highest acreage among foodgrains. Bajra also had a large acreage, although it declined sharply over the years. In 2002-05, it averaged 1467 thousand ha, which was 72 per cent of that in 1968-71.

In pulses, arhar was the most important crop in Maharashtra, and it had a noticeable growth in recent years. The area under it increased nominally till early eighties, rising from 634 thousand ha in 1968-71 to 697 thousand in 1980-83. But in 2002-05 it reached 1060 thousand ha, and constituted 29.8 per cent of A-I total. The yield rate also increased from 510 kg in 1968-71 to 669 kg in 2002-05; the latter was higher than the national average whereas the former lower. The growth in production over the entire period was by 121.6 per cent, and reached 709 thousand tonnes in 2002-05. The state's share in A-I production rose to 30.8 per cent from 17.3. The situation of gram was not good. The yield rate had risen by 90 per cent over the entire period till 1997-00, but it remained below the national average.

Non-Foodgrains

The performance in non-foodgrains was significantly better. The areas under them rose to 9597 thousand ha in 2000-03 from 7407 thousand in 1991-92, and the relative share in all-India total increased from 12.27 per cent to 14.88. The growth in production was significantly higher than in food-grains. The index of production (taking 1979-82 = 100) for them averaged 171.5 during 1998-01 as against 124.1 in foodgrains.

Among the crops, the highest acreage was always under cotton, accounting for more than a quarter of total. The growth in production was substantial. In sugarcane, the growth in area was noticeably high; over the entire period of three-and-half decades, it was by 177 per cent. The yield rate, on the other hand, declined in recent years after a substantial rise in early eighties. Despite the fall, in 2000-03 it was 39.5 per cent higher than the A-I average—being respectively 78,601 and 56,344 kg. The growth in production over the entire period was by 228 per cent. In value term, the production averaged Rs. 3979.57 crore in 2000-03, rising from Rs. 2665.66 crore in 1990-93; in the all-India total, the state's share rose to 20.95 per cent from 17.62. In the following three years, the production recorded a sharp fall. At the average of 28,332 thousand tonnes, it was only 11.3 per cent of A-I total. Both the area and the yield rate declined; the former to 423 thousand ha, and the latter to 66229 kg—nominally higher than the A-I average.[1]

In oilseeds, the most important crop in Maharashtra continued to be groundnut, despite a sharp fall in area. In 2000-03, the area under it was only 57.3 per cent of that in 1990-93. The next important oilseed in recent years was sunflower. But both the area and the yield rate had declined. The area in 2000-03, was only 67 per cent of that in 1990-93. The yield rate declined to only 500 kg in 2000-03 as against 536 kg at the national level. In the following three years, 2003-06, the production increased to 158.7 thousand tonnes, and constituted 13.4 per cent of A-I total. This was solely due to the growth in area to 318 thousand ha; the yield rate declining to 489 kg. The situation of safflower worsened noticeably. In oilseeds as a whole, Maharashtra's situation was not good. In the A-I total production in value term, its share increased from 7.29 per cent in 1990-93 to 9.76 in 2000-03. (GOI 2006a).

Among other crops, chillies and onions were important. The area under chillies declined continuously and the yield rate remained very low. In 2003-06, chillies had only 97.4 thousand ha, 62.4 per cent of that in 1968-71.

In fruits and nuts as a whole, the state had a good position. Total area under them stood at 586 thousand ha in 2002-03, which was 15.5 per cent of the national total; in production, the share was 18.6 per cent. The yield rate this year was 14,336 kg, 20 per cent higher than in all-India; in 1998-01, at the average of 16,581 kg, it was 43 per cent higher. In fruits, banana had a noticeable growth. The yield rate in 2000-03 was more than double the national average, being respectively 62,857 and 27,734 kg. The value of output averaged Rs. 988.07 crore, and constituted 18.5 per cent of A-I total. In the following three years, 2003-06, the production averaged 4537 thousand tonnes, and constituted 32.2 per cent of A-I total. The area increased to 72.2 thousand ha and the yield rate to 62,871 kg. In mango, Maharashtra had as much as 434 thousand ha in 2003-06—rising from 152.9 thousand in 1999-02—and constituted 21.9 per cent of A-I total; the relative share in production, however, came to only 5.32 per cent The yield rate had declined to 1461 kg from 3,400 kg; the latest was only a quarter of the A-I average.

In citrus fruits, Maharashtra had a very good position. The area under them increased from the average of 133 thousand ha in 1998-01 to 240 thousand in 2003-06; the latest constituted 33.6 per cent of all-India total.

The highest growth in production was in Mousambi. Cashew nuts made a noticeable progress in Maharashtra. The area under it increased by six times between 1980-83 and 2000-03. The yield rate, although declined in 2000-03, was still higher than the national average by 20.7 per cent. The production increased by as much as 11.2 times over the period. In value term, it had risen from Rs. 33.98 crore in 1990-93 to Rs. 288.91 crore in 2000-03; the state's share in A-I total rising from 6.87 per cent to 26.6. In the following three years, 2003-06, the situation improved further. The production averaged 159 thousand tonnes, and constituted 28.8 per cent of A-I total. The yield rate reached 1014 kg, 47 per cent higher than in all-India. (*ibid*.; GOI 2006a).

In vegetables, roots and tubers, Maharashtra had a very poor situation. In floriculture, Maharashtra's situation was very poor. The value of production (at 1993-94 prices) averaged only Rs. 59.11 crore in 2000-03, and constituted 3.71 per cent of A-I total; a decade earlier, in 1990-93, it was Rs. 30.33 crore and 3.01 per cent.

Land Resource

The reporting area (RA) of the state is relatively good. At 30.758 thousand ha, it constituted 10.05 per cent of all-India total. Land not available for cultivation was also relatively low. It had risen from 9.58 per cent in 1999-00 to 10.17 in 2005-06; at the national level, the latest was 13.92 per cent. Among the selected states, Maharashtra's was the second lowest. The proportion of net area sown was as much as 56.8 per cent in 2005-06, 10.3 points higher than in all-India. The NSA per thousand population declined from 182 ha in 2000-01 to 171 ha in 2005-06; the latest at the national level was 130 ha. The cropping intensity was, however, very low. The GCA as percentage to NSA was only 113 in 2005-06 as against 136 in all-India. The fallow land was quite high. It had risen from 7.29 per cent of the RA in 1973-74 to 8.39 in 2003-04; the latest was higher than in most of the states. The culturable waste land was, however, only 2.89 per cent in 1999-00 as against 4.52 in all-India. The proportion of forest area was also low, declining from 21.5 per cent in 1970-71 to 16.9 in 2003-04; the latest at the national level was 22.8 per cent.

Agro-climatically, Maharashtra is divided into nine zones. Areas with assured and well distributed rainfall are limited, being confined to Konkan and eastern parts of Vidarbha. Large areas of the state, in the eastern parts of the Bombay-Deccan, are frequently affected by famine or scarcity conditions. According to the Fact Finding Committee of 1960, areas liable to chronic scarcity covered 17,006 sq miles, with a population of 34.16 lakh. (GOM 1979).

Although the availability of land for agriculture is relatively good here, great caution is necessary in converting agricultural land to non-agricultural use. Nature takes hundreds of years to create the top soil with fossils and humus for the growth of flora; once it is surrendered to industries, it can neither retain nor regain its fertility.

Land-Holding System

The pattern of land-holding by the farmers, which greatly influences the productivity of land, did not change adequately over the years. The share of bottom 50 per cent of households in land-ownership rose to only 2.63 per cent in 1982 from 1.88 in 1953-54; at the national level, the latest was 3.52 per cent. For the top five per cent, it remained unchanged at 38.95 per cent. The proportion of households owning no land in 1982 was as much as 21.24 per cent, declining from 28.56 in 1953-54; in all-India, it was from 23.09 per cent to 11.33. In recent years also the situation was very poor. In 2003-04, landless hhs. constituted as much as 38.3 per cent as against 31.1 in all-India; Maharashtra's was the second highest. The proportion with large holdings continued to be relatively high. This poor performance was due to the failure to implement the land-ceiling legislation properly. The amount of land declared surplus by September 1999 came to only 752.7 thousand ha, lower than in two of the states. The land distributed was 652.6 thousand ha to 141.4 thousand families;

the latter constituted a mere 2.59 per cent of all-India total. The amount distributed per beneficiary, however, came to as much as 4.62 ha, around five times the national average. In recent years, the situation worsened much. Total number of beneficiaries till June 2005 came to 135.3 thousand—around a fifth of that reached in 1999—and the relative share in A-I total at 2.54 per cent.

The measures to correct the land-holding system came very slowly. The land ceiling Act, Maharashtra Agricultural Lands (Ceiling on Holdings) Act, 1961 came almost a decade after the abolition of intermediary interests. And then, the ceiling was fixed at a very high level. It could be between 18 and 126 acres, depending on the quality of land. Allowance was also made for size of family, subject to an outside limit of twice the ceiling area. The feudal interests, visualising the possibility of more radical measures, carried out all the changes that could save them from loss of land. Changes in ownership were brought by sale, partitions and other methods. (Nanekar, K R 1968: 217).

The ceilings were revised and lowered 13 years after the 1961 Act, in October 1975. Under the new law, by December-end 2001, 2.99 lakh hects of land were declared surplus. Of this surplus, 34.5 hects were given to the Maharashtra State Farming Corp. Ltd., and 2.60 lakh hects to 1.40 lakh landless persons and 75 co-operative farming societies. Rest of the land were not distributed due to being involved in litigations or is uncultivable. In allotting land, backward class landless persons were given preference and 1.06 lakh hects—i.e., 40.8 per cent of the total—went to 71,570 of them. The allottees were given financial assistance at the rate of Rs. 2,500 per hector. Till March 1998, 1.37 lakh allottees were covered. (GOM 2002:172).

The tenancy Acts, implemented between 1957 and 1965, also proved largely ineffective. Bulk of the small tenants were successfully terrorised by the landlords into "voluntarily" surrendering their tenancies. A committee on the impact of land reform in Maharashtra had found that only in one-third of all tenancy cases did the tenant get a part or whole of the land leased in by him. The proportion of the total leased in area passing into the hands of tenants was as low as eight per cent in the former Central Province's districts of the state, 13 per cent in Marathwada, 20 per cent in the non-coastal parts of Western Maharashtra and 33 per cent in the former Berar districts. (Correspondent 1973:I). Till March 2001, the right of ownership was conferred on about 14.92 lakh tenants in respect of 17.36 lakh hects. Every tenant holder was to be provided Khate-Pustika for keeping proper record of his land and keep these updated. Till March 1998, out of 92.59 lakh land-holders, only 73.11 lakh were issued these books.

The tenancy Acts failed to change the tenancy practices or to reduce the insecurity of tenure. Many of those who had continued to be tenants were reduced to the status of labourers. Their security of tenure now depended on the chance element of good relations between them and the landlords. Rents also continued to be exorbitant in spite of the reasonable maxima fixed by the

Tenancy Acts of 1951 and 1958. The latter had fixed it at one-sixth of the gross produce or two to five times the land revenue whichever was less. (Nanekar, KR 1968: 218).

The proportion of tenant holdings in Maharashtra had, however, declined noticeably over the years. In 1991-92, tenant holdings constituted only 6.9 per cent of total, declining from 10.6 in 1981-82. The latest was lower than in all but three of the states. The proportion of area under tenancy became only 5.5 per cent as against 8.3 per cent at the national level. The terms of lease also changed noticeably. The share of produce system accounted for only 20.9 per cent of the holdings in 1991-92, declining from 48.5 in 1981-82, whereas that under the fixed money system increased from 11.0 to 36.2 per cent. At the national level, it was in reverse direction; the proportions in the latest year being respectively 34.4 and 19.0 per cent. The reliability of these data is, however, doubted. Land rich households generally under-report the extent of tenancy. (NSSO 1997; Rawal Vikas 2008).

As regards the size of operational holdings, it is relatively big in Maharashtra. The proportion of marginal holdings had declined from 43.6 per cent in 1991-92 to 40.0 in 1995-96 and then increased to 43.7 in 2000-01; the latest at the national level was as much as 63.2 per cent. In area, the marginal holdings accounted for 13.2 per cent in 2000-01 as against 18.7 in the latter. The proportion of sub-marginal holdings had declined from 28.3 per cent in 1991-92 to 10.4 in 1995-96; at the national level, the latest was 17.2 per cent. The small holdings constituted a large proportion here; being at 29.7 per cent in 2000-01 as against 19.0 in all-India. The related share in area was respectively 25.5 and 20.2 per cent. In 1970-71, small holdings constituted 21.7 per cent, below the national average.

The large holdings had a sharp fall over the years; declining from 8.67 per cent of total in 1970-71 to 3.04 in 1991-92 and only 1.09 in 1995-96. The latest was below the national average as against much higher earlier. The area under them declined to 9.45 per cent from 20.3 in 1991-92. The proportion of medium holdings also dropped from 22.4 per cent in 1970-71 to 8.8 in 1995-96. In recent years, however, their share increased noticeably. In 2000-01, medium and large holdings together accounted for 26.6 per cent of total as against 17.8 in all-India. The relative share in area rose to 61.3 per cent, from 36.7 in 1995-96; the latest was almost equal to the A-I average as against much higher earlier.

On fragmentation of holdings, Maharashtra's situation was relatively good. Number of parcels per holding declined from 3.78 in 1961-62 to 3.04 in 1981-82 as against from 5.66 to 4.04 at the national level. Average area per parcel decreased to 0.98 ha from 1.23 over the period compared with from 0.47 to 0.41 in the latter. After another decade, in 1992, a noticeable improvement came. Number of parcels per holding declined to only 1.8 in Maharashtra and for all-India to 2.2. (Thangaraj, M 1994; NSSO 1997).

Irrigation Facility

The importance of a good irrigation facility in Maharashtra may be realised from the fact that a major part of the state lies in the rain shadow of the Western Ghats with an average rainfall of between 600 and 750 mm. Heavy rains occur only over the Ghats and the coastal districts of Thane, Kolaba and Ratnagiri. The growth in irrigation facility was, however, very low. The net irrigated area had risen from 1072 thousand ha in 1960-61 to 1835 thousand in 1980-81 and 2959 thousand in 2000-01, i.e., by only 176 per cent over the period of four decades. The gross irrigated area had risen by 199 per cent, from 1220 thousand ha to 3647 thousand (GOM 2002). The relative position among the states was extremely poor. The NIA as percentage to NSA increased from 8.0 in 1971-72 to 15.4 in 1991-92, and after another 14 years, in 2005-06, stood at 18.9; at the national level, the latest was 42.4 per cent, rising from 22.6 in 1971-72. Among the major states, Maharashtra's was the lowest coverage. A recent Maharashtra government white paper has brought out that water in reservoirs and dams for irrigation was diverted to industry and urban development leading to drought-like conditions in many parts of rural Maharashtra. Even after spending a whopping Rs. 70,000 crore, the irrigation potential of the state rose by a mere 0.1 per cent. (TST 2012 z97, z98).

The coverage of foodgrains area by irrigation was very low. As regards the source of irrigation water, wells always had the dominating share; rising from 57.1 per cent in 1973-74 to 64.6 in 1999-00 and further to 69.3 in 2005-06; the latest at the national level was only 58.8 per cent. The share of canals had risen from 20.3 per cent in 1973-74 to 35.4 in 2003-04 but declined again to 30.7 in 2005-06; the latest was 5 points higher than the A-I average. The use of pump sets was very low here, and had a sharp fall in recent years.

District-wise, the availability of irrigation facility varied widely. In 1998-99, the gross irrigated area as percentage to GCA varied between the highest of 55.4 in Bhandara and the lowest at 1.0 in Ratnagiri; as many as nine districts had eight per cent or below, with the state average at 16.4. Nearly two decades earlier, in 1980-81, the variation was much less. The highest was 36.7 per cent in the same Bhandara and the lowest at 2.9 in Akola, with 12.1 per cent at the state level; eight districts had less than half the state average. (GOM 1990, 2003)

Naturally, the proportion of area sown more than once remained very low in a large number of districts. In 1998-99, at the lowest it was only 4.2 per cent in Ratnagiri while the highest was 67.7 per cent in Kolhapur, with 24.5 at the state level; seven districts had less than 10 per cent of the area sown more than once. Earlier, in 1984-85, the variation was slightly higher; the highest being 44.4 per cent in Bhandara and the lowest at 2.5 in Yavatmal, with 12.4 per cent at the state level. For 13 districts, the coverage was less than 10 per cent.

Maharashtra's irrigation potential was not high. In major and medium irrigation, it accounted for 7.01 per cent of the national total, and in minor irrigation at 5.96 per cent. The utilisation of the potential was also very slow. In

1969, the potential created was only 8.54 per cent of the ultimate potential as against 15.21 in all-India. After another nearly three decades, in 1997, it reached 56.4 per cent, at par with the A-I average. In minor irrigation also, the development of ground water lagged behind; being at only 37.0 per cent in 2003 as against 41.1 in all-India. The utilisation of the created potential was much worse.

This low level of utilisation caused significant loss to the state, both in terms of production and employment generation. And it was due to a host of problems, some of which arose from the construction phase itself. Irrigation schemes were declared to have been completed for commissioning even when the network of field channels and land leveling work remained incomplete. This inevitably led to concentration of the use of water at the head reaches of the distribution system, which led to adoption of water intensive crops like sugarcane and banana. Subsequently when the work of land leveling and construction of field channels were completed, the users in the head reaches declined to give up their claims on intensive use of irrigation water.

These problems were again largely related to the issues of costs of operation and maintenance of the systems and pricing of water. The revenue realised from sale of water did not even meet the O&M expenditure of the schemes, let alone meeting depreciation charges, etc. To look at the situation in the eighties: Between 1980-81 and 1986-87, total working expenses had risen by more than three times, from Rs. 1088 lakh to Rs. 3436 lakh. More than half of it went for salary and wages, leaving little for actual maintenance work. The gross receipts had, on the other hand, risen by only 45.6 per cent in this period, from Rs. 1021 lakh to Rs. 1487 lakh. In the receipts, the contribution from sale of water decline to only 24.99 per cent in 1986-87 from 52.51 in the preceding year. The proportion of working expenses covered by gross receipts declined from 93.82 per cent in 1980-81 to 43.26 in 1986-87. (GOI 1993a, 1996a). In recent years the situation worsened further. In 2003-04, the gross receipts per ha came to only Rs. 130, declining from Rs. 206 in 1991-92; the working expenses per ha stood at as much as Rs. 3050 in 2003-04.

This widening gap between the receipts and expenditure resulted in the paucity of funds for O&M, and consequent unsatisfactory performance of the irrigation network. The fund shortage was mainly due to low water rates. The low water rates also caused a rapid rise in the irrigation subsidies.

Provision of Inputs

Fertilisers

The use of fertilisers also remained low in Maharashtra. The per hectare consumption in 2001-04 averaged only 71.3 kg., rising from 26.83 kg. in 1980-83 and only 2.41 kg. in 1962-65; each of these was much below the national average—being respectively 90.2, 42.62 and 4.33 kg. The extent of disparity has narrowed considerably in recent years. In 2005-06, at 99.7 kg., it was only

5.8 kg. less than the A-I average. The proportion of average cultivation expenses going for fertiliser/manures is, however, relatively high. In 2002-03, it stood at 26 per cent.

District-wise, the consumption of fertiliser varied greatly. In 2001-02, out of 33 districts, six were in the range of 100-150 kg/ha, 11 with 95-100 kg, 10 districts with 50-75 kg, and six in the range of 25-50 kg. More than a decade-and-a-half earlier, in 1984-85, the highest consumption was 117 kg in Kolhapur and the lowest at four kg in Beed, with the state average at 28 kg; seven districts had below 20 kg while four with above 40 kg. The growth in total consumption between 1984-85 and 2002-03, varied between the highest of 1468 per cent in Beed and the lowest at 43.5 in Dhule, with 184 per cent at the state level. Five districts had below 100 per cent growth, while seven with above 300 per cent. Even after the highest growth, however, Beed had a consumption of only 59.67 kg in 2002-03 as against 77.01 kg at the state level. (based on the GCA of 1994-95). (FAI 1985, 2003).

Behind the low consumption, non-availability of fertilisers, apart from other factors, played an important role. The non-availability was both due to low production and inadequacies in distribution. The production of fertilisers generally fell short of consumption by a wide margin. In 2002-03, for example, there was a deficit of 125.8 thousand tonnes in N and 264.2 thousand in P_2O_5. The capacity utilisation in Maharashtra was very low. In N it was 74.9 per cent this year as against 86.1 at the national level; and in P_2O_5, 58.6 and 70.6 per cent, respectively.

The situation of related infrastructure was also not good. The soil testing facility has been very poor. Total number of S.T. laboratories stood at only 44 in 2000-01, with the analysing capacity at 392.45 thousand number, constituting 4.90 per cent of all-India total. Even this capacity remained unutilised to a large extent. The quality control facility was, however, relatively good. The annual analysing capacity stood at 12,340 in 2002-03, which was 9.86 per cent of A-I total and third highest among the states. Number of fertiliser sale points was also high.

On the use of non-chemical nutrients also the state's situation was not good. The production of rural compost stood at only 16.094 lakh tonnes in 1995-96, a mere 0.71 per cent of A-I total. Smaller states like Punjab and West Bengal produced many times more. It may be noted that the state had a target of producing 10.50 lakh tonnes at the end of Third Plan. (GOI 1961a: 36). The area under green manure was also very low. The average for 1994-97 came to 0.72 lakh ha, a mere 2.33 per cent of A-I total; the state had a target of covering 0.81 lakh ha by March 1966.

Provision of Bank Credit

On the provision of credit to agriculture, the organised sector of banking here did not play the role expected of it. In the all-India total flow to the sector from all agencies, the state's share stood at only 10.4 per cent in 2003-04. The per hectare credit came to only Rs. 915, around 65 per cent of the A-I average. In the aggregate of credit, the highest proportion came from the co-operative sector, although it declining from 63.8 per cent in 1986 to 55.5 in 1996-97 and then rose to 58.4 per cent in 2002-03. The share of SCB declined to 37.2 per cent from 42.7 in 1996-97. At the national level, the SCBs had provided as much as 49.3 per cent in 2002-03 and the Co-operatives only 41.4 per cent. The role of RRBs was insignificant in Maharashtra. In the total flow, its share declined from 2.11 per cent in 1986 to 1.8 in 1996-97, and then rose to 4.44 in 2002-03. Even the latest was less than half that for All-India.

In co-operative credit, the performance of PACS—the most important institution—was far from satisfactory. The growth in credit over the entire period between 1969-70 and 2002-03 was by only 58 times as against 97 times in all-India. The per hectare credit came to Rs. 2527 in 2002-03, which was only 3.52 per cent higher than the A-I average; in 1997-98, it was 31.7 per cent higher. Maharashtra's share in A-I total declined from 15.03 per cent to 13.2. The holding size-wise distribution of credit, however, improved considerably over the years.

The performance of SCBs was very poor until recently. In the all-India total credit outstanding from them, the state's share rose to 10.2 per cent at March-end 1995, from 8.4 in 1980, but declined again to only 7.33 in 2004. As regards the RRBs, their relative position among the states was very poor. Agricultural advances outstanding per hectare came to only Rs. 36.22 in 1989 as against Rs. 92.06 in all-India. In the following years also it remained low. Region-wise, the provision of agricultural credit varied widely. As regards PACS, during 2000-03, the total loans per hectare annually averaged as much as Rs. 1904 in the Western region as against the lowest of Rs. 529 in Vidarbha, with Rs. 1341 at the state level. The crop loans per hectare were respectively Rs. 1351, 421 and 1011.

Marketing Facilities

The marketing facility in Maharashtra has been relatively good. The storage capacity as percentage to total foodgrains production stood at 32.0 in 1993 as against the national average of 21.4; Maharashtra's was higher than in all but three of the states. In the co-operative sector, its capacity in 2003 was 14.2 per cent of A-I total. The cold storage facility was, however, very poor. The state accounted for only 3.83 per cent of A-I total in 2005; in terms of the state's production of fruits and vegetables, it was only 3.1 per cent as against 12.1 per cent at the national level.

The availability of market in Maharashtra was not bad. The number per 100 sq. km. stood at 2.7 in 1993, the third highest among the states. As regards communication facility, the road length had improved noticeably over the years, and stood at 1241 km per 100 sq km in 1999 as against only 768 km for All-

India. In 2002, however, it declined. The road condition was also relatively good; proportion of unsurfaced being half that at the national level. In rural areas, however, the situation was very poor. The availability of goods vehicles was relatively good; the state accounted for 14.0 per cent of A-I total in 2003. The facility of co-operative marketing in the state had risen quite fast. Number of processing societies in the state was much higher. On Maharashtra's relative position among the states, the situation of only the PAMS may be looked into.

Inter-district disparities in availability of marketing facilities were very high. The average area served by a regulated market in 1994-95 varied between the highest of 205.06 sq km in Solapur and the lowest at 2.74 in Ratnagiri. There were 16 districts, out of the total of 30, with above 100 sq km per market. (GOM 2000). On co-operative marketing facility also the variation was high. In 1998-99, average number of members per society was at the highest 3,143 in Yavatmal and the lowest at 25 in Beed, with the state average at 776; 8 of the districts had below 500 members while only four with above 2000. The financial strength of the societies also varied greatly. The owned capital per society in 1998-99 was at the highest Rs. 99.10 lakh in Akola and the lowest at Rs. 33 thousand in Beed, with state average at Rs. 14.06 lakh. There were 13 districts with below Rs. 10 lakh. (GOM 2003).

II: THE ALLIED ACTIVITIES

Animal Husbandry

As in crop farming, in animal husbandry also Maharashtra did not have a good performance. The value of livestock output (at 1993-94 prices) annually averaged only Rs. 7787.32 crore in 2000-03 and constituted 8.69 per cent of A-I total. The growth in output in relation to 1990-93 was by only 43.2 per cent, lower than at the national level. In poultry also the situation was similar. In the A-I total value of egg production, Maharashtra accounted for only 8.73 per cent in 2000-03. In the average monthly income of a farmer hh, animal farming had contributed only 5.85 per cent in 2002-03, which was less than a third of that in Gujarat. (GOI 2006a; NSSO 2006a). A detailed look is given below.

Livestock

The livestock population of Maharashtra had a very low growth. The total number in 2003 stood at only 204.60 lakh, constituting a mere 4.22 per cent of A-I total; in 1992, it was as much as 8.5 per cent, with the number at 174.46 lakh. The growth over the period was by only 17.3 per cent as against 137.1 per cent for All-India. All the categories of livestock are, however, not equally important and the rearing pattern varies considerably from place to place. In 2003, the number of in-milk bovine in rural Maharashtra stood at 30 per 100 households as against 36 in rural India. For ovine, it was respectively 51 and 64, and on poultry 84 and 123. Three decades earlier, in 1971-72, the numbers in these categories were respectively 49, 128 and 137 as against 54, 99 and 101 at the national level. (NSSO 2006b).

Cattle and Buffaloes

As noted in the preceding chapter, cattle are kept both for work and milk production. The proportion used for work only stood at 37.0 per cent in 1992, declining from 40.0 in 1961; at the national level, the fall was sharper, 40.4 to 26.9 per cent. The growth of cattle population as a whole was not high here. Between 1972 and 1992 it was by 62.6 per cent, nominally higher than at the national level. The growth was particularly low for females, by only 83.9 per cent as against 92.8 per cent in all-India. The proportion of cross-bred in the cattle was relatively high. In 1992, it constituted 10.2 per cent as against 7.4 in the latter. Percentage of females in them was as much as 78.3, 8.9 points higher than at the national level. The situation of milch cattle was also good. In the total females, it was 63.3 per cent in 1992 as against 56.1 at the national level. The proportion in milk was, however, not good; being respectively 48.4 and 54.6 per cent. The situation of cross-breds was much better, percentage of milch cattle in them was 15.7 as against 10.02 in all-India. The proportion in milk was still better, being respectively 21.55 and 12.71 per cent.

In recent years also, the relative position was more or less the same. In 2003, the state had 163.03 lakh cattle, constituting 8.80 per cent of A-I total, which was higher than in all but three of the states. In the total number, the proportion of cross-bred increased to 17.03 per cent as against 13.33 at the national level. In the A-I total number of cross-breds, Maharashtra's share came to 11.25 per cent, which was the second highest among the states.

On buffaloes, the situation was much worse. In the all-India total number, the state's share came to only 6.28 per cent in 2003. In the total number, the proportion of females was relatively high. In 1992, at 85.2 per cent, it was 6 points higher than the national average. In terms of households, per thousand hhs, there were only 298 buffaloes in 2002-03 in rural areas as against 514 in rural India. In urban areas, it was respectively 11 and 22. In buffaloes, adult males numbered only 23 in 2002-03 in rural areas as against 36 in all-India; on adult females, it was respectively 201 and 294. On young stock, the situation was still worse; numbering only 74 per '000 hhs compared with 184 in rural India.

The adult male buffaloes were kept mainly for work only; at 13 per '000 hhs in rural areas, it was 56.5 per cent of the total. At the national level, however, it was still higher—being 25 and 69.4 per cent. In adult females, the number in milk was 126 and constituted 62.7 per cent of the total; In all-India, it was 172 and 58.5 per cent. Earlier, the situation was still better. In 1992, there were 140 adult females in milk per '000 hhs, 70 per cent of total adult females.

Milk Output

The growth in milk production was substantial in Maharashtra, but the relative share in A-I total output remained small. In 1999-02, it stood at 7.18 per cent, rising from 5.16 in 1981-82. The per capita production in 1999-02 came to only 175 kg, which was 78.5 per cent of the A-I average. In value term, the state's production had constituted 9.15 per cent of A-I total in 2000-03, rising from 8.90 in 1990-93, with a growth of 54.3 per cent. The per capita production in 2000-03 was Rs. 568 as against Rs. 584 at the national level. In the total production of milk, the share of buffalo was relatively low here. In 1994-95, it was only 47.0 per cent as against 54.0 at the national level.

Goats, Sheep and Pig

The rearing of ovine declined noticeably in Maharashtra over the years, as noted earlier. Between goat and sheep, the former was reared in a larger number. The growth in goat population increased faster since the early seventies. Between 1972 and 1992, it was by 68 per cent as against only 14 per cent in the preceding 16 years. Both were, however, below the national average; and the state's share in A-I total declined from 9.4 per cent in 1956 to 8.6 in 1992. In the following years also the proportion remained virtually the same. Maharashtra's number in 2003 was lower than in three of the states. On sheep, maintained both for producing meat and wool, the growth had a sharp fall in recent years. Between 1992 and 2003, it was by a negligible 0.55 per cent as against 44.6 per cent in the preceding period of two decades; at the national level, it was 21.0 and 27.0 per cent respectively. The state's share in A-I total number declined to 5.03 per cent in 2003 from 6.06 in 1992.

On pigs, the state's situation continued to be very poor despite a significant growth in recent years. Between 1992 and 2003, number of pigs had risen by 16.76 per cent here compared with only 5.71 per cent at the national level; the relative share in the latter's total rose to 3.25 per cent from 2.94. In terms of households, the number per 100 hhs came to only three in both 1991-92 and 2002-03; at the national level, it was 4 and 3 respectively.

With this pattern of growth, the output from goat, sheep and pigs naturally remained low. The milk output from goat had risen from only 0.62 lakh tonnes in 1961 to 2.14 lakh in 1994-95, i.e., by 245 per cent; at the national level, it was by as much as 390.5 per cent. The relative share in A-I total output declined from 11.1 per cent to 7.80. On meat, the output exclusively from goat is not available. But meat production as a whole stood at the average of Rs. 1640 crore in 2000-03, and constituted 10.48 per cent of A-I total; in 1990-93, it was 10.09 per cent. The per capita production in 2000-03 came to Rs. 169.49 as against Rs. 152.29 at the national level.

On the production of raw wool, the situation was very poor. The growth, in value term, between 1990-93 and 2000-03 was by only 19.4 per cent as against 43.2 per cent at the national level. The relative share in the latter's total declined from 4.07 per cent to 3.39. In terms of quantum, and over a longer period, between 1961 and 1995-96, there was an absolute fall in production, and the relative share in A-I total declined from 5.86 per cent to 3.61. An important reason behind this situation is that the production of wool did not receive much attention. In the composition of sheep, cross-bred constituted only 1.14 per cent in 1992 as against 4.75 per cent at the national level. (*ibid.*).

The inter-district variation in rearing of livestock was very high. The number per 100 human population in 1992 varied between the highest of 107 in Gadchiroli and the lowest at 17 in Thane, with the state average at 45; only six districts had above 60. On cattle, in terms of area, the number per sq km was at the highest 180 in G. Mumbai and the lowest at 45 in Gadchiroli, with state average at 74; it was below 60 in three of the districts. Number of cows and buffaloes in milk per 1000 population this year varied between the highest of 94 in Kolhapur and the lowest at 8 in G. Mumbai, with 47 at the state level; 11 of the districts had above 60, while five with below 40. The inter-district variation in number of working cattle and buffaloes was much greater. Per 1000 hects of NSA, the highest in 1992 was 1294 in Gadchiroli and the lowest at 158 in Solapur, with state average at 364; only three districts had above 1000 while ten districts with below 300. (GOM 2000).

On ovine, the inter-district variation was still higher. In 1992, number of goats was at the highest 9.15 lakh in Ahmednagar as against the lowest of 32 thousand in G. Mumbai. There were five districts—Solapur, Nashik, Jalgaon and Pune, apart from Ahmednagar—with above five lakh each, accounting for 33.7 per cent of the state's total. On the other hand, eight districts, with below 2 lakh each, accounted for only 10.06 per cent of total. The rearing of sheep was more localised and, therefore, the variation was much greater. Nine of the districts—Ahmednagar, Satara, Pune, Solapur, Sangli, Nashik, Kolhapur, Dhule and Beed—together accounted for 78.7 per cent of the total number. None of the other districts could reach even one lakh; the highest was 4.05 lakh in Ahmednagar.

Poultry

On poultry rearing, at least till early nineties Maharashtra made a significant progress. Between 1972 and 1992, the number of poultry had risen by 163.5 per cent and the relative share in A-I total rose to 10.48 per cent from 8.82. Among the selected states, Maharashtra's latest was the second highest. In recent years, however, there was a noticeable fall. In 2003, the relative share in A-I total came to only 7.76 per cent, which was lower than in three of the states. In terms of households, Maharashtra had only 84 poultry per 100 hhs in 2002-03, declining from 192 in 1992 and 137 in 1971-72. In relation to the A-I average, the latest was only 68.3 per cent.

On the composition of poultry, no recent data are available. In 1992, in fowls—constituting the overwhelming proportion—improved variety accounted for only 36.6 per cent and the balance desi; at the national level, the proportion was still lower, being only 34.8 per cent. In the total of poultry, ducks constituted only 0.01 per cent this year as against 3.45 per cent at the national level.

As regards the output from poultry, Maharashtra's situation was not bad. In 1999-02, the state accounted for 9.73 per cent of A-I total egg production, which was the second highest among the states. In value term, the situation worsened considerably in recent years. In 2000-03, Maharashtra accounted for only 8.73 per cent of A-I total, declining from 10.21 in 1990-93. The growth over the period was by only 42.2 per cent compared with 66.3 in all-India. The per capita availability in 200-01 came to only 34 gms, nominally higher than the national average. The national Institute of Nutrition in Hyderabad has prescribed consumption of 180 eggs a year for an individual; India presently has 43. The number in China is 312 and in Japan 346.

The district-wise variation in poultry rearing was very high. In 1992, the highest number reared was 40.46 lakh in Pune and the lowest at 2.19 lakh in Wardha. Out of 30 districts, 12 were with above 10 lakh each and they accounted for 71.2 per cent of the state's total. Seven districts—viz, Ahmednagar, Sangli, Solapur, Nashik, Satara and Thane, apart from Pune—together contributed 50.9 per cent. Around a decade earlier, in 1983, the concentration was still higher. Pune alone had 28.76 lakh poultry; none of the other districts could reach even half this level. Eight of the districts together accounted for 55.9 per cent of the state's total.

The scope for raising the production from the sector was not low. Number of cattle reared by some of the classes of land holdings was very low. In 2002-03, per thousand hhs, the number reared by 0.005- 0.040 ha class was only 381 here as against 426 at the national level. The next class, 0.040-0.5 also had respectively 330 and 409. Similarly, the highest size, above 20 ha, had 705 as against 847 at the national level. Moreover, there was no rearing of C-Bs by this class as against 116 in the latter. There was also scope for substituting the non-descript cattle by C-Bs. The rearing of buffaloes could also be raised by at least some of the size classes. The lowest size had only 25 buffaloes as against 262 at the national level; for the next size, 0.002-0.005 ha, also it was respectively 172 and 297. (NSSO 2006b).

On sheep and goat, the number reared was less than the national average in four of the size classes, beginning from 0.040-0.50 ha, with 132 and 191 respectively, to 5.0-7.5 ha class with 171 and 229. The scope for increasing the number was particularly high in poultry. Number of fowls and ducks was below the national average in four of the size classes. The rearing was highly concentrated in 0.002 ha or less, with 419 per thousand hhs; in four of the size classes it varied between 217 and 256 and the rest had below 150.

Marketing

On the product marketing facility, the situation of only co-operative dairying in the state is looked into. The present condition of the milk co-operatives is in general extremely poor. But in the past they played a significant role in the growth of milk production. The dairy related co-operative movement in the state had started as early as late 1950s, when the government dairy department was set up in 1958. The primary milk producers' co-operative societies began to be started with the main objective of providing various services to the members. Their activities included, besides collection and marketing of milk, organising inputs supply and providing veterinary services and provision of credit on concessional terms. In due course, a number of milk schemes was started on the Anand pattern in Gujarat.

The programme of 'Operation Flood' (OF) was launched in the state in 1970-71 with the main objective of building the dairy industry on co-operative lines. In the beginning it was launched in two districts only, Jalgaon and Kolhapur. However, under the 'OF-II', 19 more districts were covered. The National Diary Development Board prepared a perspective plan for dairy development in 1983, and in March 1986 the government's policy on co-operativisation was announced. In 1987, a committee was appointed to evaluate the programme in the state. The study found that the success of a co-operative depended on the level of milk procurement, plant utilisation, terms and conditions of finance, nearness to urban markets, and the role of government as well as management in running the cooperatives.

It was due to the differences in situation on these factors that only a few regions were contributing the bulk of milk production. In 1991-92, Pune, Nashik, Aurangabad and Konkan together accounted for 85.6 per cent of milk output; the respective shares being 32.24, 21.21, 19.76 and 12.39 per cent. On the other hand, Amravati region was contributing only 8.12 per cent and Nagpur 6.28. The total production this year was 39,546 lakh litres. In the total number of primary milk societies at 12,513, Pune accounted for 32.75 per cent, Nashik 25.31, Aurangabad 20.42 and Amravati 11.31 per cent. The procurement per milk society this year was as much as 1.19 lakh litres in Pune, 0.82 lakh in Nashik, 0.45 lakh in Nagpur and 0.36 lakh in Aurangabad whereas Amravati had only 0.10 lakh and Konkan 0.14. The procurement as percentage to production in these regions were respectively 38.17, 30.92, 14.43, 11.71, 4.33 and 1.32 (quoted in Shah, Deepak 1997). To identify the reasons behind low procurement, a detailed look is given into the situation in two of the districts—Jalgaon in a poor state and Kolhapur with good performance.

Fishery

Maharashtra has relatively large fishery resources. In marine fishery, it has a coastline of about 720 km. Though the territorial water area is only 1.32 lakh sq km, the continental shelf extends up to 180 metres having an area of

1.12 lakh sq km. Out of this total area, fishing takes place in only up to 70 metres depth. The potential of fish catch from marine area has been estimated at 6.3 lakh tonnes per year; of which the production in 2000-01 came to only 4.03 lakh tonnes. In inland water, Maharashtra has rivers of about 3.2 thousand km and canals about 12.8 thousand; both together constituting 8.61 per cent of A-I total. In reservoir water areas, the state's share is 13.7 per cent. There is also a brackish water area of 80,000 ha. The area suitable for exploitation under inland fisheries is, however, only 3.20 thousand sq km, and in brackish water 18.6 thousand ha.

The growth in fish production in Maharashtra has not been good. Over a period of three decades, between 1967-69 and 1996-99, it had risen by only 263 per cent; the relative share in national total rose to 13.4 per cent in 1984-87, from 10.3, but declined again to 10.6 in 1996-99. In recent years, it worsened further. The production in 2001-04 averaged 532 thousand tonnes, and constituted only 8.60 per cent of A-I total, lower than in three of the states. In the total production, the share of marine fishery had declined from 91.5 per cent in 1967-1969 to 76.5 in 2001-04 . The production from inland water was very low.

Behind this poor performance, an important reason was the low level of Plan expenditure. At least till the end of seventies, the expenditure remained very low. In the Third plan, it rose to Rs. 309 lakh from Rs. 138 lakh in the preceding plan, but in the following two plans the growth was nominal. In the Sixth plan, however, it rose to Rs. 1385 lakh, a 311 per cent rise over the Fourth plan's. In the following three plans again the growth decelerated; the expenditure reached Rs. 4901 lakh in the Ninth Plan, i.e., only a 254 per cent rise over the Sixth Plan's.

Forestry

Maharashtra has a substantial forest area but its quality deteriorated much over the years. The total forest area in the state at the end of 1950s stood at 166.27 lakh acres, of which 140.58 lakh—i.e., 84.5 per cent—were in charge of the Forest Department, 16.32 lakh under the Revenue Department and the balance privately owned. The major portion of the last two were given to pasture and grazing. Of the area under Forest Department, about 13.15 lakh acres were scrub lands with poor productivity, about 25 lakh acres functioned mainly as means of soil conservation, and another 25 lakh acres were remote and inaccessible; only the balance of 77 lakh, i.e., 55 per cent, were under exploitation.

Of the land under Revenue Department, a sizeable part consisted of reserved forests; and the portions that were not under cultivation were progressively taken over by the Forest Department. The private forests were also mostly taken over by the government. Of the scrub forests with the Forest Department, about 10,000 acres were afforested by the end of Second plan. Of the areas under regular exploitation, about 49 lakh acres had optimum conditions for natural regeneration. The balance of 28 lakh acres needed planned plantation programme. In early sixties, there was an annual plantation programme of about 10,000 acres, and it was to increase greatly in the following plans.

The proportion of forest area reserved increased from 58.8 per cent in 1960-61 to 75.8 in 1997; another 14.6 per cent was under protected area in the latest year. Thus reserved and protected together accounted for 90.4 per cent; at the national level, it was 86.3 per cent. This change in legal status, however, could not save the forest areas from depredation by unscrupulous elements. Actual forest cover (AFC) as percentage to the RFA stood at only 72.3 in 1997 as against 82.8 in all-India. The proportion of dense forest area was also only 37.0 per cent this year as against 48.0 in the latter.

The growth in expenditure on forests was very low. Between 1972-73 and 1999-00 it was by only 32.3 times as against 40.2 times in All-India. The plan expenditure on forestry increased substantially only since the early '80s. The Sixth Plan spent Rs. 54.61 crore on it, which was 19 times the Third Plan's outlay (Rs 283.46 lakh). In the following plans again the expenditures were very low. After a sharp fall in the Seventh—to only Rs. 18.62 crore, it increased to Rs. 352.60 crore in the Eighth Plan and Rs. 394.60 crore in the Ninth; the latest was only a 7.2-fold rise over the Sixth Plan's.

The production situation worsened noticeably. Forest produce per ha of forest area declined from Rs. 129 in 1988-89 to Rs. 120 in 1998-99. The production of timber in 2001-02 was expected to decline to 1.21 lakh cm, valued at Rs. 67.0 crore, from 1.67 lakh cm and Rs. 84.7 crore in the preceding year. On firewood, it was expected to rise to 4.17 lakh cm from 2.48 lakh. The estimated value of minor forest produce in 2001-02 was Rs. 66.8 crore. (GOM 2002: 173). The relative position of Maharashtra among the states was not bad. In 1998-00, timber production stood at the average of 75,300 cu metres, and constituted 5.13 per cent of A-I total; among the selected states, it was the third highest. In fuel wood, at 7,49,468 cum, it was as much as 17.1 per cent of A-I total; and among the states, next only to Karnataka. (GOI 2003c, 2001). These figures probably do not take into account the production that was illegally removed.

Maharashtra's performance in agriculture, etc., as a whole does not appear good, if the extent of public capital formation (PCF) in the sector is considered. The per hectare PCF had risen from the average of Rs. 548 in 1980-83 to Rs. 956 in 1998-01; both were significantly higher than in All-states. Average for the entire period came to Rs. 748 as against Rs. 584 in the latter The share of public investment in it was also much higher than in A-S.

The diversion of agricultural land for non-agricultural use was high here, and this was often done without giving adequate consideration to the environmental damages caused. A recent example on this is the Lavasa project, near Pune. In June, 2011, an expert appraisal committee of the environment ministry had recommended conditional approval for the first phase of its 2000-hectare hill town project. Soon after the work started, the state government had to file a case against the promoters of the project for violation of the Environmental Protection Act. But the project overcame this obstacle soon when the environment ministry granted clearance, subject to "strict compliance" of certain terms and conditions. This Rs. 3000 crore project, involved large scale cutting and filling and change of drainage pattern. The construction had begun prior to obtaining the environment clearance. (TST 2011 z10, z31, z29).

NOTES

1. In August-September, 2009, there was an acute scarcity of sugar in the country. In 2008-09, the deficit between demand and supply reached eight million tons, and the country became a net importer of sugar, from an exporter in the preceding year. This was mainly because many farmers switched over to wheat cultivation, abandoning cane, as the former became more profitable after the government raised its purchase price. Various factors contributed to this situation. Sugar is used mainly by industry, only 34 per cent is consumed by people. There is demand for an urgent correction in sugar policies. Only richer farmers owning hundreds of acres of land reap the benefits. There are huge issues of power supply, labour problems and sugar price controls primarily driven by vote bank politics. In November 2012, sugarcane farmers in western Maharashtra, were up in arms against the politically strong lobby of cooperative sugar mills. Their main demand was a better price of Rs. 3,000 pe tonne of sugarcane. (TST 2009 z17; z85).

16

INDUSTRIAL GROWTH AND STRUCTURAL CHANGE

Maharashtra has always been in the forefront of industrialisation in the country. With less than 10 per cent of the country's population, the state accounts for around a quarter of its gross value added from the industrial sector. During 2003-06, in the state's GSDP at current prices, the share of industry averaged 27.4 per cent, and of manufacturing at 18.4 per cent. In the national total GSDP from industry, Maharashtra's share came to 13.22 per cent. The industries, however, continue to be heavily concentrated in a few districts. There is also a serious problem of environmental pollution from industry. A detailed look is given below on the pattern of industrial growth over the years.

At the beginning of the Third five-year plan (1961), the concentration of industries in the Bombay region was extremely high. The census of manufacturing industries in 1958 had found that out of the state's total number of working factories at 1228, Greater Bombay alone had 789, i.e., 64.3 per cent, and for the Bombay division at 904 and 73.6 per cent, respectively. Poona division had 205 factories, with Poona having 84. In terms of value of production, the share of Bombay division alone was 82.9 per cent, with Greater Bombay at 76.8 per cent; the Poona division accounted for another 11.5 per cent. On the other hand, Nagpur division accounted for only 4.78 per cent of total, and Aurangabad division a measly 0.80 per cent. (GOM 1964: 20.3). The Third five-year plan, the first plan after the creation of the new state, in stead of lamenting over the high level of industrial concentration appreciated it. The document stated: ".... the high level of automatic industrial growth that has taken place in the Bombay-Poona belt is not inconsistent with the proposed agro-industrial development of the state as a whole." (GOM 1961: 67).

It was due to this sort of nonchalant attitude towards industrial concentration that in 1984-85, Greater Bombay was still accounting for 46.88 per cent of the state's total factory workers; and another 21.31 per cent came from Thane and Pune. Number of factory workers per lakh population was 5,774 in Greater Bombay, followed by Thane 3,102 and Pune 2,778 as against the lowest of 91 in Gadchiroli. As many as 13 districts, out of 29, had less than 500, with the state average at 1651. After another one-and-half decade, in 1998-99, also there was no striking improvement. While Mumbai's share in total employment declined to 28.9 per cent, for the Konkan division—comprised of four districts—it was still 44.6 per cent. Number of factory workers per lakh population this year stood at 3,221 in Greater Mumbai and for the Konkan division at 2,413 compared with below 500 for as many as 12 districts.

Factory Sector

In the factory sector, Maharashtra's relative position worsened considerably over the years. In the all-India total value of output, its share was almost static at 24 per cent till the end of 'seventies but declined to 22.7 in 1990-91 and further to 18.5 in 2003-04; the next year, however, it increased to 21.5 per cent. The per capita output was the highest until the end of nineties, when it was overtaken by Gujarat. However, even in 2004-05, at Rs. 35,649, it was 132 per cent higher than the national average. The size of factories here increased greatly over the years. In the all-India total number of factories, the state's share declined to only 13.5 per cent in 2003-04, from 21.4 in 1962.

On the provision of employment also the situation was similar. Till 1999-00, Maharashtra was the highest employer, accounting for 14.9 per cent of A-I total, but in 2004-05, at 12.4 per cent, it was next to Tamil Nadu. The productivity of the employees had risen remarkably over the years. The output per worker in 2004-05 stood at Rs. 44.06 lakh, which was 74 per cent higher than the national average; in 1977-78, it was only 37 per cent higher. The growth over the period was by 58.7 times as against 46.2 times at the national level. The fixed capital per employee also increased rapidly—being by respectively 49.2 times and 28.7 times—and became higher than the national average from lower earlier. In 2004-05, at Rs. 11.81 lakh, it was 52 per cent higher. The emoluments per employee were also high. In 2004-05, at Rs. 1.14 lakh, it was the third highest. The FC/output ratio was low; being always one of the lowest. NVA/FC was high, although the relative position had deteriorated greatly in 2004-05. The NVA/output ratio went below the national average in 2004-05, from higher earlier. (*ibid.*).

Structural Change

The industrial structure of Maharashtra changed noticeably over the years. In terms of employment, the average daily employment continued to be the highest in textiles (including wearing apparel), although it declined quite sharply after mid-eighties. The employment provided in 1961 stood at 368 thousand, but in 1986 it declined to 293 and then to only 229 thousand in 2000. Food products etc came next and the average daily employment in it increased from 90.2 thousand in 1961 to 119.6 thousand in 1986, and then to 165.2 thousand in 2000. Among other industries, only four—viz, machinery and equipment, basic metal and metal products, chemicals and chemical products and transport equipment—had provided above one lakh each in the last two decades or so. Among them, the highest growth was in chemicals and chemical products; rising from 34 thousand in 1961 to 94.7 in 1976 and 127.9 thousand in 2000. In the total employment provided by the sector, the share of these six industries came to 76.5 per cent in the latest year, declining from 80.3 in 1981 and 82.5 per cent in 1961. (GOM 2002: T-59).

For a more detailed picture, we look into how the situation changed over the last one decade. In 1989-90, six industries—viz, cotton textiles, machinery and equipment, basic chemicals, food products, electricity and transport equipment—together accounted for 61.7 per cent of total persons engaged; the share of the first two combined was at 27.2 per cent. After four years, in 1993-94, among the six industries, only cotton textile and transport equipment had reduced the number engaged. The combined share of the six industries declined to 59.0 per cent. In value of output, the situation changed quite drastically over this five-year period.

To look into some of the technical coefficients: Among the major industries, the C/O ratio had risen noticeably particularly in metal and alloys, metal products and cotton textile—being respectively from 0.29 to 0.48, 0.18 to 0.44 and from 0.28 to 0.46. The fall was sharp only in basic chemicals, from 0.98 to 0.38. The highest ratio was in electricity, declining from 1.49 to 1.39. The NVA/O ratio continued to be the lowest in food products, declining from 0.11 in 1989-90 to 0.10 in 1993-94. The sharpest fall was in cotton textiles, from 0.26 to 0.014; and the highest rise in textile products, from 0.17 to 0.38. At the state level, the ratio increased from 0.20 to 0.23.

In many of the industries the growth in fixed capital was very high, but it rarely had any impact on the NVA/O ratio and not much in labour productivity also. In metal products, for example, total F.C. rose by as much as 435 per cent in this five-year period, and in per person engaged (PE) by 321.5 per cent. But the NVA/O ratio remained at the same 0.22, and the output per PE rose by only 76.8 per cent. In metal and alloy, the rise in F.C. was by 166.6 per cent and in per PE by 173 per cent; the NVA/O increased from 0.12 to 0.18, and the output per PE by only 65 per cent. In machinery and equipment, the F.C. increased by 118 per cent and in per PE by 101, but the NVA/O ratio fell from 0.25 to 0.24 and the output per PE increased by only 67.1 per cent. At the state level, total F.C. rose by 106.4 per cent and in per PE by 90.1; the NVA/O increased from 0.20 to 0.23 and the output per PE by 70.8 per cent. (CMIE 1997a).

After another six years, in 1999-00, the relative share in total output changed as follows: For food products, a rise to 14.0 per cent from 10.9 in 1993-94; textiles to as much as 8.01 per cent from only 0.80; in metal products, from only 2.26 to 10.9 per cent; and in refined petroleum products and rubber etc from 10.5 to 12.2 per cent. The fall was sharpest in basic chemicals and other chemical products, from 28.0 per cent to 18.7; in machinery and equipment it was from 13.4 to 7.9 per cent; and in metal and alloys from 7.29 to 5.62 per cent.

The inter-industry variation in some of the technical coefficients continued to be very high. The C/O ratio during 1997-00 averaged as much as 0.77 in leather and leather products, wood, and paper products, etc., as against 0.38 for all industries in the state. In non-metallic mineral products and basic and fabricated metal products it was 0.60, and in textiles, wearing apparel, etc., at 0.51. The lowest was in food products, beverages and tobacco products, at 0.22. The variation in FC/NVA in this period was still higher. The highest was 4.43 in leather, wood and paper, etc., followed by non-metallic mineral products etc at 4.36 as against 1.63 in food products, etc., and the lowest of 1.60 in refined petroleum, chemicals, rubber and plastic products, etc. For all industries together, it came to 2.01. (GOM 2002: T-39).

Small-Scale Industries

The Organised Sector

Maharashtra's situation on the organised sector of SSI has not been good. Over a period of 16 years, between 1972-73 and 1987-88, number of units had risen by only 70.6 per cent as against 265.5 per cent in all-India; the relative share in A-I total number declined from 10.9 per cent to 5.08. In production also the growth was low, and the relative share declined from 20.3 to 17.5 per cent. However, the state continued to be far ahead of any other state.

On the provision of employment by the sector, the state's position was very poor. In the A-I total employment, its share declined to only 9.71 per cent in 1987-88 from 14.5 in 1972-73; the growth here being only around a third of that at the national level. The productivity of the employees had, however, risen fast; being by 855 per cent as against 646 in the latter. Per employee, it continued to be the highest among the states, and in relation to the national average the latest was 80 per cent higher. This was, however, accompanied by a very high level of fixed assets per employee.

The situation of the technical coefficients was on the whole very good The NVA/P ratio had declined, but the latest, at 33.1 per cent, was still 9.2 points higher than in all-India. The C/O ratio decreased from 0.43 to 0.17, anc the latest was 5 points lower than the national average. The NVA/C ratio alsc improved similarly. The capacity utilisation by the sector was very good. I 1987-88, at 74.6 per cent, it was far higher than in any other state. Th technological situation of the units was also good. Percentage of unit consuming energy in 1987-88 was as much as 93.9. The units were, howeve heavily concentrated in urban areas; the rural share this year was only 20.3 pe cent, less than half of that at the national level. In total employment also rura areas accounted for only 22.1 per cent. (*ibid.*).

Structural Change

The composition of the industries changed noticeably over the 16 yea since 1972. The highest contributor to total output in 1972-73 was met products, with 19.0 per cent, followed by chemicals 18.2, i.e., the two combine at 37.2 per cent. At a great distance came a group of six industries—vi. machinery and parts, paper products and printing, rubber and plastic, electric machinery and apparatus, basic metal and alloy industries and transpo equipments and parts—together contributing 44.09 per cent; their individual share varied between 8.79 and 5.28 per cent.

In 1987-88, the share of the first two industries declined sharply; for metal products to 10.31 per cent and basic chemicals to 6.87. The highest contributor this year was rubber, plastic, etc., with a share of 19.5 per cent, followed by food products 12.0; that is, a combined total of 31.5 per cent. In 1972, they had provided only 11.27 per cent, with the respective shares at 8.08 and 3.19 per cent. Apart from these four industries, there was a group of six—viz, basic metal and alloy, machinery and equipment, electrical machinery and apparatus, textile products, non-metallic mineral products and paper, etc.—together contributing 37.72 per cent; their individual shares varying between 9.63 and 4.43.

In the all-India total production in some of these industries, Maharashtra's share was quite a high. In 1987-88, for rubber, plastic, etc., it was as much as 27.80 per cent, in machinery and equipment 23.03, in metal products 21.42, basic chemicals 20.30, electrical equipments, etc, 19.78, in transport equipment 19.49, paper, etc., 19.32, non-metallic mineral products 18.94, in textile products 16.23 and in basic metal and alloy 16.13 per cent.

The Unorganised Sector

On the unorganised sector of industry also Maharashtra's relative position was on the whole quite good. The NSSO survey in 2000-01, found the state having an annual gross value added of Rs. 7595.06 crore, constituting 12.6 per cent of A-I total, which was the highest among the states. The relative share in number of enterprises was, however, only 7.3 per cent, lower than in four of the states. On the provision of employment, the situation was not good. At 29.72 lakh this year, it was only 8.02 per cent of A-I total. The productivity of the workers was, however, the highest here. At Rs. 25.6 thousand per worker, it was more than double the A-I average.

As regards the rural-urban distribution, as in case of the organised sector, here also the rural share was very low. In 2000-01, the rural areas accounted for only 24.7 per cent of total output as against 44.3 at the national level. In number of enterprises, it was respectively 53.9 and 70.1 per cent. In the provision of employment also the rural share was only 41.8 per cent as against 64.7 per cent at the national level. The productivity of rural workers averaged only Rs. 15.1 thousand, less than half that in urban areas. The growth status of rural enterprises was also not good. Percentage of units reporting contracting was 12.2 and stagnant at 62.1; both were, however, below that in all-India.

The size of enterprises in rural areas was very small. OAMEs—i.e., those without any hired worker—constituted as much as 92.4 per cent as against 62.3 per cent in urban areas. Moreover, rural OAMEs working perennial constituted only 87.6 per cent here compared with 91.6 at the national level. The enterprises faced a variety of problems. Shortage of capital was reported by 59.0 per cent of rural OAMEs as against 49.6 per cent in all-India. The problem of power cut was reported by 15.7 per cent, higher than in the latter. Among other problems, the competition from larger units was reported by 51.0 per cent here as against the national average of 22.2 per cent.

The proportion of NDMEs in rural Maharashtra was only 4.9 per cent, lower than at the national level. The distribution of workers among the three types in rural areas was in the ratio of 75.3: 8.2 :16.5, and in urban areas at 34.0: 27.2:38.8. Each of the types in rural areas had lower productivity per worker than in urban areas. For OAMEs, it was respectively Rs. 12.5 thousand and Rs. 16.7 thousand; on NDMEs, Rs. 24.5 and Rs. 37.4 thousand; and on DMEs Rs. 22.6 and Rs. 44.3 thousand; each of them was, however, significantly higher than the national average.

To look at some of the structural ratios: In 2000-01, the fixed assets to employment ratio for rural OAMEs in Maharashtra was 17051.75 as against 10184.06 at the national level. The output to employment ratio was also high, at 23947.46 and 17410.40 respectively. The output to fixed assets was, however, low; being 1.40 and 1.71 respectively. The value-added to fixed assets was also low; only 0.73 here compared with 0.86 in all-India. (NSSO 2002b).

As regards the industrial composition of the output, it was heavily concentration in a few industries. In the total annual GVA (rural+ urban) in 2000-01, the share of wearing apparel etc was 15.2 per cent, followed by textiles 14.9, food products and beverages 12.3 and furniture manufacturing 10.69. Thus, these four industries together accounted for 53.1 per cent. Another 22.2 per cent came from wood and wood products, etc., fabricated metal products (except machinery and equipment) and electrical machinery and apparatus, distributed almost equally. The concentration was heavier in rural areas. Here, four groups of industries—food products and beverages (21.1 per cent), wood and wood products, etc., (19.5), basic metals (15.6) and wearing apparel, etc., (15.3)—together accounted for 71.5 per cent.

Causal Factors

Infrastructure

The relative position of Maharashtra's infrastructural situation worsened considerably over the years. The infrastructure development index, taking all-India = 100, declined continuously from 120.1 in 1980-81 to only 107.1 in 1992-93; both were below as many as five of the states. The situation in neighbouring Gujarat was always better. (CMIE 1997a). Among the infrastructural items, two, availability of power and transport and communication facility, are critically important. A brief look is given below on how their situation changed over the years.

Power

On power, Maharashtra's relative position on availability of power worsened considerably. In the all-India total of energy generated, the state's share declined from 15.9 per cent in 1980-81 to 12.6 in 1998-99 and further to 11.9 in 2004-05. The energy available in 2004-05 was 82,075 mkwh and constituted 14.6 per cent of A-I total. But the T&D losses were very high; rising from the average of 17.3 per cent in 1980-83 to 33.3 in 2002-05. In recent years, the situation worsened considerably. In 2010-11, with the generation at 65,791 mkwh, the relative share was below 10 per cent. In the total electricity generated, thermal provided 91 per cent and the balance from hydro.

The relative position on industrial consumption of electricity (utility) continued to be very good. In the total sale to ultimate consumers, the share in Maharashtra declined from 69.0 per cent in 1973-74 to 35.2 in 1998-99 and then rose to 40.9 per cent in 2004-05. The per capita consumption had risen from 115.4 kwh in 1973-74 to 222.4 kwh in 2004-05; the latest was 5.55 times the national average. In 2008-09, the share of industrial consumption rose to as much as 59.1 per cent; for agriculture it was 13.7 and domestic 17.7 per cent. CMIE 2011).

District-wise, the industrial consumption of electricity varied greatly. Despite the relatively happy situation, the power shortage in the state was not low.

The obsession with industrialisation must stop. The demand for energy is increasing fast but the supply is obstructed by a number of factors. Coal mining activities are opposed by people living near coal mine deposits. The construction of dams for hydro-power projects cause enormous damage to the environment and displace people living in the upstream. Nuclear power projects are probably much more dangerous and everywhere people living in the surrounding areas of the proposed sites are opposing their construction. Therefore, before going for an increase in the installed capacity in power, the government should raise the efficiency in utilisation of the existing capacity.

There is urgent need to evolve a fresh utility management approach. 'Optimization' of the existing capacity should be done first, and only then 'augmentation'. A judicious blend of supply-side and demand-side management (DSM) is necessary. Presently there is virtually no DSM at all. An Integrated Resource Planning and Least-cost Utility Planning has to be applied. A proper DSM can generate electricity through savings. The power distribution/ delivery network suffers from many deficiencies. The ills of the system are many—"ill-trained workforce, poor reliability, high-line losses, low voltage profiles, overloading of transformers, poor maintenance, absence of conservation measures, power theft, haphazard layouts, whimsical load connection, inadequate clearance, and so on." (Devasahayam, MG 2012a). In installing new capacity, emphasis should be on renewable energy sources like solar energy, wind power, tidal power, biofuels and small hydro-power, which continue to remain largely unexploited. The environment polluting thermal or the hazardous nuclear power, or even of big hydro-power projects should be least resorted to.[1]

Transportation Facility

As regards the transportation facility, the road density had risen noticeably over the years. The quality of roads in Maharashtra was always relatively good. The proportion of unsurfaced in 2002 stood at only 21.4 per cent as against 42.8 per cent at the national level. The situation of motor vehicle density was also not bad. In 2002-03, per sq km of area, it numbered 26.43 as against 20.39 in all-India; Maharashtra's was, however, lower than in five of the states. Nearly three decades earlier, in 1975, the relative position was much better; with a density of only 1.35 vehicles, it was the highest among the states.

Inter-district, there was great variation in the transportation facility. The disparity in road length has been noted in Chapter 2; here the situation of two more variables may be looked into. The proportion of unsurfaced roads in 1994-95 varied between the highest of 43.0 per cent in Sangli and the lowest at 1.68 in G. Mumbai, with the state average at 18.1 per cent; seven districts had above 25 per cent unsurfaced, while three with below five per cent.

Institutional Finance

Working Capital

On the provision of working capital, Maharashtra's situation was very good. In March 2007, the credit outstanding from scheduled commercial banks (SCBs) stood at Rs. 230197.2 crore, rising from Rs. 36330.4 crore in March 1996—i.e., a growth of 533.6 per cent; the relative share in all-India total increased from 29.7 per cent to 31.0. The number of accounts, however, had a sharp fall; after rising to 420,471 in 1999-00 from 209,993 in 1995-96, it declined to 217,409 in 2006-07. In the A-I total, these constituted respectively 7.85, 4.54 and 6.68 per cent. (CMIE 2008a).

In the credit to industry, the share of manufacturing and processing had declined from 94.0 per cent in March 1996 to 78.2 in March 2007, with a growth in credit by only 427.4 per cent. Among the industries, the combined share of four—chemicals and chemical products, engineering, basic metal and metal products and textiles—had declined from 67.3 per cent to 53.1 over the period; for the first two together, it was from 38.2 per cent to 21.9. Three decades earlier, at December-end 1977, the four industries together had contributed 73.1 per cent, with the first two at 39.4 per cent.

From this flow of credit, the SSIs were not benefited to the desired extent. In the all-India total outstanding with the sector, Maharashtra's share declined from 23.5 per cent in 1968 to 18.3 in 1983, and in the following years increased to 19.2 per cent in 1995 and 24.0 in 2004. The relative share in number of accounts had declined to only 6.4 per cent in 2004 from 7.5 in 1983 and as much as 20.2 in 1968. The growth in number of accounts was by less than a third of that in all-India. The average amount per account in 2004 was nearly four times that in all-India.The inter-district distribution of credit was very heavily concentrated in a few, in keeping with the locational concentration.

Long-Term Finance

On the provision of term finance also Maharashtra's situation was very good. The cumulative total of assistance from all the institutions together had constituted 23.84 per cent of all-India total in March 2001, rising from 18.8 in 1990; the latest was four times that in the largest state Uttar Pradesh. On per capita basis, the assistance was always far higher than at the national level; the latest was 2.53 times higher. This high level of assistance was mainly because the term financing institutions did not give any importance to the development of the backward states.

In the provision of credit, the role of the all-India institutions had, however, declined considerably over the years. In the cumulative total till March 2001, their share came to only 25.3 per cent as against 41.1 per cent in that till March 1990. The leading institution IDBI, however, continued to provide a large amount of assistance to Maharashtra. The per capita cumulative from it till March 2001 came to Rs. 2,923, which was more than double that at the national level; the assistance till March 1990 was only 50.9 per cent higher than in the latter.

Of the state level institutions, the role of the State Financial Corporation was not good. In the all SFCs' cumulative total assistance till March 2001, Maharashtra's share came to only 9.22 per cent, declining from 18.1 per cent in that till 1972. The per capita assistance was below the national average in both the time-points. The provision from the SIDC was, however, very high. The per capita cumulative till March 2001 came to Rs. 595, which was 3.5 times the national average and highest among the states; in 1990, it was only 41 per cent higher.

The assistance to the SSIs from the term finance institutions was very low. Particularly depressing was the role o the SFC, the only state-level institution providing finance to them. The cumulative total assistance from it till March 2001 came to only Rs. 2,003 crore, and constituted 7.83 per cent of all-SFCs' total; in 1990, it was 8.96 per cent. In the total assistance from the SFC, the share of SSIs declined to 54.7 per cent in the cumulative till 2001, from 74.9 per cent in that till 1990; the former was 16.6 points below the national average. The SIDBI, a subsidiary of the IDBI, however, gave high importance to the SSIs here. The per capita cumulative assistance from it till March 2001 came to Rs. 550, which was 67.8 per cent higher than at the national level. (*ibid.*).

Promotional Measures

Maharashtra probably did not need any special promotional measures for attracting industries to the state, for the overall industrial climate itself was relatively good here. This is evidenced by the fact that even in the era of licensing, the state had received a large share of the LOIs and licences issues by the government. The problem with Maharashtra was not so much of attracting investment to the state, but of bringing industries to the backward regions. For promoting small-scale industries many measures were taken. At the instance of the government of India, there were policies like protection and reservation, exclusive purchase from the sector, price preference, and the provision under the PMRY of setting up self-employment ventures. The first one had introduced exclusive manufacturing in the SSI sector in 1967, beginning with 17 items and reaching a peak of 873 in October 1984. This policy was, however, considerably relaxed in the period of liberalisation.

For the SSIs there are also schemes like co-operative industrial estates (IE), District Industries Centres, the package scheme of incentives, and industrial co-operatives by village artisans. Under the scheme of IE, land is acquired by the government and handed over to the society on lease. The society contributes 20 per cent of the project cost and the government provides matching share capital at the rate of 20 per cent to cover land leveling, development of roads, etc. Government also guarantees the 60 per cent loan component. Total number of estates developed increased from 33 in 1970-71 to 59 in 1980-81 and 95 in 1994-95. District-wise, number of IEs varied greatly. In 1994-95, while Thane had as many as nine IEs and Pune, Buldhana and Nagpur six each, for seven districts it was only one each. The performance of many of the IEs was very poor. The industrial area acquired in Thane was 5580.6 hects as against the lowest of 68.5 hects in Beed. Number of industrial plots developed was as much as 8,949 in Thane as against only 32 in Gadchiroli. For 10 districts, it was less than 500 plots while four had more than 2000. The allotment of plots also varied greatly. In Bhandara, the number allotted was only 19.1 per cent of that developed, in Yavatmal it was 33.2 per cent and in Buldhana 49.0 as against 83.8 per cent at the state level.

This level of inter-district variation was due to a variety of factors. But a study conducted as early as 1966 had emphasised that the success of an IE depends to a very great extent on its location, particularly with regard to nearness to markets and raw materials sources and availability of entrepreneurs, skilled workers and socio-economic overheads like transport and communication. The report noted that the sites of IEs were often not selected after thorough studies of locational advantages and disadvantages as well as potentiality of development. (GOM1966). Such deficiencies continue to plague the functioning of many of the IEs even today. Some of the IEs were located at sites far away from the sources of raw materials required for their industries and also from their markets. Due to the absence of industrial background in the neighbourhood, some of the estates could not develop primary or ancillary industrial activities. The government's assistance in overcoming the difficulties were also far behind what was required. The most important problem of the estates in Maharashtra was often of consolidating their achievements and placing them on a sound footing. Instead of improving the already established estates, the government went on establishing new ones. It was argued that the IEs should be located in the interior for ensuring balanced industrial growth. But this policy was not balanced with the need for locating the estates in the best possible sites.

The DICs set up to serve the tiny units, also had poor performance. They were to provide financial assistance by way of margin money to rural artisans/ tiny units having investment in plant and machinery of below Rs. 2.00 lakh, and located in rural areas and towns with population up to one lakh (1971 census). The assistance was limited to 20 per cent of the total investment or Rs. 40,000 whichever is less. The expenditure under the scheme had a sharp fall in recent years—to only Rs. 67.41 lakh in 2000-01, from Rs. 92.28 lakh in 1998-99. Number of beneficiaries had, however, risen from 382 to 9,937, and consequently the assistance per beneficiary dropped to Rs. 678 from Rs. 24,157. (GOM 2002a).

That these measures were not very effective in spreading SSI units to backward areas is evident from the fact that the SSI Census in 1997-98 had found only 13.4 thousand units, out of the total of 29.86 thousand in Maharashtra—i.e., 45 per cent—in backward areas; at the national level, it was 62.20 per cent. (SIDBI 2002: 27).

On further industrialisation of the state, however, a note of caution is necessary. The air and water pollution are increasing rapidly and affecting human health. The increased global warming will cause immense harm to the state. It has been estimated by the National Environmental Engineering Research Institute that Mumbai would face damages worth Rs. 35,00,000 crore by 20[illegible] because of climate change. The government, however, is not listening to saner voices. The setting up Special Economic Zones—whose objective is to promote exports at any cost—is progressing rapidly. Till October 2006, 75 SEZs were permitted to be set up in the state. The land allotted for them totalled 30,827 hectares, constituting 17.6 per cent of all-India total. The government of Maharashtra is competing with Gujarat in attracting industries to the state. On 3 January 2013 , wary of ceding further ground to it, the Congress-led coalition government announced a new industrial policy, offering a number of sops to investors in SEZs that now cover more than 32,000 ha of rural land acquired from thousands of farmers in the peripheries of Mumbai, Nagpur, Pune, Nashik, Amravati and Thane. The biggest concession on the offer is business houses, apart from investing in industries, can also use 30 per cent of the total land allotted to them for developing residential complexes and townships. The coalition partner Nationalist Congress Party took serious exception to developing urban townships on quintessential agricultural land till recently owned by farmers. Desperate to stop businesses from moving to neighbouring Gujarat, Maharashtra government was compelled to incorporate several compromises in its industrial policy draft. (TST 2013 d).

These SEZs will cost the people dearly. The government has also planned to set up a number of new thermal power plants on the Konkan coast to generate nearly 20,000 MW of power. Moreover, the Jaitapur nuclear power plant, spread over 968 hectares of land is to be constructed here, despite strong opposition from people. The project is to have six third generation pressurised reactors, each with 1650 megawatts capacity. The project has not been subjected to an independent rigorous scientific techno-economic scrutiny and safety audit. (TST 2011 z22; 2012 z50).

NOTES

1. The recent world-wide trend in managing the energy supply may be given a brief look. The progress in use of alternative sources of energy is still in significant has stated that if even one per cent of it could be captured, the use of fossil fuels could be done away with. But it is proving difficult because the oil, coal and gas companies are paying US senators across the board to crush any move to reduce their use. Renewable energy presently accounts for only about 10.9 per cent of domestic primary energy production in the United States; and in China it is about 26 per cent. India has a potential in renewable sources of more than 10,000 MW but the present installed capacity is only 2,039 MW. (TST 2011 z22, 2012 z52).

On wind energy India installed capacity on it stood at 17,351.54 MW in 2011-12, rising from 5,350.77 MW in 2005-06. The energy generated over the period increased from 5.991 billion units to 23.353 billion. Had the installed turbines produced at their full potential, the generation would have risen from 39.34 BU in 2005-06 to 137.96 BU in 2011-12. This under utilisation of capacity was mainly due to the fact that wind is a variable resource: wind speed is high during the monsoon months, but very slow in the winter.

As regards the use of nuclear power, Public opinion has turned against it all over the world following the Fukushima Daiichi disaster in March 2011. While the full impact of it is yet to be assessed, it is considered the worst in the history of nuclear disasters. Nearly 80,000 residents had to be evacuated from their homes. It has been estimated that decommissioning of the crippled Fukushima nuclear plant will take 40 years and cost $14.8 billion. (TST 2011 z50). Decades ago, nuclear energy appeared to lead the race as an energy alternative. Presently, world-wide there are approximately 450 reactors generating 15 per cent of the earth's electricity requirement. Number of reactors in the world increased from only 15 in 1960 to 245 in 1980 and 416 in 1990.

The advantages of nuclear energy were apparent: abundant power, cheaper than through gas or coal plants, no carbon emissions, no blots on the landscape except an occasional containment dome and cooling tower. However, the hopes of a burgeoning nuclear industry were dashed after the three Mile Island nuclear accident in Pennsylvania in 1979 and the Chernobyl disaster in

April 1986. The explosion in Chernobyl had affected nine million people, and an area of 155,000 sq km is still severely contaminated. Despite the hazards China has, however, planned to construct more than 50 NPPs by 2015. (Rajappa, Sam 2012; TST 2012 z82).

The Government of India has also decided to import 40,000 MWe worth of reactors over the next 20 years. These are to be installed in a string of nuclear power plants (NPPs) along the coastline. This is a sure recipe to kill the fishing industry and deprive millions of fishermen of their livelihood. Koodankulam (KDK) in Tamil Nadu—built with Russian assistance—is the first of this string of coast-based NPPs. Four mega desalination units, each producing 106,000 litres of water an hour, is provided for the first unit of the KDK. These units will suck in enormous quantities of sea water along with microscopic to tiny sea flora and fauna of myriad sea creatures, which will be killed in the desalination plants. (TST 2011 z34, z10; 2012 z8, z47, z49, z55, z60).

Even on hydro-power there is need for great caution, for the construction of large dams has serious consequence for the river ecology, apart from bringing immense sufferings to the people displaced by them. According to recent estimates, of the world's 177 large rivers, only one-third are free-flowing. Once a free-flowing river is dammed, very important changes take place in its ecology as well as the environment of downstream villages. Dams hold back not just water but also silt and nutrients that replenish farm lands and build protective wetlands. The world's biggest dam, Three Gorges in China has caused severe problems to the environment, shipping, agriculture, etc., (Saighal, V 2011).

The phenomenon of reservoir-induced seismicity is also a big problem. The earthquake of magnitude 8 on the Richter scale that occurred in Sichuan province of China on 12 May 2008, killing 87,000 people, has been presumed to be triggered or induced by the reservoir of the famous Zipingpu dam nearby. (Arpi, Claude 2011). In the Three Gorges Project, the seismicity at the Chinese site has increased by 30 times after impounding of water and more than 3,000 small quakes have been reported.

** Destruction of the 7,500 km Indian coastline, along with its bio-diversity, is going apace everywhere. Within 500 metres of the coast, there are 1,262 settlements, 1,023 structures, 143 existing ports and another 76 proposed ports. Within 10 km, there are 27 power plants and another 59 proposed power plants. In a stretch of just 150 km in Maharashtra, 15 power projects with a combined 25 gigawatts of generating capacity, six captive ports and six mega-shipyards are coming up. The coastal management zone has been replacing the coastal regulation zone to enable changing of rules. (TST 2012 z69).

17

ABSOLUTE POVERTY AND THE MEASURES

Although Maharashtra is one of the most developed states, the absolute poverty remained very high here, as noted in Chapter 2. The proportion of BPL population in 2004-05 stood at 30 per cent, which was significantly higher than at the national level. If proper price adjustment is made, it will be more than double this figure. The consumer expenditure here continued to be very low. In 1977-78, 62 per cent of the rural population were living with MPCE below the rural average of Rs. 61.83. After another two decades, in 1999, agricultural labourer, constituting 42.49 per cent of rural hhs, had MPCE of only Rs. 391, nominally higher than the national average. Percentage of population with calorie undernourishment in 2008 stood at 27.0 here as against 20.0 in all-India. (GOI 2009c).

Inter-district, the poverty situation varied greatly. Even in 2004-05, the consumer expenditure in rural areas stood at the highest of Rs. 871 in Pune and the lowest at Rs. 352 in Gadchiroli, with Rs. 568 at the state level; 13 districts had below Rs. 500. In urban areas, the highest was Rs. 1570 in Greater Mumbai and the lowest at Rs. 474 in Bid, with Rs. 1148 at the state level. The proportion of BPL population naturally differed much. In rural areas, this year, at the highest it was 65 per cent in Gadchiroli and the lowest at 2.3 in Sindhudurg, with 29.6 at the state level; in five of the districts it was above 50 per cent. In urban areas, the highest was as much as 80.4 per cent in Bid as against the lowest of 11.7 in G Mumbai, with 32.1 at the state level.

Social group-wise, the situation of the backward classes were extremely poor. The MPCE for STs in rural areas stood at only Rs. 384 in 1999-00, which was below the national average; for as much as 45.5 per cent, it was below Rs. 300. For SCs, it stood at Rs. 429, which was lower than in three of the states, although higher than at the national level. The proportion with below Rs. 300 was 35.3 per cent, higher than in all-India. After five years, in 2004-05, The MPCE for both STs and SCs—at Rs. 418 and Rs. 457, respectively—became lower than at the national level.

The occupational distribution was very unfavourable for both the categories in Maharashtra. The proportion of labour hhs in SCs in rural areas stood at as much as 70.2 per cent in 1999 and for STs at 59.9 per cent as against 61.4 and 48.5 per cent, respectively in All-India. Agricultural labour hhs constituted 61.5 per cent in SCs and 54.8 in STs; in all-India, it was respectively

51.4 and 39.7 per cent. The proportion in self-employment was very low. For SCs this year, only 10.7 per cent were agricultural and 6.1 per cent non-agricultural as against 16.4 and 12.0, respectively in All-India. For STs, the proportions were respectively 18.8, 4.9, 36.2 and 5.2 per cent. The possession of land was extremely low. For 71.5 per cent of SC hhs it was below 0.40 ha, and in STs at 58.9 per cent; the latter was higher than in All-India by as much as 12.6 points. The extent of illiteracy with the backward communities was also not low.

The most important factor behind high level of poverty is probably the low wage rates. The proportion of labour households had risen from 34.0 per cent in 1964-65 to 46.5 in 1987-88 and further to 47.2 in 2004; these were much higher than at the national level. The real wage rate for males had risen from Rs. 2.63 in 1974-75 to Rs. 6.62 in 1993-94; both were below the national average. In recent years, the relative position worsened further. In 2004-05, the average daily wage rate in agriculture stood at only Rs. 52.97 for men and Rs. 31.90 for women as against Rs. 61.23 and Rs. 44.59, respectively at the national level. For casual workers as a whole in rural areas, it averaged only Rs. 44.94 in 2004 as against Rs. 50.70 in the latter. The productivity of agricultural labourers had also declined substantially; in 2004-05, it was 19 per cent below the national average as against higher in 1993-94.

Activity-wise, the wage rates in agriculture were much below the national average. In 2009, for men, in ploughing it was only Rs. 90.25 as against the all-India average of Rs. 100.83; in relation to Kerala's, it was only 31.8 per cent. In sowing, at Rs. 86.00, it was lower than in six of the states. In weeding, the rate was only Rs. 69.71 as against Rs. 78.47 at the national level; in winnowing, Rs. 68.57 and Rs. 78.41, respectively; and in well digging, Rs. 107.78 and Rs. 116.15. For unspecified unskilled labour, it was only Rs. 69.81 as against Rs. 85.72 in the latter. Only in threshing Maharashtra's was higher than at the national level; being respectively 90.00 and Rs. 83.49. The rates for women were very low. In sowing, for example, it was only Rs. 50 as against Rs. 63.54 in all-India. (GOI 2009a).

The enforcement of the Minimum wage Act, 1948 has been very poor, even in recent years. In 2003-04, 1,25,776 irregularities were detected through 1,13,043 inspections. Of the total number detected, only 79,629 could be rectified. Number of claims settled was only 117 and the number prosecuted 287. Fines realised was Rs. 2,80,000. (GOI 2005a).

The measures for ameliorating rural poverty began very late, and then also their implementation remained very poor. However, first a brief look may be given into how the agricultural labourers were treated in the first two decades.

Wage Employment Programmes

In early 'seventies, a number of employment schemes was initiated in Maharashtra. Some of them were started by the state government in response to the severe drought conditions in the state during 1971-74, and some sponsored by the Union government. Among the schemes, particularly important was the Employment Guarantee Scheme launched in May 1972 by the state government. During the drought period, the EGS was used as a relief programme and after the drought it continued as an anti-poverty programme. The first serious effort to organise the programme came in 1975-76. In view of the importance of this programme, a detailed look is given to its operation first.

Nationally-Sponsored Programmes

The implementation of the Centrally sponsored programmes was in general very poor. Under the NREP, started in 1981, not only the employment created was low, there were other deficiencies also. Considering a period of only four years, during 1985-89, in the All-India total of persondays created, the state's share came to only 6.8 per cent, lower than in as many as five of the states. The utilisation of available fund was very low, and so too of the foodgrains; the latter, at 46.3 per cent, was the lowest among the states. The cost per pd averaged only Rs. 16.88 in this period, lower than in all but two of the states. The performance on the RLEGP, launched in 1983, was also not much better. The employment created during 1985- 89 constituted 9.13 per cent of A-I total, which was below that in three of the states. The utilisation of available fund and the foodgrains remained low here also. Foodgrains could be utilised to the extent of only 69.9 per cent as against 87.4 per cent at the national level. The quantum utilised, however, constituted as much as 47.6 per cent of A-I total. The cost per pd was very low; being the second lowest among the states. Towards the end of 'eighties, as noted in Chapter 7, a major change came in the wage-employment programmes in the country. In April 1989, the JRY was created and with it the NREP and the RLEGP were merged. The mode of operation of this scheme was radically different from the earlier ones. The performance of this scheme in Maharashtra was very poor, as will be evident from the analysis below.

JRY/JGSY

The employment created under the JRY had declined sharply towards the end of 'nineties. During 1997-00, it came to an annual average of only 424 lakh pds as against 854 during 1989-95. This fall in employment was, however, a part of the all-India trend. At the national level actually the fall was sharper, and consequently, Maharashtra's share in the latter's total increased from 10.2 per cent in 1989-95 to 12.2 in 1997-00. Among the major states, Maharashtra's continued to be the third highest. The expenditure under the scheme was relatively low here, and the cost per pd continued to be much below the national average. The wage rate for JRY workers was the lowest here.

From the employment created, the weaker groups were benefited to a very small extent. The proportion going to the landless workers declined from 35.7 per cent in 1989-95 to 32.0 in 1997-00; both were much below the national average. Social group-wise, the share of SCs/STs in the total increased from 48.9 per cent to 50.0 over the period. Both were the second lowest among the states.

Since 1999-00, there were two major changes in the employment programmes. The first one made employment creation a secondary objective, and consequently the employment created in Maharashtra in 2000-01 came to only 316 lakh pds, that is, significantly below the preceding years'. The next change was the creation of Sampoorna Gramin Rozgar Yojana in January 2002, and merging with it the EAS. The employment creation continued to decline in the state. At 674.7 lakh pds in 2004-05, it constituted only 8.25 per cent of A-I total. In the total created, the share of landless workers came to only 29.7 per cent as against 39.9 per cent at the national level. (*ibid.*).

On the sub-schemes also Maharashtra's performance was very poor. Under the Million Well Scheme, over a period of eleven years, 1988-99, the state had constructed a total of 75,252 wells, constituting 5.77 per cent of A-I total, which was lower than in four the major states. The cost per well increased greatly; rising from the average of Rs. 33 thousand in 1988-95 to Rs. 49 thousand in 1995-99; the latter was significantly higher than the national average.

On the IAY also the situation was not good. In the A-I total number of houses constructed during 1985-95, the state's share came to only 5.86 per cent, and in the following four years it increased to 7.33 per cent The cost per house was doubled over the period and became higher than at the national level. The utilisation of available fund reached 112 per cent during 1995-99, but the physical achievement remained only 77 per cent of the target. In recent years, Maharashtra's situation worsened much. In 2008-09, up to January 21, the state had constructed 47,767 houses, constituting only 4.33 per cent of A-I total. The achievement in relation to target came to only 41.2 per cent as against 51.8 per cent at the national level.

On the EAS, launched in December 1993, also Maharashtra's performance was not good. In the national total of employment created during 1993-00, the state's share came to only 7.5 per cent, which was lower than in five of the states. The cost per personday was very low; at the average of Rs. 41 in this period, it was the lowest among the major states. From the employment created, the weaker sections were benefited to a very small extent. The relative share of SCs/STs in the total created during the seven-year period came to only 49.8 per cent as against 55.8 per cent at the national level. The situation of landless workers was still worse.

In terms of coverage of households, the provision of employment by public works as a whole had a sharp fall here. Per 1000 hhs, the number participating stood at only 33 in 1999-00, declining from 85 in 1993-94 and 118 in 1987-88. The latest was below the national average as against much higher earlier. (*ibid.*).

The NREGA, introduced in 2006-07, also had a very poor performance in Maharashtra. In the three years of 2006-09, the state had created only 40.8, 39.0 and 45 pds of employment per hh, and all these were below the national average. Total number of man-days of work created in the latest year was only 400 lakh and constituted a mere two per cent of All-India total. The proportion of hhs. completing 100 days of employment were a negligible 1.5 per cent in 2006-07 and 1.8 per cent in 2007-08. The statutory wage rate, applicable to the NREGA, was very low here. At Rs. 69, it was lower than in all but two of the states. It may be noted that the scheme could not spend even half the amount allocated to the 12 districts selected in the first phase. In Chandrapur, for example, a total of Rs. 51.35 crore was allocated during 2005-06 and 2006-07 but only Rs. 8.04 crore could be spent. (GOI 2008; Datar, Chhaya 2007).

Self-employment Programmes

On the most important self-employment programme, the IRDP, launched in 1980-81, Maharashtra had a poor performance. Number of families assisted had a sharp fall, declining from a total of 5.92 lakh in 1992-95 to 4.54 lakh in 1996-99; the latest was 8.6 per cent of A-I total, and among the major states lower than in three. After the restructuring of the scheme in April 1999, it declined further; to only 70,146 in 2004-05, constituted 6.40 per cent of A-I total. In terms of households, however, the situation was relatively good. Although the number Per 1000 hhs had declined from 77 in 1993-94 to 62 in 1999-00, the latest was 10 points higher than at the national level.

As regards the nature of organisation, the proportion of members from Self-Helf Groups had a sharp rise in recent years, to as much as 84.4 per cent in 2004-05 from only 17.7 in 2000-01; at the national level, the latest was 71.0 per cent. The nature of assets provided was also somewhat different here. In 1993-94, for example, milch animal accounted for 42.9 per cent of total beneficiaries, followed by sheep/goat at 22.1, drought animals 10.4 and pumpset 3.9 per cent; at the national level, it was respectively 40.3, 8.1, 11.3 and 8.1 per cent. (NSSO 1998c).

Among the beneficiaries, social group-wise, the SCs/STs had very low share; accounting for only 42.9 per cent of total in 1992-95 as against 62.6 per cent in all-India. In the following years also there was not much improvement; being at 48.7 per cent in 2004-05. The situation of women, however, improved greatly in recent years; rising to as much as 75.8 per cent of total in 2004-05 from 38.5 in 2000-01; at the national level, the latest was 54.5 per cent. MPCE class-wise, the distribution was very unfair here; a significant proportion came from the ineligible category. In 1999-00, per 1000 beneficiaries, the number in Rs. 950+ category was as much as 51, higher than in all but three of the states. The lowest class, below Rs. 225, on the other hand, had only 40.

The subsidies provided was relatively low in Maharashtra. The per capita subsidy in 1996-99 came to Rs. 6,405, rising from 3,419 in 1992-95; the latest was lower than in all but two of the states. On the credit per beneficiary also the situation was not much better. Although the amount was a little more than doubled over the period, the latest was below that in as many as five of the states. After the restructuring of the scheme, both the subsidy and the credit became very low here. In 2000-01, the subsidy disbursed totalled Rs. 17.54 crore and credit Rs. 28.50 crore, which were less than a fifth of that disbursed annually during 1996-99.

On the sub-schemes of the IRDP also Maharashtra's performance was not good. Under the TRYSEM, during 1992-99, the total number trained here constituted only 5.49 per cent of all-India total, which was below that in four of the states. The proportion of SC/ST in them was very low; being only 34.3 per cent in 1992-96 as against 45.2 per cent at the national level. The placement of the youths was also not good. During 1992-96, it came to 52.6 per cent of the total trained, below that in four of the states. The expenditure per trainee was, however, relatively high.

The performance on the DWCRA was slightly better. During 1992-99, a total of 14,056 groups were formed, constituting 6.31 per cent of A-I total, which was higher than in all but three of the states. The groups were, however, of smaller size here, and consequently the relative share in number of beneficiaries was less. The expenditure per group was noticeably higher than at the national level; at the average Rs. 27,035 in this period, it was 59.7 per cent higher. The total expenditure on the scheme, consequently, came to as much as 10.1 per cent of A-I total.

The situation of SITRA, launched in July 1992, was also similar. To look at the performance in only two of the years: The total number of beneficiaries here during 1997-99 came to only 22,192 and constituted 6.31 per cent of all-India total, which was lower than in three of the states. The expenditure per beneficiary was relatively high. At Rs. 2330, it was higher than the national average and among the major states, higher than in all but three. The relative share in A-I total expenditure, therefore, came to 7.05 per cent. It may be noted here that after the launch of the SGSY, the schemes like TRYSEM, DWCRA, SITRA, etc ceased to be in operation.

For the Backward Regions

The absolute poverty is visibly much more in the regions which are traditionally backward. Therefore, after the bifurcation of the state in May 1960, the Third Five-year Plan began a special effort to remove the imbalance in development. The main reason behind the backwardness of certain regions was the low agricultural productivity, and this in turn was mainly due to being frequently affected by scarcity conditions. The scarcity areas are largely in the districts of Ahmednagar, Solapur, Pune, Satara and Sangli in western Maharashtra and in the districts of Aurangabad, Bhir and Osmanabad in Marathwada. Except for certain small portions protected by major irrigation, agriculture in these districts is dependent on rainfall which is inadequate and unevenly distributed. The soils are undulating and shallow and, therefore, not retentive of moisture and are liable to heavy erosion. Konkan was another area that needed special attention. Except for pockets of paddy cultivation, the entire area had formidable problems of economic land utilisation. The area suffered from depleted production potential due to prolonged soil erosion. Vidarbha also suffered from water scarcity and other problems and needed special attention.

The Third Plan proposed to make additional allocation to Vidarbha and Marathwada regions so that the shortfall in the earlier plans could be wiped out by the end of Fifth Plan. But the increase was not much. For Konkan area, adjustments were made in the district-wise allocations on district-level schemes, and this brought an additional allocation of Rs. 3.71 crore to the Konkan districts compared to the rest of the Bombay Division. The increase in allocations to Vidarbha and Marathwada, particularly the former, was also not high. On irrigation, the allocation in proportion to population came to Rs. 19.48 crore for Vidarbha and the actual provided was Rs. 21.37 crore. For Marathwada, it was respectively Rs. 13.31 crore and Rs. 24.49 crore. On the scarcity areas, the Third Plan had a total outlay of Rs. 30.0 crore, constituting 29.7 per cent of the state's total. Purpose-wise, major and medium irrigation received Rs. 14.48 crore, constituting only 21.2 per cent of the state's total; and on minor irrigation, respectively Rs. 1.55 crore and 17.1 per cent. Contour bunding was provided Rs. 11.73 crore, 65.6 per cent of the total. (GOM 1961).

From around mid-seventies, the pattern of allocation for the disadvantaged areas changed radically. The drought-prone areas programme was started in 1974-75 with the objective of an integrated development of the identified DPAs. The emphasis was on optimising the use of land and water resources and providing gainful occupation to the weaker sections. The DPAP was implemented in 12 districts of Maharashtra—viz., Ahmednagar, Solapur, Satara, Sangli, Pune, Nashik, Aurangabad, Osmanabad, Beed, Jalgaon, Dhule and Buldane—out of which six received Central assistance. Later, the GOI identified 148 blocks as DPAP, spread over 25 districts in the state. The funding pattern also changed. The Fifth Plan spent only Rs. 29.23 crore on it against an outlay of Rs. 39.50 crore. (GOM 1981: 54).

In the following plans, there was virtually no growth in expenditure. The Sixth Plan spent only Rs. 26.48 crore—i.e., an absolute fall over the preceding plan's—and constituted 17.6 per cent of the total for rural development and a mere 0.41 per cent in the grand total. The Seventh Plan raised it to Rs. 32.92 crore, but the relative share declined to 2.09 per cent 0.30 per cent, respectively. In the Eighth Plan, the expenditure rose to Rs. 60.35 crore, but the relative shares were still only 2.13 per cent and 0.31 per cent. In the next Plan, the situation worsened much; with the expenditure at Rs. 80.44 crore, the relative shares came to 1.81 and 0.17 per cent. Thus, the DPAP was virtually a total neglect.

For Tribal Areas

The depressing situation of the tribals in Maharashtra has been noted earlier. Here, only a few facts about the extent of government's neglect of tribal development may be noted. Even at the level of Union government there was hardly any initiative worth the name. The executive power conferred to it under the Constitution's Fifth Schedule was totally violated, as noted in Chapter 12. The governors never used the wide ranging powers given to them for protecting the tribals. On the pattern of tribal development, the S C Dube committee, 1972, had defined the task as their social and economic development through fast and time-bound integrated area development and other programmes. The suggestions were, however, not concretised in terms of specific programmes in different states, suited to each scheduled area/Tribe. The strategy for integrated development led to the evolution of the tribal area sub-plan (TASP) concept in the Fifth Plan (1974-79). The area under TASP in Maharashtra was spread over 50.267 sq km in 51 Tehsils in the total population of this area at 37.14 lakh in 1971, tribals constituted 58 per cent. (GOI 1981a).

The resource allocation for the TASP continued to be very low. Although the state government had decided in early eighties that the plan allocation for the tribal areas should be equal to the percentage of tribals in the state's population (9.27), in actual practice it remained much less. In the Sixth Plan (1980-85), the TASP outlay was only Rs. 313.27 crore, constituting 4.88 per cent of the state's total. (GOM 1985: 38). In the Seventh Plan, it was respectively, Rs. 434.85 crore and 4.14 per cent. In the Eighth plan also the outlay constituted only 6.26 per cent, with the amount at Rs. 1159.18 crore. (GOM 1992). Even these funds often remained unutilised to a large extent.

The planning for tribal areas itself was generally defective. The study group on tribal sub-plan in the Ninth Plan had brought out that most of the over 300 different schemes being implemented in the tribal areas had outlived their utility. Further, most schemes were a copy of those being implemented in the non-tribal areas and were not suitable for the tribals. The impact of most of the schemes were negligible. The report also stated that the funds for the regional development boards were not being used in the tribal areas. Anything done in the tribal areas is done in the name of and with the funds allocated for tribal development, but it often goes to the non-tribals. (Kulkarni, S D 1980).

The fate of the protective measures taken by the government to prevent exploitation of the tribals were also not much better. Around mid-seventies, two laws were passed for restoring certain already alienated lands of the tribals. Of these, while the Maharashtra Land Revenue Code Tenancy Laws (Amendment) Act 1974—on lands alienated in contravention of the laws in force—was implemented more or less satisfactorily, the Maharashtra

Restoration of Land of Scheduled Tribes Act 1975—on land transferred to non-tribals by way of sales, etc., under the laws in force then—could not be implemented due to stay orders from the Supreme Court. The regularisation of the so-called encroached lands also could not be implemented properly because of deficiencies in the government resolutions. On the exploitation of tribals by traders, however, the Maharashtra State Tribal Development Corporation, set up in 1973, did some good work, particularly after the Maharashtra Tribal Economic Condition (Improvement) Act 1977 came into operation. Under the monopoly procurement scheme, the activities of the corporation were extended to 59 tahsils of the 14 districts by mid-eighties. The quantum procured during 1980-85 varied between 803 and 916 thousand quintals.

The exploitation of tribals by unscrupulous officials, however, continued almost unabated. Recently it was found that about 20,000 Pawra tribals living in the 30 villages of Chopda taluka of Jalgaon district were denied the lease to forest land although they fulfilled the eligibility criteria under the Forest Rights Act, 2006. They had submitted their claims to the Forest Rights Committee that recommends the cases to the sub-divisional committee. But as the FRC did not present the claims before the village committee, this gave the sub-divisional committee a convenient excuse to reject them. As a protest to this, the Adivasis boycott the polls held in April , 2009. (TST 2009r).

In this scenario of utter neglect of the tribals' development, it is no surprise that in recent years there has been demands for separation of some of the areas from the state. People in the highly underdeveloped Sironcha taluka in Gadchiroli district had been openly demanding the taluka's transfer from Maharashtra to Andhra. Similar demands are being raised in the equally backward Bhamragad taluka of the district. The Naxalite violence has also become more acute in recent years. The district most affected is Gadchiroli, followed by Gondia and Chandrapur. (TST 2007j).

But no ad hoc measures are going to solve the problem. In 2009, in Gadchiroli, 15 policemen were killed in an encounter in February, and again in October, another 17 in an ambush at a police station. The latter happened, on the very next day of a stern warning from the Union home minister. Recently, on March 27, 2012, at least 13 CRPF personnel were killed and 17 others were injured due to a high intensity landmine blast near Pushtola village in Gadchiroli district. (TST 2007j; 2009g; 2009m, z34; 2012 z6). The only way out of violence and disorder in a radical change in the attitude of the government and a determined attack on the poverty.

PART V: THE ECONOMY OF GUJARAT

18

RESOURCE MOBILISATION AND DEPLOYMENT

I: THE GOVERNMENT BUDGETS

Before gong into the details of changes in resource mobilisation and expenditure, a brief look may be given to the situation of some of the broad indicators of fiscal health. The gross fiscal deficit (GFD) of Gujarat had worsened noticeably over the years. As percentage to the GSDP, it averaged (-) 4.80 during 2002-05, rising from (-)1.82 in 1993-96; the latest was higher than the All-States' average. The revenue deficit as percentage to fiscal deficit averaged as much as 81.2 in 2000-03 as against 62.0 for All-States. The own revenue receipts/own revenue expenditure averaged only 0.588 in 2000-03, declining from 0.830 in 1990-93; the latest was lower than in six of the states. The composite index on budgetary health, based on eight fiscal indicators, had also declined from 69.46 in 1990-95 to 41.56 in 2000-03; the latest was lower than in six of the states. As regards recent years, the per capita GFD in 2009-10 came to as much as Rs. 2640, which was 55.4 per cent higher than in A-S (1699). The gross revenue deficit was still worse. At the per capita of Rs. 1168, it was nearly five times that in A-S (Rs 245). (GOI 2000b, 2004; CMIE 2006a, 2011c).

Resource Mobilisation

On the total budgetary resources mobilised, Gujarat's situation was not bad. The per capita total receipt in 2000-03 averaged Rs. 5,267, which was 36 per cent higher than in A-S; in 1975-78, it was only 1.75 per cent higher. Among the states, Gujarat's latest was the highest. In the total receipts, however, the share of revenue receipts had a sharp fall, to only 62.0 per cent in 2000-03 from 88.7 in 1975-78; the latest was much below the A-S average. The per capita receipt, however, remained higher than in the latter; At Rs. 3,268 in 2000-03, it was higher by 28.9 per cent. The growth in capital receipts was very high, by 58.8 times in this period as against 46.3 times for A-S. The per capita receipt in 2000-03 was Rs. 1,999, which was 51 per cent higher than in A-S; in 1975-78, at Rs. 56.52, it was only 19.0 per cent higher. In recent years, the state's budgetary situation worsened considerably. In 2009-10, the per capita total receipt stood at Rs. 10,382 as against Rs. 9,100 for A-S—i.e., the former only 14.1 per cent higher. The proportion of revenue receipt in the total increased to 69.3 per cent, but it was 4.9 point below that in A-S The per capita revenue receipt came to

Rs. 7,196, only 6.6 per cent higher than in the latter. The capital receipt constituted a much as 30.3 per cent of total, and the per capita receipt came to Rs. 3,186, which was 35.6 per cent higher than in A-S. (CMIE 2011c).

Revenue Receipts

In the revenue receipts, the contribution of tax revenue had worsened over the years; being down to 65.0 per cent in 2000-03 from 70.2 in 1975-78. The growth in tax revenue over the entire period was by 28.6 times as against 32.0 times for A-S. Per capita tax revenue came to Rs. 2,124 in 2000-03, which was 18.4 per cent higher than in A-S; in 1975-78, it was higher by 32.4 per cent. The relative position of non-tax revenue naturally improved. The growth in NTR over the period was 36.3 times here as against 22.7 times for A-S. The per capita NTR in 2000-03 came to Rs. 11,437, 54.2 per cent higher than in A-S. On the collection of own revenue, the situation was not good. As percentage to GSDP, it came to only 9.20 in 2006-07, which was lower than in most of the states.

In recent years, in 2009-10, the situation of tax revenue improved considerably. Its share in total revenue increased to 78.3 per cent, which was 9.6 points higher than in A-S. The per capita tax revenue came to Rs. 5635 as against Rs. 4637 in the latter—i.e., the former 21.5 per cent higher. The situation of non-tax revenue worsened noticeably. Per capita NTR came to only Rs. 1561 as against Rs. 2113 for A-S. (CMIE 2011c).

Tax Revenue

In the tax revenue, the proportion of own collection was naturally high in an industrialised state like Gujarat. It rose to as much as 86.3 per cent in 2000-03 from 76.6 in 1975-78; at the level of A-S, the latest was only 71.4 per cent. The tax transfer from the centre was relatively low. As regards the composition of OTR, it is evident that the taxes on commodities and services continued to provide the overwhelming proportion—to the extent of 91-92 per cent till 1997; the latest at the level of A-S was 89.7 per cent. In recent years also it was similar. In 2002-05, it provided 90.4 per cent as against 87.2 in the latter. The share of taxes on property, etc., declined from 8.05 per cent in 1975-78 to 6.42 in 1988-91 and then recovered to 7.63 in 1997-00; at the level of A-S, the latest was 9.73 per cent. In 2002-05, it rose to 8.62 per cent as against 11.4 per cent in A-S. The taxes on income had provided only 0.98 per cent in 1997, declining from 1.76 in 1988-91; for All-States, the latest was 1.57 per cent.

Intra-group, in the taxes on commodities and services, the share of sales tax rose to as much as 77.4 per cent in 1988-91 from 69.0 in 1975-78, and then declined to 70.1 in 1997. Within sales tax, the proportion contributed by both the state sales tax and the central sales tax declined whereas that from motor spirit and lubricant was more than trebled—rising to 20.79 per cent in 1997 from 6.57 in 1975-78. The collection from state excise was very low due to the prohibition policy. The entertainment tax and taxes on goods and passengers also had a sharp fall. The fastest growth was in duties on electricity. The collection had risen 72.7-fold between 1975-78 and 1997-00; and the relative share rose to 18.9 per cent from 6.8. In the total OTR, it had provided 17.3 per cent in 1997, which was around five times that in A-S. Taxes on vehicles also had a high growth, but still it provided only 6.52 of the OTR in 1997-00, rising from 3.93 in 1988-91; at the level of A-S the latest was 5.88 per cent. As regard the recent situation, in 2002-05, the central sales tax had provided 13.67 per cent of total from commodities and services, rising from 10.7 in 1997-00.

Non-Tax Revenue

In the NTR, the proportion of own collection had shown a decline. After rising to 68.3 per cent in 1975-78, from 57.3 in 1965-68, it declined again to 64.0 per cent in 2000-03; the latest was, however, much higher than the A-S average. On per capita basis, the ONTR in 2000-03 came to Rs. 731.64, which was 122.9 per cent higher than in A-S, and in relation to Maharashtra 43.8 per cent higher. The Grants from the Centre had risen by only 43.2 times between 1965-68 and 1997 as against 67.6 times in Maharashtra. The per capita grant, however, remained high until recently. In 2002-05, it came to Rs. 431 as against Rs. 214 in the latter. In recent years, the situation was very poor. In 2009-10, it stood at only Rs. 620 as against Rs. 1014 in Maharashtra and the A-S average at Rs. 1312.

The composition of the ONTR changed noticeably over the years. The relative share of economic services declined to only 20.2 per cent in 1997-00 from 37.9 in 1988-91. This was a part of the general trend; at the level of A-S also it had declined from 52.0 per cent in 1975-78 to only 19 per cent in 1997-00. In recent years, however, its share increased again to as much as 51.3 per cent in 2002-05, and for A-S to 44.1. In economic services, the highest contributor continued to be industries, providing as much as 69.2 per cent in 1997. Among other items, major and medium irrigation had provided 15.7 per cent in 1997-00, rising from 8.0 in 1988-91. The contribution from forestry, etc., had a sharp fall over the years.

Capital Receipts

As noted earlier, the capital receipts acquired an increasing importance over the years. Its composition also changed noticeably. Until recently, the highest proportion always came from Central loans, providing as much as 48.4 per cent in 1997—compared with only 35.6 per cent in A-S—declining from 51.6 per cent in 1988-91. But in 2002-05, the central loans contributed only 15.5 per cent; the per capita receipt was, however, still as much as Rs. 387—46.6 per cent higher than the A-S average. More recently, in 2009-10, it came down to only Rs. 15 as against Rs. 87 in A-S. In the composition of the loans, non-plan loans accounted for the highest proportion. In 1997-00, it was as much as 69.5 per cent, declining from 74.5 in 1988-91; at the level of A-S, the latest was only

46.2 per cent. The loans under state plan schemes came next with a share of 30.3 per cent in 1997-00, declining from 48.9 in 1975-78; at the level of A-S, the latest was 43.4 per cent. The centrally sponsored schemes had a very small share.

The contribution from internal debt was generally low. In 1997-00, it had provided 11.7 per cent of total, rising from 7.2 in 1988-91. In recent years, however, it increased to as much as 27.6 per cent in 2002-05, with the amount at Rs. 3647 crore—a 5.4-fold rise over 1997-00. The sharpest fall was in recovery of loans and advances; the relative share declining to 3.11 per cent in 1997-00, from 15.3 in 1988-91. In 2002-05 also it provided only 2.76 per cent as against 5.37 per cent at the level of A-S. Among other items, deposits and advances had contributed as much as 22.9 per cent in 1997-00, rising from only 6.31 in 1988-91. Small savings, PF, etc., made a very small contribution here; providing only 6.31 per cent in 1997-00 as against 14.4 per cent at the level of A-S.

The debt burden of the state had risen rapidly over the years. Between 1981 and 2003, it was by 39.7 times as against 28.4 times for A-S. The per capita debt in 2003 came to as much as Rs. 9,244, the highest among the states. The debt as percentage to GSDP rose to 37.0 in 2003-07 from 20.41 in 1990-91 and 14.55 in 1980-81; the latest was, however, still 3.2 points below the A-S average. In the composition of the debt, the relative share of central loans had declined while that of internal debt rose rapidly. The former's was down to 40.2 per cent in 2003, from 65.0 in 1981; the latest was higher than in A-S as against lower earlier. The proportion for internal debt was more than doubled in this period, rising from 23.9 per cent to 52.7; in A-S, the latest was 48.2 per cent. The burden of interest payment became very heavy. In 2002-05, it constituted 29.9 per cent of total revenue as against 25.0 per cent in A-S.

Trend in Expenditure

The budgetary expenditure of the government of Gujarat was quite high. The per capita total expenditure in 2002-05 came to Rs. 5,981 as against Rs. 4,768 for All-States, i.e., the former 25.4 per cent higher; earlier, in 1975-78, it was 18.0 per cent higher. In recent years, in 2009-10, it came to Rs. 10,419, which was 16.4 per cent higher than in A-S. The proportion of developmental in the total increased from 58.7 per cent in 1975-78 to 68.3 in 1997-00; the latest was 8.9 points higher than the A-S average. The per capita development expenditure in 1998-01 came to Rs. 3,107, which was 76 per cent higher than in A-S. In recent years, the situation worsened much. In 2002-05, the share of developmental was only 59.3 per cent, 3.9 points higher than in A-S. The per capita expenditure came to Rs. 2,531 as against Rs. 1,947 for A-S, i.e., the former 30.0 per cent higher. As percentage to GSDP, the development expenditure was very low in recent years; being only 9.9 in 2006-07 as against 12.0 for All-States. (RBI 2009).

As regards revenue versus capital, the former's share had risen to 83.0 per cent in 2000-03, from 64.7 in 1975-78, but declined again to 71.4 per cent in 2002-05; each of these was below the A-S average. The per capita revenue expenditure, however, continued to be higher than in the latter. In 2002-05, it was respectively Rs. 4,270 and Rs. 3,517—i.e., the former 21 per cent higher. The growth in revenue expenditure was by as much as 50 times between 1975-78 and 2000-03 as against only 39 times for A-S. As percentage to GSDP, the revenue expenditure had risen from 12.52 in 1993-96 to 18.37 in 2000-03; the latest for A-S was 16.67. The capital disbursements had a much lower growth. Between 1975-78 and 2000-03 it was by only 18.3 times; even this was higher than in A-S. The per capita disbursement was always higher than in the latter. In 2002-05, it was respectively Rs. 1,710 and Rs. 1,232, i.e., the former 38.8 per cent higher; earlier, in 1988-91, also it was similarly placed. This was despite a large share of the capital receipts going to meet the revenue deficit. In 2000-03, it was to the extent of 54.7 per cent as against 41.5 per cent at the level of A-S. Below, a look is given to the pattern of changes in the composition of expenditures.

Revenue Expenditure

In the revenue expenditure of Gujarat, the proportion of developmental was relatively high. In 1997, it stood at 68.3 per cent, declining from 71.5 in 1988-91; the latest was still 9 points higher than in A-S. In the development expenditure, the proportion going to social services was relatively low, being always lower than in A-S. The per capita expenditure was, however, noticeably higher than in the latter. The expenditures on the other items were very low. In 2002-05, welfare of SC, etc., had a per capita of Rs. 97 which was 28.6 per cent higher than in A-S. On water supply, etc., it was only Rs. 38.55 as against Rs. 59.23 in the latter; and in social security, etc., at Rs. 45 and Rs. 68, respectively. On nutrition, however, at Rs. 58, it was more than double that in A-S (Rs. 26.82); and in urban development, at Rs. 92 as against Rs. 43 in the latter. More recently, in 2009-10, the per capita expenditure on some of the items were as follows: family welfare at Rs. 59 as against Rs. 48 in A-S; water supply, etc., at Rs. 126 and Rs. 93, respectively; Nutrition Rs. 160 and Rs. 97; and welfare of SC. etc., Rs. 182 and Rs. 181.

On economic services, Gujarat spent a relatively large amount. The situation of agriculture etc was very poor. As regards nondevelopment expenditure, it had risen sharply over the years; and the relative share rose to as much as 40.7 per cent in 2002-05, from 31.4 in 1997-00 and 28.0 in 1988-91. The per capita N-DE in 2002-05 came to Rs. 1,740 as against Rs. 1,570 at the level of A-S. The single most important item here was interest payment. Its relative share rose to 61.0 per cent in 2002-05, from 49.0 in 1997 and 28.0 in 1975-78; at the level of A-S, the latest was only 48.2 per cent. The per capita expenditure on it came to Rs. 1,062 in 2002-05 as against Rs. 757 for All-

States—i.e., the former 40.3 per cent higher. In 2009-10, at Rs. 1483, it was 49.5 per cent higher.

The highest growth in expenditure was in pension payment. The last category under revenue expenditure, compensation and assignments to local bodies and PRIs, had a very low growth, and the relative share declined from 0.87 per cent in 1975-78 to 0.34 in 1997. The per capita expenditure in 1997 was only Rs. 11.01, less than a third of the A-S average (Rs. 39.09). In the following years also there was no noticeable improvement. In 2002-05, the relative share increased to 0.51 per cent, which was less than a third of that in A-S. The per capita expenditure came to only Rs. 22 as against Rs. 67 in the latter. More recently, in 2009-10, also the situation was very poor. The per capita expenditure was only Rs. 18.30 as against Rs. 178 in A-S.

Capital Expenditure

In the capital disbursements of Gujarat, a welcoming feature is the high growth of development expenditure. In economic services, the most important item was irrigation, etc., and its share rose to 74.5 per cent in 1997, from 65.5 in 1988-91 and 23.5 in 1975-78. The per capita expenditure in 1997-00 came to Rs. 292 as against only Rs. 84 in A-S, i.e., the former 248 per cent higher; in 2002-05 also the situation was similar, being respectively Rs. 510 and Rs. 157. The next important item was transport. etc., and its share increased from 13.5 per cent in 1997-00 to 20.1 in 2002-05. The per capita expenditure in 2002-05 came to Rs. 115 as against Rs. 88 in A-S. In 2009-10, however, it was below the latter's—being respectively Rs. 275 and Rs. 328. On agriculture etc the relative share was not high, and the per capita in 1997 came to only Rs. 40; even this was, however, 129 per cent higher than in A-S (Rs 17). In 2002-05, there was a sharp fall; the per capita came to Rs. 25.42 as against Rs. 26.88 in A-S.

In social services, with a high growth in expenditure, the relative share rose to 19.2 per cent in 1997-00 from 11.6 in 1988-91. The per capita expenditure in 1997 came to Rs. 93, which was 120 per cent higher than in A-S. In 2002-05 also it was in a similar position; being respectively Rs. 235 and Rs. 116. In social services, water supply, etc., accounted for the highest proportion; rising from 58.3 per cent in 1988-91 to 70.8 in 1997. The per capita expenditure in 1997-00 came to Rs. 66, which was four times that in A-S. In 2002-05, at Rs. 92, it was only 102.6 per cent higher.

Plan Expenditure

The plan expenditure in Gujarat was quite high. As regards the sectorial pattern of expenditure, in the earlier plans, the highest proportion always went for irrigation and power. It increased from 34.0 per cent in the Second Plan to 53.5 in the Fourth; in the following plans it declined, and in the total for nine five-year plans it came to 34.4 per cent. Social and community services came next, and received an average of 32.5 per cent for all the plans together; a noticeable increase, however, came only since the Seventh Plan (1985-90). The relative share of agriculture etc had a sharp fall over the years; from 24.86 per cent in the Second plan to 13.63 in the Fourth and 6.71 per cent in the Eighth plan. In the following two plans also it averaged only 8.04 per cent. Transport etc was also in a similar situation; and the average for all the plans together came to only 4.9 per cent of total. The allocation to industry, etc., varied between four and seven per cent. For a comparison with the All-states' pattern, a look is given to only the latest Tenth plan's per capita outlays (based on 2001 population). Social services, with the highest allocation in this plan, gave a per capita of Rs. 2,982, which was 73.1 per cent higher than in A-S (Rs. 1,723).

Local Bodies

Panchayat Raj Institutions

The panchayats in Gujarat had a three tier system since April 1963, on the basis of the Gujarat Panchayat Act 1961. After the 73rd amendment of the Constitution, the Gujarat Panchayat Act 1993 was passed. There are presently 13,507 Village Panchayat, 184 Taluka Panchayats and 19 District Panchayats. The devolution of powers and responsibilities to PRIs was relatively good here. A devolution index prepared by the IIPA shows Gujarat with 53.07 in 2009 as against the national average of 45.04. Gujarat's rank among the states was seventh. (GOI 2011a).

The revenue resources of the PRIs had a noticeable rise after mid-seventies. Whereas between 1963-64 and 1973-74 it was by only 314.8 per cent—from Rs. 26.70 crore to Rs. 110.76 crore—in the following two decades it was by as much as 1025 per cent, the amount reaching Rs. 1245.88 crore in 1993-94. The expenditure also increased similarly, from Rs. 25.50 crore in 1963-64 to Rs. 112.57 crore in 1973-74 and then to Rs. 1158.45 crore in 1993-94—i.e., a 45.4-fold rise over the period of three decades. A detailed look is given below to the pattern of change since early 'nineties.

The relative position of Gujarat among the states was quite good. The per capita total revenue of PRIs, for all tiers together, came to Rs. 770.46 in 1995-98, which was nearly three times the all-States' average and second highest among the states. The proportion of own revenue in the total was, however, very low; being at only 1.9 per cent in 1995-98 as against 3.7 per cent at the level of A-S. It had actually declined from 2.7 per cent in 1990-91 to 1.8 in 1997-98. The situation of village level PRI in it was very poor. The per capita total revenue came to only Rs. 38 in 1995-98, which was around half that in A-S and lowest among the states. The proportion of own revenue in the total was, however, as much as 29.0 per cent, nearly three times that in A-S.

In the revenue collection by the PRIs, the own revenues came mainly from the village level; in 1995-98, it was to the extent of 77.2 per cent. This was, however, much below the A-S average, and lowest among the states. In the own revenue of PRIs, the contribution of tax revenue was relatively high. The contribution of non-tax revenue to the OR was, therefore, very low. As regards the expenditures, for all tiers combined it was very high but at the village level it was extremely low. A notable aspect of the expenditure at village level in Gujarat is that the proportion going for core services (water supply, street lighting, sanitation and roads) was quite high.

Urban Local Bodies

The financial situation of the ULBs in Gujarat was very good. The state accounted for 9.47 per cent of all-States' total revenue from ULBs in 1995-98, which was next only to Maharashtra. The per capita TR came to Rs. 692, 39.0 per cent higher than in A-S. The proportion of own revenue in the total was also relatively high. At 74.9 per cent in 1995-98, it was 6.5 points higher than in A-S. The per capita OR in this period came to Rs. 518, which was 51.9 per cent higher than in the latter. In the following years, the relative position improved further. In 2002-03, at Rs. 494.48, it was 90.1 per cent higher. The own revenue in Gujarat could finance as much as 74.6 per cent of total expenditure in 2002-03 as against only 52.6 per cent at the level of A-S. Earlier, in 1998-99, also it was in a similar position.

In the own revenue, the contribution from taxes was very high. During 1995-98, it was to the extent of 89.6 per cent, which was the highest among the states. The per capita own tax in 1998-99 came to Rs. 360, nearly double the A-S average. In 2002-03, it improved further to 123 per cent higher, with the amount at Rs. 390.85. Transfers to the ULBs in Gujarat were very low. The per capita in 2002-03 came to only Rs. 112.60, substantially below the A-S average.

Transfers as a whole were, however, not low. As percentage to the state revenue, it declined from 24.57 in 1998-99 to 16.7 in 2002-03; both were much higher than in A-S. The per capita transfer in 2002-03 came to Rs. 565, which was 138 per cent higher than in the latter.

PART II: THE BANKING SYSTEM

Co-operative Credit Institutions

The co-operative credit system in Gujarat was on the whole quite strong. Taking all tiers and types of societies together, their working capital had risen by 19.4 times between 1961 and 1981 and in the following 17 years, by another 9.09 times. The working capital per society increased from Rs. 1.18 lakh in 1961 to Rs. 9.89 lakh in 1981 and Rs. 58.83 lakh in 1998; i.e., a 49.9-fold rise over the entire period. In the working capital, however, the owned fund constituted only 10.86 per cent in 1998, declining from 17.92 in 1981 and 21.75 in 1961. The growth in membership of societies was low. Per society it had risen from 150 in 1961 to 210 in 1981 and 260 in 1998. (GOG 2000).

The relative position among the states was, however, very good. The state accounted for 13.1 per cent of all-India total working capital in 1998, which was next only to Maharashtra. The working capital per society came to as much as Rs. 208.87 lakh, 51 per cent higher than the national average. In the working capital, deposits had contributed as much as 66.5 per cent this year, which was incomparably higher than at the national level. Deposit per society was nearly double that in the latter. In the A-I total deposit, the state's share came to 17.2 per cent.

In the total number of societies, primary societies naturally constituted the bulk. Among them again, the PACS and the PNACS were particularly important. In the total number of societies, they constituted respectively 14.7 per cent and 9.43 per cent in 1998; in 1981, it was 23.7 and 7.61 per cent. Below a detailed look is given to their operation.

Primary Agricultural Credit Societies

The PACS in Gujarat were not in a very strong position. Number of societies had declined, and the growth in membership was low. Over a period of nearly four decades, 1961 to 1998, the membership had risen by only 227.8 per cent. The relative position of Gujarat's PACS among the states had worsened noticeably. The working capital per society which was much higher than the national average in 1970, became substantially lower in 1998, being only 70.8 per cent of the latter's. The situation of deposit per society was still worse; being a little more than a tenth of all-India's in 1998 as against 41.0 per cent higher in 1970. The lending activities also became low. Loans outstanding per society in 1998 was only 78 per cent of that at the national level as against 133 per cent higher earlier. The membership per society in 1998 was around a third of that in all-India. In recent years also on the whole the situation remained more or less the same. In March 2005, the working capital per society came to only Rs. 44 lakh, which was 63.8 per cent of that at the national level. The deposit per society was only Rs. 1.7 lakh as against Rs. 17.4 lakh in the latter. The borrowings per society was also much below that in all-India. The loans outstanding per society improved substantially, but it could not cross the national average. The proportion of overdue continued to be high.

Non-Agricultural Credit Societies

The situation of PNACS in the state is better than that of PACS. Between 1961 and 1998, number of societies had multiplied 5.5 times and of membership 13.5 times. The growth in working capital was as much as 832 times—from Rs. 15.53 crore in 1961 to Rs. 12927.45 crore in 1998. Per society, it had risen from Rs. 1.85 lakh to Rs. 278 lakh. The contribution of owned fund in it had, however, declined from 26.9 per cent in 1961 to 16.4 in 1981 and 11.2 in 1998. The growth in deposits was very high, and its relative share rose to 74.5 per cent in 1998 from 61.4 in 1981. The lending activities increased greatly, and per society it rose to Rs. 130 lakh in 1998, from Rs. 1.07 lakh in 1961, i.e., by 121 times. The level of over dues was low, and 80 per cent of the societies showed profits. (GOG 2000).

The relative position of Gujarat's PNACS among the states was, however, not good. In the all-India total working capital of PNACS, the state's share declined from 14.0 per cent in 1970 to only 4.39 in 1998. The working capital per society stood at only Rs. 12.17 lakh in 1998, which was a mere 40.8 per cent of the national average; earlier, it was much higher than in the latter. The deposit mobilisation also moved similarly. Per society, it came to only Rs. 5.91 lakh in 1998, around half the national average. The relative share in working capital declined to 48.6 per cent, from 66.1 per cent in 1970, but it became much higher than in the latter. The lending activities increased noticeably but the relative position had a sharp fall. The amount outstanding per society in 1998 came to Rs. 8.67 lakh, a mere 46.0 per cent of A-I average; in 1970, it was higher than in the latter. The situation of overdue also worsened. The inter-district variation in operation of the PNACS was very high.

As regards the variation in share capital of the societies, per society in 1980-81, at the highest it was Rs. 3.31 lakh in Mahesana and the lowest at Rs. 60 thousand in Kachchh, with the state average at Rs. 2.12 lakh. On deposit per society, the variation was much higher. The highest was Rs. 100.82 lakh in Surendranagar and the lowest at Rs. 33 thousand in Dangs—i.e., the former 305.5 times the latter—with Rs. 15.46 lakh at the state level. The borrowings per society were very low in most of the districts. At the highest it was Rs. 5.20 lakh in Gandhinagar and the lowest at Rs. 15 thousand in Vadodara—i.e., the former 34.7 times the latter—with the state average at Rs. 2.37 lakh; six districts had borrowings of less than Rs. 50 thousand. On loan operations, the outstanding per society varied between the highest of Rs. 29.33 lakh in Rajkot and the lowest at Rs. 2.08 lakh in Dangs, with the state average at Rs. 15.16 lakh. (GOG 1985).

Commercial Banks

The performance of SCBs in Gujarat has not been good. In deposit mobilisation, the state's share had declined from 8.0 per cent of A-I total in 1971 to 6.75 in 1983, 5.07 in 2006 and further to 4.72 per cent in 2010. The per capita deposit in the latest year came to Rs. 36,663 as against the national average of Rs. 38,400; in 1983, it was 36.0 per cent higher than in All-India. The rural situation has also worsened. In 2004, The rural share of total deposit came to only 11.0 per cent in 2010, declining from 14.1 in 2004; at the national level, the fall was from 12.9 per cent to 9.22 in this period The rural deposit per office had risen from Rs. 7.96 crore in 2004 to Rs. 15.5 crore in 2010; both were higher than in All-India—being respectively at Rs. 6.08 crore and Rs. 13.01 crore.

On credit deployment, the situation was very poor. At March-end 2006, the state accounted for only 3.86 per cent of A-I total, declining from 5.36 in 1993. The per capita credit in 2006 came to only Rs. 10,869, which was 78.3 per cent of the national average, and in relation to Maharashtra's, only 22.3 per cent. Earlier, in 1993, the relative position was much better; Gujarat's being

10 per cent higher than the national average. In recent years, there was some imnprovement. In 2009-10, the per capita credit came to Rs. 27,570, which was 99.4 per cent of All-India's. The C-D ratio continued to be much below the latter's. In 2006, it was respectively 55.1 and 72.4 per cent. The rural situation was extremely poor. The relative share in total credit had declined from 17.3 per cent in 1993 to 10.4 in 2004 and further to 8.78 in 2006; the latest was nominally higher than in All-India. The rural C-D ratio stood at only 41.8 per cent in 2006, which was 14 points below the national average. Another distressing aspect is that the small borrowers were largely neglected. In 2006, they accounted for only 15.0 per cent of total credit, below the A-I average.

Regional Rural Banks

The RRBs also had a very poor performance in Gujarat. The state's share in all-India total deposit in 2010 stood at only 2.78 per cent, rising from 2.62 in 2004, 1.8 in 1989 and 0.79 in 1981. The deposit per office had risen from Rs. 3.72 crore in 2004 to Rs. 9.31 crore in 2010; the latter was nominally higher than in All-India but the former lower. The growth in number of accounts between 1981 and 2000 was by as much as 40.9 times, more than four times that in all-India. The relative share in A-I total number was, however, still only 2.36 per cent.

As regards loan operations, the amount outstanding had risen by as much as 719 times between 1981 and 2006 as against only 45.7 times in all-India. The state's share in A-I total rose to 2.98 per cent in 2002 from 0.31 in 1981, but in 2006 it declined to 2.55 per cent. The amount per branch had risen by as much as 103 times over the entire period as against only 29 times for All-India; the latest was, however, below the latter's. The C-D ratio had declined, and in 2006 it went below the all-India average. The loan recovery situation of Gujarat's RRBs was relatively good. The recovery as percentage to demand in 2001 stood at 77, which was 6 points higher than the A-I average.

The inter-RRB performance in Gujarat varied noticeably. The deposits per branch in March 2002 was at the highest Rs. 566 lakh in Kutch GB and the lowest at Rs. 186 lakh in Junagadh-Amreli Bank, with Rs. 312 lakh at the state level. The borrowings varied between the highest of Rs. 73.43 lakh in Jamnagar GB and the lowest at Rs. 15.57 lakh in Valsad-Dangs—i.e., the former 4.7 times the latter—with the state average at Rs. 46.27 lakh. On loans outstanding, the highest amount per branch this year was less than double that in the lowest, being respectively Rs. 186.1 lakh in Jamnagar and Rs. 99.7 lakh in Junagadh-Amreli, with Rs. 143.6 lakh at the state level. The C-D ratio was only 0.24 in Kutch as against the highest of 0.61 in Jamnagar, with the state average at 0.46. (NABARD 2003).

The efficiency level of banks varied greatly. The proportion of Non-performing Assets in 2002 was only 1 per cent in Jamnagar GB as against 34 per cent in Surat-Bharuch GB, with the state average at 14. The recovery as percentage to demand was as much as 96 in Junagadh-Amreli compared with 44 in Banaskantha-Mehsana. The productivity per employee varied noticeably. The highest was Rs. 135 lakh in Kutch as against the lowest at Rs. 76 lakh in Junagadh-Amreli, with state average at Rs. 109 lakh. The productivity per branch varied to a much greater extent. The highest was Rs. 701 lakh in Kutch and the lowest at Rs. 286 lakh in Junagadh-Amreli, with state average at Rs. 455 lakh.

More than a decade earlier, in 1989, also the inter-bank disparities were similar. The highest deposit per branch was 2.96 times the lowest—respectively Rs. 23.45 lakh in Kutch and Rs. 7.91 lakh in Sabarkantha-Gandhinagar GB—with Rs. 15.88 lakh at the state level. On loans outstanding, the variation was higher the highest being 3.15 times the lowest—Rs. 15.36 lakh in Kutch and Rs. 4.88 lakh in Junagadh-Amreli—with the state average at Rs. 11.85 lakh. The situation of C-D ratio was much better then. (NABARD 1990).

19

HUMAN RESOURCE DEVELOPMENT: EDUCATION AND HEALTH

EDUCATION

Gujarat's educational situation has been relatively good, as noted in chapter 2. The situation of some more indicators may be looked into here. The proportion of 15 years and above not literate in 1995-96 stood at only 38.9 per cent in Gujarat, which was 12 points below the national average. In rural areas, however, at 48.0 per cent, it was only 5.6 points below the latter's; for females, the proportion was as much as 63.9 per cent. After nearly a decade, in 2004, on seven years and above, percentage not literate was found to be 37.4 in rural areas, only 1.5 points below the national average. In females, 51.2 per cent were not literate, which was higher than the all-India average.

On the literates, Gujarat's situation was worse. In 2004, in rural areas (among seven years and above), 34.0 per cent were below middle school, with females at 28.2; both were higher than at the national level. The proportion with secondary and above stood at only 11.5 per cent, which was just at par with the latter's; for females, at 7.6 per cent, it was nominally higher. Social group-wise, the state's position was not bad. District-wise, there were great variations in the educational situation.

Schooling Facilities

The availability of schools in Gujarat was not bad. The growth in number of schools was by 63.0 per cent between 1980-81 and 2005; the relative share in A-I total, however, declined from 11.7 per cent to 8.23. On secondary schools also the situation was not bad. Number of schools had risen by 253 per cent over the period. As regards the management of schools, as in Maharashtra, here also the proportion of government schools was very low. At the Primary and Middle levels, local bodies accounted for as much as 78 per cent in each in 2004-05; almost the entire balance constituted private schools. In High schools also government-managed formed only 3.23 per cent; private aided constituted 65.3 per cent and private schools 28.1. At Pre-degree/ HS level, the proportions were respectively 4.35, 72.6 and 19.8 per cent. At the national level, the pattern was quite different. (GOI 2007a).

On the availability of rooms in schools, the situation at primary level was very poor. Average number per school in 1994 came to only 1.92, which was below the national average. Number of teachers in schools was very low. The pupil-teacher ratio in primary schools increased to 60 in 2000-01 from 41 in 1980-81; at the national level, the latest was only 43. On middle schools, the ratio increased from 38 to 45 over the period. After four years, in 2004-05, however, the ratio declined to 35 in primary schools and 39 at the middle level. Average number of teachers per elementary school in 2005 came to 5.3. Among the teachers, number of females was high here. Per 100 male teachers, there were 113 females at the primary level and 96 at middle level; in all-India, it was respectively 64 and 60. The P-T ratio in high schools was relatively good. It had risen from 24 in 1980-81 to 29 in 2000-01 and 34 in 2004-05; the latest was higher than the national average. Among the teachers, the proportion of females was only 31 per 100 males in 2004-05, which was half the national average.

The enrolment situation in Gujarat was good only at the primary level. The net attendance ratio was also similarly placed. There were many reasons behind the high drop-out rate. The provision of incentives for attracting students to schools was, however, very good here.

Adult Education

Adult education, as elsewhere in the country, did not receive the attention it deserved. According to the 1971 census, Gujarat had about 41.75 lakh illiterates in the age-group 15-35. By the end of 1979-80 about 9 lakh were covered by the Adult Education Programme (AEP). The 1981 census, however, found the number of illiterates to have risen to 47.85 lakh. The backlog of illiterate adults in April 1985 was estimated at 41.62 lakh. Almost all the programmes on adult education emphasised involvement of voluntary agencies.

The GOI guidelines had required all adults to be covered by the AEP during the Seventh Plan (1985-90). The plan, however, targeted to cover only 24 lakh, both through the centrally assisted AEP and the state AEP. The outlay on AEP increased from Rs. 250 lakh in the Sixth Plan to Rs. 700.40 lakh in the Seventh and Rs. 2020 lakh in the Eighth Plan; the proportion for state AEP had declined to 55.7 per cent in the Eighth Plan from 71.4 in the preceding plan. The Total Literacy Campaign—financed by the GOI to the extent of two-thirds—was launched in 1989.

The TLC was estimated to cover 42 lakh illiterate adults in Gujarat by March 1997. It was to be implemented in 17 districts, as Gandhinagar and Bhavnagar had already achieved total literacy. The performance of the programme was relatively good here. By March 1998, 61.17 lakh adults, constituting 8.4 per cent of all-India total, were made literate. The proportion under the TLC was, however, only 67.1 per cent compared with 72.3 per cent in All-India. The achievement in relation to target came to 59.2 per cent, which was 17.7 points higher than the national average On the post-literacy phase also the state's performance was relatively good. The proportion completing

PL-I by the end of Eighth Plan was 49.4 per cent of the target, 9.4 points higher than the national average.

In recent years, the AEP has been revised and greatly expanded. In the Tenth Plan (2002-07), the activities of the Jan Shiksha Sansthan—concerned particularly with vocational and occupational development of the disadvantaged groups — have been extended to rural areas. The scheme of continuing education has also been greatly expanded to include removal of residual illiteracy, imparting equivalency, individual interest programme, skill development, setting up of rural libraries and a number of other activities. The State Literacy Mission Authority has been suitably strengthened for this purpose. The role of NGOs has been increased significantly in every sphere.

Higher Education

Above the school level, on the whole Gujarat's situation was not bad. Number of colleges in general education had risen from 33 in 1950-51 to 101 in 1960-61 and 210 in 1966-67. But in the following three decades it was not even doubled; reaching 317 in 1997-98. After another six years, in 2003-04, the state had 422 colleges, and constituted 4.48 per cent of A-I total. (GOG 1969:18, 2000; GOI 2007). The enrolment in colleges had risen by 5.5 times between 1950-51 and 1966-67, from 17 thousand to 93 thousand; but in the following years, it reached only 1.33 lakh in 1980-81, and constituted 3.85 per cent of A-I total. The situation of professional education was much better. The enrolment in engineering, technology etc in 1980-81 constituted 9.56 per cent of A-I total, and in medicine at 5.77 per cent. In agriculture and forestry, it was 5.81 per cent and in education 8.20. The situation of below degree level diploma/certificate was, however, not good. Total enrolment in 1980-81 constituted 4.71 per cent of A-I total. Within it, the share of engineering etc was as much as 94.0 per cent compared with 57.5 at the national level.

After two decades, in 2000-01, the situation improved noticeably. The enrolment in polytechnic institutes stood at 30,508 and constituted 7.72 per cent of A-I total, which was the third highest among the states. On technical industrial arts and crafts schools, the share in A-I total came to as much as 13.61 per cent, the second highest. At the degree level, the enrolment in engineering etc constituted 6.74 per cent of A-I total, and in medicine 6.8; in education, it was only 3.31 per cent. In general education, the enrolment at PG level constituted 6.11 per cent of A-I total.

In recent years, Gujarat's relative position had worsened noticeably. In 2004-05, in the A-I total enrolment in higher education, its share came to 5.48 per cent. The GER stood at 10.67 per cent, nominally higher than in all-India. In the total enrolment, girls constituted 42.5 per cent, which was the third highest among the states. The enrolment in polytechnic improved further. Numbering 45,564, it constituted 11.72 per cent of A-I total, which was next only to Tamil Nadu. At the degree level and above, the situation of both engineering and medicine worsened. In the state's total enrolment, the former accounted for 5.39 per cent and the latter only 1.48. In the A-I total enrolment in engineering etc, Gujarat's share declined to 5.0 per cent, and in medicine etc to 3.72 per cent. In general education, at the P.G. level, the state's share in A-I total increased to 7.59 per cent. In the total enrolment, the share of Arts was relatively low; being only 47.9 per cent as against 59.4 in the latter. The P-T ratio in higher education as a whole was very high here; being at 40 this year as against 25 at the national level.

Overall, the professional education received high importance in Gujarat. In 2006-07, the state had 493 institutes, constituting 44.1 per cent of total number in higher education as against 27.7 per cent at the national level. In general education, on the other hand, it was respectively 47.9 and 58.8 per cent. In the A-I total number in professional education, the state's share came to 8.79 per cent, and in general education at 4.49. (GOI 2009).

Pattern of Expenditure

Gujarat's expenditure on education has been very low. In terms of the state's GDP, even the highest reached in the nineties, 4.25 per cent in 1999-00, was below the A-S average and among the major states, lower than in all but two. In the total budgetary expenditure also education's share was low, and had declined from 20.7 per cent in 1990-91 to 11.47 in 2004-05; both were below the A-S average. The per capita expenditure on education was, however, always higher than in the latter. In 2004-05, at Rs. 744, it was 11.5 per cent higher. Earlier, in 1994-97, it was still better; being higher by 37.9 per cent, with the amount at Rs. 116. It may be noted, however, that the revenue expenditure on education (Centre/state) in 2004-05 came to only Rs. 856 as against the all-India average of Rs. 969. (GOI 2007a).

As regards the Plan expenditure in education, the relative share in grand total had a sharp fall. In the Third Plan, with the expenditure at Rs. 20.71 crore, it came to 8.63 per cent. But in the subsequent plans, this proportion could never be reached again. In the next Plan, it was 6.22 per cent, with the outlay at Rs. 28.00 crore. The Sixth Plan raised it to Rs. 61.60 crore, but the relative share came to only 1.64 per cent. The following three Plans had (Rs. crore) 104.96, 317.00 and 1734.72, respectively; and the relative shares at 1.61, 2.76 and 6.20 per cent. (GOG 1992).

Stage-wise, the expenditure was very low at the elementary level. The recurring expenditure on education in Gujarat was quite high. In the grand total of recurring expenditure, the share of higher educational institutions was relatively low. At 15.1 per cent in 1980-81, it was the second lowest among the states. On per capita basis, however, the expenditure was very high. At Rs. 95.79, it was 10.9 times the national average and far higher than in any other state.

Health and Family Welfare

Health and Health Care

The health condition of the people of Gujarat does not appear good, at least from the angle of life expectancy, as noted in Chapter two. The life expectancy at birth went below the national average in 2001-06 from higher earlier. Among the major states, Gujarat's was lower than in as many as seven in case of males and eight on females. The incidence of certain diseases was noticeably high. On blindness, in 1992-93, per lakh population, 447 were suffering from complete blindness and 2819 from partial; both were much higher than the national average. The incidence of malaria and tuberculosis was also not low. The former, at 3228, was higher than in four of the states.

Among other indicators of health, the situation of infant/child mortality was not bad. The neo-natal mortality rate had declined from 42.3 in 1992-93 to 34 in 2005-06; the latest was five points below the national average and higher than in three of the states. For children under five, it had declined from 104 to 61 over the same period. The latest was 13 points below the national average but higher than in three of the states. The incidence of anaemia was also very high in Gujarat. Percentage of children suffering from any anaemia increased from 75 in 1998-99 to 80 in 2005-06; the latest was higher than in as many as six of the states. The rural-urban disparity was very high; the proportion in 1998-99 being 84 and 74 per cent, respectively. The underweight children constituted as much as 47 per cent in 2005-06, rising from 45 in 1998-99; the latest was higher than in as many as 10 of the states. The maternal health situation also worsened in recent years. The proportion of ever married women suffering from any anaemia increased from 46.3 per cent in 1998-99 to 55.3 in 2005-06.

There is considerable variation from the angle of location, mother's education, etc. The preventive measures taken were far from satisfactory. The proportion of children aged 12-23 months fully immunised declined from 53.0 per cent in 1998-99 to 45 in 2005-06; the latest was lower than in all but four of the states. The registration for paediatric care was also low; the coverage in 1995-96 being only 55.2 per cent, below that in five of the states. As regards inter-district variation, A survey in 2002-04 found the proportion of children fully immunised at only 19.2 per cent in Dohad as against the highest of 91.7 in Navsari. On maternal healthcare, Gujarat's situation was significantly better. The proportion of births in medical institutions stood at 46.3 per cent in 1998-99, which was 12.7 points higher than at the national level. On the intra-state variation in maternal care, only the situation of the proportion receiving at least two TT may be looked into. District-wise, during 2002-04, at the highest the coverage was 91.1 per cent in Navsari and the lowest at 46.0 in Dohad; only nine districts had above 80 per cent. The variation on the basis of certain social characteristics was also high.

Infrastructure

The infrastructural situation was quite good here. Number of sub-centres per lakh population was always higher than at the national level, although it declined from 23.79 in 1986 to 15.67 in 1999; even the latest was higher than in all but three of the states. The availability of PHCs was, however, not good, being below the national average. On the availability of dispensaries, located mostly in urban areas, the situation was quite good. In 1991, the number per lakh population was nearly five times the national average, being respectively 15.22 and 3.25. On hospitals also the state had a very good position; at 4.34 per lakh population, it was more than three times the latter's. The availability of beds made a notable progress over the years, rising from only 39 per lakh population in 1961 to 146 in 1991; the latest was the highest among the states. The rural situation was, however, much worse.

As regards medical personnel, number of doctors per lakh population reached 53 in 1991 from 26.2 in 1971; at the national level, the latest was 47.2. The rural situation was, however, very poor. Average number of doctors per PHC came to only one in 1999, which was below the national average. The numbers under the Indian systems of medicine and homeopathy were also very low. In 2001, it stood at only 4.4 per lakh population as against 67.1 in all-India. The growth in number of nurses was noticeably high. The non-allopathic medicines progressed only towards the end of nineties. The number of institutions on Ayurvedic and homeopathic together increased from 573 in 1990 to 1,031 in 1999-00; most of it, however, came only in the last year.

Behind the health problems of the people, lack of proper sanitation facility was an important factor. In 1998, as noted in Chapter 2, 89.8 per cent of the rural households were without any latrine. The energy used for cooking was also firewood and chips to the extent of 80.1 per cent of the hhs in 2004. On the drinking water facility also the situation is far from satisfactory. This year, tap water was available to 47.0 per cent of hhs and tube well/ hand pump to 38.6 per cent; at the national level, it was respectively 24.8 and 56.4 per cent. (IIPS 2001; NSS 2006).

Family Welfare

The maternal healthcare situation has been noted earlier; here only the measures for birth control are looked into. The fertility rate in Gujarat was very high at least till mid-seventies. The rural-urban disparity in TFR was substantial. The NFHS-1993 found it at 3.17 and 2.65, respectively. Level of education-wise, illiterates had 3.59 as against 2.83 for literate but less than MSC. Religion-wise, Muslims had as much as 3.34 as against 2.96 for Hindus. Social class-wise, the STs had very high TFR, being at 3.34 as against 2.98 for SCs. The mean number of children ever born to women ages 40-49 also varied similarly. In rural areas, it was 4.64 as against 4.01 in urban areas; education-wise, illiterates had 4.81 compared with 3.68 for less than MSC. (IIPS 1995a).

The measures taken for reducing the birth rate were relatively high. The mean age at effective marriage was also relatively high here; at 20.3 years in 1996, it was higher than in all but Punjab. Percentage of women aged 20-24, married before age 18 was only 40.7 this year as against 50.0 at the national level. The situation improved further in the following years; being down to 33.5 per cent in 2005-06. Women ages 15-19 who were already mothers/pregnant constituted only 12.7 per cent this year as against 16.0 per cent in all-India. These achievements were largely due to the quality of services provided by the family welfare department. The care taken during sterilisation was found to be very good in as much as 70 per cent of cases in 1992-93 as against only 42.6 per cent at the national level. Percentage of currently married women's need for family planning services satisfied increased from 79.0 per cent in 1992-93 to 91.8 in 2005-06. The exposure to media was also good here. (*ibid.*).

All these, however, varied considerably from the angle of location, educational level, social classes, etc. The knowledge of legal minimum age at marriage in 1992-93, was there with only 14.9 per cent in rural areas about males and 24.8 per cent on females; in urban areas, it was respectively 39.7 and 50.3 per cent. Education-wise, among the illiterates, only 6.5 per cent knew about males and 14.0 per cent on females; for those with MSC, it improved to 49.6 and 65.2 per cent, respectively. Social class-wise, Only 8.5 per cent of STs knew about males and 17.0 per cent for females. These variations were largely due to the differences in exposure to media. The proportion of married women not regularly exposed to any media was as much as 56.3 per cent in rural areas as against 23.1 per cent in urban areas. Education-wise, for illiterates it was 65.0 per cent compared with only 14.8 per cent for those with MSC.

Pattern of Expenditure

This nature of performance in health and family planning was largely due to the low level of expenditure on them. The per capita revenue expenditure on health during 1997 averaged only Rs. 192.79, which was lower than in five of the states, although higher than the national average by 12.2 per cent. The growth in expenditure was relatively low. Between 1975-78 and 1997, it was by 22.1 times, lower than in all but three of the states. The total expenditure on health was also similarly placed. The per capita in 2002-05 came to Rs. 179.28, which was lower than in six of the states.

As regards the distribution over different heads, hospitals and dispensaries naturally accounted for the highest share, although it declined continuously from 48.6 per cent in 1960-61 to only 29.3 in 1992-93. The latest was lower than in three of the states. The per capita expenditure was below the national average in two out of the three time points considered. The expenditure on maternal and child health was very low. In each of the time points, the per capita was below the national average. In 1992-93, at Re 0.19, it was around a quarter of the latter's. On the national disease programme also the state spent a relatively low amount. Of the three time points, only in the last one it was higher than the national average. On family welfare, the expenditure was relatively high. The per capita had risen from Rs. 1.48 in 1975-76 to Rs. 11.73 in 1992-93; both were higher than the national average. (*ibid*.).

As regards the situation in recent years, as noted in the preceding chapter, the state's spending here is quite low. The revenue expenditure on medical and public health in 2002-05 annually averaged Rs. 769 crore, and constituted 5.31 per cent of all-states' total. The per capita expenditure was nominally higher than in A-S. On water supply and sanitation, the annual average came to only Rs. 203.7 crore and constituted 3.28 per cent of A-S total. The per capita, at Rs. 38.55, was 65.1 per cent of the latter's. On family welfare also, with the annual average at Rs. 120.7 crore—constituted only 4.98 per cent of A-S total—the per capita came to Rs. 22.84, nominally higher than in A-S. (Rs 23.12).

Plan Expenditure

The plan expenditure on health remained low until the recent plans. Including water supply and sanitation, the Third Five-year Plan had spent only Rs. 16.02 crore, constituting 6.67 per cent of the grand total. The next plan also had an allocation of only Rs. 23 crore. In the Sixth Plan, although it rose to as much as Rs. 220.76 crore, the relative share came to only 5.87 per cent. In the Seventh Plan, the growth itself was nominal; being fixed at Rs. 271.8 crore, constituting 4.53 per cent of the grand total. In the following two plans, the outlays rose noticeably—to respectively Rs. 663 crore and Rs. 3,832 crore, and constituted 5.77 per cent and 13.68 per cent of the respective grand total.

In these outlays/expenditure, water supply and sanitation accounted for the lion's share in the recent plans. In the Seventh through Ninth plan, it was respectively 62.1, 63.5 and 78.3 per cent. This was a belated recognition of its critical importance. The per capita expenditure on water supply and sanitation had risen from Rs. 2.62 in the Third Plan to Rs. 44.23 in the Sixth and Rs. 593 in the Ninth Plan, i.e., a 226-fold rise over the entire period. On medical and public health, on the other hand, it was respectively Rs. 5.14, Rs. 20.54 and Rs. 164.66—i.e., only a 32-fold rise.

As regards the distribution over the minor heads, the situation in only three of the plans are looked into. Under Medical and Public Health, the minimum needs programme naturally got the highest priority. Its share in the total increased from 28.7 per cent in the Sixth Plan to 46.5 in the Seventh and 48.7 per cent in the Eighth Plan; the outlays were respectively Rs. 20.09, Rs. 47.92 and Rs. 118 crore—i.e., a 5.9-fold rise. This was followed by control of communicable diseases, with a share of 20.4 per cent in the Eighth plan, declining from 27.5 in the Seventh and 46.6 per cent in the Sixth Plan. Of the remaining items, medical education and research and indigenous systems of medicine had received relatively large amounts. The outlay on the former increased from Rs. 6.60 crore in the Sixth Plan to Rs. 11.97 crore in the Seventh and Rs. 27 crore in the Eighth Plan; the relative shares were respectively 9.43, 11.61 and 11.16 per cent. On the ISM, the outlays were Rs. 1.20 crore, Rs. 3.00 crore and Rs. 14.00 crore, respectively.

Under water supply and sanitation, rural water supply had received a total of Rs. 114.21 crore in these three plans together, and constituted 18.0 per cent; for urban water supply, it was respectively Rs. 86.82 crore and 13.7 per cent. On sanitation, rural areas received attention only in the Eighth Plan, with a provision of Rs. 315 crore; in the Seventh Plan, it was a negligible Rs. 70 lakh, and in the Sixth no provision at all. Thus, the rural areas were largely neglected.

20

AGRICULTURAL GROWTH AND TRANSFORMATION

As in other states, here also agriculture continued to be of critical importance. In the rural workforce, the proportion of agricultural workers constituted as much as 76.7 per cent even in 1991, declining from 82.6 in 1981 and 88.2 in 1961; the latest was only three points below the national average. In recent years, the NSSO survey in 2004 found that per 1000 households, there were 310 agricultural labour hhs in Gujarat as against the A-I average of 254. This importance of agriculture notwithstanding, in the GSDP, its share averaged only 16.27 per cent in 2003-06, Rs. 30,961 crore out of Rs. 190,304 crore; around a decade earlier, in 1993-96, it was 23.03 per cent. (CMIE 2009). A detailed look is given below on the pattern of growth in agriculture and allied sectors over the years.

I. CROP FARMING

Gujarat's growth in agricultural production was quite good till early eighties. In the pre-green revolution period, between 1952-53 and 1964-65, the state had a compound annual growth of 4.55 per cent as against 3.01 in all-India. In the post-green revolution period also, between 1968-69 and 1981-82 it had a growth rate of 3.23 per cent compared with 2.16 in all-India. In the following years, however, the situation worsened sharply. Between 1980-81 and 1994-5, the state had only 1.96 per cent as against 3.40 in the latter. In the all-India total value of output, Gujarat's share rose to 6.2 per cent in 1980-83, from 5.9 in 1962-65, but declined again to 5.2 in 1992-95 and further to 4.61 in 2000-03. The yield rate was below the national average in the pre-GR period, but became higher since the early 'seventies. In recent years again it became lower. Below, a look is given into the pattern of growth in different crops.

Gujarat had a very poor performance in food-grains. The area under it declined continuously, from the average of 4964 thousand ha in 1968-71 to 3249 thousand in 2000-03. The proportion of GCA under food-grains was only 35.1 per cent in 2005-06 as against 63.1 at the national level; in 1970-71, it was respectively 56.73 and 78.78 per cent.The yield rate was always below the national average; and in 2000-03, it came to only 68.2 per cent of the latter's. In 2003-06, however, a significant recovery came.

Gujarat devoted a large proportion of the cropped area to non-foodgrains; rising from 52.47 per cent of the GCA in 1966-69 to 60.17 in 1990-93 and then to 65.5 in 1997-00. In the all-India total area under NFG, the state's share came to 10.45 per cent in recent years. The highest acreage among NFGs was always in groundnut. But both the area and the yield rate fluctuated widely from year to year.

In the next important crop, cotton, also Gujarat is the largest producer in the country.In sugarcane also Gujarat's performance was not bad. The area under it increased noticeably, with the yield rate showing significant growth. The production had risen by as much as 590 per cent between 1968-71 and 1980-83, but in the following years till 2002-05 it was by only 66.3 per cent. Among oilseeds, apart from groundnut, sesamum, castor and rapeseed and mustard were important. The area under each of them had risen noticeably over the years. Castor had nearly a seven-fold rise between 1968-71 and 1990-93, and then recorded a fall in 2002-05. In sesamum also the state's situation was very good. Among other crops, tobacco had a substantial acreage, despite a sharp fall in recent years. In vegetables, roots and tubers as a whole, the situation was not good. Among other vegetables, tomatoes was in a relatively good position. The yield rate in 2002-05 came to 17,987 kg as against 16,476 kg in all-India. In fruits and nuts, the acreage remained low despite a relatively high yield rate. The situation of mangoes was also not bad. The area under it had risen from 34.1 thousand ha in 1991-94 to 86.5 thousand in 2003-06. In citrus fruits as a whole, Gujarat had a significant progress in recent years. The area under it increased from 8.1 thousand ha in 1991-94 to 28.1 thousand in 2003-06.

It may be noted here that the importance of cultivation in the farmers' income is relatively low in Gujarat. In 2002-03, in the average monthly income of a farmer's household at Rs. 2684—which was 26.9 per cent higher than at the national level—only 43.4 per cent came from cultivation as against the national average of 45.8 per cent. The proportion from wages was 34.5 and 38.7 per cent, respectively. The farming of animals provided a very large share here; at 17.0 per cent, it was the highest among the states. (NSSO 2006a).

Inter-District Disparities

Among the districts, there were great variations in the production situation of different crops. In food-grains, in the most important crop bajra, the highest acreage in 1990-93 was in Banaskantha, averaging 247 thousand ha, and there were six districts—viz, Mehsana, Kheda, Bhavnagar, Surendranagar, Kachchh and Rajkot—with 71 thousand to 125 thousand ha. The combined share of these seven districts came to 71.3 per cent; earlier, in 1981-84, it was 73.7 per cent. Over the period, each of these districts excepting Surendranagar, had recorded declines. The sharpest fall was in Kachchh, from 112 to 73 thousand ha. As regards the yield rate, the highest in 1990-93 was

1480 kg in Junagadh and the lowest at 625 kg in Jamnagar, with 978 kg at the state level. In 1981-84, the disparity was higher; the highest being 1625 kg in Valsad and the lowest at 466 kg in Surendranagar, with 999 kg at state level. Over the period, the yield rate had declined in nine of the districts; the sharpest fall was in Panchmahal, from 1122 kg to 746 kg. The highest increase was in Surendranagar, from 466 kg to 700. (GOG 2000; CMIE 1996).

In jowar, the next important crop, the variation in yield rate was much higher. The cultivation of rice was much more heavily concentrated in a few districts. Wheat was grown more extensively in the state. In pulses, arhar, the most important crop, was heavily concentrated in five of the districts—viz, Bharuch, Vadodara, Sabarkantha, Surat and Panchmahals. Their combined share in total area came to 90.2 per cent in 1990-93, rising from 84.0 in 1981-84; for the first two together, it was as much as 62.3 per cent in 1990-93. Number of districts growing arhar had, however, increased over the period. The variation in yield rate was relatively low.

Among non-foodgrains, the production of oilseeds was concentrated in seven districts—viz., Rajkot, Junagadh, Jamnagar, Amreli, Banaskantha, Mehsana and Bhavnagar; together accounting for 82.6 per cent of total area in 1996-97, with the first three at 45.6 per cent. The yield rate this year was at the highest 2078 kg in Gandhinagar (with very low acreage) and the lowest at 722 kg in Dangs, with 1334 kg the state average. Groundnut, the most important crop, was concentrated in five districts, viz, Rajkot, Junagadh, Jamnagar, Amreli and Bhavnagar; together accounting for 89.5 per cent of total area in 1996-97, with the first three at 64.5 per cent. The yield rate varied between the highest of 1831 kg in Kheda (with only 8,000 ha) and the lowest at 973 kg in Kachchh, with 1313 kg for the state. (GOG 2000).

The Factors Behind

Land Resource

The availability of land resource is the first basic factor behind the production situation, and here Gujarat was not in a good position. The state accounted for only 6.15 per cent of the country's geographical area; and within it again the proportion of not available for cultivation was as much as 19.9 per cent in 2005-06 compared with 13.9 per cent in all-India. Other uncultivated land, excluding fallow, constituted 14.9 per cent as against 8.8 in the latter. The forest area was extremely low, constituting only 9.83 per cent of the RA this year. Per thousand people, it came to only 35 ha in 2003-04, declining from 65 ha in 1970-71; the latest was only 53.8 per cent of the national average.

The proportion of net sown area in the state was, however, relatively high; being at 52.2 per cent of the RA in 2005-06 as against 46.5 in all-India. Per thousand people, the NSA this year came to 183 ha as against 130 in the latter. District-wise, there was extreme of variation in resource endowment. The reporting area itself varied greatly. The highest was 19 times the lowest, being respectively 1233 thousand ha in Banaskantha and only 65 thousand in Gandhinagar. The proportion of barren and uncultivable land was very high in a number of districts. In 1996-97, at the highest it was 37.4 per cent of the RA in Kachchh, followed by Jamnagar 15.4, with the state average at 13.8 per cent. In relation to 1977-78, the quantum had increased in all but five of the districts. In Jamnagar, it was by as much as 43.6 thousand ha, in Vadodara by 22.7 thousand, Banaskantha by 16.6 thousand and in Amreli by 12.8 thousand. The forest areas were concentrated in nine of the districts—viz., Kachchh, Panchmahal, Junagadh, Dangs, Banaskantha, Bharuch, Surat, Sabarkantha and Valsad—together accounting for 75.5 per cent of the total in 1996-97; the first three together with 37.7 per cent.

Land-holding System

The system of land-holding by farmers greatly determines the efforts made to raise the productivity of land. But the ownership of land, despite measures, continued to be heavily concentrated in a small segment of farmers. The top five per cent of farmers owned as much as 31.74 per cent of total in 1982, declining from 35.95 in 1953-54; at the national level, the concentration was still higher, they owned 37.55 per cent in 1982. For top 10 per cent also it was in a similar position. The share of the bottom 50 per cent had risen from 1.53 per cent to 3.37 per cent in this period; at the national level, the latest was 3.52 per cent. The proportion of households owning no land had declined from 30.48 per cent in 1953-54 to 16.83 in 1982; at the national level, the latest was only 11.33 per cent. Among the major states, Gujarat's was higher than in all but two. The proportion with sub-marginal holdings was, however, low here; being at 23.9 per cent in 1982 as against 36.9 per cent at the national level. In recent years, Gujarat's situation worsened much. The proportion of landless hhs in 2003-04 stood at as much as 35.37 per cent, i.e., more than double that in 1982.

The Ceiling Legislations

This situation was largely due to the absence of proper implementation of the ceiling legislation. By 1982, only 146.5 thousand acres of land, constituting 3.67 per cent of A-I total, could be declared surplus. After another six years, at the end of June 2005, the situation worsened further. The quantum distributed by then came to 59.37 thousand ha, i.e., half of what was reported in 1999. Total number of beneficiaries, however, showed a small rise, with the land distributed per beneficiary declining to 1.78 ha. The land distributed in relation to that declared surplus increased to 64.8 per cent as against 71.6 per cent in all-India. Number of litigation cases was very high here. In June 2005, it stood at 1278—with total area at 67,962 acres—constituting 9.07 per cent of all-India total. The reasons behind this poor implementation are more or less the same as in most other states. The first Land Ceiling Act was passed in 1960 and it came into force from September 1961. The villages were classified into different categories, on the basis of the type of land, the mode of irrigation, productivity of land, etc., and the ceiling limits were fixed. The Act was amended in 1974, but it could not be brought into force until April 1976 due to litigation. Further delays came due to an instruction from the government not to proceed further on possession and distribution of land. This ban was lifted only in March 1980. Consequently, till November 1980, only 7478 ha of land could be taken possession, and out of it, only 1447 ha were disposed of on a permanent basis and 1686 ha given on eksali basis. The surplus land in five of the districts were kept reserved for affectees of the Narmada Reservoir Project.

Abolition of Intermediaries

On the abolition of intermediaries, steps were taken in the fifties itself. The Bombay Tenancy and Agricultural Lands Act had provided for transfer of ownership to permanent tenants with effect from April, 1957. In addition, thirty different tenure abolition laws were enacted for the purpose. Peasants were allowed to become owners of the land either on payment of occupancy price or without paying it. The last tenure of Devasthan Inam was abolished in November 1969. This tenure was already abolished in Saurashtra and Kachchh by two Acts in 1951 and 1958, respectively. By the end of 'seventies, all the areas of the state were covered by the Raiyatwari Tenure. The implementation of these Acts conferred occupancy rights to 12.6 lakh tenants in respect of 10.00 lakh hectares till March 1985. The tenants who could not pay the purchase price were allowed another nine months to pay up. Arrangements were also made for advancing loans to such tenants. (GOG 1985: 127).

On the security of tenure, some important steps were taken in early fifties. In the former Bombay area, permanent tenants got complete security of tenure. For other tenants, it was subject to landlord's right to resume land not exceeding three economic holdings (12 to 48 acres) on condition that every tenant retained half the area leased. A landlord was required to give notice for resumption to the tenant by 31st December 1956.

In the Kutch area, a landlord owning and cultivating personally less than one-third of family holding could resume the entire area leased (family holding varied from 12 to 45 acres). In other cases, it could be up to three family holdings after leaving half the leased land with the tenant. Consequent on these measures, the incidence of tenancy in Gujarat was greatly reduced. In 1991-92, the state had only 3.7 per cent of tenant holding, declining from 4.8 per cent in 1981-82; the latest was a third of the national average. In terms of area, the proportion under tenancy increased from 2.0 per cent of total to 3.3 per cent over the period; at the national level, it was from 7.2 to 8.3 per cent. Recent data are not available, but it is well known that concealed tenancies do exist here as in other states. (NSSO 1997). The terms of lease also changed noticeably over the years. The fixed money system gained much in popularity by early nineties, while the share of produce system declined.

Irrigation Facility

The provison of irrigation facility is a crucial factor in Gujarat's agriculture as it is highly dependent on the monsoon. Out of the total of 19 districts, parts of 10 districts are drought-prone. Particularly drought-prone are the districts of Saurashtra. In 1999, the government had to declare 8,666 villages as 'scarcity hit' in the wake of monsoon failure. The mean annual rainfall in the state varies from 350 mm in Kachchh to nearly 2000 mm in The Dangs. (GOG 2000a). Despite this alarming situation, the progress in irrigation facility was very slow. In 1965-66, percentage of irrigated area to total cropped area stood at only 10.5, and after another one-and -half decade, in 1980-81, also it could not reach 20. Even in 2005-06, the net irrigated area as percentage to NSA stood at only 34.4 in, rising from 25.5 in 1991-92; the latest was eight points below the national average.

As regards the source of irrigation water, there was a heavy dependence on ground water. Its share declined from 82.7 per cent in 1965-66 to 57.3 in 1980-81 but increased again to 77.4 per cent in 1998-99 and further to 86.6 in 2003-04; in 2005-06, however, it declined to 80.8 per cent; at the national level, the latest was 58.8 per cent. The share of canals increased from 13.5 per cent in 1965-66 to 17.4 in 1980-81 and 20.8 in 1998-99, but in 2005-06 it declined to 17.7 per cent; the latest was eight points below the national average. District-wise, the irrigation facility varied greatly.

Potential and Utilisation

Behind this poor situation, an important reason is the limited water resources for irrigation. There are also physical limitations on the availability of storage and diversion sites due to the flat nature of the terrain in the region through which the principal rivers flow. The ultimate irrigation potential of the state through surface water is estimated at 39.40 lakh ha, including 17.92 lakh through Sardar Sarovar (Narmada) Project (SSP) and 3.48 lakh through minor irrigation schemes. The ground water resources are also limited without augmentation by the SSP. In fact, some of the ground water resources have been depleted due to advancing ingress of salinity. (GOG 1992: 264).

As regards the potential created, on surface water, till June 1991 it came to 14.05 lakh ha, with 12.21 lakh through major and medium schemes (MMS). On ground water, it was 19.08 lakh ha. The maximum utilisation on this date was 10.18 lakh ha under surface water; and on ground water at 16.43 lakh ha. The relative position among the states was very poor. The public capital formation in irrigation had a very low growth in Gujarat.

Problem Areas and the SSP

This dismal ground-water situation was accentuated by poor surface water resources. Rivers in north Gujarat are seasonal in nature, carrying stream flows only during three or four months of the year. The major and medium irrigation schemes here were designed for run-off of very low dependability. In most years there is no spill-over from these reservoirs into the downstream. In April 2000, as against the total capacity of 2,018 m cm in 13 major and minor dams, the storage available was only about 6 mcm. (Kumar, M D 2002). There were proposals to link the hydrological systems of north and south Gujarat to reduce water stress in the former. The SSP itself had envisaged supplying water to the irrigation projects in north Gujarat, and also to recharge the depleted aquifers. (GOG 1989; Ranade, et al 2004).

The problems of Saurashtra and Kachchh are also of no small magnitude. Continuous heavy withdrawals of groundwater for irrigation and water supply, combined with decreased recharges, have created problems of ingress of salinity in the groundwater. An area of more than one lakh hectares was affected as early as in 1980. (GOG 1981). The problems were, however, largely due to neglect of these areas by the government. Most of the state's irrigation development budgets were spent on schemes benefiting central Gujarat, and no significant schemes came up to solve the problems in the drought-prone areas. For example, for 10 years, while the Kadana and the Ukai dams were being built, Kachchh and Saurashtra did not receive any worthwhile scheme. In recent years again, 131 schemes of the drought-prone areas could not take off as bulk of the irrigation budget was spent on the SSP. During the Seventh, Eighth and the Ninth Plan, the outlay for the SSP averaged 78.0 per cent of the grand total on irrigation.

The expenditures on a number of important areas were drastically cut. The SSP is built on the river Narmada, one of the major west flowing rivers in the country. It passes through the states of MP, Maharashtra and Gujarat, traversing a total distance of 1312 km before falling into the sea. The total catchment area of the river is 27,610 sq miles. The Narmada is the single largest source of flow irrigation in Gujarat. It is stated that, without the waters of Narmada Gujarat will be able to irrigate only 30.0 per cent of the cultivated area, even including ground water; but with Narmada waters, it can be raised to 43 per cent.

The SSP is an inter-state multipurpose project with cost and benefit to be shared by the participating states of MP, Maharashtra, Gujarat and Rajasthan. The cost of the project was estimated at Rs. 6406.04 crore (at 1986-87 prices) in October 1988, to be shared by Gujarat to the extent of 76.5 per cent, MP 13.8, Maharashtra 6.54 and the balance by Rajasthan. The cost had, however, escalated to Rs. 13,180 crore at 1991-92 prices. The work comprised of 29 major, 135 medium and 3,500 minor dams. As per the implementation programme, the main components were to be completed by the year 2000. (GOG 2000a). However, in 2007, the project was yet to be fully completed. In Gujarat, the project was to provide irrigation facilities to 17.92 lakh ha of land spread over 3,393 villages of 12 districts. About 75 per cent area of the command is drought-prone. The project will also provide about 10 lakh acre-feet of water for drinking, municipal and industrial uses to about 135 urban centres and 8,215 villages. The state will receive 16 per cent share of the electricity produced by its two power houses, with a total installed capacity of 1450 MW. The irrigation potential was to be created in a phased manner, reaching a cumulative total of 8.75 lakh ha by 1996, 13.75 lakh by 1998 and ultimately 17.92 lakh by 2000. (GOG 1992: 271-72, 277).

Apart from the monetary cost of the project, the costs in terms of human sufferings and damage to the environment are also not negligible. Because of the river's peculiarly narrow path, the 214 km long SSP reservoir has submerged a total of 245 villages in the three states. As many as about 150,000 families have lost their land to the Narmada canal. The people downstream of the dam, living in about 200 villages and a few cities like Bharuch were also severely affected. It was estimated that the number of people to be affected by the SSP would not be less than a million, of whom only those affected by the dam were to be considered as PAPs. As regards the environmental cost, the project was to submerge around 13,000 ha of forest land. The ministry of environment had first refused to give clearance and then reluctantly gave a conditional clearance in 1987, under political pressure. (Oza, Nandini 1997; Iyengar, S 2002).

Provision of Inputs

Bank Credit

On the provision of credit to agriculture from the organised sector of banking, Gujarat's situation was quite good. In the all-India total credit to agriculture, the state's share had risen from 6.4 per cent at June-end 1986 to 7.78 in 2002-03; the credit per hectare in 2002-03 came to Rs. 5,194, which was 39 per cent higher than the national average. In the credit flow to agriculture, co-operative credit was the leading source. Its share had risen from 49.6 per cent in 1986 to 51.4 in 1996-97 and further to 59.9 per cent in 2002-03; the latest was 18.5 points higher than the A-I average. The relative share of SCBs had declined from 48.8 per cent to 34.9 over the period.

In co-operative credit, the growth in provision from the leading institution, PACS was relatively low. Over the entire period between 1969-70 and 2002-03 it had risen by only 48 times as against 97 times at the national level The growth in credit per hectare was also by 51 and 91 times, respectively. The SCBs' performance was very poor. The credit per hectare was always below the national average. In the credit provided by the SCBs, the small land-holders were largely neglected. The performance of the RRBs was much worse. In March 1989, the per hectare credit to agriculture, etc., came to only Rs. 33.22, which was around a third of the national average. In the A-I total of loans outstanding, the state's share was only 2.21 per cent; in number of accounts, it was still worse, only 1.81 per cent. The share of agriculture, etc., in the total was, however, as much as 74.4 per cent here compared with 53.2 per cent in all-India.

In the loans outstanding to agriculture, etc., allied activities accounted for only 26.9 per cent this year as against 30.8 at the national level. In number of accounts, however, it was respectively 41.0 and 34.0 per cent. Naturally, the amount per beneficiary was low; being at Rs. 2,179 as against Rs. 2,610 in all-India. In agriculture, the proportion for crop loan was very low, being at 27.5 per cent as against 33.7 per cent in the latter. The amount outstanding per hectare came to only Rs. 9.14, less than a third of the national average. The lending for agricultural investment was relatively high; being at 45.6 per cent of total as against 35.5 per cent in the latter.

Marketing Facilities

Proper development of warehousing and marketing facilities are essential for the growth of agricultural production. Warehousing facility helps not only in minimising the wastage of agricultural produce, but also in stabilising the prices as the farmers are not compelled to go for distress sales immediately after harvesting. The government's efforts in this direction, however, proceeded very slowly. The State Warehousing Corporation, which is in charge of developing the warehousing facility, had a storage capacity of only 73,000 tonnes in 1980. The target for the end of Eighth Plan was 2.41 lakh tonnes but only 1.59 lakh could be created.

The relative position of Gujarat among the states was, however, not bad. In 1993, the storage facility as percentage to total food-grains production came to 58.4 as against only 21.4 at the national level; among the selected states, Gujarat's was the highest proportion. In recent years, however, the situation worsened. In the marketing of agricultural produce, the co-operative societies had an insignificant role in Gujarat. Number of societies was large but their membership remained very low. Purchases by the societies were large; the relative share in A-I total being 11.8 per cent in 1998. The district-wise variation in performance of PAMS was very high. On the transportation system, Gujarat's situation was relatively good. In 1996, percentage of villages connected with all-weather roads stood at as much as 90 compared with only 48 at the national level. On the road length in the state, however, the situation was not good. In 1999, per one hundred sq km, there were only 476 km of roads as against 768 km in all-India. Earlier, in 1975, it was respectively 23 and 36 km. The proportion of unsurfaced roads was, however, very low. The availability of motor vehicles was very good in Gujarat. In 2003, the density per sq km stood at 33.20, which was 62.8 per cent higher than at the national level. The proportion of goods vehicles in the total had, however, declined to 5.7 per cent this year, from 9.5 in 1975. Inter-districts, there was great variation in the transportation facility.

II: ALLIED ACTIVITIES

Animal Husbandry

Gujarat's overall situation in animal husbandry has not been good. The total value of output from livestock annually averaged Rs. 4443.02 crore in 2000-03 and constituted 4.96 per cent of A-I total. Per capita, it came to Rs. 878.12, nominally higher than in all-India. In poultry, the situation was very poor. Per capita production in this period averaged only Rs. 6.32, around a fifth of all-India's. The animal husbandry's contribution to a farmer's income was, however, relatively high. In 2002-03, in the average monthly income of a farmer household, animal farming as a whole had contributed as much as 17.0 per cent, four times that at the national level; the incomes were respectively Rs. 455 and Rs. 91. Below, a detailed look is given to the situation.

Livestock

The livestock population of Gujarat was very low. It had declined from 185.98 lakh in 1992 to 142.31 lakh in 2003; the relative share in A-I total declining from 3.95 per cent to 2.93. The rearing practices are substantially different here from that in most other states. In 2002-03, number of in-milk bovine per 100 hhs in rural Gujarat came to 52 as against 36 in all-India; in ovines, it was respectively 58 and 64. Three decades earlier, in 1971-72, the situation was much better; the state had 67 in-milk bovine and 122 ovines as against 54 and 99, respectively at the national level. Number of donkeys and camels were relatively large here. In 2003, the former numbered 65 thousand, and constituted 10.0 per cent of A-I total; and the latter at 53 thousand and 8.39 per cent. (NSSO 2006b; GOI 2003b).

Cattle and Buffalo

The growth in number of cattle was negligible in Gujarat. The proportion of females in cattle had risen from 37.0 per cent in 1972 to 47.4 in 1992; both were below the national average. In 2002-03 also the state had only 286 adult females per 1000 hhs as against 380 in all-India. Percentage of cross-bred in cattle was only 2.81 in 1992, around a third of that in all-India; and in 2002-03, at 8.6 and 13.3 per cent, respectively. In cross-bred again, females constituted only 51.8 per cent in 1992 as against 69.4 in all-India.

A good aspect of the situation in Gujarat is, however, that the proportion of milch cattle in females was very high. In buffaloes, Gujarat's situation was much better. In 2003, it numbered 71.40 lakh and constituted 7.29 per cent of A-I total, rising from 6.3 per cent in 1992. In terms of hhs, per 100 hhs, there were as many buffaloes in 1991-92 compared with 59 at the national level. In 2002-03, however, the situation worsened somewhat; the numbers being respectively 81.7 and 51.4. The growth in number of buffaloes was higher here than at the national level. Between 1961 and 1992, it was by 80.5 and 64.4 per cent respectively, and in the following years by 35.5 and 16.3 per cent.

The proportion of females in buffaloes was also very high. In 1992, it stood at as much as 92.5 per cent compared with 79.4 at the national level; among the major states, Gujarat's was the highest proportion. The situation of milch buffalo in females was also not bad. At 61.2 per cent this year, it was higher than in all-India. The proportion in milk was 69.9 per cent, the second highest among the states. As regards the composition in recent years, in 2002-03, per '000 rural hhs, there were 751 female buffaloes as against 425 at the national level. In adult females, the number in milk was 340 as against only 172 in the latter. Number of dry females was, however, very high here; being at 160 compared with 102 in all-India. The young stock also numbered as much as 232 as against 131 in the latter. As regards male buffaloes, most of them were young stock, to the extent of 81.5 per cent. Number of adult males used for work only was only 7 as against 25 at the national level.

Milk Output

These changes in pattern of bovine rearing had a good impact on milk production. Gujarat's share in all-India total output of milk increased from 3.80 per cent in 1961 to 7.96 in 1971-72. In the following years, however, it declined to 6.53 per cent in 1981-82 and averaged 6.60 per cent in 1999-02. The per capita production in 1999-02 averaged 109.5 kg, which was 34.5 per cent higher than in all-India; earlier, in 1971-72, at 67.0 kg, it was 63.4 per cent higher. In value term, the per capita output had risen from the average of Rs. 599 in 1990-93 to Rs. 774.28 in 2000-03; these were respectively 26.9 and 32.5 per cent higher than at the national level.

Inter-district, there was great variation in the output of milk, as may be inferred from the pattern of rearing cattle and buffalo. In 1992, four of the districts—viz., Kheda, Mehsana, Valsad and Sabarkantha—together accounted for 67.9 per cent of the total number of cross-breds in the state. On buffaloes, five districts—Kheda, Mehsana, Panchmahals, Sabarkantha and Banaskantha—had a combined share of 50.6 per cent. Per '000 ha, Kheda had 997 buffaloes, Sabarkantha 844 and Panchmahals 783 as against the state average of 479 (based on the GCA of 1996-97). On CBs, Valsad had as many as 95.1 and Kheda 88.1 as against the state average of 21.0; four of the districts had less than two CBs. On the rearing of indigenous cattle also the variation was not low. (GOG 2000).

That there was scope for further increase in milk production, becomes evident from a look at the pattern of owning of bovines by size-class of holdings. In 2003, number of buffaloes per '000 hhs was at the highest 688 in 5.0-7.5 ha, which was much higher than at the national level, being 549. In the latter, the highest buffalo-owning size was 20 ha and above, but in Gujarat this size had no buffalo at all. Here the lower size-classes were owning a much larger number than at the national level. Thus, there was scope for increased buffalo owning by larger holdings. Larger rearing was particularly possible in case of CBs. Each of the size-classes in Gujarat, except one (5.0-7.5 ha), had lesser number of CBs per '000 hhs than at the national level. (NSSO 2006b: 51).

Goat and Sheep

The goat population of Gujarat had a very low growth. In sheep, the situation was worse. Over the entire period of 31 years, 1961 to 1992, their number had risen by only 36.9 per cent, with the last two decades at 17.8 per cent; at the national level, the situation was worse. The following period of 11 years, till 2003, had a negligible 1.68 per cent rise here as against 21.0 per cent in all-India. The state's share in A-I total number had declined from 4.31 per cent in 1972 to 3.35 in 2003. As regards the composition of sheep, the cross-breds had constituted only 0.69 per cent in 1992 compared with 4.75 per cent in all-India. Age-wise, the proportion of one-year-and-above was relatively high; being at 78.6 and 62.2 per cent, respectively. As regards the output, goats are maintained both for meat and milk. As regards the inter-district disparities in rearing of ovines, goats were relatively well spread out throughout the state.

Poultry

In poultry, Gujarat's situation was extremely poor. The NSSO survey in 2002-03, found the state having only 52 poultry per 100 hhs compared with 123 at the national level. Three decades earlier, in 1971-72, the numbers were respectively 85 and 101. In the all-India total number of poultry, Gujarat's share had declined from 1.97 per cent to 1.67 over the period. The composition of poultry was, however, relatively good here. In fowls, the improved variety constituted 41.5 per cent in 1992 as against 34.8 per cent at the national level.

The output from poultry was naturally very low. During 1999-02, the egg production averaged 505.1 million number, and constituted only 1.57 per cent of A-I total; among the selected states, Gujarat's was the lowest. The per capita production came to only 14 grams per day, less than half the national average. In value term, the production averaged Rs. 319.7 million in 2000-03, which was 0.94 per cent of A-I total; in 1990-93, it was 1.90 per cent.

The rearing of poultry was heavily concentrated in a few districts. In 1992, four districts—viz., Valsad, Kheda, Panchmahals and Surat—together accounted for 65.6 per cent of total; for the first two combined, it was 40.9 per cent. Another three districts — Vadodara, Bharuch and Sabarkantha—together contributed 15.8 per cent. Thus, the combined share of these seven districts came to 81.4 per cent. A decade earlier, in 1982, the concentration was still higher. The first four districts had provided 70.1 per cent; and for the seven districts combined, it was 87.5 per cent.

Infrastructure

Behind the poor performance in animal husbandry an important reason was the lack of adequate facilities. Around two-and-half decades after economic planning began, in April 1974, the state had only 211 vet hospitals/dispensaries, six intensive cattle development blocks, five cattle breeding farms, 70 sheep extension centres, two sheep breeding-cum-marketing centres, nine poultry breeding farms (extension) and three intensive poultry development projects (IPDPs). The cross-breeding of local cows began only towards the end of 'seventies and by March 1985, 40 cross-breeding centres were established. The Sixth Plan had a target of performing 4.67 lakh artificial inseminations but only 2.90 lakh could be reached. On poultry, the Fifth Plan had set up six new IPDPs and four district poultry extension centres. For sheep, two intensive sheep development blocks and 18 sheep extension centres were started. Assistance was also provided for setting up 984 sheep units. The cross-breeding of sheep, however, began only in the Sixth Plan. Fodder development also received attention only in the 'eighties, and by March 1985, there were five seed production farms and six village fodder farms. (GOG 1985: 39, GOG 1981:108).

District-wise, the facilities vary greatly. In 1998-99, per VD/BVD, there were as many as 114.1 thousand livestock in Valsad as against the lowest of 18.6 in Gandhinagar, with the state average at 43.4. Even the availability of FAVC was very low in a number of districts. In Junagadh, one centre had to look after as many as 84.7 thousand livestock as against the lowest of 11.8 in Gandhinagar, with the state average at 35.4. On the availability of artificial insemination centres, the disparity was very high. The number per centre/sub-centre was at the highest 82.6 thousand in Banaskantha as against only 1.38 in Kheda, with 5.41 at the state level.

For the infrastructural deficiencies, the government's lack of initiative was primarily responsible. The plan expenditure on animal husbandry remained very low until recent years. The Third Five-year Plan had spent only Rs. 149 lakh on it against the outlay fixed at Rs. 233 lakh. In the Sixth Plan, the outlay was raised to Rs. 17.70 crore. In the following two plans again the growth was very low; the outlays fixed being respectively Rs. 18.20 crore and Rs. 30.70 crore. The Ninth Plan, however, raised it to as much as Rs. 76.00 crore. The relative share in grand total of plan outlay had declined continuously—from 0.62 per cent in the Third Plan to 0.47 in the Sixth and 0.27 in the Eighth and Ninth.

As regard the distribution over different heads, to look at the situation in only three of the Plans: In the Sixth Plan, the highest share naturally went to cattle development, at 37.5 per cent of total, followed by poultry development 24.4 per cent; veterinary and animal health (VAH) received 15.3 per cent and sheep and wool development 12.1. Thus, these four items together accounted for 89.3 per cent of total. In the Seventh plan, the highest proportion of 38.0 per cent went to VAH, followed by cattle development 29.9 and poultry development 10.3. In the Eighth Plan also the pattern was similar. The highest of 41.5 per cent went to VAH, followed by cattle and buffalo development 31.2; poultry development received only 5.5 per cent and fodder development 5.2.

Development of Fisheries

Fisheries is a major economic enterprise in Gujarat. There are 771 fishing villages inhabited by 3.09 lakh fishermen population (livestock census 1988). The state has 78,033 active fishermen engaged in the marine sector and 37,162 in inland fisheries. The contribution of fisheries to the state domestic product came to an annual average of Rs. 1498 crore in 2002-05, and constituted 0.92 per cent; in 1993-96, it was respectively Rs. 617 crore and 1.00 per cent.

Gujarat's performance in fish production was quite impressive. Between 1961-64 and 1979-82, the annual average production had risen by 181 per cent, from 0.83 lakh tonnes to 2.33 lakh. In the following years, it was still faster, being by 207 per cent till 1997-1999 (calendar years), the production reaching 7.15 lakh tonnes. In the total production, the contribution of inland fishery came to only 6.11 per cent in 2001-04. The relative position of Gujarat among the states was very good. In the all-India total production of fish, the state's share came to 11.5 per cent in 2001-04, declining from 13.6 in 1996-99; both were the second highest among the states. In marine production alone, however, Gujarat was always the largest producer; the relative share in A-I total came to 22.9 per cent in 2001-04, with the production averaging 667.9 thousand tonnes. In inland production, the state's situation was very poor.

The high production notwithstanding, the state's potential remained largely unexploited even in marine fishery. Gujarat is in an enviable position in marine fishery resources. It has the longest coastline in the country, about 1663 kms, constituting roughly one-third of the total. The state also has a vast sea board forming about 1.65 lakh sq km, with 30,022 sq km within a distance of 20 km from the shoreline. The most prominent features of the coastline are the two indentations, the Gulf of Kachchh and the Gulf of Khambat, together covering around two-thirds of the coastline. There are also a large number of creeks and low lying potential resources of about 3.67 lakh hectares.

The marine waters surrounding the Saurashtra peninsula are considered the richest fishing grounds, consisting of the most important commercial varieties like Pomfrets, Hilsa, Goldara, Perches, Sharks, Cat fish, Bombay ducks and Tuna, besides different Crustaceans. Total standing fishable stock of Gujarat was estimated at around 8.00 lakh tonnes in mid-sixties, with demersal stock up to 40 fathoms at 3.38 lakh tonnes and beyond at 1.95 lakh. The Gulf of Kachchh also offers scope for the growth of different types of Oysters. (GOG 1969: 119; Sen Gupta, R et. al. 2000).

The inland water resources are also substantial. Gujarat has 200 rivers and rivulets and 18 major tanks and ponds. It was estimated in early 'nineties that village ponds provide 20,519 ha of waters, reclaimable seasonal ponds 6000 ha, conversion of water logged areas into ponds 95,000 ha, existing reservoirs 140,000 ha, minor irrigation tanks 44,025 ha and rivers 1192 kms. (GOG 1992: 171). Gujarat's relative position among the states is also quite good.

The measures for utilising the water resources proceeded very slowly, and inadequate berthing and landing facilities continued to hamper marine fishery. In early 'nineties, Gujarat had one major port, 11 intermediate ports and 28 minor ports. Number of full-fledged fishery harbours was only three, and there were 216 fish landing centres. Number of fishing boats had risen quite rapidly; reaching 16,817 in 1991, from 4,945 in 1970-71. The proportion mechanised in them had risen from 25.4 per cent to 51.6. Number of motorised boats in 1991 was 2,857 and of mechanised trawlers at 2,814. These were very inadequate for exploiting the deep sea resources and the pelagic columns, and the fishing efforts were too much concentrated on the 40 fathoms line. The government's assistance for mechanisation was very low till mid-seventies; being provided to a total of only 1946 fishing vessels during 1951-74. (GOG 1992, 1986).

Forestry and Wildlife

Gujarat is one of the highly deficit states in forest resources. Only about 10 per cent of its land area is under forest as against 23.3 per cent at the national level. The per capita forest area was only 0.06 ha in 1991, less than half the national average (0.13 ha). Out of the total forest area of about 15.59 lakh hectares, less than half could support productive forests. In early 'nineties, forests supplied only 30 per cent of the need for timber, 10 per cent of small timber and 27 per cent of fuel wood requirements. The acute shortage of almost all trees based products led to theft of timber and fire wood a regular feature. Naturally, the condition of the forests deteriorated. The proportion of dense forest in the recorded forest area was only 32.6 per cent in 1997 as against 48.0 per cent in all-India. Even the proportion of actual forest cover became very low here.

The inter-district distribution of forest areas are extremely uneven. In 1996-97, five districts—viz, Kachchh, Panchmahals, Junagadh, Surat and Bharuch—together accounted for 52.5 per cent of total, with the first one alone at 15.3 per cent. Another five districts—viz, Sabarkantha, Valsad, Jamnagar, Banaskantha and The Dangs—combined contributed 31.3 per cent. Thus, ten districts, out of 19, accounted for 83.8 per cent of total. The proportion of forest area to the district's geographical area was at the highest 59.84 per cent in Dangs, followed by Panchmahals 24.41, Valsad 23.77, Junagadh 18.88, Surat 18.59 and Sabarkantha 17.19. The forest area had declined considerably over the years in a number of districts. In relation to 1977-78, in Kachchh, it was by as much as 57.2 thousand ha, in Jamnagar by 44.1 thousand, Panchmahal by 11.6 thousand and Dangs by 10.1 thousand. (GOG 2000).

The measures for protecting the forests were very inadequate. Even the classification of forest areas remained less favourable for their protection. The reserved and protected areas together reached 76.4 per cent of total in 1997, from 67.5 in March 1979 and 43.8 in 1961; the latest was 7.2 points below the national average. The management of these areas continued to be very poor. The state's total forest area had risen from 15426.45 sq km in 1960-61 to 19655.04 in 1980-81 but declined again to 18815.14 sq km in 1996-97.

In the absence of proper measures, the problems of soil erosion and salinity continued to aggravate. Till March 1980, soil and moisture conservation and afforestation works were carried out in only 0.78 lakh ha. A number of plantation schemes were undertaken but the quantum of work done was very low. Plantations were raised in about 0.22 lakh ha on desert border, 0.37 lakh ha by fast growing species, and economic plantations in about 0.59 lakh ha. Under the farm forestry scheme, nearly 500 lakh seedlings were distributed but their survival rate was generally very low. In the following years, the progress was quite fast; the total cumulative plantation area reached 29.81 lakh ha in 1999, constituting 9.55 per cent of A-I total. The proportion of block plantation in it was, however, only 43.4 per cent, 24 points below the all-India average.

Measures were also taken for protecting the forest from fire and from grazing. The expenditure on the former had risen from Rs. 0.73 lakh in 1970-71 to Rs. 43.93 lakh in 1990-91 and Rs. 79.39 lakh in 1997-98, i.e., by 109 times over the entire period. The area closed to grazing increased from 1675.67 sq km in 1970-71 to 6792.52 in 1980-81, but in the following years it declined and averaged only 3423.08 sq km during 1993-98. (GOG 2000).

The government's expenditure on forest increased noticeably over the years. Between 1972-73 and 1999, it was by 63.4 times as against 40.2 times at the national level. In the all-India total expenditure on forestry, the state's share rose to 8.16 per cent from 5.17. The per hectare expenditure in the latest year came to Rs. 1628, which was three times the national average. The revenue from forest however, remained very low. Per hectare it came to only Rs. 118 in 1999, a mere 40 per cent of the national average. Earlier, the situation was still worse. The revenue as percentage to expenditure came to only 7.27 in 1999 as against 54.3 at the national level.

As regards the Plan expenditure, a noticeable growth came only since the Sixth Plan. This plan had provided for an outlay of Rs. 90 crore, which was 40 times the Third Plan's (Rs. 2.24 crore). In the following three plans, the growth decelerated; the Ninth Plan provided Rs. 800 crore, i.e., 8.9-fold rise over the Sixth Plan's. The pattern of expenditure changed noticeably over the years. The community forestry project was launched in the Sixth plan, and it was provided as much as 68.7 per cent of the total. The works to be covered were strip plantations, village woodlands, and reforestation of degraded forests. Plantation schemes were provided 7.3 per cent and a similar proportion for forest conservation and development. In the Seventh Plan, their shares were respectively 72.0, 8.40 and 5.51 per cent. In the Eighth Plan, however, the proportion for community forest project declined to 53.5 per cent, whereas that on forest conservation and development was raised to 17.0 per cent and for forest produce to 13.4.

The changes in expenditure brought a noticeable change in production. The production of timber declined from 229.8 thousand cms in 1985-86 to only 20.1 us and in 1990-91. The average for 1990-93 came to 27.3 thousand and increased to 35.6 thousand in 1995-98. The production of fire wood rose to 459.1 thousand cm in 1985-86, from 179.6 thousand in 1980-81; since 1990-91, however, it declined and averaged only 25.2 thousand in 1995-98. The value of forest produce had risen from Rs. 19.87 crore in 1980-81 to Rs. 48.98 crore in 1985-86, but during 1995-98 it averaged only Rs. 25.20 crore. (GOG 2000). The relative position among the states had worsened noticeably. In 1998-00, Gujarat accounted for only 1.94 per cent of A-I total production of timber, and in fuel wood 0.47 per cent. In minor forest produces, in T/K/B leaves it was 3.26 per cent and in gums 11.8 per cent.

In the management of forest, the system of people's participation had a poor success here. In January 2004, the area under joint forest management stood at only 160.5 thousand ha, constituting 10.6 per cent of the total forest cover area; at the national level, it was as much as 25.7 per cent. Among the selected states, Gujarat's was lower than in all but two. Total number of families involved was 149,191, and constituted 1.78 per cent of A-I total.

This level of performance in agriculture, etc., was not in keeping with the extent of public capital formation in the sector. The per hectare public capital formation had risen from the average of Rs. 595.69 in 1980-83 to Rs. 1323 in 1998-01—i.e., by 122 per cent; the latest was 76.7 per cent higher than in all-states. For the entire period, the per hectare investment averaged Rs. 798 as against Rs. 584 in A-S—i.e., the former 36.6 per cent higher.

NOTE

- The sharp fall in area under tobacco is a welcome change, for its cost to the economy and hazard to people's health are too high. A study in 2011 has found that the use of fuel wood between 1962 and 2002, for tobacco curing and the manufacture of cigarettes and other smoking consumable had destroyed and degraded 680 sq km of scrub forests, or nearly 808 million tonnes of wood, through successive extraction.

21

INDUSTRIAL GROWTH AND STRUCTURAL CHANGE

Gujarat has always been relatively developed industrially. Around mid-sixties, the state accounted for 8.42 per cent of all-India total value-added from the factory sector, which was the fourth highest among the states. However, the industrial base was very narrow, being dominated by the textile and the engineering industries ancillary to textiles. Moreover, the industries were mainly concentrated around the major city centres. In the following years, Gujarat made a rapid stride in industrialisation. Industry's contribution to the state's GDP rose to 41.6 per cent in 2002-05, from 39.1 in 1993-96; for manufacturing alone, the latest was 29.6 per cent. In the all-India total GDP from industry, Gujarat's share came to 7.05 per cent in 2002-05, and in manufacturing only at 9.21 per cent. (CMIE 2008).

FACTORY SECTOR

Segment-wise, the factory sector had a very good performance in Gujarat. Between 1977-78 and 2004-05, its gross output had risen 61.8-fold, from Rs. 4,222 crore to Rs. 260,749 crore. The state's share in all-India total output rose to 15.6 per cent from 10.9. Among the major states, Gujarat's was next only to Maharashtra. As regards the provision of employment, the number employed had risen by 29.3 per cent between 1977-78 and 1999 as against only 15.2 per cent in all-India; the relative share in latter's total rising to 10.07 per cent, from 8.98. In 2004-05, however, it stood at 9.20 per cent. The productivity of the employees was very high.

Structural Changes

The industrial structure diversified noticeably over the years. By the end of seventies, the share of textile group in factory labour force declined to 48 per cent, from 76 in early 'sixties, whereas chemicals and engineering raised their shares by two and half times to 20 and 18 per cent respectively. This trend towards diversification continued in the following years also, as evident from a detailed look at the changes in the 'nineties.

In the provision of employment, in 1989-90, five industries, viz, cotton textiles, basic chemicals, machinery and equipment, food products and wool, silk, etc., together accounted for 63.8 per cent of total; in 1993-94, their share declined to 61.6 per cent. If non-metallic mineral products is included, the combined share rises to 71.5 per cent in 1989-90 and 68.4 in 1993-94. Among the five industries, basic chemicals had raised its share to 16.4 per cent from 13.5 over the period, whereas for cotton textiles it declined from 20.6 to 14.82 per cent.

As regards the industry-wise changes in some of the technical coefficients, over the five-year period, the FC/O ratio had risen from 0.47 to 0.67 in basic chemicals, in metal and alloy from 0.15 to 0.50, rubber, plastic, etc., from 0.16 to 0.35, paper, etc., from 0.28 to 0.46, cotton textiles from 0.25 to 0.43, non-metallic mineral products from 0.83 to 0.91 and wool, silk, etc., from 0.22 to 0.30. Noticeable fall came in electricity, from 2.03 to 1.27, and in transport equipment from 0.23 to 0.08. The growth in fixed capital over the period was very high for a number of industries. As against a 151.7 per cent rise for all industries, metal and alloys had 105.5 per cent, and its share in the total for all industries rose to 8.00 per cent from only 1.74. In basic chemicals, the increase was by 204.5 per cent and the relative share rose to 36.6 per cent from 30.2. Rubber, plastic, etc., had 304.7 per cent rise, and the relative share increased from 4.47 to 7.20 per cent. Electricity, with the second highest amount of FC, had only a 54.6 per cent rise, and the relative share declined from 34.9 per cent to 21.7. The employees' productivity did not always increase in keeping with the growth in FC. For the industry with the highest growth in FC, metal and alloy, the output per employee had risen by only 171 per cent with the FC per employee rising by 898 per cent In basic chemicals it was respectively 64.6 and 134 per cent.

Small-scale Industries

The situation of the SSI sector in Gujarat was much worse. The growth in number of units was low, and the relative share in A-I total declined from 7.3 per cent in 1972-73 to 5.9 in 1987-88. The production had, however, risen by as much as 1619 per cent, and the state's share in A-I production stood at 8.3 per cent in 1987-88, higher than in all but three of the states. The NVA/Production ratio was very low, and declined from 32.3 per cent to 14.8; the latest was 9.1 points below the A-I average. In employment, the state's share in A-I total number had risen from 6.93 per cent in 1972-73 to 7.56 in 1987-88; the latest was higher than in most of the states. The rural share of the employment was, however, very low; being at only 20.7 per cent in 1987-88, 12.6 points below that at the national level.

The productivity of the employees was not bad; being always higher than in all-India. The growth was, however, low; at 611.5 per cent over the period, it was lower than in most of the states. This moreover, was assisted by a large amount of fixed assets. As regards the recent situation, the Census in 1997-98 found the state having only 34.45 thousand units, constituting 5.92 per cent of A-I total. The employment provided this year was 9.87 lakh, which was 6.22 per cent of the latter's. The amount of fixed investment was relatively high; at 8.96 per cent of A-I total, it was the third highest among the states. Average investment per unit came to Rs. 3.52 lakh as against Rs. 2.26 lakh in all-India. (SIDBI 2002).

Structural Change

Over the 16-year period, 1972-73 to 1987-88, the industrial structure of the SSI sector here had changed greatly. In 1972-73, four industries, viz., chemicals, machinery and parts, metal products and basic metal and alloy, together accounted for 61.8 per cent of total output. But in 1987-88, their share was only 42.7 per cent. The contribution of chemicals had declined to only 7.6 per cent from as much as 17.7, and of Metal products from 14.8 per cent to 6.5. Basic metal and alloy had, however, raised its share from 12.2 per cent to 14.3. Another group of five industries, viz, mineral products, rubber and plastic, hosiery and readymade garments, transport equipment and wood products, together provided 26.2 per cent in 1972-73; in 1987-88, their share rose to 33.1 per cent. This was, however, solely due to the rapid growth in rubber, plastic and petroleum; its share in the total rising from 5.53 per cent to 20.8. The fall was sharp in transport equipment, etc., to only 1.93 per cent from 4.69. The fastest growth in output in this period was in food products; with a 69.6-fold rise, its relative share rose to 10.0 per cent from only 2.47. Electrical machinery and apparatus and paper etc were the two other items recording a noticeable rise.

As regards the inter-industry distribution of fixed investment, in 1987-88, four industries, viz, rubber, plastic and petroleum, machinery and equipments, chemicals, and mineral products, together accounted for 51.2 per cent of total, with the first one alone at 18.0 per cent. The fixed investment per unit was the highest in rubber, plastic, etc., at Rs. 5.56 lakh, followed by chemicals Rs. 5.16 lakh; the lowest was in wood products, at Rs. 1.19 lakh. The C/O ratio was highest in mineral products, at 0.63, and the lowest at 0.15 in basic metal and alloy and food products.

The Unorganised Sector

The performance of the unorganised sector in Gujarat has been relatively good, despite the worsening over the years. The annual GVA of the sector stood at Rs. 41616 million in 2000-01 and constituted 6.91 per cent of all-India total. This was a fall from the earlier level; the relative share had declined from 10.65 per cent in 1989-90 to 9.63 in 1994-95. The rural share of the GVA was, however, very low; being at only 23.0 per cent in 2000-01 as against 44.3 per cent in all-India. Earlier, in 1989-90, it was still worse, being respectively 17.4 and 52.6 per cent.

The enterprises in Gujarat were of relatively large size. On the provision of employment, the situation was much worse. In 2000-01, the state's share in A-I total was only 4.01 per cent, declining from 5.5 in 1994-95. In the total employment again, the rural share was only 37.8 per cent in 2000-01 as against

64.7 at the national level. Earlier, it had declined from 42.3 per cent in 1989-90 to 31.0 in 1994-95. The emoluments of workers in Gujarat were very low. Per hired worker, for rural-urban combined, it averaged only Rs. 8.42 lakh annually in 2000-01 as against Rs. 120.19 lakh at the national level. However, in rural areas, the relative position was significantly better; being Rs. 23.9 thousand and Rs. 18.5 thousand, respectively. (*ibid.*). Despite the low emoluments, the productivity of the employees was noticeably higher.

Enterprise type-wise, the proportion of workers engaged in OAMEs was very low here. In 2000-01, it was only 43.4 per cent as against 67.6 per cent in all-India. In rural areas also the situation was similar, although the proportion was much higher. Percentage of workers in DMEs was much higher here than at the national level; at 35.5 per cent this year, it was double that in the latter. In rural areas, the relative position was still better; being respectively 30.6 and 12.1 per cent. The productivity of workers in each of the type of enterprises was significantly higher than in all-India. In rural OAMEs, it was higher by 48.0 per cent and in NDMEs by 45.0 per cent. (ibid.).

The situation of some of the technical co-efficient of the unorganised sector in Gujarat was very poor. In rural OAMEs, the output/ input ratio in 2000-01 came to only 2.25, lower than in most of the major states. The output/ fixed assets ratio was only 1.42 as against the national average of 1.71. The value added/fixed assets was also 0.79 and 0.86, respectively. As regards the industry-wise structure of the unorganised sector, it was heavily concentrated in a few industries. The relatively good position notwithstanding, a substantial number of enterprises faced a number of problems.

Overall, the health of the unorganised sector units in Gujarat was relatively good. In 2000-01, in rural areas, per 1000 MEs, the number expanding was 161, which was 14 points higher than at the national level, and among the major states, higher than in all but three. The numbers stagnant and contracting were respectively 622 and 115 as against 665 and 117 in all-India. Rural-urban combined, however, the situation was not so good. Only 143 units were expanding as against 156 at the national level. The proportion stagnant was 615, higher than in four of the states.

The above noted industrial growth, though impressive in several ways, remained selective in geographical spread. In early eighties, three districts, viz, Ahmedabad, Vadodara and Surat, together accounted for 60.0 per cent of the total workers in factories, with Ahmedabad alone at 37.9. In the nineties also there was not much change. In 1996, about 62 per cent of total investment and 46 per cent of employment in the manufacturing sector were concentrated in the top three districts. Conversely, the share of bottom three districts was about one and three per cent, respectively. At the taluka level, the top 25 talukas, that is, 13 per cent of total, were accounting for 67 per cent of total number of units, 70 per cent of employment and 86 per cent of investment. (Shah, Amit et al 2001: 3).

Causal Factors

Infrastructure

On the infrastructural facilities as a whole, Gujarat's situation was quite good. An index of infrastructure development, calculated by using 13 indicators, gave Gujarat 122.9 in 1992-93, taking all-India =100, and it was steady at this level for many years. Gujarat's latest was higher than in all but four of the states. (CMIE 1997a).

Among the infrastructural items, the power situation in the state was quite good. The installed capacity in 1998-99 constituted 7.5 per cent of all-India total, which was the third highest among the states. In recent years also it was in a similar position; being at 6.48 per cent in 2004-05 and 7.5 in 210-11. On power generation also the trend was similar. The gross electricity generation had risen from 46,834 mkwh in 2008-09 to 61,828 mkwh in 210-11. In both, thermal had provided 93 per cent. But the balance in the latter came entirely from hydro, whereas in the former hydro provided only 1.97 per cent and the balance was gas-based. The supply from hydro had risen from 921 mkwh to 4,164 mkwh in this period. The capacity utilisation in Gujarat was always much higher than in All-India.

The non-utilities sector in the state is also in a very good position. In 2004-05, the installed capacity in electricity stood at 2970 MW, and the gross generation came to 13527 mkwh, both were much higher than in any other state; Gujarat's share in A-I total came to 15.5 per cent and 18.9 per cent, respectively. In 2010-11, the generation increased to 20,714 mkwh, which was 62 per cent higher than the second highest—Chattisgarh. The exploitation of non-renewable sources was also relatively good. The power available from it stood at 2,009 mkwh in 2009, which was lower than in only four of the states—Andhra, Tamil Nadu, Karnataka and Maharashtra. (CMIE 2011).

Despite this relatively good position, the power shortage in Gujarat continued to be high. During 2000-02, it averaged 10.6 per cent as against 7.65 at the national level. Behind the shortage, T& D losses were an important factor. It had risen from average of 20.3 per cent in 1980-83 to 27.7 in 2002-05; in 2006-09 it was 25 per cent.

The industrial consumption of electricity in Gujarat had risen rapidly over the years. Between 1980-81 and 2004-05, under low and medium tension it was by 646 per cent and under higher tension at 145.6 per cent. On the transportation facility, Gujarat's situation was not good, as noted in the preceding Chapter. The road density continued to be below the national average. In 2002, per '000 sq km of area, it stood at 702 kms, which was 92.9 per cent of the national average; in 1975, at 230 kms, it was 63.9 per cent. The road condition is, however, relatively good. The proportion of unsurfaced road was only 9.68 per cent in 2002, declining from 15.31 in 1990-91. Inter-district, there was great variation in the situation, as noted in Chapter 2.

On the availability of motor vehicles, Gujarat was in a very good position. The density per sq km had risen from only 10.47 in 1990-91 to 33.20 in 2003; both were much higher than at the national level. The proportion of goods vehicles in them had, however, declined from 9.5 per cent in 1975 to 5.7 in 2003.

Institutional Finance

Working Capital

In the provision of working capital to industries, the SCBs played a significant role here. At March-end 2007, the total amount outstanding to the sector stood at Rs. 53826.7 crore, constituting 50.8 per cent of the grand total to the state; at the national level, it was only 38.1 per cent. In the all-India total credit to industries, Gujarat's share came to 7.26 per cent. Earlier, in March 1996, the share of industry was as much as 61.1 per cent as against 48.0 in all-India. In the industrial credit, the share of manufacturing etc had decline from 94.4 per cent to 74.7 over the period; the growth being by only 383.4 per cent as against 510.6 per cent for industry as a whole. (CMIE 2008a).

In the credit outstanding with manufacturing etc at Rs. 40219.6 crore in 2007, three industries, viz, textiles, chemicals and chemical products and basic metal and metal products, together accounted for 50.5 per cent, with the share of first one at 19.4. Three more industries—petroleum, coal, etc., engineering and food manufacturing and processing—together received 25.7 per cent, with the first one at 10.5. A decade earlier, in March 1996, the first group had received 62.1 per cent of total, with textiles alone at 27.7. The second group's share was 22.5 per cent, with engineering alone at 11.9. Still earlier, in December 1977, textiles alone accounted for 41.9 per cent of total credit, followed by chemicals, etc., 15.9, engineering 12.5, basic metals, etc., 7.92 and food manufacturing 6.79 per cent.

From the SCBs' credit to industries, the small-scale units were benefited to a very small extent. In 2004, in the A-I total credit outstanding with SSIs, the state's share was only 4.93 per cent, declining from 8.0 in 1983; the latest was lower than in four of the states. The growth in credit over the period was by only 7.37 times as against 12.0 times in all-India. In the number of accounts assisted, the state's share stood at only 2.97 per cent in 2004, declining from 8.2 in 1968. The average amount per account in 2004 was higher than in all-India by as much as 65.4 per cent.

22

ABSOLUTE POVERTY AND THE MEASURES

The poverty situation in Gujarat was much less acute than in most other states, as has been noted in Chapter 2. The proportion of BPL population in 2004-05 stood at only 16.75 per cent, which was below the national average by as much as 11.52 points, and in relation to Maharashtra by 13.2 points. This was, however, an increase over 1999-00. The situation of MPCE also worsened in recent years. The proportion in rural areas with below Rs. 380 in 2004 was 18.2 per cent, only two points below the rural-India's. In 1987-88, at 24.9 per cent, it was lower by 15.6 points. Percentage of population with calorie undernourishment in 2007 was 23.3 as against 20.0 in all-India.

The inter-district disparities in MPCE continued to be very high, and consequently in the proportion of BPL population. In 2004-05, in rural areas, the MPCE was at the highest Rs. 1012 in Gandhinagar as against the lowest of Rs. 349 in Dangs, with Rs. 596 at the state level. In urban areas, the highest was Rs. 2422 in Gandhinagar and the lowest at Rs. 604 in Kheda, with the state average at Rs. 1115. The variation in proportion of BPL population was much higher. This year, in rural areas, at the highest it was 88.4 per cent in Dangs as against a negligible 0.0 in Junagadh, with 18.9 at the state level; four districts had above 40 per cent. In urban areas, the highest was 52.9 per cent in Kachchh and the lowest at 0.6 in Gandhinagar, with 13.3 at the state level.

Social group-wise, the poverty among the STs was worse than in SCs. In 1999, the STs—constituting 21.3 per cent of hhs—had an MPCE of Rs. 438 in rural Gujarat as against Rs. 388 at the national level, i.e., the former 12.9 per cent higher. After five years, in 2004-05, at Rs. 484, it was 13.6 per cent higher. For SCs, at Rs. 522 in 2004-05, it was higher than the national average by only 9.87 per cent. In relation to the state's non-backward community (NBC), the amount for STs had declined from 66.9 per cent in 1999-00 to 58.8 in 2004-05; and for SCs from 70.1 to 63.4 per cent.

In urban areas also, the situation of SCs was much better than that of STs. In 2004-05, the MPCE for SCs was 24.3 per cent higher than in all-India, rising from 7.06 per cent higher in 1999-00; for STs, it was respectively 7.35 per cent higher and 4.2 per cent lower. The disparity with the NBC—in contrast to rural areas—decreased significantly. For STs, it rose to 71.4 per cent of the latter's from 62.6; and for SCs from 61.7 to 73.2.

Behind the disparities, the occupational distribution of the communities was an important factor. The proportion of STs in rural labour was very high in Gujarat, being at 57.2 per cent in 1999-00 as against 48.5 at the national level; in agricultural labour, they constituted respectively 44.7 and 39.7 per cent. In self-employment, the proportion agricultural was 31.1 per cent and in non-agriculture only 3.2 per cent as against 36.2 and 5.2 per cent in all-India. In agriculture, a large proportion of the STs were cultivating very small plots; those with less than 0.40 ha constituted as much as 60.0 per cent as against 46.3 per cent in all-India. For SCs, the situation was much worse. The proportion in rural labour was as much as 68.5 per cent, seven points higher than at the national level.

The wage rates in Gujarat continued to be very low, and this was an important reason behind the poverty of labour households. The proportion of labour hhs in rural areas had risen from only 18.5 per cent in 1964-65 to 50.5 in 1987-88 and then declined to 44.4 in 2004; even the latest was 7 points higher than in all-India. This pressure of employment kept the real agricultural wage rate (at 1960-61 prices) at only Rs. 1.7 in 1995 as against Rs. 4.1 in all-India; for non-agricultural labourers, it was respectively Rs. 3.7 and Rs. 8.8. In recent years, in 2004-05, the average daily wage rate in agriculture came to Rs. 55.48 for men and Rs. 30.14 for women as against Rs. 61.23 and Rs. 44.59 at the national level. For rural casual workers as a whole, it stood at Rs. 45.20 as against Rs. 50.70 in the latter. In urban areas, the relative position was still worse.

To look at the activity-wise situation in agriculture: In 2009, for ploughing, the rate for man was only Rs. 98.97, which was below the national average and among the major states lower than in six; the highest was Rs. 269.55 in Kerala. In sowing, at Rs. 87.17, it was lower than in five of the states; and in weeding, at Rs. 72.96, lower than in seven. In transplanting, Gujarat had only Rs. 64 as against Rs. 81.73 at the national level; in harvesting, Rs. 70.27 and Rs. 84.82 respectively; in threshing Rs. 73.83 and Rs. 83.49; and in winnowing Rs. 71.23 and Rs. 78.41. In unspecified unskilled labour, the state had only Rs. 69 as against Rs. 85.72 at the national level. (GOI 2009a).

The labour productivity in Gujarat was, however, not low. In 2004-05, per agricultural labourer it stood at Rs. 12,292, which was 14 per cent higher than in all-India, rising from 5.3 per cent higher in 1993-94. In manufacturing, the situation was still better. In 2004-05, at Rs. 56,802, it was 76.6 per cent higher than in all-India.

A very important reason behind the low wage rates is the non-existence of organisational support for the labourers. An NSSO survey in 1993-94 found 88.9 per cent of agricultural labourers reporting non-existence of any Union/Association in their activity, which was the second highest among the states. For non-agricultural workers in rural areas, it was 80.6 per cent compared with 66.6 per cent in All-India. (Jha, Praveen 2007). Naturally, the implementation of the Minimum Wages Act 1948 was very poor here. In 2003-04, for example, 1,01,364 irregularities were detected with 1,20,550 inspections. The number that could be rectified was only 57,977. Number of claims filed was 4,052, of which only 1,134 were settled; 1.080 person were prosecuted. (GOI 2005a).

Wage Employment Programmes

The employment created by different employment programmes in Gujarat had a sharp fall. To look into the overall situation first: Per 1000 hhs, the number participating in public works had declined from as much as 178 in 1987-88 to only 60 in 1993-94 and further to 19 in 1999; the latest was only 65.5 per cent of that at the national level. In 1987-88, Gujarat's was the highest among the states and 2.78 times the national average.

Scheme-wise, the first one, Crash Scheme for Rural Employment, operated during 1971-74, had created a total of 143.07 lakh person-days (lpds), constituting 4.71 per cent of all-India total. The average cost per person-day came to Rs. 3.87, slightly less than in the latter; among the 18 major states, Gujarat's was lower than in nine. In the assets created, roads received a very high priority. In the total expenditure in this three-year period, its share came to 87.2 per cent as against 71.3 for the 16 states. The expenditure on land development, on the other hand, constituted only 4.0 per cent, a quarter of that at the national level. The share of minor irrigation was also low, being 8.8 and 12.8 per cent, respectively. The total road length created came to 5,150 kms, and constituted 6.57 per cent of A-I total.

The Food for Work Programme, launched in 1977 and continued till September 1980, also did not have a good performance. An evaluation study in August-October, 1979 found that in the two districts studied (Amreli and Panchmahal), the total person-days created was 24,357 in 1978-79, constituting 7.76 per cent of the total for 20 districts studied. The average per family, however, came to only 324.8 pds as against 446.3 in the latter. This was despite a much higher level of increase over the pre-launch situation; being by 38.5 per cent compared with 10.9 per cent for all districts. Average wage per family also remained very low; rising from Rs. 1,024 prior to its launch to Rs. 1,423 after; for all-districts, it was from Rs. 1,981 to Rs. 2,332. (GOI 1980).

The National Rural Employment Programme, replacing the FWP in 1980, had a very poor performance in Gujarat. To look at the situation over a period of four years: During 1985-89, total number of pds created was only 511.13 lakh, constituting 3.46 per cent of A-I total; among the selected states, it was lower than in all but two. The target itself was low; and this was with an achievement of as much as 149.8 per cent. The utilisation of available fund was, however, only 89.3 per cent, lowest among the states. The cost per pd came to Rs. 22.63, lower than in five of the states. The utilisation of foodgrains was very high here, being the highest among the states.

The situation of RLEGP was much worse. The pds created in this four-year period constituted only 2.19 per cent of all-India total; among the selected states, it was lower than in all but two. Here also the target itself was low, and the achievement 20 per cent higher. The utilisation of available fund was, however, low; being only 90.6 per cent as against 100 per cent at the national level. The cost per pd came to as much as Rs. 24.31, higher than in all but three of the states. The utilisation of foodgrains was very high here also, being the second highest. (*ibid.*). The quality of planning and implementation appears to be very poor.

The JRY

The Jawahar Rozgar Yojana, created in April 1989, brought a major change in the wage-employment programmes, as noted in chapter 7. Gujarat's performance in this scheme was also not good. Total of persondays created during 1989-95 constituted only 2.6 per cent of A-I total, with the share in expenditure at 3.2 per cent. The cost per pd came to Rs. 42.87, higher than in all but two of the states. In the following years, the situation worsened further. Total of pds created in 1997, constituted only 1.80 per cent of A-I total. The number created annually averaged 62.3 lakh, which was less than a third of that during 1989-95. The cost per pd increased noticeably; at Rs. 95, it was 42 per cent higher than at the national level. Among the beneficiaries from the employment, the share of SC/ST was always high. During 1989-95, it was as much as 65.7 per cent, around 17 points higher than the national average. In the following years also the situation was similar. The proportion of landless was, however, very low.

On the sub-schemes also Gujarat's situation was not good. Number of wells constructed under the MWS came to only 4.22 per cent of A-I total during 1988-95, and declined to 2.89 in 1995-99. The expenditure per well increased from Rs. 31 thousand in the first period to Rs. 43 thousand in the second; the latest was higher than in all but two of the states. The level of fund utilisation was relatively good; averaging 89.1 per cent during 1992-99 as against 83.8 at the national level. On the IAY, the situation was still worse. Number of houses constructed under it constituted only 2.62 per cent of A-I total during 1985-95, and increased to 3.31 in the following years. The expenditure per house was very low, rising from Rs. 12,000 in the first period to Rs. 15,000 in the second. In recent years, there has been some improvement in the situation. In 2008-09, up to January 21, the state had constructed 54,962 houses, which was 4.98 per cent of A-I total. The achievement in relation to target was 58.3 per cent, which was higher than at the national level.

The proportion of total expenditure going for wage payment was very low here. The employment created was very low. A serious drawback in the implementation of the programme was that a very large proportion of the participants came from above the poverty-line income (Rs. 6,401 and above);

accounting for as much as 62.3 per cent of total this year as against 56.96 per cent at the national level. In the BPL category also, the higher income groups had relatively high representation. Of the 37.7 per cent, half came from the class of Rs. 4801-6400. The quality of assets created under the JRY was found to be relatively good. The misappropriation of fund was relatively low here.

The EAS

The Employment Assurance Scheme, launched in 1993, also had similar performance. Total number of pds created till March 2000 came to 462 lakh, constituting only 2.07 per cent of A-I total. The level of fund utilisation was very low; average for the seven-year period came to only 51.1 per cent as against 67.9 per cent at the national level. The cost per pd was, however, noticeably higher; averaging Rs. 72 and Rs. 59, respectively. In the employment created, the share of SC/ST averaged 58.6 per cent, which was lower than in all but three of the states.

The employment programmes underwent several changes since April 1999, as has been noted in Chapter 7. After the changes, Gujarat's relative position in employment creation improved but nominally. In 2004-05, at 264.68 lpds, it constituted 3.24 per cent of A-I total. This number was around double that created annually by the two schemes together towards the end of nineties. Among the beneficiaries, the situation of landless was very poor; at 36.8 per cent of total, it was lower than in all but two of the states.

In recent years also Gujarat's situation on provision rural employment was very poor. The person-days created by the NREGA, launched in 2006, per rural hh. declined from 43.7 in 2006-07 to 29.6 the next year and only 25 in 2008-09; the latest for All-India was 48 pds. Percentage of hhs. completing 100 days of employment in the first two years were respectively 5.4 and 3.9 as against 10.2 and 10.8 in all-India. Among the beneficiaries, the proportion of landless was very low; at 36.8 per cent in 2006-07, it was lower than in seven of the states. The share of wages in total expenditure was very low; and the average wage cost per pd came to only Rs. 56 as against Rs. 65 in all-India. The NREGA wage rate itself is very low here; at Rs. 50, it was the lowest among the states. (GOI 2008, 2008a, 2011a).

This is a very sad situation in a state of the stature of Gujarat. But it needs to be noted that even the provision of 100 days per family is unlikely to meet the demand in years and areas of severe drought. Serious thought should be given to guaranteeing 180 days of work, at least in the most backward districts. Corruption in running the scheme also needs to be tackled firmly. And for this, an essential first step is computerisation of all stages of NREGA work, beginning from registration of workers. There is, however, no real substitute for powerful people's vigilance.

Self-Employment Programmes

Operation of the IRDP/SGSY

On the IRDP, the first SEP launched for BPL population in 1980, Gujarat's performance was not good. To look at the situation since early 'nineties: The state's share in All-India total number of families assisted had declined from 3.14 per cent in 1992-95 to 2.44 in 1996-99. After the scheme's restructuring in April 1999, Gujarat's share in A-I total number of swarozgaris stood at 2.50 per cent in 2004-05. The proportion covered by SHGs was very low here. The participation in the scheme in terms of hhs had declined from 92 per thousand in 1993-94 to 46 in 1999. Among the beneficiaries, the proportion of SC/ST was very low; constituting only 51.8 per cent during 1992-95 as against 62.6 per cent in All-India. MPCE class-wise, the lower classes had high participation here.

The quantum of subsidy provided was relatively high in Gujarat. During 1992-95, per beneficiary it came to Rs. 4,121 as against Rs. 3,896 at the national level. In the following years, the situation improved further. In 1999, at Rs. 12,657, it was 22.6 per cent higher than in All-India. The provision of credit was, however, very low. (ibid.).

The implementation of the IRDP suffered from many deficiencies. On the sub-schemes of the IRDP also Gujarat's performance was not good. Under the TRYSEM, the total number trained during 1992-99 came to 57 thousand and constituted 3.67 per cent of A-I total. In the total number, the proportion of SC/ST was 57.2 per cent, 12 points higher than at the national level. As regards placement of the youths, at 45.2 per cent of the total number trained during 1992-96, it was below the national average. The expenditure per trainee was very low. Average for the entire period came to Rs. 3,167, which was below the A-I average.

The DWCRA was in a worse position. The total number of members during 1992-99 constituted only 2.46 per cent of A-I total; among the selected states, it was lower than in as many as six. The expenditure per group was, however, much higher here than at the national level; being respectively Rs. 25,188 and Rs. 16,933. The SITRA, launched much later, was in a better position. During 1997-99, total number of beneficiaries came to 21,350 and constituted 6.07 per cent of A-I total; among the major states, it was higher than in five. The expenditure per beneficiary was, however, very low. At the average of Rs. 1,760 in the two years, it was much below the national average.

For the Backward Areas

Apart from specific programmes for the BPL population, measures were also taken for the development of special problem areas. The Fourth five-year Plan had classified these areas into: (i) Scheduled areas and other economically backward areas, (ii) Flood affected areas, (iii) chronically drought affected areas, (iv) Border areas, (v) Desert areas, and (vi) Scheduled Tribes population. Fifty-six talukas of the state, i.e., 30 per cent of total, were declared as more backward, based on the situation of 11 indicators of development. The fund allocation for these areas was, however, very low. The Fourth Plan had provided a total of about Rs. 44.90 crore for all these areas together, constituting only 10 per cent of the total outlay for the Plan. In the total outlay, the scheduled and other economically backward areas received 53.3 per cent; and the flood affected, chronically drought affected and Border areas together 35.5 per cent .

In the outlay for the economically backward areas, irrigation and power received 63.8 per cent, with the share of power in it at 71.9 per cent, followed by roads 11.3 and agricultural programmes 9.40 per cent; in agriculture, forest received as much as 87.9 per cent. In the outlay for flood affected areas, irrigation and flood control was provided 68.2 per cent. In drought affected areas, agriculture received 35.9 per cent and social services 35.0. In desert areas, almost the entire amount was for agricultural programmes. In the allocation for scheduled tribes, with the lowest amount of Rs. 1.77 crore, 53.2 per cent went for education, followed by economic upliftment 12.4. (GOG 1969: 55).

In the following years, many changes came but the allocation for the problem areas did not increase much. For example, in the Sixth plan, the desert areas (DDP) and the drought prone areas (DPAP) together had received Rs. 19.50 crore, constituting 1.71 per cent of the grand total. In the following Seventh Plan, the allocation declined to Rs. 15.36 crore and the relative share to 0.96 per cent. The Eighth plan had no provision for the desert areas but the DPAP received Rs. 18.65 crore and constituted 0.16 per cent. In the Ninth plan, although the allocation rose to as much as Rs. 80.06 crore for the DPAP and the DDP together, the relative share came to only 0.29 per cent.

It may be noted here that the number of backward talukas fixed at 56 in 1970, remained the same in the following decades also. The committees set up for development of the backward areas made many recommendations but these were not given due attention. After the submission of the Hathi committee report in 1971, the government had decided to give additional financial assistance of Rs. 75 lakh per year for minor irrigation and road works. But it was provided to only 33 talukas. The Patel Committee in 1984 warned against the earlier measures of allocating Rs. one or two lakh per taluka as a special grant, and recommended "strategic intervention on a long scale". (Patel, Surendra J 1991). The government, however, ignored it and continued with the past pattern of providing ridiculously small sums. The level of grant was raised from 'Rs. two lakh' to 'Rs. two to three lakh'. Prices had gone up three times over the 14 years, and therefore, the real value of the grant in 1985 was less than half that in 1979.

Tribal Area Sub-Plan

For the tribal areas, under the tribal area sub-plan, introduced in 1976, 32 talukas with majority tribal population were covered. Another 15 pockets of tribal concentration were also included in it. These areas are mainly in the eastern hilly belt of the state, spread over eight districts. The total area covered by the sub-plan is 27,189 sq km, constituting 13.89 per cent of the state's total. Eighty-one per cent of the state's tribal population lived in this area in 1971.

The TSP's aims were high, to eliminate all forms of exploitation of the tribals and speed up the process of their development. Steps were take to save the tribals from land alienation, exploitation in forest labour and for securing their essential consumption needs. Production-oriented programmes and infrastructure development were emphasised and generation of employment opportunities was given priority. The measures taken were, however, insignificant from the angle of the need. The policies were implemented lackadaisically, and the fund allocations were very low.

To look at the level of plan expenditures: In the Sixth Plan (1980-85), an outlay of Rs. 459.65 crore was fixed for the TSP, constituting 14 per cent of the grand total. This was expected to be supplemented by special central assistance and other central programmes and institutional finances. In the total outlay under TSP, agriculture and allied programmes received 28.2 per cent, followed by social and community services 23.5 per cent and water development 19.9. The following Seventh plan raised the outlay to only Rs. 540.96 crore, and the relative share declined to 9.02 per cent. In this plan, transport and communication was given the highest of 22.8 per cent, followed by agriculture and allied programmes 16.7, mid-day meal scheme 15.2 and water development 14.8 per cent.

In the following plans, there was no allocation for the TSP. Based on the recommendation of the Patel committee, noted earlier, additional funds in the form of 20 per cent additional discretionary outlay was provided for the 56 most backward districts in the decentralised district planning. In the Eighth Plan, it came to only Rs. 301 crore. Another Rs. 359.40 crore was provided under the welfare of backward classes, 37.8 per cent of which was for tribal development. Special projects for the welfare of tribals were also initiated around mid-eighties for attracting institutional finance. The activities of the Tribal Development Corporation, set up in October 1972, were accelerated around this time. The corporation provides soft loans to tribal co-operatives and share loans. Some of the schemes relating to co-operation, social welfare and cottage and small industries were transferred to it.

None of these measures were implemented with the sincerity they deserved. Fund diversions and delay in implementation of projects were common. The sufferings of the tribals multiplied also due to the anti-people forest policy of the government. An increasing number of so-called development projects alienated the tribals from their land. Though by law the sale of tribals' land to non-tribals is prohibited, large tracts of their land were acquired by the state. Lands were acquired for wild life sanctuaries, construction of dams and industrial complexes. As much as 20,171 ha of land were lost for only four irrigation projects—viz., Daman Ganga (7544), Sardar Sarovar (7470), Karjan (3677) and Kakrapara. Total number of ST families affected was 6,466. (Shah, Ghanshyam 2002). The living condition of the affected people (PAP) greatly deteriorated everywhere due to lack of proper rehabilitation measures. A brief look is given below into the nature of resettlement and rehabilitation (R&R) provided to the oustees.

R & R of the PAP

Panam Irrigation Project

The Panam irrigation project, located in the Panchmahals district, had dislocated 22,348 persons, the third highest in the state. The dam is across Panam river and has a length of 269.45 metres with height at 56.36 metres. The construction of the project began in February 1972 and the dam was completed in late 1978. The main canal and distributaries were completed in 1984. The command area of the project is irrigated by a 110 km long canal. The gross command area served by the canal is 62,750 hectares, of which 41,116 hects are cultivable. The area submerged due to construction of the dam was 8,980 hects, of which 5,985 hects (66.6 per cent) were cultivable land. Besides, 3,730 houses and 1140 wells were flooded out. The project affected 42 villages, of which six were fully submerged, 12 affected to the extent of 75 per cent and five were half affected. Total population affected was 22,348 in 3,546 families. The evacuation of the first batch of affected people began in May-June 1974 and by the end of 1978, majority of the affected families were shifted to the newly created resettlement sites. The affected families were grouped into: fully affected as those whose agricultural land as well as house were submerged; and partially affected were expected to experience submergence of a part or whole of their agricultural land or of their houses. Sixty per cent of the families (2,124) were classed as fully affected.

For rehabilitation of the families, 19 sites were prepared on the forest land. Out of a total of 2,292 resettled families, 2,274 were given either house plots or agricultural land or both in the sites, depending upon the extent of submerged property. Another 1,002 affected agricultural families did not get additional land in lieu of their submerged land because their unsubmerged holdings exceeded the government's land allotment norms; they received cash compensation for their submerged land and remained in the old village. There were another 220 affected families which also remained in the old villages because they hoped to be able to cultivate naturally fertile land after the monsoon when the reservoir's water level went down.

These rehabilitation policies came gradually as the project was being implemented. The resolution relating to the allotment of agricultural land and residential plots was issued in May 1973; that for the provision of basic amenities at rehabilitation sites and free industrial training classes in October 1975; and that for the ad hoc grant and provision of transportation facility came in July 1976. This passing of the resolutions over a period of more than three years revealed the piecemeal character of the rehabilitation effort. We give a brief look below on the findings of a study on the implementation of the resolutions and the situation of the oustees. (Gumber, Anil 1992).

The rehabilitation effort was very slow and implemented only partly. The allotted forest land was yet to be transferred to the revenue department, and this prevented the conferring of land rights on the allottees. The absence of land titles deprived the resettlers the credit from banks, assistance under any poverty alleviation programme and benefits from agricultural extension services. The availability of basic facilities was not at par with those in the neighbouring revenue villages. It was found that no attention had so far been paid to the health facilities for the people at the resettlement sites or the affected area. The people had to approach a private doctor in the vicinity or travel a long distance to avail the services of the public hospital. Provision for a free vocational training programme (with some stipend for the trainees) in carpentry, masonry, turning, etc., laid down in the policy remained yet to be implemented. There were also no steps so far to electrify the resettlement sites and the affected villages.

In mid-eighties, there were many things yet to be done in the resettlement sites that could have improved the living condition of the people. In 15 out of 19 resettlement sites more than 900 acres of agricultural land were left unallotted. This land could be allotted to the landless families or put to some other use. The utilisation of the Panam reservoir water was also distressingly poor. With a fish catchment area of 6,000 hectares, the annual catch came to only about 20 tonnes. Similarly, some of the households in the affected area were engaged in collection of minor forest produce, but they were unable to get adequate price in the local market. An important reason behind the poor situation of the oustees here is that they were neither organised nor assisted by voluntary agencies to fight for better rehabilitation.

Sardar Sarovar Project (SSP)

The cost and benefits to be derived from the SSP have been noted in Chapter 20. Here we look at only the tortuous course that the resettlement and rehabilitation of the PAP took. The dispute between Gujarat and Madhya Pradesh over the extent of use of water led to the setting up of a tribunal, the Narmada Water Dispute Tribunal (NWDT) in 1969. The Tribunal submitted its final report in 1978, and ordered the Gujarat government to bear the total cost of rehabilitation in all the three states of Gujarat, Maharashtra and MP.

On the oustees, the Tribunal made a basic provision for the allotment of two ha of irrigable agricultural land to each landholding family losing 25 per cent or more of agricultural land. Family included husband, wife, minor children and other dependent on the head of the family. Further, every major son was treated as a separate family. (Iyenger, Sudarshan 2002). This was a path-breaking recommendation because earlier, in most of the projects the persons losing land were given cash compensation which hardly enabled them to buy alternate land. The recommendation of a minimum of two ha of agricultural land, however, had a serious lacuna. It failed to take into account the fact that in tribal settlements a large number of families do not own but only operate land for production, due to the community ownership of land. Secondly, the NWDT provision ignored female headed households and the landless.

Not only this, the three state governments were not inclined to even abide by the NWDT provisions. In the Resolution issued by the Gujarat government in June 1979, a crucial change was made which killed the spirit of the NWDT provision. The entitlement of a minimum of two ha of irrigated land to 'each land owning family' was changed to 'each land holding'—operated jointly by two or more families. On the strength of this resolution, the government offered a minimum of two ha of its waste land—located far away from the submergence villages—to each holding and not to each family. The tribals living in the first five affected villages refused the government offer. The government took the stand that those who rejected the offer could buy land on their own from the cash compensation paid.

However, by the end of 1983, the tribals began organising themselves and the matter was taken to the court; the government stood exposed. An NGO, the ARCH Vahini, also began to take interest in the PAP. In August 1983, they wrote a detailed letter to the World Bank describing the dependence of tribals on forest land for their survival. The Bank, till then, knew nothing about the problem of encroachers in the submergence zone, as the government had never supplied the information to it. The government treated the tribals cultivating forest and government waste land as 'illegal encroachers', and, therefore, not to be considered as PAP eligible for alternative agricultural land.

In May 1985, the World Bank entered into a loan agreement with the government of India and the three state governments. Besides the techno-economic aspects of the project, the R&R conditions were also negotiated. The chief negotiator, Thayer Scudder, built upon the NWDT Award and secured land entitlement for the encroachers and the landless in the submergence villages. The government of India agreed to release the forest land for this purpose. The loan agreement had also provided for the right to choose the agricultural land to the displaced families.

The struggle, however, continued as even after signing the loan agreement (LA) the GOG attempted to violate its spirit in the implementation. The non-compliance with the provisions in the LA came to the notice of the World Bank Mission in April 1987, and the Mission members visited the interior-most villages and declared in presence of the government officials that all encroacher and landless families were entitled to a minimum of two ha of land of their choice. The government initially declined to do it, but as the Bank took a tough stand ultimately it had to yield. Three government resolutions were issued in December 1987 incorporating these changes.

In the implementation of policy, a major issue was the total number of affected persons. The highest number was estimate by the Narmada Bachao Andolan: 1,50,000 tribals in 245 submergence villages, 1,70,000 farmers by the canal network, and 40,000 by the Shoolpaneshwar Sanctuary. It stated further that thousands of families would be displaced due to the Catchment Area Treatment and Compensatory Afforestation, and thousands of landless labourers due to transfer of private lands to the tribals. (ARCH-Vahini 1993). The Independent Review Mission estimated the number of families at 40,000 as against the original estimate of 6,603 by the NWDT.

The implementation of the reformed R&R policy was in two phases: 1988 to 1993 and 1993 to 1997. The second period coincided with the withdrawal of the project from the World Bank and also the absence of the review mission, which meant no pressure from any external agency. However, by December 1993, a large majority of Gujarat and Maharashtra families had been allotted land, and there were very few cases of allotment of bad quality land. The Land Purchase Committee and the Joint Inspection Committee were in place and working well till 1992.

From early 1993, the discipline in the LPC got diluted, and some sub-standard purchases of land took place. This happened particularly when the MP government pressurised the Gujarat government to first buy land, prepare sites and then invite the displaced tribals and others to choose and select sites. There was also a pressure to buy land faster. One of the NGO members stopped attending meetings, protested and then resigned. The progress of work became slow. Between December 1993 and March 1996, only 1075 families were allotted land, of which 828 were from MP. The MP government was not happy with the resettlement efforts by the government of Gujarat. Thus, even the PAPs of SSP, despite a long struggle and being assisted by the World Bank and NGOs, did not get a satisfactory R&R. It may be noted here that the construction of dams over rivers not only brings immense sufferings for the people upstream, but also have serious long-term costs. Studies have found that hydropower reservoir emit more green-house gas per unit of power produced than thermal plants. Organic matter ferments in the base of reservoirs and produces methane which is let off into the atmosphere at the spill ways. The reservoirs also arrest the sediments that are carried by the rivers to the coasts and prevent their erosion. The sea waves' natural tendency to hit coast and cause erosion is greatly neutralised by the inflow of sediments brought in by the rivers.

The attitude of the government towards the tribals comes out more vividly if a look is given into the manner in which their land right movements were suppressed. The situation in only two of the districts are considered.

PART VI: SUMMING UP

23

SUMMARY AND CONCLUSIONS

I

If development is not to lead to disorder, extreme of inequality, both inter-personally and spatially, must be avoided at any cost. Peoples' level of consciousness gradually rise and ultimately they revolt against the injustices perpetrated by the dominant section. It is to guard against such eventualities that the Constitution of India, in the Preamble itself laid down the objective of securing for all its citizens, "Justice, social, economic and political", and "equality of status and opportunity". The Directive Principles of State Policy aimed at assuring adequate means of livelihood to everybody, free and compulsory education, improved public health, and many other good things.

But all these were virtually thrown overboard, and the Constitution was reduced to a propaganda material. Within a decade, voices of dissent began to appear and ultimately took a violent form in many parts of the country. The deficiencies in the Constitution became apparent soon after it came into operation, and by the year 1980 there were 45 amendments. The deceptive nature of India democracy became transparent. The Party in power at the Centre never represented the majority of voters. And the elections gradually became a farce, with muscle and money power playing the dominant role. Corruption became rampant everywhere in the country; and in recent years the Prime Minister himself was encouraging it. Mega scams are coming to light almost daily.

A small section of people began wallowing in riches while grinding poverty became the lot of a vast number. The resource mobilisation remained extremely low and their deployment perverse. The rate of saving was below 20 per cent till the end of'eighties and in the following years also it was not much higher. The role of public sector remained far below what the situation demanded. The plan expenditures were low, and it was further diluted by corruption and inefficiency. The politicians-contractors-bureaucrats nexus grabbed a large part of it.

The growth of the economy was very low. Over a period of nearly five decades, between 1950-53 to 1994-97, the per capita income was only a little more than doubled, rising from Rs. 1136 to Rs. 2606. The diversification of economic activities was far from satisfactory. The secondary sector's share in national product had risen to only 26.1 per cent in 2004-05 from 21.6 in 1973-74.

A large portion of the workforce continued to be engaged in the low productive agriculture, and farmers committing suicide became quite common in recent years. The proportion of BPL population remained high. The provision of basic facilities was virtually nonexistent in rural areas.

The educational and health situation continued to be distressingly poor. Even after three decades of development efforts, the literacy rate in 1981 stood at only 36.2 per cent, with females at 24.8. The proportion with middle school and above constituted only 26.7 per cent in rural areas in 2004. On health, The IMR was as much as 60 even in 2003, with rural areas at 74. The proportion of children under-three suffering from anaemia was 79 per cent in 2005-06. The control over population growth was almost a total failure.

This is the background in which the Central and Western Indian states pursued their development efforts. Their contribution itself was significant to this pattern, as they together accounted for 39.2 per cent of the country's population. Among them, however, there were wide differences in terms of resource endowment. Two of the states, Uttar Pradesh and Madhya Pradesh, were land-locked, while the other two had long coastlines and relatively developed to begin with. Between the first two again, the latter was the largest in terms of area while the former most populated. The major findings of the study are noted below for each of the states.

II

Uttar Pradesh had the worst performance among the four. Most of the socio-economic indicators were in a distressingly poor state. The literacy rate in 2001 was only 57.4 per cent, with females at 43; among the states, both were lower than in all but Bihar. The health condition of the people was one of the worst. The IMR was as much as 73 even in 2005, which was 16 points higher than the national average. The under-5 mortality rate was 96, 22 point higher. The birth rate was also very high. The hygienic condition continued to be extremely poor. A sanitary latrine was available to only 22 per cent of the households in 1998. The human development index in 2001 was lower than in all but two of the states. The intra-state disparities were extremely high in every parameter. The IMR was as much as 134 in Budaun as against only 36 in Ballia.

Behind this depressing situation, the main factor was the abominably low quality of political leadership. Their only concern was somehow to grab the offices, and for this they did not hesitate to encourage the mafia and the criminal elements. There were frequent changes in the government and the administration suffered. Naturally, the resource mobilisation was low, and their deployment perverse. Inefficiency and corruption were rampant.

The per capita total budgetary receipts was always below the all-states' average, and declined from 77.5 per cent of the latter's in 1975-78 to 61.5 per cent in 2000-03. Naturally the expenditure level remained very low. The capital expenditure was very low here, and it was largely because a large proportion of capital receipts was going to meet revenue deficit; in 2000-03, it was to the extent of 42.6 per cent.

The situation of co-operative credit system was very gloomy. The most important institution, PACS, had an working capital per society of only Rs. 11 lakh in 1998, which was around a third of the national average. The deposit mobilisation per society came to one-twelfth of that at the national level. In recent years, the situation worsened further. Naturally, the lending activities remained low. The loans outstanding per society was only Rs. nine lakh in 2005, around a quarter of the national average. The PNACS were in a still worse situation. This extremely low resource mobilisation and deployment naturally implied inadequate provision of facilities in different areas. In the sphere of education, the availability of schools was very low. In the area of health, the MCH activities were at a very low level. Children aged 12-23 months fully immunised was only 23 per cent in 2005-06, around half that at the national level. The maternal healthcare was also similarly placed. The proportion of pregnant women registered for pre-natal care was only 54.4 per cent in 2004 as against 69.8 in all-India. The situation of health infrastructure was distressingly poor. The availability of Sub-centres was very inadequate. And then there was acute scarcity of doctors. Average number of doctors per PHC was only 0.59 in 1997. Number of nurses, per lakh population, was 9.24 in 1991, a quarter of that at the national level. The family planning measures were very inadequate. The TFR was always significantly higher than the national average.

The productive sectors suffered from utter inadequacy of facilities, and the production remained low. On the provision of facilities, the situation of irrigation was quite good. In the allied sectors, the situation of animal husbandry was not bad. The performance of the industrial sector was very poor. An important factor behind this situation was poor infrastructure.

While the performance of the productive sectors was poor, the direct poverty alleviation measures also did not get the needed attention. The employment created under the wage employment programmes had a sharp fall over the years. Per thousand hhs, the number participating declined to only 29 in 1999 from 51 in 1993-94. The implementation of the programmes were thoroughly vitiated by inefficiencies and corruption. The rules laid down in the JRY manual were largely violated. Even the NREGP, launched with much fanfare, was almost a total failure. The wage rates in UP were in general very low. The implementation of the IRDP was also not much better. As in case of the employment programme, the lower income groups did not receive the due attention. On the operation of the PDS UP's situation was very poor. Even after the recent changes, benefits to the poor households were extremely low. The system continued to be thoroughly riddled with corruption and inefficiency. The situation of the poor is unlikely to improve noticeably unless there is an aggressive assertion through proper organisation.

III

Madhya Pradesh, despite having ample resources, had a very poor performance. Over the period of nearly four decades, between 1960-63 and 1994-97, its per capita income had risen by only 567 per cent as against 939 per cent at the national level. Its per capita income averaged Rs. 14695 in 2003-06, constituting only 62.4 per cent of all-India's; and for Chhattisgarh, at Rs. 18106, it was 76.9 per cent. The economic diversification was very low. The poverty situation continued to be very depressing. Percentage of rural households with MPCE of less than Rs. 380 was as much as 42.1 even in 2004, more than double that at the national level.

The social indicators of development were in a very poor state. Even after three decades of efforts, the literacy rate stood at only 27.9 per cent in 1981, which was eight points below the national average. The female literacy rate was 28.8 per cent even in 1991. At higher levels, the proportion with middle school and above in rural areas was only 16.4 per cent in 2004, with females at 7.4; both were the lowest among the states.

Behind this poor situation lay the same factors as in UP. Self-seeking, short-sighted political leadership lacked the determination to bring the right type of development. The resource mobilisation was low, and it was largely squandered away on non-essential purposes. The growth in budgetary receipts was very low, and MP's share in A-S total stood at only 5.75 per cent in 2000-03. The per capita receipt came to Rs. 2,801, which was only 72.5 per cent of A-S average.

The budgetary expenditure naturally remained very low. The per capita total in 2000-03 was much below the A-S average. In the total expenditure, the proportion of developmental was high; but the per capita amount was very low. The revenue expenditure had a rapid growth, and the relative share rose to as much as 83.2 per cent in 2000-03. At the sub-state level, the situation of PRIs in resource mobilisation improved significantly in recent years.

The ULBs were also similarly situated. The per capita total revenue averaged only Rs. 278 in 1995-98, which was a little over half the A-S average. The own revenue in it was extremely low; the per capita came to Rs. 78, less than a quarter of that in A-S. In the following years, however, the situation improved greatly; rising to Rs. 362 in 2002-03, which was 39 per cent higher than in A-S. On expenditure, the ULBs were in a very poor situation. The per capita in 1995-98 came to only Rs. 353, less than a twelfth of the A-S average. The proportion of total going for core services was only 36.1 per cent as against 57.8 per cent in the latter.

The performance of the banking system was also not good. The co-operative credit institutions had a very poor performance. In 1998, the state accounted for only 4.2 per cent of the A-I total working capital for all societies together, declining from 7.3 per cent in 1958. In the working capital, the share of deposit was extremely low.

In this situation, the provision of facilities in different sectors naturally remained utterly inadequate. In the area of education, in 1994, 71 per cent of the primary schools had two rooms or less. At upper primary, the average number of rooms was 3.9 as against 5.1 at the national level. The schools were mostly without drinking water facility, not to speak of urinal and lavatory facility. The drop-out rate was very high until recently. The incentive system for attracting students to schools was, however, relatively good. The coverage by scholarship, free education, provision of midday meal, etc., were significantly higher than at the national level.

On health, the preventive measures taken were utterly inadequate. Percentage of children fully immunised was only 40 in 2005-06, lower than in most of the states. The maternal healthcare was in no better position. The proportion of pregnant women registered for ante-natal care was only 57.4 per cent in 2004, 13 points below the national average. The infrastructure for medical care was in a very poor state. In 1999, the average rural area covered by a Sub-centre was as much as 36.5 sq. km. and for a PHC 258 sq. km. Number of beds per lakh population in rural areas in 1991 was only 4. The availability of medical personnel was extremely low. In 1991, number of doctors per lakh population came to only 16.9, around a third of the national average. On birth control, the measures were at a very low level.

The productive sectors also suffered from inadequate facilities and poor quality of governance. The state's share in A-I total value of agricultural production declined from 8.8 per cent in 1992-95 to 5.56 in 2000-03. The yield rate was always much below the national average. Foodgrains, accounting for the lion's share of cropped area, had a very poor performance. The irrigation facility in the state continued to be utterly inadequate.

As regards the allied sectors, the performance in animal husbandry was very poor. The state's share in A-I total milk production had declined from 9.70 per cent in 1990-93 to 7.92 in 2000-03. On meat, the per capita production came to only Rs. 30.57 in 2000-03, which was a fifth of the national average. In poultry, the egg production was only half that at the national level. In fishery, the state's situation was extremely poor, despite having large water resources. On forest resources, the state was in a very good position; but their management was extremely poor. The forests were exploited ruthlessly without taking any commensurate measure for their regeneration.

The performance of the industrial sector was also not good. On the factory sector, the state's share in A-I total output declined to only 4.47 per cent in 2004-05, from 6.35 in 1999. The per capita output declined from 80.4 per cent of the A-I average to 55.5 per cent. The relative share in A-I total employment was only 3.67 per cent in 2004-05. The productivity of the employees, however, increased greatly. The SSI sector was also in no better position. As regards the unorganised sector, in 2000-01, the state accounted for only 3.42 per cent of A-I total GVA, declining from 4.56 per cent in 1994-95. In employment, the relative share was 4.0 per cent, lower than in all but two of the states.

The scheduled tribes—constituting around a quarter of the state's population—probably suffered the most. They continued to be exploited by traders and moneylenders, and a large number of them also suffered displacement by industrial projects. The measures taken by the government were far behind what was necessary. Even the expenditure on tribal welfare remained very low until recently. The implementations were also marred by officials' collusion with the contractors and politicians The injustices perpetrated on them for decades have now given rise to violent protests.

IV

Maharashtra, the third largest state in the country, is much better placed than most others. It is the most industrialised state, and its SDP generally the highest. In 2003-06, the per capita income averaged Rs. 33,277, which was 41 per cent higher than in all-India. The suctorial diversification of income was already high and it increased further. In 2002-05, agriculture had provided only 13.5 per cent. In employment, however, agriculture continued to bear the main burden. In 2004, 78.7 per cent of the usually working persons in rural areas were in agriculture. This heavy dependence on the low-productive agriculture implied an aggravated poverty situation. In 1999-00, the proportion of rural population with MPCE of below Rs. 380 was as much as 37.7 per cent. The rural-urban disparity is very high here. In 2004, the rural MPCE was only Rs. 569, which was 45.2 per cent of that in urban areas. This is really a shameful situation for a state of the stature of Maharashtra.

The social indicators of development were on the whole in a good position. The literacy rate was always much higher than at the national level. In 2001, at 76.9 per cent, it was next only to Kerala. At higher levels also the situation was good. On health, the IMR declined noticeably over the years; and in 2005, at 38, it was the lowest among the states. The proportion of malnourished children was, however, very high; being higher than at the national level. The hygienic conditions were very poor. Percentage of households without latrine was as much as 93.1 in 1998.

Maharashtra's biggest failure was in reducing the regional imbalance in development. This situation was primarily a product of the class character of the government, leading to inadequate resource mobilisation and neglect of the weaker sections. The growth in budgetary receipts was very low in Maharashtra.

The growth in expenditure was very low; and the per capita total expenditure in 2000-03 was higher than the A-S average by only 20.6 per cent as against 36.6 per cent higher in 1975-78. In the total expenditure again, the proportion of developmental was low and declined over the years. In terms of revenue versus capital, the former had a sharp rise and constituted as much as 88.1 per cent of total in 2000-03. In the revenue expenditure, the proportion of developmental had a sharp fall, and constituted only 59.2 per cent in 1997-00. In the developmental, the share of social services increased noticeably, and the per capita in 2002-05 came to Rs. 1581, nearly double the A-S average. The non-developmental expenditure had a rapid growth, and the per capita in 1997 was as much as Rs. 1169, 36.4 per cent higher than in A-S. In the NDE, interest payment accounted for the highest proportion, which, however, was below the A-S average. In administrative services, police had the highest share; and the per capita expenditure came to Rs. 190 in 2002-05 as against Rs. 168 in A-S. The highest growth in expenditure was in compensation and assignments to LBs etc; and the per capita became 49 per cent higher than in A-S in 2002-05, from lower earlier.

The capital disbursements had very low growth, and it was largely because a large portion of capital receipts went to meet the revenue deficit; in 2000-03, it was to the extent of 62.2 per cent. The per capita capital expenditure in 2002-05 came to Rs. 1,547, only 25.6 per cent higher than in A-S; in 1997-00, it was 37.3 per cent higher. The proportion of developmental in it was, however, relatively high; and the per capita in 1997-00 came to Rs. 376, which was 55 per cent higher than in A-S. The debt burden of the state was relatively low.

At the sub-state level, the PRIs' performance in mobilising resources was quite good. The banking system in Maharashtra was quite strong. In the co-operative sector, the state accounted for 28.8 per cent of A-I total working capital for all tiers in 1998. In the working capital, deposit constituted as much as 63.2 per cent.

The commercial banks were in a much better position. The state's share in All-India total deposit mobilised by them was 23.2 per cent in 2006. The per capita deposit was 148 per cent higher than in A-I. On credit deployment, the situation was still better; the relative share in A-I total being 32.8 per cent. The rural situation was, however, distressingly poor. The relative share in total credit stood at only 1.95 per cent in 2006. Inter-district disparities were very high. The RRBs also performed very poorly. In the A-I total credit outstanding in 2006, the state's share came to only 2.77 per cent; and in total deposit at 3.97 per cent. The C-D ratio had a sharp fall over the years.

In this situation, the provision of facilities in different areas naturally remained very inadequate. In the area of education, the coverage of rural population with a primary school in the habitation stood at 73.3 per cent in 1994, which was below that in five of the states. Of the production sectors, the situation of agriculture was not good. With a cropped area of 12.4 per cent of A-I total, the share in A-I production came to 10.0 per cent in 2000-03. In the production of foodgrains, the state's share was only 5.51 per cent, with that in cropped area at 11.0 per cent. In the most important crop rice, the yield rate had a sharp fall. In non-foodgrains, the state's situation was much better. The highest acreage was always in cotton, and the state became the largest producer in the country in recent years, accounting for 25 per cent of total in 2000-03. The yield rate, however, remained low. In sugarcane also the state accounted for 21 per cent of A-I production. In fruits and nuts, Maharashtra had a good position, and the relative share in A-I production reached 18.6 per cent in 2002-03.

The most serious problem in Maharashtra's agriculture is the lack of irrigation facility. The NIA as percentage to NSA was only 16.9 in 2003-04, which was less than half the national average. The cropping intensity was very low. In animal husbandry, the per capita milk production in 1999-02 came to only 175 kg. per annum, which was much below the A-I average. In meat output, the situation was relatively good. But in poultry, the production of egg was very low. In fishery, despite having large fishery resources, the state's situation was not good.

As regards industrialisation, Maharashtra has always been in the forefront of the country. The situation of the unorganised sector was also similar. In 2000-01, the state accounted for 12.6 per cent of A-I total GVA, which was the highest among the states. In employment, however, the share was only 8.02 per cent. Here also the rural share of total output was very low. The infrastructural situation for industry was quite good, although the power situation had deteriorated.

The problem with Maharashtra is not of attracting investment to the state, but of bringing decentralised industrialisation. The percolation effects of the productive sectors' growth did not benefit the poor much. The self-employment programme, IRDP, also did no better. Number of families assisted had a sharp fall over the years. As regards the PDS, it was in a very poor state until recently. Behind the poverty situation, a very important factor was the neglect of the backward regions. The plan expenditures in them were far behind what was required; most of the expenditures were going to western Maharashtra. In this situation, the extremist activities naturally increased manifold in recent years.

V

As regards Gujarat, its economic performance has been on the whole quite good. The per capita income in 2003-06 averaged Rs. 30,182, which was 28 per cent higher than all-India's. The diversification in economic activities was substantial. The primary sector's share in NSDP declined to only 18.8 per cent in 2002-05 from 44.2 in 1970-73; the secondary sector's rose to 35.8 from 23.1. In employment, however, the former continued to have a dominating position. The employment situation was quite good here. The situation of consumer expenditures had, however, worsened in recent years. In 2004, the proportion with MPCE of below Rs. 380 in rural areas was 18.2 per cent, only two points below the national average. The relative position on the BPL population had aiso worsened. In 2004-05, at 19.5 per cent in rural areas, it was four points higher than in 1999, and among the major states, higher than in four.

The social indicators were not in a good position. The literacy rate in 2001 stood at 69.1 per cent, which was lower than in four of the states. At higher levels, the situation was much worse. On health condition, the life expectancy at birth was below the national average in 2001-06; earlier, it was higher than in the latter. The proportion of malnourished children was high. The IMR was also higher than in three of the states in 200.

The inter-district disparities, as in Maharashtra, were very high. Percentage of main workers engaged in the secondary sector in 1991 was below 10 in four of the districts as against more than 20 in five. Even in 1996, three of the districts—Ahmedabad, Vadodara and Surat—together accounted for 46 per cent of total worker in the factory sector. The IMR was as much as 89 in Mehsana as against the lowest of 35 in Surendranagar. The proportion of urban population in 1991 was 10-11 per cent in four of the districts, with the state average at 34.5 per cent.

This nature of development came because the authorities did not have the urge to bring a balanced development and improve the condition of the masses. The resource mobilisation was relatively high, but the spending priorities were perverted. The aggregate of budgetary receipts had risen by 44 times between 1975-78 and 2000-03, which was the highest among the states. The per capita receipt in 2000-03 was 36 per cent higher than in all-states. In the total receipts, however, the contribution of revenue receipts had a sharp fall. The growth in capital receipts was very high.

The commercial banks' performance in Gujarat was also not good. The total deposit at the end of March 2006 came to only 5.07 per cent of A-I total. On credit deployment, the situation was still worse; being only 3.86 per cent of A-I total. The rural credit was in a deplorable state. The relative share in total credit declined to 8.78 per cent in 2006, from 17.3 in 1993. The performance of RRBs was also very poor. Their relative share in A-I total deposit was only 2.7 per cent in 2006, and a similar proportion in credit also.

The provision of facilities in different sectors remained far from satisfactory. The production sectors also suffered from inadequacy of facilities. In agriculture, the state accounted for only 1.90 per cent of A-I total production of foodgrains in 2000-03, declining from 3.56 in 1980-83. The area under foodgrains had declined continuously, and the yield rate was always below the national average. The most important crop bajra had recorded a sharp fall; the relative share in A-I production declining from 20.4 per cent in 1980-83 to 14.5 in 2002-05. In non-foodgrains, however, the state's situation was quite good. In Groundnut, Gujarat continued to be a leading producer in the country; the relative share in A-I production came to 39.2 per cent in 2002-05. In cotton also the state's situation was very good. The yield rate had risen noticeably, and the relative share in A-I production stood at 28.2 per cent in 2002-05. In fruits and nuts, the acreage remained low despite a relatively high yield rate. Banana was an important crop here, accounting for 12.1 per cent of A-I production. The irrigation facility in Gujarat progressed very slowly.

Among the allied sectors, the state's performance was good only in fishery. The relative share in A-I total fish production stood at 11.5 per cent in 2001-04, declining from 13.6 in 1996-99. The state has vast fishery resources, but the measures taken for their utilisation proceeded very slowly. And then, industrial pollution of water and construction of obstacles across rivers had reduced the catches. In animal husbandry, production of milk was quite good. The per capita output in 2000-03 came to Rs. 774, which was 32.5 per cent higher than at the national level. In the production of raw wool, the state's share in this period was 7.59 per cent. In forestry, Gujarat's situation is very poor—only 10 per cent of its land area being under forest. Even this could not be maintained properly.

On industrialisation, Gujarat was in a strong position. The state accounted for 15.6 per cent of all-India total output from the factory sector in 2004-05, rising from 10.9 in 1977-78. The latest per capita output was more than three times the national average. In employment, however, the relative share in A-I total was only 9.20 per cent. The productivity of workers increased noticeably in recent years. The infrastructural situation was relatively good here. On power, the state's installed capacity increased to 7.5 per cent of A-I total in 2010-11 from 6.5 in 2004-05. The per capita industrial consumption of electricity was very high in Gujarat. The non-utilities sector is the strongest her. As regards transportation facility, the road density was very low but the vehicle density was high. On the provision of finance, the situation of term finance was particularly good. The per capita cumulative total till March 2001 from all FIs came to Rs. 12,726, which was 164 per cent higher than in all-India. On the provision of working capital, the situation of SSIs was very poor. For promoting the growth of industries, a number of steps was taken but those on the SSIs and for the backward areas were not very effective. The industrial estates were largely concentrated in a few districts, and their management left much to be desired.

The operation of the productive sectors could not help the poor much, and the direct poverty alleviation measures were also not implemented properly. The employment created by the wage employment programmes had a sharp fall over the years. Per thousand hhs, the number participating had declined from 178 in 1987-88 to only 19 in 1999. The employment created by the JRY in Gujarat during 1989-95 constituted only 2.6 per cent of A-I total and declined to 1.80 in 1997. A large proportion of the beneficiaries were from the ineligible category. The NREGP was almost a total failure. Person-days provided per rural household in 2007-08 was only 29.6 The implementation of self-employment programme IRDP was also not much better. In the A-I total number of families assisted, the state's share came to only 2.44 per cent in 1996-99. The PDS was, however, always in a relatively good position in Gujarat.

There were also measures for the development of backward areas. But the fund allocations for them remained small. Number of talukas considered backward was 56 in 1970 and it remained the same in the following decades also. The backlog of development went on rising continuously. The development of tribal areas also received very little attention, and they continued to suffer from the anti-people forest policy of the government. Their problems were aggravated also by the so-called development projects ousting them from their land without proper rehabilitation. The tribals were left with no alternative to organising land right movements.

VI

This pattern of development is clearly a betrayal of the masses. Those who fought for the freedom of the country, did not give their lives for an India of this distressing situation after six decades of development efforts. There is virtually no government worth the name. The criminal elements are reigning supreme almost everywhere. The democratic facade is meant for cheating the people; elections were all a game of money and muscle power. The Indian Constitution has turned out to be a propaganda material. The Directive Principles of State Policy promised all good things in this world, but the actions of the government were the exact opposite of it. The basic needs of an overwhelming proportion of population are yet to be met.

Our legislators are all self-seekers, and the Parliamentarians' behaviour is in general a matter of shame. The judiciary is useless for the common man. Millions of cases are pending in the Courts. The rule of law is virtually totally absent, and more and more people are taking the law into their own hands. The police department is in general corrupt and inefficient, and has no credibility. Corruption is rampant everywhere. The politician-bureaucrat-contractor nexus is nullifying most of the development efforts. The Constitution has been distorted to serve vested interests.

It is also necessary to mention that in the context of the inter-dependence of different parts of the world, the happenings in other parts cannot be ignored. The environmental degradation is mainly a product of the unending greed of the rich people throughout the world. The energetic 'beasts' in human form were let loose on the natural resources of the world. The scientific inventions went far beyond what was needed for meeting the needs—in contrast to desires—of the people.

The carbon emissions increased manifold, and at the same time the rainforests—inhaling massive amounts of the gases—were ruthlessly destroyed. After looting the mother Earth, they turned their attention to the outer space. There is mounting concern about the depletion of the ozone layer. Many nations continue to spend huge amounts on arms build up. The US defence budget for military stores currently stands at $ 700 billion, and Worldwide military expenditure stands at around US$ 1,650 billion a year. If the military expenditure is reduced by even one-third, it can go a long way in meeting the basic needs of all present-day poor. (Saighal, Vinod 2011; TST 2009, 2012 z38).

In the fragile ecosystems of the tropical forests—where 50 per cent of the world's species reside—half of the forest cover has disappeared. Every year 13 million hectares of forest are destroyed. The nature has already started avenging, as evidenced by tsunami, earthquakes, floods and other natural calamities. In the International Court of Justice environmental issues are now the top priority. (TST, 2011 z18, z32; 2012 z21, z23).

There is an urgent need to change the objective of growth world-wide. The progress should be measured solely in terms of long-run peace and happiness. And for this, meeting the basic needs of everybody should get the highest priority. Certain minimum satisfactory norms of clean drinking water, food and nutrition, housing, etc., be achieved for all the poor throughout the world. The developed countries should come forward to help the developing ones in this pursuit, but first the latter have to direct all their attention to mitigating abject poverty in their respective countries. The limitations of the available carbon space as well as other real constraints will make it obligatory to put an immediate end to all wasteful activities. The first attack has to be on the production of armaments and ammunition, for nothing is more wasteful than this. This will not only increase human welfare and security but of all life-forms.

For these changes to come, a new global order has to be brought. The question is how the new order is to be shaped to ensure peace, justice and stability. A global federalism covering all the nations of the world is a compelling need of the hour. The European Union is a harbinger for this purpose. All the contiguous nations of the world have to come together and form their respective regional unions, and then they together will form a federal world government The world's most powerful nation the USA has to play a leading role in this process. America is not a conventional nation-state. It is a land of migrants who were fleeing repression or seeking economic gain. Almost all Americans have dual loyalty to America and to their country of origin.

NOTES

- The availability of fresh water is rapidly becoming an insurmountable problem in many places. To note a few of the facts: Nearly 97 per cent of the planet's water is salt water in seas and oceans. Close to two per cent of the earth's water is frozen in polar ice-sheets and glaciers and a fraction of one per cent is available for drinking, irrigation and industrial use. All over the globe, farmers and municipalities are pumping water out of the ground faster than it can be replenished. That the planet's fresh water is consumed in a profligate manner is beyond doubt, particularly in agriculture which accounts for 70 per cent of all water usage. Most governments subsidise irrigation water so heavily that farmers have little incentive and motivation to invest in drip systems or other water saving methods.

BIBLIOGRAPHY

Books

Abbas, Hasan 2005. *Pakistan's Drift into Extremism: Allah, the Army, and America's War on Terror,* Armonk, N.Y., M.E. Sharp.

Abbas, K.A., 1978. *Janata in a Jam* ? Bombay, Jaico Publishing House.

Aiyar, Mani Shankar 1992. *Remembering Rajiv*, Calcutta, Rupa and Co.

Ao, A Lanunungsang 2002. *From Phizo to Muivah: The Naga National Question in North-East India*, New Delhi, Mittal Publications.

ARCH-Vahini 1988. *Displacement in Sardar Sarovar (Narmada) Project: A Gujarat Experience*, Mangrol, Rajpipla.

Asian Development Bank (ADB) 2001. Report and Recommendation of the President to the Board of Directors on, Propose Loans for MP Power Sector Development Programme, November.

Austin, Granville 1999. *Working a Democratic Constitution: The Indian Experience*, New Delhi, OUP.

Bakshi, Rajni 1986. *The Long Haul: The Bombay Textile Workers Strike*, Bombay, BUILD Documentation Centre.

Basu, Sajal (ed.) 1978. *Underground Literature During Indian Emergency,* Calcutta, Minerva Associates.

Brar, Lt. Gen. K.S., 1987. *Operation Bluestar: The True Story*, New Delhi, UBS Publishers.

Brecher, Michael 1966. *Succession in India: A Study in Decision Making*, London, Oxford University Press.

Chakravary, Uma and Nandita Haksar 1987. *The Delhi Riots: Three Days in the Life of a Nation*, New Delhi, Lancer International.

Chandra, Jag Parvesh 1979. V*erdict on Janata*, New Delhi, Metropolitan Book Co.

Cohen, Stephen P., 2001. *Indi: Emerging Power*, New Delhi, OUP.

Dasgupta, C., 2002. *War and Diplomacy I Kashmir,* 1947- 8, New Delhi: Sage Publications.

Deb, Kalipada 1997. *The Challenge of Rural Development*, Five Decades of Indian Experience, M D, New Delhi.

Dhar, P.N., 2000. *Indira Gandhi, the 'Emergency', and Indian Democracy*, New Delhi, OUP.

Fertiliser Association of India (FAI) 2003. Fertiliser Statistics 2002-03, N D.

Gandhi, Arun 1983. *The Morarji Papers: Fall of the Janata Government*, New Delhi, Vision Books.

Gandhi, Rajmohan 1984. *The Rajaji Story*, 1937-1972, Bombay, Bharatiya Vidya Bhavan.

Gopal, S., 1979. *Jawaharlal Nehru: A Biography*, Vol. 2:1947-56, London, cape.

Government of Bombay (GOB) 1958. Second Five Year Plan (1956-57 to 1960-61), Bombay State.

Indian Council of Forest Research and Education (ICFRE) 2002. *Forest Statistics India* 2001, New Forest, Dehradun.

Indian Institute of Public Opinion 1967. *The Indian General Election* 1967: The Structure of Indian Voting Intentions.

Instt. of Applied Manpwer Research (IPMR) 2011. *The India Human Development Report 2011: Towards Social Inclusion, Planning Commission*, New Delhi: OUP.

International Institute for Population Sciences (IIPS) 1995. *National Family Health Survey (MCH and Family Planning)*, India 1992-93, Bombay, August.

Iyer, Ramaswamy R 2003. *Water: Perspectives, Issues, Concerns*, New Delhi, Sage Publications.

Jayakar, Pupul 1993. *Indira Gandhi: An Intimate Biography,* New York, Pantheon Books.

Jayal, Niraja Gopal 1999. *Democracy and the State: Welfare, Secularism and Development in Contemporary India*, Delhi, OUP.

Kaul, B.M., 1967. *The Untold Story*, Allied, Bombay.

Lewis John P., 1995. *India's Political Economy: Governance and Reform*, Delhi, OUP.

Limaye, Madhu 1994. *Janata Party experiment: An Insider's Account of Opposition Politics*, Vol. 1, Delhi, B.R. Publishing Corp.

Martin, Richard 2012. *Superfuel: Thorium, the Green Energy of the Future*, Palgrave Macmillan.

Mavalankar, P.G., 1979. *'No Sir': An Independent MP Speaks During the Emergency*, Ahmedabad, Sannistha Prakashan.

Mehta, Ved, 1970. *Portait of India*, New York, Farrar, Straus and Girous.

Mohan, Anand 1967. *Indira Gandhi: A personal and political Biography*, New York, Meredith Press.

Morse, Bradford and Thomas Berger 1992. *Sardar Sarovar: Report of the Independent Review*, Ottawa, Resource Future International INC, Canada.

National Bank for Agriculture and Rural Development (NABARD) 1986. Statistical Statements Relating to the Co-operative Movement in India 1981-82, Bombay.

National Council of Applied Economic Research (NCAER) 1960. Techno-Economic Survey of Madhya Pradesh, Asia Publishing House, Bombay.

Prachand, S.L.M., 1977. *The Popular Upsurge and the Fall of Congress*, Chandigarh, Abhishek Publications.

Prasad, S.N., and Dharam Pal 1987. *History of Operations in Jammu and Kashmir* (1947-48), New Delhi: Ministry of Defence, p. 28f., 379.

Rao, Amiya and B.G., (eds.) 1977. *The Press She Could not Whip: Emergency in India as reported by the Foreign Press*, Bombay, Popular Prakashan.

Schofield, Victoria 1999. *Kashmir in Conflict* , London, IB Tauris.

Singh, Jaswanth 1999. *Defending India*, Bangalore, Macmillan India.

SIDBI 2002. 2002. *Report on Small Scale Industries Sector* 2001, Mumbai, February.

Srivastava, C.P., 1995. *Lal Bahadur Shastri: A life of Truth in Politics*, New Delhi: Oxford University Press.

Tarlo, Emma 2003. *Unsettling Memories: Narratives of India's 'Emergency'*, Delhi, Permanent Black.

Visvanathan, Shiv and Harsh Sethi (eds.) 1998. *Foul Play: Chronicles of Corruption*, New Delhi, Banyan Books.

Voluntary Action Network India 1995. S*tate Panchayat Acts A Critical Review,* N. D.

Woodford, Clare and Harry Jr. 1951. *India Afire*, New York, john Day.

World Bank 2000. The Madhya Pradesh Human Development Report 1998, UNDP.

Articles

Abhyankar, Nikit 2005. "*power Sector Restructuring in Madhya Pradesh*", Economic and Political Weekly (EPW), November 26.

Acharya, Amitav 2011. "*Can Asia Lead: Power Ambitions and Global Governance in the 21st Century*", International Affairs, Vol. 87, no. 4.

Ahluwalia, Montek S., 2011. "*Prospects and Policy Challenges in the Twelfth Plan*", EPW, May 21.

Arpi, Claude 2011. "*A Tragedy to come: Development Must Respect Nature*", the statesman (Siliguri) TST, October 13.

Ashish, Sri Madhava 1993. "*Decentralised Management of Natural Resources in the UP Hills*", EPW, August 28.

Badhwar, Inderjit 1986. "*Hindus: Militant Revivalism*", India Today, May 31.

Bagchi, S 2009. "*Nehruvian dilemma, From Faith To Disillusionment With The Machine*", TST, November 11.

Banerjie, Indranil 1988. "*The New Maharajas*", Sunday, 17-23 April.

Basu, Barun Kumar 2012. "*Verdict of 2012 - 1: Congress Arrogance And Decimation*", TST, March 23.

Basu, Shantanu 2011. "*The Taxman Cometh - I: Higher Collection An Optical Illusion*", July 7.

Bandyopadhyay, J. and S. Shiva 1979. "*Agricultural Economy of Kumaon Hills*", EPW, October 13.

Bandyopadhyay, D 2012. "*Beware of the invasion: Danger of The GM Crop*", TST, March 11, 12.

Banerjee, Sumanta 2008. "*On the Naxalite Movement: A Report with a Difference*", EPW, May 24.

Banerji, Arun Kumar 2009. "*Crimson Corridor - I*", TST, 11 January.

Bathla, Seema and Sukhadeo Thorat 2006. "*Trends and Determinants of Public Investment in Indian Agriculture at the Regional Level*", Man and Development, June.

Bhalla, G.S., et al. 1997. "*Recent Developments in Indian Agriculture A State Level Analysis*", EPW, March 29.

Bhat, Ramesh, Nishant Jain 2006. "*Analysis of Public and Private Healthcare Expenditures*", EPW, January 7.

Bhatia, Sitesh 2011. "*Man-made Disasters: Earthquakes, Landslides, Floods—*", Sept. 26.

Bhatia, M.S., 1999. "*Rural Infrastructure and Growth in Agriculture*", EPW, March 27.

Burra, Neera 1987. "*Exploitation of Child Workers in Lock Industry of Aligarh*", EPW, July 11.

Chakraverti, P.R., 1965. "*The Economics of Poverty*", AICC Economic Review, December 1.

Chatterjee, Vidyarthy 2012. "*Adivasis here, Adivasis there - I*" and "..... II", September 27 and Chaudhuri, Siladitya, et al. 2009. "*Levels of Living and Poverty Patterns: A District-Wise Analysis for India*", EPW, February 28 - March 6.

Chelliah, Raja J., 2005. "*Malady of Continuing Fiscal Imbalance*", EPW, July 30.

Datar, Chhaya 2007. "*Failure of National Rural Employment Guarantee Scheme in Maharashtra*", EPW, August 25.

Dhagamwar, Vasudha 1986. "*After the Shah Bano Judgement - II*", Times of India (TMI), February 11.

Dhawan, B.D., 1980. "*Underutilisation of Groundwater Resources A Case Study of East Uttar Pradesh*", EPW, Sept. 27.

Dholakia, Archana 2005. "*Measuring Fiscal Performance of States An Alternative Approach*", EPW, July 30.

Dholakia, R.H., et al. 2005. "*Consistent Measurement of Fiscal Deficit and Debt of States in India*", EPW, June 18.

Diwakar, D.M., 2009. "*Intra-Regional Disparities, Inequality and Poverty in Uttar Pradesh*", EPW, June 27-July 10.

Dogra, Bharat 2009. "*Unorganised Sector Legislation Falls Short of Workers' Expectation*", TST, Feb. 27.

Ganguly, B.K., Kalpana Chaudhary 2003. "*Forest Products of Bastar A Study of Tribal Exploitation*", EPW, July 12.

Ganguly, Kaushik 2009. "*Issues in State Finance Outstanding Liabilities of the States*", EPW, July 25.

Ghosh, Nilabja 2004. "*Promoting Bio-Fertilisers in Indian Agriculture*", EPW, December 25-31.

Ghosh-Dastidar, A 2008. "*Decades and Years, Waiting for Adults to Tie Up the Loose End*", TST, Nov. 9.

Guha, Amalendu 1980. "*Little Nationalism Turned Chauvinist: Assam's Anti-Foreigner Upsurge* 1979-80", EPW, Annual Issue, October.

Gulati, I.S., K.K., George 1978. "*Inter-State Redistribution through Budgetary Transfers*", EPW, March 18.

Irudaya Rajan, S., 2005. "*District Level Fertility Estimates for Hindus and Muslims*", EPW, January 29.

Iyenger, Sudarshan 2002. '*Resettlement and Rehabilitation in the Sardar Sarovar Project: A Review of Policy Reforms and Implementation*', in Shinoda, Takashi (ed.) The Other Gujarat, Popular Prakashan, Mumbai.

Iyer, Ramaswamy R 2012. "*River Linking Project A Disquieting Judgement*", EPW, April 7.

Jacobsen, B.B., Kurt et al. 2011. "*Remembrance Days: Domestic Consequence of Grand Strategy*", TST Dec. 19.

Jagannathan, R., 1987. "*Welcome to Hard Times*", 6-12 September.

Jagmohan 2012. "*Vivekananda and Gandhi ......To The Unprincipled Politics of The Present Times*", January 26.

Jain, Jyotsna, Mihir Shah 2005. "*Antyodaya Anna Yojana and Mid-day Meals in MP*", EPW, November 26.

Jain, Sunil 2004. "*Vote Vajpayee*", Business Standard, February 16.

Joy, K.J., et al. 2009. "*An Alternative Energy Plan for the Konkan*", EPW, May 9-15.

Jyotishi, Amalendu, R., Parthasarathy 2007. "*Reservoir Fisheries Management Experiences of Tawa in Madhya Pradesh*", EPW, Feb. 3-9.

Kalbgh, Chaitanya 1980. "*The North-East: India's Bangladesh*?", India Today, 1-15 May.

Kannan, K.P., and N., Vijayamohanan Pillai 2001. "*Plight of Power Sector in India - I Physical Performance of SEB*"; II do. Financial Performance", EPW, January 13-19 and 20-26.

Kapur, Ashok 2009. "*Nature Serves Notice - I and II*", TST, August 23 and 24.

Kaul, Sumer 2006. "*A Parasitical Order*", TST, 24 September.

Khare, Harish 2003. "*Reloading the Family Matrix*", Seminar, June.

Khasnobis, H., 2009. "*Oceanic Challenge The Sea As A Victim of Carbon Abuse*", TST, September 2.

Khera, Reetika 2004. "*Monitoring Disclosures*", Seminar, February.

Krishnan, T.N., 1992. "*Population, Poverty and Employment in India*", EPW, November 14.

Kulkari, Nandu R 2007. "*Maharashtra in a Power Struggle*", TST, February 14.

Kulkarni, S.D., 1980. "*Problems of Tribal Development in Maharashtra*". EPW, September 20.

Lal, Deepak 1976. "*Agricultural Growth , Real Wages, and the Rural Poor in India*", EPW, June 26.

Laxminarayan, H., 1979. "*Inter Size Group and Inter State Variations in Distribution of Agricultural Assets*", EPW, June 30.

Madalgi, S.S., 1968. "*Hunger in Rural India: 1960-61 to 1964-65*", EPW, Annual No.

Maharatna, Arup 2009. "*Chaotic comfort The Flip Side of Post-Modern Innovations*", TST, July 18.

Mitra, Ashok K., 1998. "*Development and Management of Irrigation in Maharashtra With Special Reference to Major and Medium Surface Irrigation Systems*", EPW, June 27.

Mitra, Siddhartha, Sangeeta Shroff 2007. "*Farmers' Suicides in Maharashtra*", EPW, December 8.

Nachane, D.M., et al. 2002. "*Does Monetary Policy Have Differential State-Level Effects? ....*" EPW, November 23.

Nagaraj, B.S., 2003. "*Smokescreen Resort*", Indian Political Review, July.

Narayan, Hemendra 2003. "*Courage of Contradiction*", TST, September 12.

Narayanamoorthy, A., et al. 2003. "*Irrigation and Agricultural Wages An Analysis Across States*", EPW, August 30.

Neelakantan, M., 1994. "*Jawahar Rozgar yojana An Assessment through Concurrent Evaluation*", EPW, December 3.

Ninan, T.N., 1985. "*Rise of the Middle Class*", India Today, December, 31.

Ooman, M.A., 2006. "*Fiscal Decentralisation to the Sub-State Level Governments*", EPW, March 11.

Oza, N., 1997. "*Marginalisation, Protests and Political Action Tribes and Sardar Sarovar Projects*", EPW, July 19.

Pal, Mahi 2004. "*Panchayat Raj and Rural Governance Experiences of a Decade*", EPW, January 10.

Pandey, Rahul 2008. "*Skewed development*", TST, December 11.

Panikar, P.G.K., 1979. "*Resources Not the Constraint on Health Improvement A Case Study of Kerala*", EPW, Nov. 3.

Pant, Rajshekhar 2006. "*Conservation Impedes Development*", Sahara Times, January 21.

Patel, Gunwant A., 1991. "*Farmers and Fertilisers Skewed Advice*", EPW, September 28.

Patel, Sujata 2006. "*Empowerment, Co-option and Domination Politics of Maharashtra's Employment Guarantee Scheme*", EPW, December 16-22.

Paul, Samuel and M., Vivekananda 2004. "*Holding a Mirror to the New Lok Sabha*", EPW, November 6.

Pervez, Md. Shahid 2000. "*Rumble in the jungle*", TST, April 29.

Puri, Harish 1985. "*Punjab Elections and After*", EPW, October 5.

Puri, Rajinder 2009b. "*Reform, Revolution or Collapse? The Choice Before India*", TST, Dec. 15.

Purohit, Mahesh C 2006. "*Tax Efforts and Taxable Capacity of Central and State Governments*", EPW, February 25.

Rahul 1992. "*Rhetoric versus Reality The State, Jawahar Rozgar Yojana and People's Participation*", EPW, Dec. 19 Rajappa, Sam 2009. "EVMs are riggable", TST, August 15.

Rajapurohit, A.R., 1979. "*Cross-Breeding of Indian Cattle: An Evaluation*", EPW, March 24-31.

Rakshit, Nirmalendu Bikash 2012. "*Not a powder-puff: Constitutional Importance Of The President*", August 23.

Ramaseshan, Radhika 1984. "*Profit against Safety*", EPW, 22-29 December.

Ramaswamy, K.V., 2007. "*Regional Dimension of Growth and Employment*", EPW, December 8.

Ramchandran, Asha 2008. "*Parched Earth*", TST, July 10.

Ranade, Rahul, M.D., Kumar 2004. "*Narmada water for Groundwater Recharge in North Gujarat Conjunctive Management in Large Irrigation Projects*", EPW, July 31.

Ravallion, Martin 2000. "*What is Needed for a More Pro-poor Growth Process in India?*", EPW, March 25.

Rawal, Vikas 2008. "*Ownership holdings of Land in Rural India Putting the Record Straight*", EPW, March 8-14.

Reddy, Ramachandra G., 2011. "*Reform of the polls: Need To Make Democracy Meaningful*", November 17.

Roy, B.K., 2011. "*Quake and Rehab - I: Lessons From The Sikkim Earthquake*", "....II: Where Human Presence is in Conflict with Nsture", TST, December 23 and 24.

Sachar, Rajindar 2011. "*None found suitable: The Voter Must Have The Right to Decide*", September 7.

Sachidananda 1979. "*Bihar's Experience*", Seminar, November.

Saighal, Vinod 2011. "*Oceanic crisis - I : Awesome Arms Build-Up Around South China Sea*", July 19.

Saith, Ashwani 2005. "*Poverty Line versus the Poor Method versus Meaning*", EPW, October 22.

Samra, J.S., 2002. "*Joint Forest Management for Sustenance*" Yojana, Vol. 46, January.

Sangvai, Sanjay 1993. "*Politics of Submergence*", EPW, December 11.

Shakir, Moin 1980. *Election Participation of Minorities and Indian Political System*, EPW, annual issue, February.

Shankar, Kripa 1991. "*Politics of Land Distribution in Uttar Pradesh*", EPW, April 27.

Sharma, Arunayan 2010. "*As Pressing a Need as Any*", The Statesman, January 8 (NB extra).

Sharma, B., 2005. *Oustees of Indira Sagar Dam: Saga of Harsud*, EPW, January 1-7.

Sharma, H.R., 1994. "*Distribution of Landholdings in Rural India 1953-54 to 1982-83*", EPW, March 26.

Sharma Kalpana 1999. "*Chronicle of a Riot Foretold*", in Patel, Sujata and Alice Thorner, eds., Bombay: Metaphor for Modern India, Delhi, OUP.

Sharma, Mridula et al. 2005. "*Survival of Aligarh Lock Manufacturing Industry*", EPW, September 24.

Sharma, Mukul 2009. "*Passages from Nature to Nationalism: Sunderlal Bahuguna and Tehri Dam Opposition in Garhwal*", EPW, February 21.

Sharma, R.D., 2008. "*Judging the Judge*", TST, December 20.

Sharma, Sanjay 2005. "*Power Eludes MP*", Sahara Times, December 17.

Shete, N.B., et al. 1989. "*Regional Rural Banks: Problems and Perspectives of Rural Credit*", Prajnan, Vol. XVIII, 2.

Singh, S.P., B.K., Sahoo 2007. "*Diversification of Agricultural Economy Towards Horticulture and Livestock: Regional Variations, Convergence and Determinants*", The Indian Journal of Labour Economics, October-Dec.

Suryanarayana, M.H., 2009. "*Intra-State Economic Disparities: Karnataka and Maharashtra*", EPW, June 27- July 10.

Swami Sandarshanananda 2007. "*Nature, avenging angel*", TST, December 15.

Thangaraj, M., 1994. "*Trends in Fragmentation of Operational Holdings in India*", IJAE, January-March.

Thimmaiah, G., 2002. "*Finance Commission Decline of a Constitutional Institution*", EPW, November 23.

Tilak, Jandhyala B.G., 2004. "*Public Subsidies in Education in India*", EPW, January 24.

Udayakumar, S.P., 2012. "*The Koodankulam Struggle and the 'Foreign Hand*", EPW, March 24.

Unni, Jeemol 1997. "*Employment and Wages Among Rural Labourers: Some Recent Trends*", IJAE, January-March.

Vaidyanathan, A., 2001. "*Poverty and Development Policy*", EPW, May 26.

Vasudeva, P.K., 2011. "*Waters of Tibet: China and its Damaging Dams*", TST, November 28.

Veeramani, C., et al. 2005. "*Manufacturing Productivity in Indian States Does Investment Climate Matter?*", EPW, June 11.

Vijay Shankar, P.S., 2005. "*Four Decades of Agricultural Development in MP An Agro-Ecological Sub-Region Approach*", EPW, November 26.

Vir, Dharam 2012. "*Governments and Legislatures: Audit Reports and Accountability*", June 20.

Wadhwa, D.C., 2002. "*Guaranteeing Title to Land*", EPW, November 23.

Weber, Max 1946. "*Politics as a Vocation*" in Gerth, Hans and C Wright Mills, eds., *From Max Weber: Essays in Sociology*, New York, OUP.

Widmalm, Sten 1988. "*The Rise and Fall of Democracy in Jammu and Kashmir, 1975-1989*", in Amrita Basu and Atul Kohli, eds., Community Conflicts and the State in India, Delhi, OUP, 1988.

Saksena, D.N., et al. 1980. '*Study of Health and Family Welfare Schemes in Rural Uttar Pradesh*', Lucknow University.

Index

J

K

N

O